Alternative Voices in Contemporary Economics

Series Editor:
Professor Steven Pressman, Monmouth University, USA

The Alternative Voices in Contemporary Economics series provides an important platform for new and innovative approaches to economic analysis within the following traditions: Post-Keynesian, Feminist, Institutional, Marxian, Sraffian, Radical, Austrian, and Behavioural. This series offers researchers working in these heterodox traditions the opportunity to address methodological, theoretical or empirical issues. The series editor works closely with authors and editors to ensure the quality of all published works.

Other titles in the Series

Understanding the Entrepeneur
An Institutional Perspective
Christos Kalantaridis
ISBN 978-0-7546-3344-0

The Economics of Prevailing Wage Laws
Edited by Hamid Azari-Rad, Peter Phillips and Mark J. Prus
ISBN 978-0-7546-3255-9

The Ethics and Economics of the Basic Income Guarantee
Edited by Karl Widerquist, Michael Anthony Lewis and Steven Pressman
ISBN 978-0-7546-4188-9

The Future of the Welfare State
European and Global Perspectives
Edited by Bent Greve
ISBN 978-0-7546-4640-2

Gandhian Political Economy
Principles, Practice and Policy
B.N. Ghosh
ISBN 978-0-7546-4681-5

Marxist Perspectives on South Korea in the Global Economy

Edited by

MARTIN HART-LANDSBERG
Lewis and Clark College, USA

SEONGJIN JEONG
Gyeongsang National University, South Korea

RICHARD WESTRA
Pukyong National University, South Korea

ASHGATE

Published by
Ashgate Publishing Limited
Gower House
Croft Road
Aldershot
Hampshire GU11 3HR
England

Ashgate Publishing Company
Suite 420
101 Cherry Street
Burlington, VT 05401-4405
USA

Ashgate website: http://www.ashgate.com

British Library Cataloguing in Publication Data
Marxist perspectives on South Korea in the global economy.
- (Alternative voices in contemporary economics)
1. Marxian economics 2. Korea (South) - Economic conditions
- 1960- 3. Korea (South) - Economic policy - 1960- 4. Korea
(South) Foreign economic relations
I. Hart-Landsberg, Martin II. Jeong, Seongjin III. Westra,
Richard, 1954-
330.9'5195

Library of Congress Cataloging-in-Publication Data
Marxist perspectives on South Korea in the global economy / edited by Martin Hart-Landsberg, Seongjin Jeong and Richard Westra.
p. cm. -- (Alternative voices in contemporary economics)
Includes bibliographical references and index.
ISBN-13: 978-0-7546-4816-1 1. Korea (South)--Economic conditions--1960- 2. Korea (South)--Economic policy--1960- I. Hart-Landsberg, Martin. II. Jeong, Seongjin. III. Westra, Richard, 1954-

HC467.95.M37 2007
330.95195--dc22

2006031594

ISBN 13: 978 0 7546 4816 1

Printed and bound in Great Britain by Antony Rowe Ltd, Chippenham, Wiltshire.

Contents

Part III The South Korean Economy in Historical Perspective

Part IV The South Korean Economy into the Future

List of Figures

List of Tables

List of Contributors

Paul Burkett is Professor of economics at Indiana State University, Terre Haute, USA. His research focuses on the political economy of development and class struggle, and Marxism and ecology. He is the co-author, with Martin Hart-Landsberg, of *China and Socialism: Market Reforms and Class Struggle* (Monthly Review Press, 2005) and the author of *Marxism and Ecological Economics: Toward a Red and Green Political Economy* (Brill, 2006).

Dae-oup Chang is an academic activist working for the Asia Monitor Resource Centre in Hong Kong as the research coordinator. He is also the coordinator of Asian Transnational Corporation Monitoring Network, which consists of 20 labor NGOs and unions, and which is involved in developing theories and practices of organizing labor against mobile capital in Asia. He earned his Ph.D from the Department of Sociology at University of Warwick. His works on the transformation of the social form of labor in Korea and other Asian developing countries under the impact of globalization have been published in *Journal of Contemporary Asia*, *Labour, Capital and Society*, *Historical Materialism*, and *Asian Labour Update*. He is currently working on a number of research projects analyzing the way in which the social form of labor has been recomposed by the transnational corporate-driven globalization and a new labor activism emerging from the struggle against the new social domination of capital in Asia.

Joseph Halevi is Senior Lecturer for the Discipline of Political Economy, School of Economics and Political Science, University of Sydney, Australia. Halevi was born in Israel and studied and lived in Rome. He has previously taught at the New School for Social Research in New York, and at the University of Connecticut. He is periodically invited by the Universities of Grenoble, and of Nice, both in France. He has contributed several articles to the journal *Monthly Review* and co-edited two books: *Restoring Demand in the World Economy*, with Jean Marc Fontaine (Edward Elgar, 1998), and, with David Laibman and Edward Nell, *Beyond the Steady State* (St Martins' Press/ Macmillan, 1992). He is currently researching on the political economy of Europe and of East Asia in relation to the United States.

Sang-Hwan Jang is Professor of Economics at Gyeongsang National University, Korea where he teaches agricultural economics and Korean economy. He received his PhD from Yonsei University, Seoul and served as Chairman of the Policy Committee for the Democratic Labor Party of Korea from 2000 to 2003. Since 2004, he has worked as Director of the Progressive Politics Institute for this party. He spent a one year sabbatical at the Department of Economics, University of Massachusetts,

Amherst, 2003-2004. His MA thesis, "An Empirical Study on Land Reform in Korea (1985, in Korean)" was evaluated as a thoroughgoing field study, criticizing the previous estimates of the reform. He has written many articles (in Korean) on problems of the agricultural economy, farmland policy, and economic policy of Korea. His recent publications include, "Continuing Suicide among Laborers in Korea", *Labor History* (2004). Currently he is conducting research on alternative economic policy for developing countries in opposition to neo-liberalism.

Seongjin Jeong is Professor of economics and former Director of the Institute for Social Sciences at Gyeongsang National University, South Korea. He received his PhD from Seoul National University, and has written widely on Marxism and the Korean economy, including articles in *Review of Radical Political Economics* and *Rethinking Marxism*. He has also translated some major Marxist works into Korean, including books by Robert Brenner, Alex Callinicos, Tony Cliff and Roman Rosdolsky. He is currently editing *MARXISM 21*, a representative Marxist journal in Korea.

Soohaeng Kim is Professor of economics at Seoul National University, South Korea and is Honorary President of Korea Social and Economic Studies Association (KSESA), a Korean Left Economists' Group, and President of Cyber Labor University in memory of Chun Taeil. Kim is a graduate of Seoul National University, BA and MA, and Birkbeck College, University of London, MSc and PhD. He wrote a doctoral thesis on Marx's theory of crisis. His main intellectual contribution to Marxism is his translation into Korean of the complete three volumes of Marx's *Capital*.

Peter Kriesler is Associate Professor in the School of Economics at the University of New South Wales, Australia. He is also Deputy Director, there, for the Centre for Applied Economic Research, executive editor of the Australian Journal of Human Rights, and on the editorial board of the Economic and Labour Relations Review, and History of Economics Review. He is the organizer of the Annual Australian Society of Heterodox Economists Conference, which is now in its fifth year. His work has been published in numerous scholarly journals including *Cambridge Journal of Economics*, the *Journal of Post Keynesian Economics*, the *Review of Political Economy* and *Economies et Societes*. He is author of *Kalecki's Microanalysis: The Development of Kalecki's Analysis of Prices and Distribution* (Cambridge, 1987), revised and translated into Japanese (2000); editor of *The Australian Economy: The Essential Guide* (Allen & Unwin 1999); *Globalisation, Human Rights and Civil Society* (Prospect Media Ltd., 1998); and *Themes in Political Economy: Essays in Honour of Geoff Harcourt* (Routledge, 1999) . His current research relates to the Australian, Asian and European economies, Marxian and Kaleckian economics, and issues related to employment and path determinacy.

Martin Hart-Landsberg is Professor of economics at Lewis and Clark College, Portland, Oregon, USA and directs the political economy program there. His areas of teaching and research include the political economy of development with an emphasis on East Asia. He is the co-author, with Paul Burkett, of *China and Socialism: Market Reforms and Class Struggle* (Monthly Review Press, 2005) and *Development, Crisis, and Class Struggle: Learning from Japan and East Asia* (St. Martin's Press, 2000).

Seung-Ho Park is Research Professor of the Institute for Social Sciences at Gyeongsang National University, South Korea. He graduated from Seoul National University with BA and MA degrees. Having contributed to working class movements for more than ten years, he returned to Seoul National University and obtained his PhD Degree with a thesis on Marxian Critique of Left Theories of Modern Capitalism. He is one of the founding members of Cyber Labor University in memory of Chun Taeil.

Dong-Min Rieu is Associate Professor of economics at Chungnam National University, South Korea. He received his PhD from Seoul National University. He has written mainly on Marxian value theory in academic journals including: *Kobe University Economic Review*, *Review of Radical Political Economics* and *Seoul Journal of Economics*.

Richard Westra has taught at universities and colleges around the world including: The Royal Military College of Canada, Queen's University, Kingston, Ontario, the International Study Centre, East Sussex, UK and the College of the Bahamas, Nassau. Currently, he is Assistant Professor in the Division of International and Area Studies, Pukyong National University, Pusan, South Korea. His work has been published in numerous international scholarly refereed journals including: *Journal of Contemporary Asia*, *Capital and Class*, *Review of International Political Economy* and *Review of Radical Political Economics*. He has also co-edited and contributed to the volumes: *Phases of Capitalist Development: Booms, Crises and Globalizations* (Palgrave, 2001) which has recently been translated into Chinese and published by Economic Science Press, Beijing (2003); *Value and the World Economy Today: Production, Finance and Globalization* (Palgrave, 2003); *New Socialisms: Futures beyond Globalization* (Routledge, 2004); and *Sustaining Life On Earth: Environmental and Human Health Through Global Governance* (Lexington Books, 2006).

Preface and Acknowledgements

This volume is the result of our shared concern with developments in South Korea (hereafter Korea) and belief in the continued relevance and power of Marxism to provide critical insight into contemporary Korean struggles and choices. While the focus of *Marxist Perspectives on South Korea in the Global Economy* is the Korean experience, we also believe that the broader significance of that experience as well as the nature of our approach will make our work relevant to those concerned with development and social change more broadly.

In the heady days of neoliberalism, marked by United States President Ronald Reagan's denunciation of the Soviet Union as the "Evil Empire" and British Prime Minister Margaret Thatcher's pronouncement that "there is no alternative" to neoliberal globalization, advocates of Marxism as a mode of analysis and inspiration for the future found themselves routinely dismissed as irrelevant (if not literally dismissed from their positions). This was especially true within the Western academy, where the Marxist research focus on materialist explanation was sanitized and references to Marxist works were purged from bibliographies. Cowed by the neoliberal intellectual offensive many Marxist influenced scholars sought refuge in poststructuralist and postmodern analysis where their revolutionary élan could be plied subverting meaning in texts.

In no part of the academy was the abandonment of Marxism more devastating than in development studies and its related fields. Here, the retreat gained momentum from two important world-economic developments: the collapse of Soviet-style socialism and the rise of the so-called East Asian "miracle economies" (with Korea perhaps the most prominent). These developments empowered neoliberals to make the most sweeping assertions about capitalist development and the economic benefits to be derived from a global unbridling of markets.

Eventually, these assertions were challenged, most effectively by a small but increasingly influential group of left-Keynesian/statist social scientists. Drawing their lessons from the East Asian experience, these analysts advocated a new "conventional wisdom," one that celebrated the role of the developmental state rather than the market as the engine of development. The sharpness of the debate between the two positions tended to overshadow the fact that both sides shared a number of critical assumptions, the most important being that capitalism was the only system capable of supporting development. As a consequence, Marxism was pushed even further to the intellectual margins in development studies, economics, and political economy.

However, despite neoliberal and left Keynesian/statist dismissals of the importance of Marxist categories and insights (including those related to class, crisis, and imperialism), Marxist voices were never completely silenced. And, as capitalism's own accumulation dynamics led to ever-greater exploitation and instability throughout the world, including East Asia, these voices have become louder. Given the critical role played by Korea as an intellectual battleground for the debate between left Keynesian/statists and neoliberals, it is especially noteworthy that there has been a resurgence of Marxist-informed analyses of the Korean experience and by Korean scholars. There is great need for such work as the recent crisis in Korea and resulting capitalist restructuring have intensified class tensions and presented social movements there with new and difficult challenges.

This was the context for our decision to organize a conference in May 2005 on Marxist perspectives on South Korea with the goal of turning the conference papers into an edited collection. The conference was held at Gyeongsang National University in Jinju, South Korea, under the direction of the Institute for Social Sciences of Gyeongsang National University, as part of their international co-research project, "Change of Accumulation Regime in Korea: 1987-2003." Among the authors of the volume, Martin Hart-Landsberg, Sang-Hwan Jang, and Seongjin Jeong are also co-researchers with the project.

What makes this volume distinctive is that the majority of papers presented and included in this volume are by Koreans. Unfortunately because of language difficulties work by Korean authors tends to remain largely unknown outside of Korea. Indeed, language difficulties have generally forced progressive scholars in the West to rely solely on Western (or Western influenced) mainstream sources for their insights into the Korean development experience, thereby contributing to a misleading understanding of that experience. We hope that the melding of Western and Korean Marxist scholarship in this volume will provide much deserved visibility to Korean Marxist scholarship and help correct many of the misunderstandings and politically motivated misrepresentations of the Korean experience.

Finally, the editors (as well as all the contributors to the volume) wish to express their gratitude for the many comments and suggestions provided by other conference participants, including Alex Callinicos, Jin-Sang Jeong, Ohnishi Hiroshi, Moohyeon Joo, Nam-Hoon Kang, Eui-Dong Kim, Chai-on Lee, Jong-Lae Lee, and Lefteris Tsoulfidis. Financial support from a Korea Research Foundation Grant (KRF-2003-005-B00006) for the project and the conference is also gratefully acknowledged.

Martin Hart-Landsberg (Portland, OR USA)
Seongjin Jeong (Jinju, South Korea)
Richard Westra (Pusan, South Korea)
2007

Introduction

Marxist Perspectives on South Korea in the Global Economy

Martin Hart-Landsberg, Seongjin Jeong and Richard Westra

This edited volume is about South Korea (hereafter Korea). More specifically, it offers a critical examination of Korea's past growth; recent crisis; and contemporary restructuring, struggles, and challenges. Most neoliberal as well as left-Keynesian/statist economists celebrate Korea as a capitalist success story, although they have different explanations for the country's success. We disagree with this characterization of the Korean experience. In brief, as we argue below, the country's past growth was heavily dependent on historically specific conditions (including a powerful state and a supportive international economic environment), and came at high cost for most Koreans (based as it was on dictatorship and exploitation). Eventually, contradictions generated by this growth, which were intensified by changing international conditions, triggered a crisis that has undermined past industrial achievements and increased competitiveness pressures, leading to deteriorating living and working conditions for the majority of Koreans. In short, we believe that our collective examination of the Korean experience offers important insights into the limits of and contradictions inherent in capitalist growth.

As the title – *Marxist Perspectives on South Korea in the Global Economy* – makes clear, this volume is also about Marxism. In particular, it is a Marxian perspective that guides our examination of the Korean experience. This perspective differs sharply from both the neoliberal and left Keynesian/statist ones that currently dominate debates about Korea in the fields of economics, development studies, and political economy. By highlighting the relevant differences, this book also seeks to demonstrate the superiority of Marxism as a framework for understanding both the Korean development experience (and by extension capitalist dynamics more generally) and the contemporary challenges facing Koreans as they struggle to build a new, more responsive political-economy.

The Celebration of the Korean Growth Model

Korea's recent growth record has been impressive. The country's real GDP grew by an average of 9 percent during the 1960s, 9.3 percent during the 1970s, and by nearly 10 percent during the 1980s and the first half of the 1990s. Equally impressive was the country's industrial transformation. By 1996, South Korea ranked as the number one "supplier of computer memory chips, the second largest shipbuilder in the world, the third largest producer of semiconductors, the fourth largest maker of electronics, the fifth largest car maker, and the largest steel producer" (Cathie, 1997/1998, 22). On the strength of this performance, Korea went from being a "basket case" in the 1950s to a member of the Organization for Economic Cooperation and Development (OECD) in 1996.

Several other East Asian countries/economies, in particular Hong Kong, Indonesia, Malaysia, Singapore, Taiwan, and Thailand, have also been celebrated for their recent growth achievements. What makes this record of East Asian gains especially noteworthy is that it stands in sharp contrast to the performance of the rest of the third world. As the IMF explains:

> Korea, for example, experienced almost a ten-fold rise in per capita income between 1965 and 1995, while Thailand saw a five-fold increase, and Malaysia a four-fold rise. In the developing countries of the Western Hemisphere average per capita incomes doubled between 1965 and 1980 before stagnating over the next 15 years, a period much of which was dominated by the debt crisis and its aftermath. . . . While the [East Asian] success stories illustrate that dramatic improvements in living standards are possible, many countries regrettably are not realizing their potential. In relative terms, most developing countries have failed to raise their per capita incomes toward those of the industrial countries. In fact, Asia is the only major region to have registered significant relative progress, in the sense of having achieved significant convergence towards industrial country living standards (International Monetary Fund, 1997, 76-7).

Even within this group of fast growing East Asian countries, Korea has often been singled out for praise. For example, Alice Amsden (an advocate of the developmental state) has argued that South Korea "can serve as a useful model from which other aspiring industrializing countries can learn" (Amsden, 1989, v-vi). Donald Keesing, writing in a World Bank working paper, concluded that "application in new settings of the combination of what is now known and recommended – particularly in countries well along in the process of development – gives very encouraging results, even if it does not turn other countries into success stories on the same scale as Korea".[1] Similarly, in an examination of the industrialization experience of seven "of the more advanced developing countries" – Hong Kong, Malaysia, Mexico, Korea, Singapore, Taiwan, and Turkey – over the period 1981-1996, the United Nations Conference on Trade and Development (UNCTAD) concluded that "of these countries, the Republic of Korea stands alone, with a production-trade configuration similar to that of the major industrial countries" (UNCTAD, 2002a, 77).

In short, by the late 1980s, economists across a wide political spectrum were promoting the fast growing East Asian countries, and Korea in particular, as model developers whose experiences should be studied and emulated. While many of these economists did acknowledge that there were costs associated with the East Asian development process – including repression of civil, human, and labor rights, and the destruction of the environment – they generally considered them to be inconsequential compared with the benefits generated by the region's rapid growth.

1 As quoted in Linder (1986, 41)

Moreover, they tended to view them as temporary, unavoidable consequences of the transition out of underdevelopment. Thus, continued economic growth was seen as the best response to whatever problems might exist.

The only area of controversy that marred this almost unanimous endorsement of the East Asian experience was disagreement over the policies that accounted for the region's rapid growth. Neoliberal economists credited market forces, while left-Keynesian/statists credited active state industrial policy.

Neoliberal economists have generally proven quite opportunistic. They have embraced any country's experience if it appears positive, claiming that it demonstrates the superiority of market forces as an engine of development. Sadly, their positions of authority in the top universities, research institutions, and international organizations have given their claims undeserved credibility. Such is the case with the East Asian experience and neoliberal assertions of market led development. For example, in a 1987 study for the Institute for International Economics, Bela Balassa and John Williamson claimed that the East Asian newly industrializing countries (NICs; Korea, Taiwan, Hong Kong, and Singapore) had outperformed the Latin American NICs and India because of their rejection of industrial policy:

> More generally, the scope of administrative controls was much more limited in the four East Asian NICs than in Latin America and, even more, India. In the latter case, there were pervasive controls on investment, prices, and imports, and decisions were generally made case by case, thereby creating uncertainty for business and opportunities for corruption, which has remained comparatively limited in East Asia.... Capital markets, too, were freer in the East Asian NICs than in Latin America and India (Balassa and Williamson, 1987, 14-15).

Even when neoliberal economists acknowledged the existence of planning, as in the case of Korea, they dismissed its importance. According to Paul Kusnets:

> The coincidence of rapid growth and economic planning, and primacy of the Economic Planning Board in the circle of economic ministries have led some observers to misconstrue the function of planning and overemphasize the role of government in the Korean economy. Planning does not entail government control of resource allocation, but rather involves a set of activities designed to sustain rather than repress market functions. The government acts by providing information, reducing risks, and altering incentives rather than by fiat or by assuming market or enterprise functions (Kusnets, 1982, 85).

This view of the role of markets in the East Asian experience, especially in the case of Korea, was clearly wrong, and by the late 1980s a small but influential group of left-Keynesian/statist economists had begun to successfully challenge it. For example, as Alice Amsden noted:

> Korea is an example of a country that grew very fast and yet violated the canons of conventional economic wisdom. . . . In Korea, instead of the market mechanism allocating resources and guiding private entrepreneurship, the government made most of the pivotal investment decisions. Instead of firms operating in a competitive market structure, they

each operated with an extraordinary degree of market control, protected from foreign competition (Amsden, 1989, 139).

Byong-Nak Song, an economist with experience at government planning agencies and research institutes in Korea, offered a similar perspective on the critical role of the state in Korean development:

> Under the government export promotion strategy, "survival of the fittest" among competing firms was not determined in the marketplace, but through discretionary government actions. "Fitness" was judged in terms of the ability to expand exports, rather than based on profitability. If determined "unfit," firms were likely to face bankruptcy. Such firms were under constant threat of tax investigations and other punitive sanctions. On the other hand, firms that efficiently used their government-back loans to expand exports were implicitly considered fit and favored with even further support (Song, 1990, 101-2).

The debate between the old (free market) conventional wisdom and the increasingly influential new (statist) conventional wisdom was and remains important to those seeking ways of promoting development in the third world.[2] However, the sharp exchanges between advocates of these two positions have served to mask some important commonalities. Most importantly, participants on both sides appear to believe that the Korean experience demonstrates that development is possible under capitalism. In fact, they seem to share the belief that capitalism is the only system capable of supporting development. As a result those on both sides have largely dismissed the importance of class and contradictions, as well as the usefulness of Marxism for understanding Korean dynamics.

This celebration of the East Asian experience was finally brought to an end by the 1997-98 economic crisis. The immediate trigger for the crisis was a massive outflow of funds from the region. Foreign investors, increasingly worried about growing banking and trade problems throughout the region, began selling their stocks and bonds, calling in their loans, and converting their local currency receipts into dollars for repatriation. The rush for dollars began in Thailand, and then spread quickly to Indonesia, Malaysia and finally Korea. The governments of these countries responded by sharply hiking interest rates in an attempt to halt the outflows. But, by late 1997, with reserves rapidly shrinking, they were finally forced to abandon their respective pegged exchange rates, leading to a dramatic decline in currency values, and an acceleration of investor flight from the region.

With their economies in free fall from plummeting stock and bond markets, rising interest rates, and rapidly depreciating exchange rates, the governments of Thailand, Indonesia, and Korea reluctantly turned to the IMF, hoping that its support would help restore investor confidence and avert a complete economic collapse. The severity of the economic declines suffered by these countries is captured to some extent by the large contractions in their respective 1998 GDPs: -13.1 percent

2 See for example Amsden (1994).

in Indonesia, -6.7 percent in Korea, -7.4 percent in Malaysia, and -10.5 percent in Thailand.

The crisis, and especially its rapid spread throughout the region, caught both neoliberals and statists by surprise. Neoliberals had continued to praise the East Asian countries for their market-based policies right up to the very moment the crisis exploded in summer 1997. For example, Jeffrey Sachs, writing in December 1997, commented as follows:

> Consider what the Fund said about Korea just three months ago in its 1997 annual report. "Directors welcomed Korea's continued impressive macroeconomic performance [and] praised the authorities for their enviable fiscal record." Three months ago there was not a hint of alarm . . . In the same report, the IMF had this to say about Thailand, at that moment on the edge of the financial abyss. "Directors strongly praised Thailand's remarkable economic performance and the authorities' consistent record of sound macroeconomic policies" (Sachs, 1997).

However, once the extent of the crisis became clear, the neoliberal establishment made a complete about face. It now claimed that the crisis was long overdue because the massive state involvement in East Asian economies had led to cronyism and inefficient resource allocation. In fact, the Managing Director of the International Monetary Fund, Michel Camdessus, went so far as to say:

> In the less distant future, growth can be expected to rebound strongly after a relatively short, but sharp, weakening of economic activity and a rapid narrowing of external deficits. And as this process takes place, each of these countries will have the opportunity to strengthen its economy in fundamental ways. That is why I am confident that, after this period of adjustment, these economies will emerge stronger than before. Indeed, I believe that this crisis could be *a blessing in disguise* (Camdessus, 1997, emphasis added).

The adjustment the IMF had in mind amounted to a full scale restructuring of the very economies that neoliberals (including those employed by the IMF) had previously touted as exemplars of market efficiency. For example, when asked at a press conference whether it was possible to reform the Korean "system of industrial policy," the IMF's Deputy Managing Director, Stanley Fischer, replied: "I don't think [the necessary] restructuring would be possible within the Korean model. What has happened in Korea is a breakdown of economic relations caused by that system – the banks were being used to funnel money from abroad into corporations that were not being subjected to market discipline and whose financial structures were not clear" (International Monetary Fund, 1997, 387). The IMF's Managing Director was even clearer. According to John Cathie, "Camdessus, using a literary metaphor from the Spanish poet Miquel de Unamuno (who 'used his ideas as he did his boots; he wore them out and then threw them away'), urged Korea to scrap its development model and begin afresh" (Cathie, 1997/1998, 21).

Although shaken by the crisis, statists disagreed with the hastily constructed neoliberal claim that the crisis was caused by too much state involvement. In fact, they believed that the crisis was largely the result of governments mistakenly abandoning their systems of state planning and regulation in the years preceding the crisis under pressure from the IMF and other advocates of liberalization. Therefore, they continued to defend the developmental state as the only instrument capable of achieving sustainable growth. As a case in point, Crotty and Lee, advocates for the statist position, offered the following explanation for the Korean crisis:

> There is an alternative interpretation of recent events in Korea, whose adherents include numerous heterodox scholars . . . along with a few prestigious mainstream economists such as Joseph Stiglitz, former Chief Economist for the World Bank, and Harvard's Dani Rodrik. These authors argue that the major cause of the crisis was not *inherent* inefficiencies in the structure of the Korean development model, but rather *contingent* inefficiencies created by liberalization, especially in the 1990s. This liberalization process disastrously weakened the structural integrity and coherence of the traditional Korean economic system. In this view, the problem in the 1990s was not too much state intervention, but the cessation of government functions essential to efficiency within the Korean model. In particular, absent the drastic weakening of the government's traditional regulation of short-term capital inflows in the 1990s, there would have been no system-shaking financial crisis, no IMF takeover, and no radical neoliberal restructuring (Crotty and Lee, 2004).

Perhaps not surprisingly, Korea has become the main intellectual battleground for the continuing struggle between advocates of the old and new conventional wisdoms. As we have seen, Korea was perhaps the most celebrated of all the East Asian success stories. It also employed state industrial policy more extensively then did the other countries. Thus, neoliberals were especially eager to discredit its past experience and take advantage of the crisis to impose a major structural transformation upon it. For the same reasons, statists have focused their efforts on defending the Korean growth strategy and arguing against neoliberal demands for the country's restructuring.

Unfortunately, there is little of value in this ongoing intellectual battle for those Koreans struggling to overcome the devastating consequences of their country's economic crisis. The main reason is that both sides have flawed understandings of the capitalist dynamics that shaped Korea's past growth and more recent crisis. The problems with the neoliberal perspective are numerous and far greater. Neoliberals clearly misrepresented the Korean experience in the pre-crisis period. They had falsely claimed that Korean growth demonstrated the virtues of relying on the market. Statists always displayed a much more accurate understanding of the critical role state direction and regulation played in achieving that growth. Neoliberals then responded to the crisis by abandoning their previous position and arguing that the crisis was a logical consequence of past statism. However, this change in argument has driven them into a theoretical cul-de-sac.

Neoliberals have acknowledged Korea as one of the few third world success stories. By now admitting that the country's past growth was largely due to the efforts of a developmental state and not market forces, they undercut their current argument that markets are the only vehicle for development. In fact, they can offer no satisfactory explanation for why statism was able to achieve such sustained and high rates of growth, or what caused it to come to such a sudden end (Burkett and Hart-Landsberg, 2000, Chapter 13). More generally, if the only countries to have succeeded over a sustained period of time were guided by statist policies, then there is little reason to believe that privileging market forces will have beneficial results. Such theoretical twists and turns make clear that neoliberal arguments and policy pronouncements are first and foremost designed to provide ideological cover for (transnational) capitalist interests, interests that run counter to those of Korean (and other) working people.

However, the statist position also is vulnerable to criticism. In particular, even though advocates have a more accurate appreciation of the pre-crisis Korean experience, their own perspective on that experience – including the causes of the crisis, and the policy responses necessary to overcome it – is also seriously flawed. For example, statists tended to celebrate Korean growth without proper appreciation of the costs working people paid for it. Dismissing the class dimension of the Korean growth process is a serious mistake. Among other things, it caused them to downplay the significance of the major struggles that working people waged against the dictatorship and the *chaebol* dominated export orientation of the economy, struggles which did threaten the continued profitability and viability of the Korean growth strategy. And it also encourages them to imagine that working people would welcome a return to that growth strategy if it were possible.

In addition, statists still do not appreciate the historically specific conditions that enabled Korean growth to take place. Said differently, their embrace of the developmental state was largely built on the assumption that capitalism provides a supportive environment for development if the appropriate state industrial policies are implemented. In fact, statists generally believed that other countries could enjoy Korea-like successes if they adopted Korea-like policies. This view of capitalism as a stable and growth supporting economic system is a false one. And, because of it, statists were unable to grasp the changing dynamics of capitalist accumulation that eventually led to the East Asian crisis more broadly and the Korean crisis more specifically. Given their assumptions, statists were left with only one explanation for the crisis, that it must have been caused by a series of foolish government decisions to abandon a workable strategy of development.

Korea is now undergoing a major neoliberal restructuring process that was shaped by the IMF, under United States (US) direction, with the support of the large *chaebol* and the Korean state. This process has left statists in full retreat. They cannot satisfactorily explain why the state they counted on to lead the development process is itself implementing neoliberal policies. And with the triumph of the neoliberal position, statists have found little ground for their policy proposals, which are largely directed towards rejuvenating the state directed growth model of the past.

The simple truth is that both neoliberalism and statism are seriously flawed theories of capitalism and as a result unable to illuminate either the Korean experience or provide meaningful perspective on what is to be done to help defend working class interests in Korea. To highlight the superiority of a Marxist approach, we offer next, in broad brush, our own Marxian influenced understanding of the Korean experience.

The Dynamics of Growth

Korea's rapid growth over the period 1961 to 1997 is best explained by a combination of domestic and international factors. Domestically, the Korean state (a military dictatorship) played the central role in shaping the country's economic trajectory. Control over the country's financial system was perhaps the single most important factor enabling the state to successfully direct the economy. Government planners were able to use their control over the allocation and cost of capital to both promote favored producers and regulate firm activity.

By the mid-1960s, the government had decided on exports as the priority activity for all firms. Significantly, this export orientation was generally advanced as part of a comprehensive effort at national industrial development. The government regularly targeted new areas for development by encouraging the establishment of import-competing domestic firms. These new firms were protected by both trade restrictions and limits on foreign direct investment and, when judged capable, required to export as well as meet domestic needs.

A prime example of this strategy was the government's 1973 program to establish new heavy and chemical industries for both import-substituting and export-generating purposes. The government directed firms into these targeted areas with, among other things, subsidized capital. Subsidized loans grew from approximately 30 percent of total credit over the 1965-70 period, to over 43 percent over the 1971-75 period, to an estimated 80 percent of manufacturing loans in 1978. One measure of the government's success: the export share of these heavy and chemical industries rose from 13 percent in 1970 to nearly 60 percent by 1985 (Hart-Landsberg, 1993, 38).

The government was also not hesitant about undertaking key investment activities itself through public enterprises, as in the case of petroleum, chemicals, and iron and steel. It eventually decided, as part of its heavy and chemical industrialization program, that production should be primarily carried out by private firms. It therefore selected a small group of *chaebol* to dominate production of the new industries. The combined sales of the top ten *chaebol* relative to GNP soared from approximately 15 percent in 1974 to over 67 percent by 1984. By 1988, the combined revenues of the top four *chaebol* equaled approximately 47 percent of Korea's total GNP (Hart-Landsberg, 1993, 38).

This industrial strategy was underwritten in large part by labor exploitation. The dictatorship kept workers disorganized and on the defensive for most of the 1960s and 1970s through its control over the only legal labor federation, a maze of ever more restrictive labor laws, and increasingly violent interventions into labor disputes by the Korean Central Intelligence Agency and special labor police. Government efforts to contain growing labor militancy in the 1980s were expanded to include mass arrests of, and several major military assaults against, workers. Also revealing of the nature of the growth regime was that the country's celebrated "economic progress" never brought the state or its growth strategy popular legitimacy. In fact, quite the opposite was true; the dictatorship found it repeatedly necessary to intensify its repression in order to sustain the conditions needed for accumulation.

As important as these domestic factors were, the reality is that Korea's growth also depended heavily on favorable international conditions. More specifically, Korea's rapid industrial transformation received substantial support from both Japan and the United States. Park Chung Hee, the military dictator who ruled the country, had been an officer in the Japanese military during the period when Japan had colonized Korea. Japan was eager to reassert its influence in Korea and thus eager to see him succeed. Therefore, as part of the 1965 Japan-Republic of Korea (South Korea) normalization treaty, Japan gave Korea $200 million in public loans, $300 million in grants and at least $300 million in commercial credits. Hundreds of millions of dollars of additional loans and grants followed over the rest of the decade (Hart-Landsberg, 1993, 145). These funds helped Korea finance needed imports and sustain its rapid rates of growth.

The US government provided even greater financial assistance, hoping to strengthen the Republic of Korea in its ideological and military contest with the Democratic People's Republic of Korea (North Korea). One avenue for the resource transfer was Korea's participation in the US led war against the people of Vietnam. The US paid secret dollar bonuses to Korean soldiers, which generated remittances of $185 million over the period 1965-73. Almost $1 billion dollars more was earned over the same period from military and civilian activities carried out in Vietnam and through increased exports to Vietnam. An additional $1.1 billion was earned thanks to US military activities in Korea itself, including local spending, provision of goods, and construction (Hart-Landsberg, 1993, 147-8).

In the early 1980s, after Korea suffered a major economic collapse, and was in political chaos, the US and Japanese governments again offered critical financial assistance. Two weeks after the Kwangju Uprising had been brutally crushed the U.S. Export-Import Bank finalized terms to extend more than $600 million in import credits to the new military dictatorship headed by Chun Doo Hwan. The heads of Chase Manhattan Bank and First National Bank also traveled to Korea to pledge their financial support. Not long after, the Japanese government extended a massive loan of $4 billion under exceptionally generous terms (Hart-Landsberg, 1993, 148, 223).

Japanese and US support for Korea was not limited to financial assistance. Japanese corporations provided critical technology and components to *chaebol* firms, enabling them to rapidly upgrade production and boost exports. For example, during the 1980s, Korean firms depended on Japanese corporations for between 40-60 percent of their machines, 60 percent of their parts, and 50 percent of their licensed technology. The level of dependence was far greater for those firms producing critical higher value added exports, like cars, ships, and electronics (Bello and Rosenfeld, 1990, 114). The additional US economic contribution included a willingness to provide open markets for Korean exports. Thus, in 1986, South Korea's first ever trade surplus, totaling $4.2 billion, was made possible because of the country's bilateral surplus of $7.3 billion with the US.

Thus, it was a combination of "favorable" domestic and international conditions that helped produce the "Korean miracle." In contrast, neoliberal and statist explanations rested almost entirely on the role of the state, with the former deliberately and misleadingly minimizing its importance. Advocates from both schools largely ignored the domestic (class) tensions and contradictions generated by the country's growth strategy, and never grasped the significance (and temporary nature) of the wider international capitalist dynamics that supported Korean growth.

The Contradictions of Growth

The late 1980s marked the highpoint for the Korean economy. From 1986-89, the economy recorded annual rates of growth of over 12 percent and its first trade surpluses. But, at the very moment when statist promotions of the Korean model were receiving their most favorable response, tensions and contradictions generated by the country's growth strategy were beginning to destroy the viability of that strategy.

For example, decades of growth had helped the *chaebol* grow increasingly powerful. They were now able to take advantage of their export successes to weaken state control over their actions. They used their new independence to channel their profits into more lucrative speculative activities rather than productive investments. In addition, the country's rapid industrialization, by creating large working class cities and massive industrial enterprises, also helped to create the necessary conditions for labor solidarity and an explosion of working class activism. Massive strike waves swept the country in 1987 and 1988, resulting in significant wage increases for most manufacturing workers.

International trends also proved threatening to the Korean growth strategy. For example, capitalist dynamics eventually generated tensions between Japan and the US that reached a boiling point in the mid-1980s. In September 1985, under US pressure, the Japanese government agreed to support a rise in the yen relative to the dollar as part of the Plaza Accord. The yen appreciated by almost 50 percent over the period 1985-88, creating serious economic problems for Japanese corporations. Initially, Korean exporters were able to take advantage of the appreciation of the yen to increase their own sales in the US market. In fact, while the yen was rising relative to the dollar, the Korean government engineered a decline in the value of the won relative to the dollar. As a result, although the Japanese trade surplus with the US leveled off in 1987, the U.S. trade deficit with South Korea grew substantially over the years 1986-89.

In response, the US turned its attention to Korea, demanding changes in the country's currency and trade policy. Under pressure, the Korean government allowed the won to rise by 16 percent relative to the dollar in 1988 and by another 3 percent over the first half of 1989. The US also threatened Korea with trade penalties if it continued to block imports of US goods through special taxes and tariffs. The Japanese, angered at losing market share to Korean exporters, also took action. For example, "in 1990, the Japanese government decided to ban the export of 200 ultra-modern technologies to Korea until 1995" to ensure that "Japanese firms will have exploited much of the market potential of the technologies" (Bello, 1992, 88).

These developments proved disastrous for the Korean economy. The country's trade balance slipped back into deficit beginning in 1990; profits and domestic investment began falling. The government tried to respond, but with little success. It failed to regain control over *chaebol* activity, in large part because it was now too closely tied to and dependent on them. There was even less it could do to force a change in Japanese or US policy. Thus, it settled on a strategy of attacking labor in hopes of stimulating new *chaebol* productive investments and exports. But while the working-class movement was weakened, it could not be broken.

These developments also led to a weakening of the Korean planning system. With the state increasingly unable to protect *chaebol* interests, the *chaebol* became increasingly unwilling to accept continued state direction and control over their activities. They therefore demanded and won, over the first half of the 1990s, several new freedoms. Among the most important was the ability to borrow and invest internationally without government approval. US pressure also contributed to this outcome. The US government threatened to block Korea's application for admission into the Organization of Economic Cooperation and Development (OECD) unless the Korean government agreed to deregulate and open up the country's financial system (Kristof, 1999).

The international environment grew increasingly hostile for Korea throughout the 1990s. Japanese corporations had responded to the rise in the yen by investing heavily in Thailand, Malaysia, and Indonesia. This investment transformed these countries into major exporters of manufactures that increasingly competed with those produced in Korea, but with even cheaper labor costs (Hart-Landsberg and Burkett, 1998). Transnational corporations searching for even lower cost production opportunities soon flocked to China, turning that country into an even more successful producer of exports. However, one of the consequences of this activity was the regional over-production of cars, steel, petrochemicals, semiconductors, and consumer electronics, which drove down export prices and earnings throughout the region. A case in point: the unit export prices of Korea's heavy and chemical products fell by more than 46.3 percent over the years 1996-98. As a result, South Korea's export growth rate fell from 30.2 percent in 1995 to 3.8 percent in 1996 (Grilli, 2002, 182).

Korea began running bigger current account deficits and accumulating greater foreign debt. Its current account deficit rose from $4.5 billion in 1992 to $8.9 billion in 1995, and then to a record $23.7 billion in 1996. *Chaebol* profits were also forced downward: the forty-nine largest business groups recorded total profits of just $32 million on combined sales of $274 billion in 1996 – a return of just over 0.01 percent (Moon, 1997, 57). Companies sustained their operations largely by going deeper into debt. And thanks to the recently approved liberalization policies, an increasing percentage of funds came from foreign lenders. By 1997, South Korea's foreign debt totaled over $160 billion dollars, with approximately $70 billion due for repayment in less than a year.

The country was teetering on the brink of crisis. Finally, several large and important companies went bankrupt in the first half of 1997. As the financial crisis swept through Southeast Asia, foreign investors became increasingly concerned about the creditworthiness of Korean firms and by extension banks, and the adequacy of the central bank's foreign exchange holdings. As they did in Southeast Asia, they began selling their Korean stocks and bonds and calling in loans. The Korean government responded, as had other governments in the region, by raising interest rates, but it was unable to halt the run on the won; by mid-November, Korea's currency was in free fall and the country was headed into recession and the arms of the IMF.

In sum, the crisis that struck Korea was not caused by misguided liberalization. It was the result of contradictions, internal and external, that made it impossible for the state to sustain the country's growth strategy. Thus, the main lesson from this history is that the crisis that appeared so suddenly in 1997-98 was years in the making and structural. There is no way or reason to restore the state-directed, *chaebol*-dominated, export-led, growth strategy of the past. The changed international environment also means that there are vastly reduced possibilities for other countries to escape underdevelopment through adoption of Korea's past developmental state strategy.

Neoliberal Restructuring

No one disputes that Korea is now undergoing a massive neoliberal restructuring. While neoliberals celebrate it, both left Keynesian/statists and Marxists oppose it because of its devastating costs for working people. Unfortunately, most progressive academics, inside and outside of Korea, continue to embrace statist understandings of contemporary Korean capitalist dynamics, which have been little changed by the crisis. Tragically, the flawed nature of these understandings makes it much harder to build the class awareness and theoretical clarity necessary to advance a meaningful working class movement of resistance and transformation.

In general, those who embrace the statist perspective – such as Lee and Lee (2002), Chang and Yoo (2002), Chang and Jung (2005), Cho (2004), Crotty and Lee (2002; 2004; 2005), and Shin and Chang (2005) – believe that the restructuring process is promoting the establishment of a "finance-led accumulation regime". They continue to believe that the pre-crisis Korean economy was basically sound, and that the crisis was primarily the result of the Korean government's mistaken financial deregulation policies. In their view, the post-1997 neoliberal policies imposed by the IMF and adopted by the Kim Dae Jung and Roh Moo-hyun governments have further weakened the hitherto efficient accumulation regime led by a state-*chaebol* coalition in favor of the "financialization" of the Korean economy and the associated construction of "share-holder capitalism". They believe that this transformation is responsible for Korea's low growth, stagnating investment, social polarization and financial dependence and call, in opposition, for the revival of Keynesian financial repression (including capital controls) and reform of *chaebol*-corporate governance as well as separation of industrial capital from financial capital.

As explained above, we believe that the crisis was the result of deepening contradictions in the state-capitalist accumulation regime that date back to the late 1980s, not the financial liberalization that immediately preceded the crisis. We also reject statist claims that the Korean economy is being transformed into a new, finance-led accumulation regime. Rather we believe that the post 1997 neoliberal restructuring represents little more than a capitalist offensive designed to restore profitability through the intensified exploitation of the Korean working class.

The structural nature of the crisis is clearly revealed in the trend of the average rate of profit for the economy as a whole, one of the most important Marxist indicators of the health of a capitalist economy.[3] For Korea, the rate of profit of the non-agricultural business sector, measured by the ratio of pre-tax profits to the net fixed capital stock, fell from approximately 12-14 percent over the period 1970-1986 to just 5.1 percent (the lowest level since 1970) in 1996, the year before the "official" start of the crisis (Jeong, 2005). Although the profit rate has recovered, as of 2002, it was still at the relatively low level of 6.6 percent, which appears to indicate that the Korean economy has yet to fully recover. Indeed, the average rate of GDP growth was only 4.2 percent from 1998-2004, significantly lower than the 7.1 percent average for the years 1993-97.

Some left Keynesians (Crotty and Lee, 2004; Chang and Jung, 2005; and Shin and Chang, 2005), have challenged the argument that the crisis was structural in nature by citing government data that shows corporate "operating profits" as a percent of sales remaining stable through 1995. This, they claim, shows that the crisis could not have been caused by a collapse of real-sector efficiency. They believe that operating profits, which are measured prior to the deduction of interest payments, are a better indicator of real sector efficiency than ordinary profits, which are measured net of interest payments and other factors, because financial payments and financial assets are excluded from the numerator and denominator respectively. It is thus directly influenced only by real-sector variables. While they are right to focus on operating profits, they are wrong to examine the trend of operating profits relative to sales. To evaluate capitalist profitability properly, profits should be measured against the invested capital stock. Doing so produces the downward trend highlighted above.

As noted above, most left Keynesian/statists – for example, Crotty and Lee (2004) and Chang and Yoo (2002) – also believe that the post-crisis neoliberal restructuring is leading to the consolidation of a new finance dominated accumulation regime in Korea. Because, in their opinion, this "financialization" not only triggered the crisis

3 As Mohun (2004a, 87) said, "(i)n contrast to the neoclassical vision, a theory whose vision is of a society characterized by class conflict over the production and appropriation of the surplus entails that the central category of macroeconomics is not GDP and its components, and their growth over time, but the average rate of profit and its trend over time."

but is also responsible for current economic difficulties, they call for policies designed to reinvigorate the old accumulation regime. We reject this characterization of the restructuring process as well as the associated reformist policy recommendations.

According to Crotty (2002), "financialization" is generally defined by the following trends: the hegemony of financial capital over industrial capital, the dominance of direct finance through equity and bonds over indirect finance through banks and the related rise of the principle of "share-holder" capitalism, the increasing debts of non-financial corporations, the growing importance of financial assets over tangible assets for non-financial corporations, and the securitization of household financial assets.

While there appears some empirical support for these trends in the United States (and some other developed capitalist countries such as France), the same is not true for Korea. For example, the ratio of financial assets to tangible assets in the manufacturing sector rose from approximately 40 percent in the 1970s to 65 percent in the 1980s, but remained at that level through most of the 1990s, and has even decreased slightly since 1997. Moreover, although Korean nonfinancial corporations have always been highly indebted, their total liabilities have become *lighter* rather than heavier after the 1997 crisis. Indeed, the ratio of total liabilities of nonfinancial corporations to gross domestic product fell from 211 percent in 1998 to 201 percent in 2002. Looking just at the manufacturing sector, the debt to equity ratio decreased from 396.3 percent in 1997 to 123.4 percent in 2003, while the ratio of equity to total assets more than doubled over the same period, from 20.2 percent to 44.8 percent (Bank of Korea, *Financial Statement Analysis*).

Moreover, there is little to indicate that Korea is undergoing a securitization of household assets. The financial assets of Korean households are overwhelmingly composed of bank deposits. In fact, their share of total financial assets has *increased* from 42.8 percent in 1975 to 60.3 percent in 2003. Conversely, the share of equities in total household financial assets decreased from 17.2 percent to 5.8 percent over the same period. There is also little reason to believe that nonfinancial corporations have fundamentally altered their methods of finance away from bank loans towards direct issuance of equity. Although direct finance, especially stock issuance, did increased rapidly after the 1997 crisis, its overall share in total finance for nonfinancial corporations was still only 38.4 percent in 2003, which was lower than the 41.6 percent share from indirect finance (Bank of Korea, *Flow of Funds*). Loans by financial institutions still composed the largest part of the liabilities of nonfinancial corporations (33.1 percent in 2003), despite the fact that the share of stocks did increase after the crisis (from 10.4 percent in 1997 to 19.8 percent in 2003).

Duménil and Lévy (2004) propose related but different criteria for testing the hypothesis of "financialization." According to them, "financialization" occurs when the share of profits going to interest and dividends is growing, and the *financial profitability* of nonfinancial corporation, i.e., the rate of profit, considering the financial relations, converges to its *real profitability*, i.e., the rate of profit abstracting from the financial relations. Again we see little to support this hypothesis for Korea. For example, the ratio of financial outflow – that is, the sum of interest, dividends and rents relative to the operating profits of nonfinancial corporations – has remained generally stable at 50 percent since the 1980s. While it did skyrocket to 103.1 percent in 1998, it soon fell back to its long term trend (55.2 percent in 2001). More generally, interest rates have remained low in the post-crisis period: after soaring to 28 percent in early 1998, the call rate of the Bank of Korea fell steadily down to as low as 3.5 percent in mid-2004.

Finally, Korean manufacturing financial profitability has remained substantially *lower* than real profitability. In other words, in the so-called Korean "high-debt model"[4], the financial profitability of the nonfinancial corporation has generally been lower than real profitability due to a constant financial outflow, especially in the form of interest payments. In other words, contrary to the "financialization" thesis, the drain of profits from the real sector to the financial sector has been an intrinsic and constant tendency of the Korean economy. In short, in their desire to champion Korea's past accumulation regime, left Keynesian/statists mistakenly transformed an exceptional and transitory phenomenon into a structural and long-run trend.

The Korean economy did emerge from its crisis more rapidly than did other crisis-stricken East Asian economies. However, the recovery of capitalist profitability was largely due to an increase in the share of national income going to profits, or said differently, an increased rate of exploitation. The profit share of the manufacturing sector rose from 21.4 percent in 1996 to 37.8 percent by 2000. In other words, the Marxian rate of exploitation almost *doubled* (Jeong, 2004).

This intensification of exploitation is reflected in the reversal of hitherto favorable trends for the Korean working class, such as an increasing wage share of national income, decreasing income inequality, a reduction in work hours, decreasing use of irregular workers, and the securing of employment through internal labor markets. For example, the wage share rose steadily from 41.1 percent in 1970 to a peak of 63.4 percent in 1996; it was down to 58.8 percent in 2004. Income inequality among urban households fell until the mid-1990s, and then rose sharply after 1997. In particular, the ratio of the income of the top 20 percent to that of the bottom 20 percent of urban wage earners rose from 4.42 in 1995, to 5.22 in 2003, and 5.43 in 2005. Average working hours per week declined from 54.7 in 1986 to 46.1 in 1998, and have once again begun to increase. Finally, employment security has been severely weakened as a result of the aggressive labor market flexibilization pursued by Korean capital and the state in the aftermath of the crisis. The number of irregular workers, counted as the sum of temporary and daily workers, jumped from 5.4 million in 1995, to 6.97 million in 2000, and 7.27 million in 2005. Approximately half (47.9 percent) of all wage workers now have irregular status. They are paid, on average, only 50.9 percent of the hourly wages paid to regular workers, despite the fact that many were previously regular workers and continue to perform the exact same tasks (Kim, 2005).

---

4 For more discussion of the Korean "high debt model," see Wade and Veneroso (1998).

Left Keynesian/statists tend to blame neoliberal financialization for Korea's growing social "polarization" (now a buzz word in Korea), thereby identifying the problem with a particular state strategy rather than capitalism itself. Chang and Jung (2005) even go so far as to deny that the rapid growth achieved during the Park Jung Hee regime was underpinned by extreme worker exploitation and generated its own significant structural polarization through its promotion of a chaebol-driven, export-led growth process. Crotty and Lee (2005) advance a similar argument, claiming for example that "what is needed now are . . . policies ... designed to modernize the state-guided system that achieved the thirty five year Korean economic 'miracle'." Although unintended, this perspective plays directly into the hands of an increasingly popular "New Right" movement that is aggressively promoting the virtues of the viciously anti-democratic, anti-left, Park dictatorship.

Beyond the short run costs highlighted above, by systematically intensifying the country's (financial and real) external dependence, the long term consequences of Korea's ongoing neoliberal restructuring will prove even more devastating for working people. Markers of the country's deepening financial dependence include: (1) a rapid increase in the market value of foreign owned shares of Korean corporations, (2) a rapid increase in foreign direct investment, and (3) a rapid increase in the outflow of value from Korea. First, the share of market value owned by foreigners jumped from 13 percent in 1996 to 40.1 percent in 2003; this is the fourth highest in the world, trailing only Hungary (72.6 percent), Finland (55.7 percent), and Mexico (46.4 percent). More specifically, as of June 2004, foreigners owned 58.1 percent, 55.3 percent, and 70.1 percent of the outstanding shares of Samsung Electronics, Hyundai Motor, and POSCO, respectively. The growth of foreign ownership in the financial sector is especially striking, with the foreign ownership share of the eight largest urban banks growing from 12 percent in 1998, to 39 percent in 2003, and 64 percent in late 2004.[5] Crotty and Lee (2005) describe the consequences of this development as follows:

> The rising power of foreign financial firms contributed to investment stagnation, a dramatic increase in household indebtedness, and the conversion of Korea's stock and foreign exchange markets into global gambling casinos. Giant global banks are poised to complete their conquest of Korea's banking market, which means continued problems for investment finance, an increasing disconnection between banking profits and economic prosperity, and tightening constraints on more effective or progressive government policies.

5 By mid-2005, the share of foreign ownership in major Korean banks was 74 percent for Korea Exchange Bank, 100 percent for Korea-America (owned by Citibank), 100 percent for Korea First (owned by Standard Chartered), 76 percent for Hana, 84 percent for Kookmin, and 63 percent for Shinhan (Crotty and Lee, 2005). According to Crotty and Lee (2005), "by mid-2005, Korea had higher foreign bank ownership than almost all Latin American countries. ... the foreign share of all bank assets, including public banks, is about 60 percent. However the share for private commercial banks is about 80 percent in 2005."

Second, the inflow of foreign direct investment increased rapidly, especially after 1997. It jumped from $0.8 billion dollars in 1990 to as much as $15.5 billion in 1999, before falling dramatically to $2.7 billion in 2003. Most of this investment was for mergers and acquisitions of existing Korean companies, many of which were purchased at fire sale prices because of the crisis (Hart-Landsberg and Burkett, 2001, 422)

Third, the outflow of value from Korea – estimated as the sum of royalty payments, interest payment and profits remittance – also increased rapidly, from $4 billion in 1994 to $11 billion in 1998 and higher in the following years. Consequently, the ratio of the outflow of value to GNP reached 2.3 percent in 2001. If we include capital gains, the total outflow of value would be far larger (Jeong, 2004). Indeed, some foreign private equity firms, such as Newbridge Capital and Lone Star, have made astronomical profits by exploiting their "fire sale" purchases of Korean assets after the 1997 crisis.

Key signs of the growing economic dependence in the real sector include: (1) the increased dependence on exports for growth, (2) weakening inter-industrial linkages, and (3) the increased dependence on imported means of production. First, the ratio of exports to gross domestic product has increased from 27.9 percent in 1996 to a high of 44 percent in 2004. Thus, Korea's growth now depends more heavily then ever on exports, a growing share of which is tied to the fortunes of the US information technology sector. Significantly, while the relative importance of exports has grown, investment has been stagnating. In fact the investment to gross domestic product ratio has fallen from 37.5 percent in 1996 to 29.5 percent in 2004 (Jeong, 2004). If overinvestment was a partial cause of the 1997 crisis, underinvestment is now a major concern, one which suggests that the revival of chaebol profitability has little to do with the restoration of a healthy regime of accumulation.

Second, exports are becoming increasingly import dependent. Indeed, the coefficient of production, (calculated as the increase of production generated by a unit increase in exports) has fallen from 1.99 in 1990 to 1.87 in 2002, while the coefficient of imports (calculated as the increase of imports generated by a unit increase of exports) rose from 0.28 in 1993 to 0.37 in 2000 (Bank of Korea, *Input-Output Tables)*. These trends strongly suggest the weakening of inter-industrial linkages, in particular the creation of a dual economy with a dynamic import-dependent (IT/*chaebol*) export sector and a stagnating domestic (non-IT/ small and medium companies) sector. Third, the ratio of imported means of production to total consumed means of production, a critical indicator of the degree of economic dependence, has also been increasing. Specifically, the dependence on imported parts for private fixed capital in the manufacturing sector has increased from 31.3 percent in 1993 to 42 percent in 2000 (Bank of Korea, *Input-Output Tables*). This dependence can only be expected to grow if the state "successfully" completes the series of Free Trade Agreements including one with the US that it is currently negotiating.

The reluctance of left Keynesian statists to take a critical stance toward capitalism has forced them to create a variety of capitalist categories which are then labeled either good or bad. Thus, Korea's old industrial based accumulation regime is good and worthy of defense. Korea's new finance based accumulation regime is bad and must be opposed. Polarization and dependency become characteristics of the latter rather than central tendencies of capitalism itself. This stance not only mystifies the causes of the crisis, it also weakens the development of the class consciousness necessary to build a movement capable of overcoming and transforming capitalism. In fact, this stance actually encourages working class support for various rightwing movements that seek to bring back the regressive and repressive social structures and policies of the past.

Left Keynesian/statists gained a significant measure of popularity during Korea's period of rapid growth, and largely because of it. While greatly reduced because of the crisis, this popularity still gives them considerable influence over the strategic thinking of working class and intellectual activists and by extension the political orientation of those resisting the deteriorating working and living conditions experienced by most Koreans. Having dismissed Marxism and socialism as largely irrelevant, left Keynesians have little to offer activists except variants on TINA (There is no alternative – to capitalism) which shift back and forth between various "good," "consensual," "self-reliant," and "national" models of capitalism such as German, Swedish, Dutch, and Danish, etc. Indeed, the maximum goal for left Keynesian/statists appears to be the achievement of "progressive competitiveness" based on "high-road" (high skill and high tech) production techniques supported by government subsidy of education and training etc. This type of thinking has even led some left Keynesian/statists (for example Chang and Jung, 2005, and Shin and Jang, 2005) to defend the *chaebol* system on the grounds that it provides an attractive alternative to a foreign capital takeover and can serve as a foundation for strengthening the "national economy" and "stake-holder" capitalism.

Missing from this political project is any recognition of the class and contradictory logic of capitalism, embrace of a labor and class perspective, and equally important, post-capitalist imagination. And, these are precisely what must be encouraged if Korean working people are to successfully confront capitalism's restructuring process, which continues to proceed at their expense. Said differently, the task of critiquing and transforming capitalism is far from out of date; Marxism needs to be reclaimed and the socialist project renewed.

The Retreat from Marxism in the Development Debate

While we have concentrated on demonstrating the continuing relevance of Marxism for understanding and responding to developments within Korea, the Korean situation is far from unique. In fact, given that the Korean example has often been used to support left Keynesian/statist policies elsewhere we believe that the arguments made above have a wider significance. At the same time, the marginalization of Marxism as a vehicle for understanding Korean processes and struggles cannot be understood as simply a Korean phenomenon. Rather it is a reflection of broader theoretical tendencies within the social sciences. Thus, it is absolutely critical to address the question of why Marxism as an analytical paradigm came to be dismissed, if not rejected, by most contemporary progressive academics (within and without Korea), thereby allowing the development debate (especially as it concerned the Korean experience) to be reduced to the arid spat between neoliberalism and statism as described above.

Answering this question requires that we take a step back to track the "development" of development theory itself, starting in the period following World War 2 (WW2). In the 1950s, as the "formalist revolution" (Blaug, 2003) swept neoclassical economics to an unrivalled hegemonic position in Anglo-US academies, it was hardly surprising that the theorizing of development would commence under the spell of neoclassical ideological assumptions. "Modernization theory", as the formative approach to the field was dubbed (Randall and Theobald, 1998), held market society (what we refer to as capitalism) to be the telos of human history. Accordingly, the rapidly de-colonizing world, dominated by "backward" or "traditional" societies, had only to adopt market economic organization and socio-political patterns of dominant capitalist states in order to progress in a relatively frictionless fashion toward "modernization" in the image of those capitalist states. This modernization process was to be advanced across the globe by market-based trade organized according to the principles of "comparative advantage". In international practice that meant that developing states were encouraged to specialize in the production of those goods in which they had purported factor endowment advantages, essentially primary products and light manufactures.

However, by the mid 1960s, mounting evidence from across the third world indicated that the policies encouraged by modernization theory were not leading to anything remotely resembling development as experienced by the advanced capitalist states. Prices for primary products, which modernization theory claimed would rise and contribute to global factor price parity as a result of expanding demand from industrialized countries, actually fell steadily in the post war period. This occurred in part because many industrialized countries, especially in Western Europe and North America, were now generating huge surpluses of foodstuffs. Many were also successfully engineering synthetic replacements for leading third world primary product and agricultural exports. Moreover, when development along capitalist lines did occur, it tended to be concentrated in economic sectors tied to foreign export, leaving large swaths of the third world disconnected from those growth processes and increasingly impoverished.

In response to this anomalous state of affairs, a genre of scholarship best described as "critical" international political economy emerged under the rubrics of theories of "dependency," "unequal exchange," and "world-system".[6] Scholars associated with these theories were generally inspired by Marx's analysis of the ways in which the plunder and colonialism of the third world contributed to the "primitive accumulation" of early West European capitalism as well as his

6 On the general conceptual thrust of this scholarship see Brewer (1991); Kiely (1995).

revolutionary commitment to eradicating exploitation. At the same time many were critical of Marx because of their mistaken belief that Marxism held that this process of primitive accumulation would eventually spread capitalist industrialization and development across the globe.

These dependency-type approaches put forward radical critiques of modernization theory that contained several shared assumptions: Firstly, they sought to anchor the study of development within understandings of the world-systemic economic logic of capitalism. This logic, activated in the 16th and 17th century expansion of capitalism from its West European heartland, not only engendered class division and significant social inequalities in national contexts as Marx had made clear but, through world economic interaction between "core" and "peripheral" states, yielded economic outcomes in the latter qualitatively different from what capitalism produced in the former. Not development, but rather, underdevelopment followed, and this underdevelopment of the periphery was a factor in the accelerated capitalist development of the core.

Secondly, it was this divergent economic outcome of core/periphery relations, described variously as "dependent", "extroverted", "disarticulated", and so forth, that dependency-type theories argued modernization theory misinterpreted as backwardness. Third, these theories also argued that so-called free trade between core and peripheral states, played out according to the tenets of comparative advantage, operated with a wage related inequity in relative prices for core manufactured goods over peripheral primary and lower value-added manufactured products to transfer wealth from the periphery to the core. Fourthly, these theories maintained that if peripheral economies were to develop in an "introverted", "auto-centric" fashion, they had no choice but to "de-link" from the world economy and construct their economies through import-substitution industrialization (ISI), possibly even as socialist economies. Dependency-type theories thus placed a spotlight upon the role of the state as the organized force of development policy direction.

This "critical" approach was also popular in Korean progressive academic circles in the late 1970s and early 1980s. One reason was that such dependency-type theories, especially those Westernized variants influenced by the work of Andre Gunder Frank and Samir Amin, provided a disguised, and therefore safe, way for Korean progressives to engage in radical research during a time when military dictatorship made it illegal to even read Marx or Lenin. Even Park Hyun-Chai's celebrated work, *Theory of National Economy* (1978), could be regarded as a variant of dependency theory.

Despite resonating with much of the overt reality of colonialism and imperialism, these critical theories were themselves challenged from several directions. A genre of "structuralism"[7] argued that they focused far too much on circulation and exchange relations in the world economy while devoting scant attention to substantive economic relations or "modes of production". Concentrating on the latter, according to this perspective, reveals that the taproot of underdevelopment is not simply

7 See Kiely (1995, Chapter 4).

trading relations between core and peripheral areas in a capitalist world-system but the economic articulation of capitalist and non-capitalist modes of production. Put differently, structuralism maintained that the expansion of capitalism highlighted in world-systems theory did not necessarily engender capitalism everywhere. Therefore, the challenge for development studies in the view of structuralism is to analyze underdevelopment as the result of the particular historical modalities by which capitalism variously conserves, dissolves or even conjures up non-capitalist modes of production through its global expansion. Thus, development studies should examine more closely the class structures and class alliances of underdevelopment in both the national and international dimensions of social class.

Another challenge came from a so-called "orthodox" Marxism that drew one-sidedly from Marx and Lenin's writing to promote the view of imperialism as the "pioneer" of capitalism. Bill Warren, the leading proponent of this perspective, questioned the dependency-type project as a whole. Warren (1980) argued that not only would the expansion of capitalism from its heartlands ultimately decompose pre-capitalist socio-economic relations, but there was mounting evidence to support the reality of third world industrialization and development (no matter how delayed). In making his argument, Warren voiced his agreement with Marx's position on the ravages visited on the world through the primitive accumulation of capital. He also claimed agreement with Lenin that, while imperialism was bellicose and predatory, the export of capital it fostered expanded the productive forces in the peripheral states such that the logic of capital and capitalist development would ultimately prevail.

Warren's argument, however, was subject to ruthless criticism on many grounds including that despite his use of radical terminology he was doing little more than repackaging neoclassical modernization theory. He was also attacked for his quick and shallow reading of the evidence, which showed that although industrialization in peripheral states, particularly in Latin America, did occur through ISI, it continued to face obstacles caused by its inability to support the expansion of the home market, which consistently limited its overall thrust.[8]

This so-called "orthodox" Marxist approach also drew support in Korea. Some Warrenite scholars, such as Ahn (1986), intoxicated by Korea's rapid economic growth and increasing *chaebol* autonomy, even declared that "dependency is dead, long live Korean capitalism!" The popularity of this approach in Korea reached its peak in the late 1980s, which as we saw above proved to be the zenith of Korean capitalism. Significantly, many of the advocates of this position in Korea eventually became open supporters of capitalism or at best Left Keynesian/statistism.

In the end, Marxism appeared to coalesce around three positions: an "impossibility thesis" of the dependency-type that held development in the third world was forever compromised by the logic of the capitalist world-system; the "inevitability thesis" exemplified by Warren that accepted development in the third world was belated but

---

8 See Ayres and Clark (1998).

believed imperialism planted the capitalist seeds of it and capitalist logic would dissolve non-capitalist socio-economic relations; and then there was structuralism which held a more complex, mediating position, maintaining that capitalism would always find ways to link to precapitalist modes of production in ways that would co-opt these in order to strengthen capital accumulation at another pole of an economy and cement capitalist dominance over the whole.

As the number of theoretical approaches multiplied, all claiming a somewhat similar Marxist lineage yet all leading to different assessments of on-the-ground realities and possibilities, growing numbers of progressive scholars came to doubt the usefulness of what they saw as Marxist-type overarching or "meta-theoretical" explanations, particularly ones predicated on a supposed inexorable logic of capitalism working its way through history. This, in turn, led a number of them to conclude that development studies animated by Marxism had reached an "impasse"[9] and that Marxism itself had to be abandoned if the field was to regain its relevance. This retreat from Marxism in fact marked a much more pivotal turn in development studies away from development *theory* as such, at least in the strong sense of the term. As a consequence, development thinking became increasingly supportive of and influenced by post-structural and post-modern approaches (Escobar, 1995; Dirlik, 1997).

This turn towards postmodernism and post-structuralism also became popular in Korea during the 1990s. Progressive Korean scholars began dismissing the grand debates of the 1980s as futile word-mongering. Instead, they turned their attention to the development of specific alternative policies, and emphasized the importance of civil movements, especially NGOs, rather than workers' movements. Many also became attracted to and supporters of the new civilian governments led by Kim Dae Jung and Roh Moo-hyun.

Nevertheless, as the "impasse" debate ran its course, evidence of continuing industrialization in the third world, particularly industrialization in more high value added heavy and consumer durable industries previously coveted by core developed states, fed the desire for a new, more comprehensive or, once again, overarching theory to capture the complex physiognomy of what was first dubbed the new international division of labor (NIDL) and ultimately "globalization" (Hoogvelt, 1997). One response was offered by the regulation school (Aglietta 1979; Lipietz, 1987). This approach argued that analysis of capitalist development requires a "mid-range" theory which studies capitalism at an "institutional" level to capture the way the "contradictions" of capitalism are managed, thereby ensuring successful long-run accumulation across historical periods or *stages* of capitalism. By embracing the need for "levels" of theory, the regulation approach held out the promise of overcoming the charges leveled against Marxism in the impasse debate. In particular, the regulation school's call for mid-range theorizing involved grasping the discrete logic of accumulation based on the institutional "forms" of each stage. By periodizing capitalism according to the structures of accumulation that marked

9 On the "impasse debate" see Kiely (1995); Westra (2004a).

each major epoch of capitalist history, regulation theory also appeared to avoid the pitfall of seeing either development or underdevelopment as the inevitable outcome of a single logic of capital.

Regulation theory also offered a new perspective on the major changes underway in the global economy. According to the theory, it was the capitalist stage or "regime of accumulation" of *fordism*, emanating from the United States, which dominated the regulation of capital accumulation in the core capitalist countries in the period following WW2. The main characteristics of this regime included an institutional ensemble of assembly-line mass production, monopoly forms of competition, high wage and benefit bargains with labor, and Keynesian state demand management.

The theory also held that all regimes of capitalism, including fordism, ultimately fall into crisis. In the case of fordism, the specific crisis was triggered by a profit squeeze that resulted when rising investment costs to meet economy of scale requirements could no longer be offset by intensifying assembly-line work given technical limitations in the labor process. Thus the task fragmentation and functional specialization characterizing key fordist industries became the foundation for spatially separating parts of the production process, thereby enabling capitalists to recoup profits through a globalizing of fordism. Mexico and Brazil became attractive sites for fordist industrial processes because of their proximity to the US market and sizeable working classes. Korea and Taiwan were also chosen as sites because of their disciplined labor forces and colonial legacies, which included the absence of a landed class and presence of an industrial infrastructure.

Despite its provocative conceptual framework and explanation for world economic developments, regulation theory soon found itself at the center of a three-pronged attack. First, it was subjected to criticisms similar to those leveled against Marxism in the impasse debate, that regulation school's theorizing of the internationalization of fordism continued the problematic tendency of Marxism to simply "read off" the development trajectory of the capitalist periphery from the designs of core capitalism (Kiely, 1995). Second, questions were raised about its empirical rendering of East Asian development in terms of fordist institutions. For example, Amsden (1990) claimed that the meteoric economic development in Japan and the East Asian NICs represented not fordism but a discreet "post-fordist" mode of accumulation characterized by a welter of novel labor process innovations and a new capitalist business structure. Finally, it was assailed by some Marxists for not fully developing the potential of its mid-range level of theory (Westra, 1996). That is, regulation theory never elaborated upon the other "ranges" of theory that were supposed to link to its regimes of accumulation and modes of regulation. As a consequence, the conceptual lacuna in specifying the unit of analysis of capitalist development (whether as a congeries of "national" capitalisms or as a single world system) and thus the determination of capitalist trajectories were simply transposed to the mid-range level of theory rather than being satisfactorily addressed.

In Korea, regulation theory was also initially regarded as a promising alternative approach to Korean capitalism by some progressive scholars (Kim, 1988). However, following the general trend elsewhere, many of its advocates became focused on the mid-range level of analysis and the regulating aspects of capitalism, and thus drifted towards left-Keynesian/statism. Indeed, it is now rare to find any traces of Marxism in regulation school-influenced scholarship in Korea.

Marxism and Socialist Development

Paralleling and accelerating the retreat from Marxism in development theorizing was a growing crisis of confidence among progressives over whether socialism was a viable project for developing countries. Marxists generally believed that socialism was to emerge out of the historical development of capitalism, which would create the conditions for it by developing the productive forces of society and the mass working class movement that would overthrow capital. As a result, the political economic milieu of most developing countries, where capitalist development of the productive forces was limited and the working class not a significant force either numerically or politically, continued to pose a challenge to the Marxist strategic perspective.

In this context, the experience and positions of the former Soviet Union (USSR) were influential (Griffin and Gurley, 1985). The Soviet leadership argued that with the consolidation of "socialism" in the USSR, the "highest" historical stage of human development had been reached. Because of the existence of the USSR, other countries were now able to skip the evolutionary path through capitalism as long as they simulated the development of those aspects of capitalism purportedly required by socialism. This, in turn, required the leadership of "Marxist-Leninist political parties" imbued with proletarian class consciousness. This procedure for building "socialism", which characterized most of the "socialist" experiments of the 20th century, became known as "developmental socialism" (Durand, 1990).

Where no socialist revolution was on the political agenda, "socialists" were encouraged to support strategies of so-called "national liberation" in which the working class and its representatives would forge alliances with social classes deemed progressive from the standpoint of "national" capitalism. This strategic perspective meshed well with that promoted by dependency theorists, who advocated a de-linking from the capitalist world system and auto-centric capital accumulation through ISI. Of course, as previously noted, without an expanding home market few if any de-linked states could hope to acquire globally competitive technologies (Ayers and Clarke 1998). And, as the historical record of the oscillations in Latin America between "populist" and authoritarian regimes demonstrated, attempts to expand the home market generated contradictions and highly combustible social class outcomes.

To be sure, Soviet-style regimes suffered from their own structural limitations. While it is true that when comparisons were made in basic social welfare indicators between developing countries striving to construct socialism and developing countries that remained within the orbit of the capitalist world system, the former generally came out best (Navarro, 1992). However, there were other costs borne by working people in these "socialist" countries. As we have seen, "developmental socialism" was charged with developing forms of capitalist productive organization in order to build "socialism." The result was often a crude "taylorist" system of work organization coupled with odious modes of authoritarian social control, an outcome that in hindsight appears inevitable given that the logic of the effort required "channeling" capitalism to develop "socialism".

It is within this historical trajectory, with Marxism increasingly wracked by internal debate and "socialism" as a post-capitalist world system teetering on the edge of collapse, that statism arose as the accepted critical opposition to a reinvigorated neoliberalism. Significantly, much of the conceptual accouterment of statism comes from a highly selective and limited engagement with both dependency-type theories and Marxism. For example, the statist eschewing of world economic analysis and focus upon comparative case studies owes much to the increased attention dependency theorists gave to so-called "situations of development" (Cardoso and Faletto, 1979). Similarly the assumed centrality of the state's role in development owes much to the Marxist analysis of the concentrated power and class dimensions of the state and the historical evidence Marxist studies marshaled on the necessary support the state provides to capital accumulation.

Not surprisingly, the statist research program suffers precisely because of its rejection of key tenants of Marxism, including its focus on the fundamental contradictions of capital accumulation and the class distributive social outcomes and crises tendencies that perpetually play themselves out across capital's national and international development trajectories. It is this theoretical shortcoming that allowed left-Keynesian/statists to reify the post-WW2 epoch of so-called "economic nationalism" (Brown and Lauder, 2001), in which the Keynesian welfare state embedded in a world economy of fixed currencies and capital controls constituted the development template. Influenced by this one-sided understanding of capitalism's "golden age", many on the left became convinced that capitalism was amenable to substantive reform and progressive and even socialist goals.

The Necessary Resurrection of Marxist Analysis

Marxists have, of course, continued to challenge their opponents in the impasse debate. Among other things, they have pointed out how those critical of Marxism have often violated their own purported commitment to "difference" by tarnishing all Marxist-influenced theories with the same brush. They have also objected to the way their opponents have transformed their critique of meta-theories into a broader dismissal of the importance of the categories and insights that inform them (Kiely, 1995). For example, rejection of a particular overarching world-systemic explanatory framework certainly does not lead logically to the conclusion that world systemic analysis *per se* can or should be dispensed with.

More generally, Marxist efforts to develop mediations between the accumulatory and social class logic of capitalism, on the one hand, and the spatial logic of capitalism on the other (the main concern of dependency-type theories), have much to contribute to our knowledge of global capital accumulation and its crises tendencies (Arrighi, 1994; Harvey, 2006). Further, as conceptual categories, the terms core/periphery perdure in analytical force only now capturing the modalities by which core and periphery emerge as potentially geographically indeterminate "social relationships" at the heart of both developed and third world societies (Hoogvelt, 1997).

Though structuralism itself foundered over the impasse debate question of reading underdevelopment in terms of its functionality to global capitalism, the emphasis it placed upon social class and the national and international class dimensions of the capitalist mode of production breaths new life in the theory of "transnational historical materialism".[10] In fact, the research agenda of transnational historical materialism intertwines several threads of earlier Marxist analysis to offer a potent critique of current globalization. Similarly, the concern of regulation theory with the NIDL and spreading global fordism is refocused by transnational historical materialism into a consideration of the "transnational relations" of US corporate capital and the US ruling class. Here, the work of the Italian Marxist Antonio Gramsci on class *hegemony*, a conceptualizing of class power deriving from consent rather than overt coercion (though coercion always lurks in the background), is used to examine the class articulations following WW2 that bound ruling classes of Western Europe and Japan to a common reconstructive project under US auspices. Transnational historical materialism is also developing a Marxist analysis of the concentrated power of the capitalist state in terms of the "internationalizing of the state", to capture the ways in which the US capitalist state promoted the international processes leading to the de-regulation and global financial market dominance characteristic of current neoliberal globalization.

While the regulation school's periodizing of capitalism in terms of fordism and its global spread was justly criticized during the impasse debate for its functionalist tendencies, the project of theorizing phases of capital accumulation has emerged as an indispensable tool in many of the most vibrant schools of Marxist thought.[11] The reality is that the critical assumptions underpinning neoclassical economics – that abstract modeling of economic conditions of "perfect competition" and "general equilibrium" directly yield insights into the complex real world economy, insights that policymakers can confidently follow – have been proved bankrupt again and again, as have their associated policies. By contrast, it appears clear that capitalist history is marked by world historic phases of development, each characterized by a leading economic sector, concomitant technology bundle, geo-spatial core and an institutional/policy architecture supporting market operation. In this sense, the constituents of a phase are the matrix through which capital receives the modicum of coherence it requires for relatively long periods of accumulation.

10 Overbeek (2000) offers a succinct summary of this perspective.

11 Albritton, Itoh, Westra and Zuege (2001) provide an anthology of the important schools of though in this vital area of Marxian research.

On the question of the post-war phase of capitalism that regulation theory dubbed fordism, debate still continues over what other appellation best reflects its key characteristics and the role to be accorded to particular constituents in guaranteeing the accumulation and expansion of capital. At the same time, there is consensus among the competing theories that global capitalism and the economies of major capitalist states operated with a requisite symmetry up to the early 1970s, at which time the world economy was beset by stagnation and crisis. There also tends to be widespread agreement that the so-called golden age of accumulation reified in statist literature cannot be reinstated, as it was contradictions generated by the capital accumulation process that marked that period which begat the accumulation restructuring associated with neoliberalism in the first place. Questions do remain, however, about whether processes of neoliberal globalization do in fact constitute a new phase of capitalism (Westra, 2003a).

As noted above, the problems development studies faced in reconciling claims for inexorable logical tendencies of capital with evidence of divergent historical outcomes of capitalist development were in part responsible for the turn in development theory away from Marxism and toward post-structuralism and post-modernism. Though the promise regulation theory held out for resolving such theoretical problems was ultimately not fulfilled, this hardly warrants the conclusion that these problems are irresolvable and that Marxists must chose between clinging to a crude determinism or embracing the post-modern play of meaning in the study of local narratives of development.

For example, work influenced by the Japanese Uno approach to Marxism (Westra 1996; 2006) also offers a "levels of analysis" perspective for the study of capitalist development which incorporates mid-range theoretical analysis. However, it develops the mid-range level within the context of the elaboration of other ranges of theory. More specifically, it offers argumentation over the epistemology and role of each level to demonstrate how levels operate within a division of labor to produce knowledge of capitalism. It also maintains that Marx's economic theory of capitalism is not a meta-theory of the sort post-modernism rants against, as its direct subject focus is but a single subset of human social relations – material reproduction – studied under the historically delimited conditions of capitalism, a historically transient society.

Mid-range theory or what the Uno approach refers to as "stage theory" offers a synchronic or structural analysis of the constituents of a phase of capitalism and deals simultaneously with the unit of analysis question as well as the functionalism attributed to Marxism. Said differently, stage theory is neither a theory of national capital nor international capital yet theorizes each synchronically as structures of accumulation for a stage. Historical outcomes cannot be read off stage theory precisely because stages are theorized as structures and are concerned with predominant "types" of capital. And, stage theory in the Uno approach is epistemologically distinct from the level of "historical analysis" which is the empirical, transformatory and agency oriented level of theory that studies the impact of capital's logic on modern history as one determinate force alongside other social forces such as race and gender.

In Korea, however, Unoist theory never won much of a following. One reason is that although it provided an important critique of Soviet-style "socialism" – arguing that while the USSR de-commodified labor power it reinstated forms of extra-economic compulsion for work reflective of pre-capitalist societies – its primary contributions to Marxism in the area of the study of capitalism remain highly theoretical. In Korea, Uno influenced scholars have rarely involved themselves in revolutionary praxis. As a result, Unoist theory in Korea is usually regarded as a kind of history of Marxology rather than a living revolutionary Marxist tradition.

Strikingly, the demise of the Soviet-style experiment that led not only opponents of socialism but also some Marxists to accept the premise of TINA has also energized socialists of varying persuasions to rethink the theory and practice of socialism in a new light. Review of this burgeoning literature (Westra, 2001; 2002; 2004a) indicates that a plethora of issues at one time believed to interminably compromise socialist aspirations are now being routinely addressed. For example, sophisticated models have been devised which display how computers can contribute to the processing and transmission of economic information with the sort of efficiency once seen as the sole prerogative of markets. Similarly, in response to the discrediting of Soviet-style central planning, Marxists have been forthcoming with new models of democratic, decentralized, participatory planning in which economic decisions are articulated through iterative micro, meso, and macro planning bodies. Acknowledging that the Soviet-style command economy was a highly ineffectual innovator, Marxists have also developed new formulas by which participatory socialist economies can marshal the "tacit knowledge" of society to innovate in the most creative ways that also conform to socialist desires to lessen work alienation. Marxism has also branched out to meet head on "green" critiques of industrial society to demonstrate how Marx's writings capture the anti-environmental thrust of capitalism and point the way to the building of eco-sensitive future socialist societies (Burkett, 1999).

But probably the greatest boost that Marxism and its vision and call for a socialist future could ever receive is the dismal failure of decades of neoliberalism, and globalization under its impetus, to contribute to the betterment of the human condition. In the US, the much vaunted exemplar of neoliberalism, 25 percent of children are born into poverty and an estimated 100,000 are living on the streets. This has been accompanied by a fall in wages for men in the 25 to 34 age group – the period when families are often formed – of 26 percent since 1972 (Anelauskas, 1999, 209, 71). Instead of the advertised world of NICs, neoliberalism has bequeathed a world of NNEs or nonviable national economies and UCE's or ungovernable chaotic entities (De Rivero, 2001). A study cited in the conservative *Economist* (2005c) names 46 such potentially "failed states". Instead of realizing a middle class dream for humanity, neoliberalism portends a nightmare scenario where it is estimated half of the worlds' urban population will be living in slums and shanty-towns by 2020 (Davis, 2004, 17). And, neoliberalism holds out a bleak future for today's youth with 50 percent of the one billion young people between 15 and 24 already living in poverty (World Watch Institute, 2004, 153).

As the above makes clear the struggle to replace capitalism remains critical, even in countries like Korea, which are widely celebrated as capitalist success stories. We know well that this is no easy struggle. But, we also strongly believe that socialist intellectuals, working to reclaim and reinvigorate Marxism as part of that struggle, can help promote the class based movements, structural understandings, and new visions necessary to ensure its ultimate success. We hope that in some small way this volume, which attempts to clarify and addresses the challenges facing those struggling for change in Korea, can contribute to that process.

PART I
Marxian Method and South Korean Capitalism

Introduction to Part I

With the resurrection of Marxist theory across the various areas of the development field fecund debate has sprung up over Marxist methods analysis. To be sure, no single method has yet achieved paradigmatic status, yet great progress has been made in Marxism in this quest. The three chapters in Part I, then, all deal with questions of Marxian methods of analysis and the potential utility of these methods for the study of capitalist development in South Korea. Part I, therefore, makes an important contribution to the broad literature on Marxist theory and method as well as to the literature on thr Korean economy. The opening chapter of Seongjin Jeong, "Trend of Marxian Ratios in Korea: 1970-2003", attempts to estimate key Marxian ratios, productive/unproductive labor ratio, rate of surplus value, and rate of profit, for the Korean economy during 1970-2003, by applying the method of Shaikh and Tonak (1994) and using macroeconomic data, including Input-Output Tables. Jeong finds that the increasing world economic trend toward growth of unproductive labor in capitalist economies commenced in Korea only in the late 1980s. He argues that the extraordinarily high level of productive labor during 1970-80s was crucial to the rapid economic growth of this period. Jeong further estimates that the rate of surplus value in Korea remained at a fairly stable level, around 140%, during 1980-2000, with a slightly increasing trend during 1990s. Unlike the rate of surplus value, the rate of profit of non-farm business sector in Korea is estimated to have fallen significantly since late 1980s, after maintaining a high plateau during the era of Park Chung Hee. Contrary to Institutionalist-Keynesian consensus which argues that the economic crisis of 1997 was anything but the crisis of "fundamentals", Jeong attempts to prove the hypothesis that Marxian tendency of rate of profit to fall was clearly behind it. Jeong also argues that recovery of the rate of profit since 1997 crisis was enabled by increasing exploitation of working class as well as by enormous devaluation of capital.

While Jeong's chapter analyses the long-term dynamics of capital accumulation in Korea, by estimating various Marxian ratios, including the rate of profit, Dong-Min Rieu's chapter, "Estimating Sectoral Rates of Surplus Value: Methodological Issues", focuses on the methodological issues involved in the estimation of the surplus value in Korea. Although both Jeong and Rieu use same data of Input-Output Tables in order to estimate the rate of surplus value, they differ in that Jeong estimates the rate of surplus value for the whole Korean economy in terms of price, applying the method of Shaikh and Tonak, while Rieu estimates sectoral rates of surplus value in terms of labor time by applying the conventional procedure of 'reversing' Marxian transformation from value to price, originally submitted by Okishio. Rieu argues that the so-called "New Interpretation" empirical variants are not superior to the conventional method of "reverse" transformation in that the former ignores the problem of differential sectoral rates of surplus value and fails to reflect Marxian perspective of the labor theory of value.

Both of these chapters exemplify the empirical relevance and theoretical potentials of Marxism in the analysis of the contemporary Korean capitalism, totally neglected or rejected by Keynesian/statism as well as mainstream neoliberal economics.

In his chapter "State, Market, and Stages of Capitalism in South Korean Development", Richard Westra operationalizes the Japanese Uno approach (Uno, 1980) to Marxian political economy to deal with two abiding methodological problems in Marxist theory that are of high relevance for understanding South Korean capitalism. First, it is striking, Westra argues, how, given the fashion in which the debate over South Korean development swirls around claims over the relative efficacy of market and state in the development process, market and state emerge as exceedingly reified concepts in the literature with scant attention paid to the historicity of their analytical separation. Westra subsequently maintains that it is only on the basis of Marxian analysis of the "ontological peculiarity" of capitalism that this analytical separation can be clearly understood. Second, the chapter expounds upon Uno's work to argue that the study of capitalist development requires a "levels of analysis" approach where the historical explanatory power of economic theory is mediated by a mid-range stage theory of capitalism. Westra's chapter then proceeds to explore causal matters regarding the specific operation of the capitalist market and role of the specifically capitalist state in Korean development through the lens of the theorizing of stages of capitalist development in the Uno approach. The chapter demonstrates how an adequate explanation of the newly industrialized country phenomenon in Korea is produced when the historical situation of Korean development is examined within the analytical contours of the stage specific accumulation modalities and institutional architecture of capital in the post-World War 2 stage of capitalism. The chapter ends by seeking to make sense of the new twists and turns in the state/market debate that follow on the heels of the Asian economic crisis in the closing years of the twentieth century. Westra maintains that far from a return to some historically non-existent "market" economy, the transformations of the global economy involved in neoliberalism constitute a movement away from capitalism rather than the indications of an emergent new phase. And that the current travails of the Korean political economy flow from the dislocations punctuating world economic change rather than from the varying policy choices over market and state as argued in the Left Keynesian/mainstream literature.

Chapter 1

Trend of Marxian Ratios in Korea: 1970-2003

Seongjin Jeong

Introduction

This chapter estimates key Marxian ratios, including the rate of surplus value for the Korean economy over the period 1970-2003. In doing so, it substantially revises and updates existing studies – for example, Jeong (1990; 2004), Park (1994), Seong (1996), Kim (2000) and Kim (2005) – using the method of Shaikh and Tonak (1994) and more accurate data on productive and unproductive labor. Moreover, in contrast to most previous works, which usually do not go beyond estimation, this chapter uses the estimated Marxian ratios to explain the long-term dynamics of the Korean economy.

This chapter is composed of three interrelated parts. The first presents new estimates of productive and unproductive labor in Korea, based on new data sources. This represents the first comprehensive examination of productive and unproductive labor in Korea. The second presents estimates of the rate of surplus value for the Korean economy, using input-output tables and the method of Shaikh and Tonak (1994). The final part presents estimates of the rate of profit for the non-farm business economy and uses the results to demonstrate the validity of the Marxian falling rate of profit theory in explaining the unraveling of Korea's state capitalist social structure of accumulation after 1987 and the economic crisis of 1997.

Productive and Unproductive Labor: 1970-2003

Data

While the distinction of productive and unproductive labor is unnecessary or even irrelevant to the measurement of capitalist profitability, it is crucial to the estimation of the rate of surplus value, that is, the ratio of surplus value created to variable capital (wages paid to workers who create the surplus value). This is true despite the fact that it has recently become fashionable for some "alleged" Marxists to reject the importance of this distinction. For example, Hardt and Negri (2000) argue that because of the growth of immaterial labor, there is no longer any relevance to this distinction. But, denying the importance of the difference between productive and unproductive labor is tantamount to rejecting the Marxian labor theory of value itself, because the distinction between the two forms of labor reflects the insights that lie at the foundation of the theory. Moreover, as we shall see, the distinction remains a powerful analytical tool for explaining the dynamics and contradictions of modern capitalism, and more specifically, the Korean economy.

Although there are many controversial issues involved in using official statistics to classify labor as productive or unproductive, this chapter adopts the method developed by Shaikh and Tonak (1994). That means we reject the older traditional Marxist approaches, including those used by Soviet economists, which held that only material goods producing labor was productive and all service producing labor was unproductive. Rather, this chapter will define service work, as long as it is not involved in circulation or supervision, as productive. Therefore, as Table 1.1 shows, business, cultural, entertainment and personal services will be classified as productive labor, while trade, finance, and public services will be classified as unproductive labor.[1]

Table 1.1 Classification of Productive and Unproductive Sectors in Korea

<table>
<tr><th></th><th></th><th>Industry</th><th>Industry Number (404 Industries Basic Classification)</th></tr>
<tr><td rowspan="11">Primary Flow</td><td rowspan="10">Productive Sectors</td><td>Agriculture and Fishing</td><td>1-30</td></tr>
<tr><td>Mining</td><td>31-45</td></tr>
<tr><td>Manufacturing</td><td>46-304</td></tr>
<tr><td>Electricity, Gas and Water</td><td>305-311</td></tr>
<tr><td>Construction</td><td>312-328</td></tr>
<tr><td>Transportation and Communication</td><td>333-351</td></tr>
<tr><td>Education and Research</td><td>375-376, 379, 380</td></tr>
<tr><td>Medical, Health and Sanitary</td><td>383, 387</td></tr>
<tr><td>Other Productive Services (Business, Cultural, Entertainment and Personal Services, etc)</td><td>362-365,369-371, 389-401</td></tr>
<tr><td>Restaurants and Hotel</td><td>331-332</td></tr>
<tr><td rowspan="6">Unproductive Sectors</td><td>Retail and Wholesale Trade, Equipment Rental</td><td>329-330, 366</td></tr>
<tr><td rowspan="5">Secondary Flow</td><td>Finance, Insurance and Real Estate Legal and Accounting Services Advertisement</td><td>352-357, 359-360, 361, 367, 368</td></tr>
<tr><td>General Government</td><td>372-373</td></tr>
<tr><td>Public Services (Public Education, Research, Medical, Health, and Educational Services etc.)</td><td>374, 377-378, 381-382, 384-386, 388</td></tr>
<tr><td>Miscellaneous etc.</td><td>402-404</td></tr>
</table>

Source: The Bank of Korea, 2000 Input-Output Tables, 2003.

1 In this respect, this chapter corrects the limitations of Jeong (1990), Park (1996), and Kim (2000), all of which adopted the traditional material conception of productive labor.

Another empirical issue of importance to the distinction between productive and unproductive labor concerns the recognition that unproductive labor exists in the productive sectors. For example, the general rule is that supervisory labor should be classified as unproductive even if it was employed in a productive sector. Unfortunately, it is not a simple matter to apply this rule. Previous studies in Korea, including Jeong (1990) and Seong (1996), used statistics on workers and wages by "industry by occupation" as found in the *Survey Report on Wage Structure* published by the Ministry of Labor, and identified productive labor as in Figure 1.1. As a result, only production occupations (including service, skilled, craft, operative, and elementary labor) in productive sectors were classified as productive labor, while all labors in unproductive sectors and non-production occupations (including manager, professional, technician, clerks, and sales labor) were counted as unproductive labor. However, the Ministry of Labor stopped publishing this data after 1991. In addition, several changes in standard job classifications since then make a consistent construction of time series impossible, even if it were possible to access the raw data set.

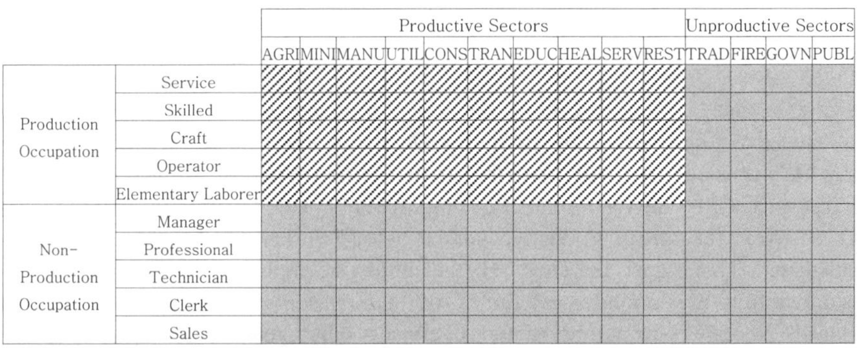

Figure 1.1 Classification of Productive and Unproductive Workers using Occupation Categories

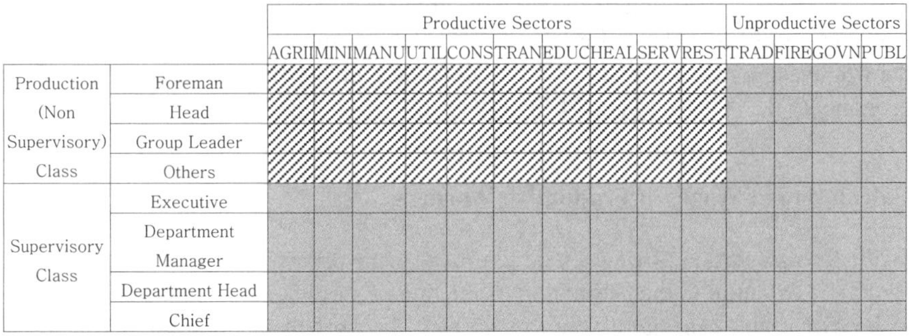

Figure 1.2 Classification of Productive and Unproductive Workers using Job Class Categories

To resolve the difficulties, this chapter uses a hitherto unexplored data source, that is, statistics on the number of workers and wages by "industry by job class" that are found in the *Survey Report on Wage Structure*, which is also published by the Ministry of Labor. The full name of the relevant table is "Age, Duration of Services, Days Worked, Hours Worked, Monthly Wages, Annual Special Payments and Number of Workers by Industry, Educational Attainment, Job Class and Sex" (from now on abbreviated as "Job Class Data"). Fortunately, the Ministry of Labor has provided this data since 1980. Figure 1.2 illustrates how it will be used to classify productive and unproductive labor in this chapter. As Figure 1.2 shows, only the production job class (that is foreman, head, group leader, and other non supervisory class) in the productive sectors are classified as productive labor, while all labor in unproductive sectors and supervisory class (including executive, department manager, department head, and chief) are counted as unproductive labor. Indeed, other empirical Marxian studies, for example, Shaikh and Tonak (1994) and Mohun (2003; 2004c), adopted a similar methodology to that illustrated Figure 1.2 for classifying and estimating productive and unproductive labor.

Calculation of Number of Productive Workers

Using the method described above, the ratio of productive workers to total workers is calculated as follows. First, the ratio of productive workers for each productive sector (Lp_i^*/L_i^*) is calculated by dividing the number of non supervisory employees in each industry (Lp_i^*) by the total number of employees (L_i^*), as reported in the "Job Class Data". Next, the ratio of productive workers to total workers for the whole economy is calculated. This is done as follows: (1) the number of employees for each industry (L_i) is drawn from the "Employment Tables" of the *Input-Output Tables*, published by the Bank of Korea; (2) the number of non supervisory employees for each industry (Lp_i) is calculated by applying the ratio of productive labor for each productive sector (Lp_i^*/L_i^*) to the number of employees in each industry (L_i); (3) the total number of productive workers for the whole economy is calculated by summing (2) for all industries, that is, $\sum(Lp_i^*/L_i^*)* L_i$; (4) finally, the ratio of productive workers to total workers for the whole economy is calculated by dividing the total number of productive workers for the whole economy ($\sum(Lp_i^*/L_i^*)* L_i$) by the total number of employees for the whole economy ($\sum L_i$), that is, ($\sum(Lp_i^*/L_i^*)* L_i$)/ ($\sum L_i$).

Calculation of Wages of Productive Workers

While the calculation of wages paid to productive workers, that is, Marxian variable capital, is essential to the estimation of the rate of surplus value, it is also important in its own right, especially when measuring the growth of unproductive labor in the country. Wages paid to productive workers for the whole economy (Wp) is calculated as follows: (1) from "Job Class Data", the average wage of productive workers for each industry (wp_i) is calculated by dividing the wage bills of productive workers (Wp_i^*), reported in "Job Class Data", by Lp_i^*; (2) like wp_i, the average wage of unproductive workers in each industry (wu_i) is calculated by dividing the wage bills of unproductive workers (Wu_i^*) by the number of unproductive workers (Lu_i^*), where both items are drawn by deducting Wp_i^* from total wage bill of that industry (W_i^*), and deducting Lp_i^* from total number of workers of that industry (L_i^*), as reported in "Job Class Data", respectively; (3) the virtual wage bills of productive workers in each industry (Wp'_i) are drawn by applying wp_i to Lp_i, while the virtual wage bills of unproductive workers for each industry (Wu'_i) are drawn by applying wu_i to $Lu_{i;;}$ (4) the ratio of the wage bills of productive workers to the total wage bills for each industry is calculated by dividing Wp'_i by (Wp'_i+Wu'_i); (5) the wage bills of productive workers for each industry (Wp_i) is calculated by multiplying the ratio of (4), that is, $Wp'_i/(Wp'_i+Wu'_i)$, to "Compensation of Employees" of each industry (W_i), drawn from the *Input-Output Tables*; (6) finally, the total wages of productive workers for the whole economy (Wp) is calculated by summing (5) for all industries, that is, $\sum (Wp'_i/(Wp'_i+Wu'_i)) *W_i$, while the total wages of unproductive workers for the whole economy (Wu) is calculated by deducting Wp from total wages of all workers W, that is, $\sum W_i$.

Results

The results of these calculations are illustrated in Figures 1.3 through 1.10. Figure 1.3 shows the trend of the ratios of productive workers to total workers by industry from 1980-2003. For the manufacturing sector, the ratio of productive workers to total workers remained at a high of approximately 95% till 1987, thereafter declining steadily to 80.3% in 2003. For the construction industry, the ratio remained at a high of approximately 80% till 1987, before declining to a low of 56% in 2003. Generally, this ratio remained relatively constant at high levels for most industries over the decade of the 1980s, and then declined over the following decade. The same basic trend appears to hold for the ratio of wages of productive workers to total wages by industry, as illustrated in Figure 1.4. For example, the ratio of productive wages to total wages in the manufacturing sector increased from 79.9% in 1980 to 88.2% in 1988, and then decreased to a low of 71% in 2003.

These trends all suggest that the ratio of productive labor only began to decrease since the late 1980s. Figure 1.5 and Figure 1.6, which are drawn from several sources, provide important supporting evidence for this conclusion. The *Report on Mining and Manufacturing Survey*, published by the National Statistical Office, provides the most accurate and longest time series for the manufacturing sector. Highlighting the trends based on this source, Figure 1.5 shows that the ratio of productive workers to total workers in the manufacturing sector declined by only 6 percentage points from 1970 (86.2%) to 1987 (79.9%), but by more than 10 percentage points from 1987 to 1997 (69.3%). Figure 1.6, which looks at wages, reveals a similar trend; after remaining relatively steady, the ratio of wages of productive workers to total wages in the manufacturing sector began a steady and rapid decent over the decade of the 1990s.

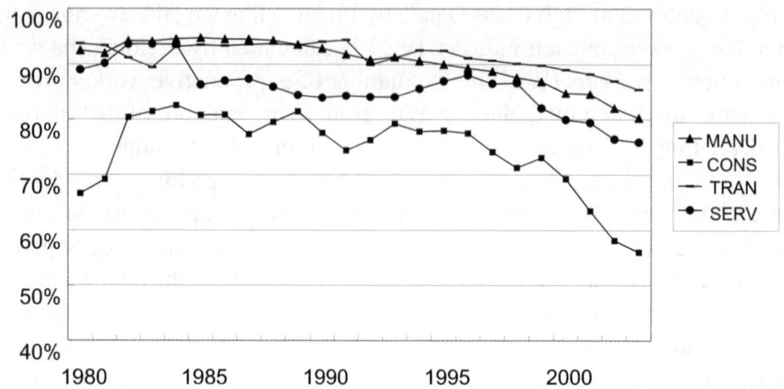

Figure 1.3 Ratio of Productive Workers (Lp/L) by Industry, 1980-2003

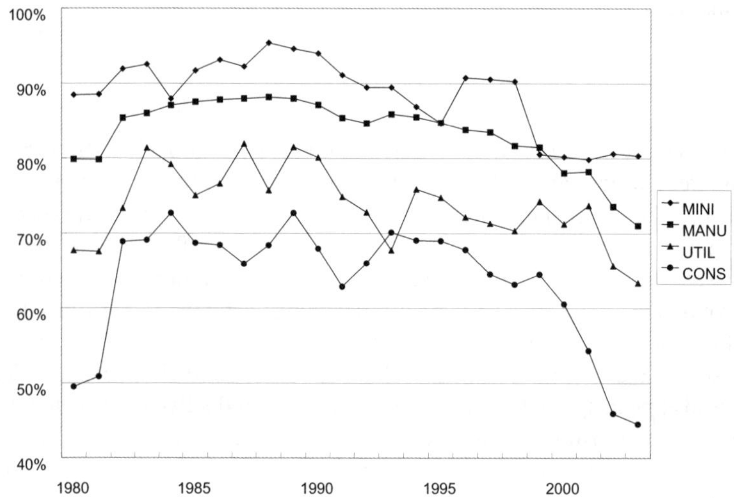

Figure 1.4 Ratio of Productive Wages (Wp/W) by Industry, 1980-2003

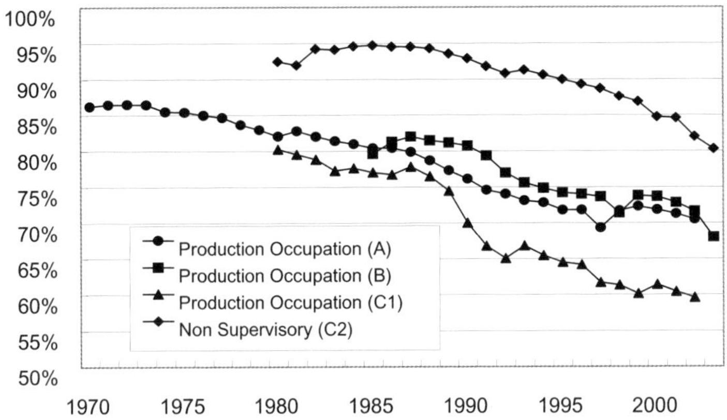

Figure 1.5 Ratio of Productive Workers (Lp/L) in Manufacturing Sector by Data Source, 1970-2003

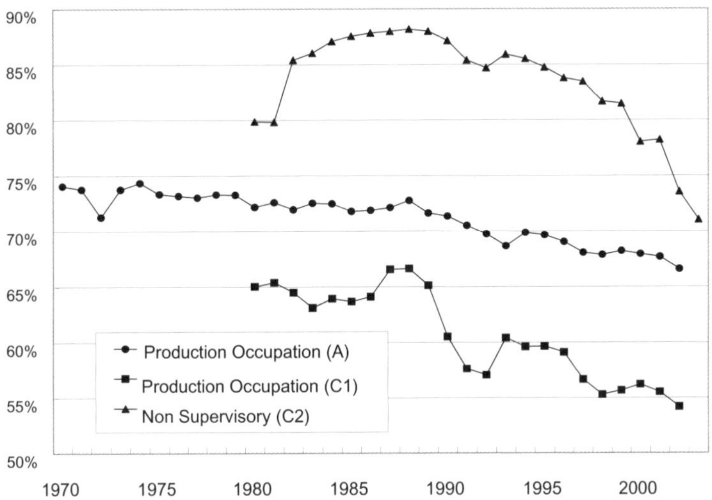

Figure 1.6 Ratio of Productive Wages (Wp/W) in Manufacturing Sector by Data Source, 1970-2003

By comparing the ratio of productive workers and the ratio of productive wages for all industries for each year from the above figures, we find that the former is always higher than the latter. The reason is that the average wage for productive workers is lower than that for unproductive workers. As we see in Figure 1.7, the average wage of productive workers in manufacturing was approximately 30% of that earned by unproductive workers in manufacturing in 1980. Although the gap narrowed over the 1980s and 1990s, with productive workers making 65.5 percent

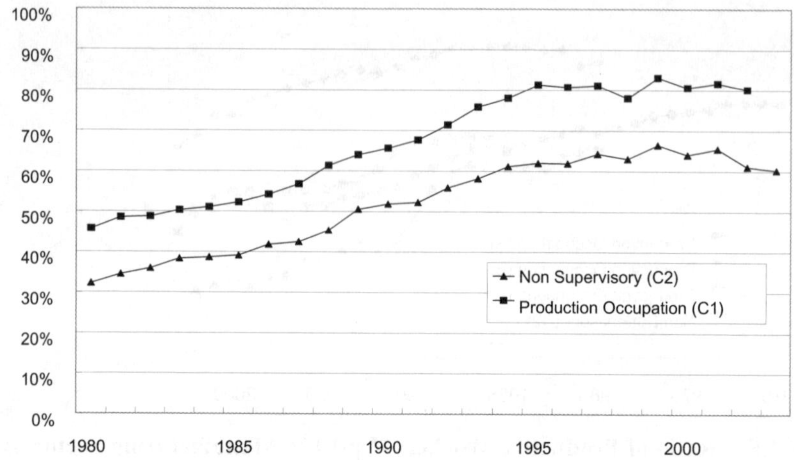

Figure 1.7 Ratio of Average Wage of Productive/Unproductive Workers (wp/wu) in Manufacturing Sector, 1980-2003

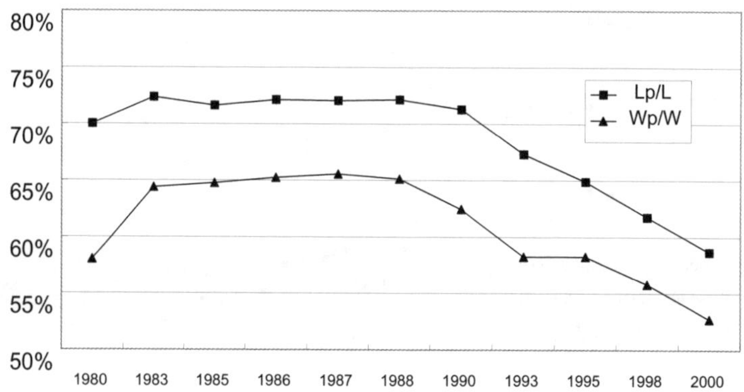

Figure 1.8 Ratio of Productive Workers and Wages of all Industries in Korea, 1980-2003

of what unproductive workers made in 1999, there has been little or no improvement since the economic crisis of 1997.

Figure 1.8 illustrates the ratios of the number and wages of productive workers to total number and wages for all workers in the economy from 1980-2000. The ratio of the number of productive workers to total workers remained relatively stable

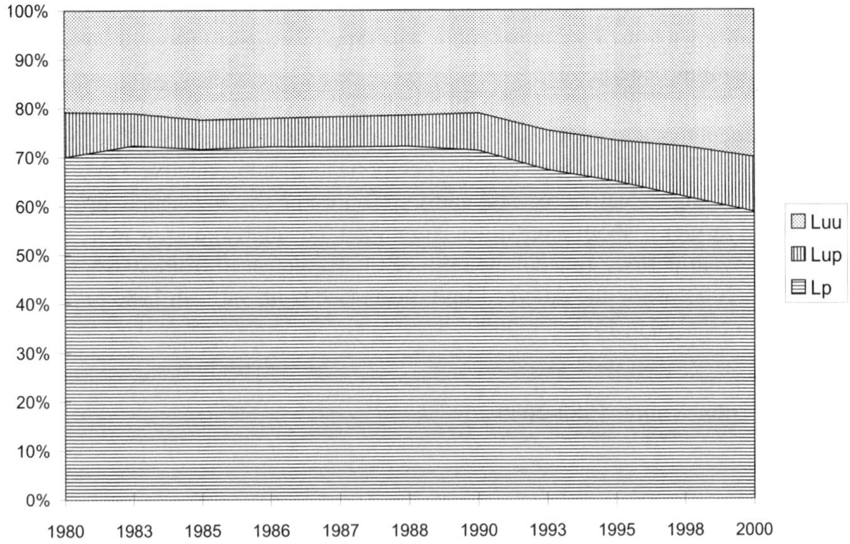

Figure 1.9 Composition of Productive/Unproductive Workers of all Industries in Korea, 1980-2003

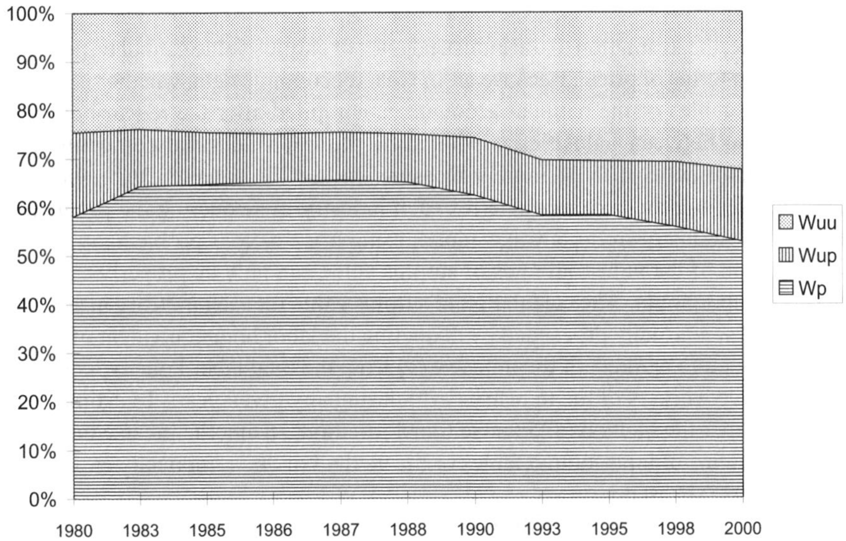

Figure 1.10 Composition of Productive/Unproductive of all Industries in Korea, 1980-2003

between 70-75% over the decade of the 1980s. However, it rapidly declined during the 1990s, hitting a low of 58.7% in 2000. The ratio of wages of productive workers followed a similar pattern.

Figure 1.9 and Figure 1.10 highlight trends in the compositions of numbers and wages of productive and unproductive workers for the whole economy during 1980-2000. Figure 1.9 shows that between two components of unproductive workers, Luu (all workers in unproductive sectors) and Lup (unproductive workers in productive sectors), the former is about three times larger than the latter, and grew more rapidly over the relevant period. Indeed, the ratio of Luu/L increased from 20.8% in 1980 to 30.1% in 2000, while the ratio of Lup/L decreased from 9.1% in 1980 to 5.8% in 1986, then increased to 11.2% in 2000.

Rate of Surplus Value: 1980-2000

Method

To estimate the rate of surplus value for the national economy, two additional issues must be addressed. The first concerns whether to estimate the rate of surplus value in price terms or labor hour terms. The second is whether to use data from input-output tables or the national accounts. This chapter follows the approach of Shaikh and Tonak (1994) in concluding that when it is the national rate of surplus value that is being estimated price terms are satisfactory and that input-output tables are essential.

Of course, the estimation of the industrial rates of surplus value cannot be properly performed in terms of price. Because all the macroeconomic data, whether it is from input-output tables or the national accounts, is compiled after the redistribution of surplus value between industries, mediated by the inter-industrial competition, is done, it cannot be used to accurately measure the surplus value created. In other words, calculating the surplus value for each industry by deducting the productive wages of the industry from its value added, using price data, is problematic. Thus, the estimation of the industrial rates of surplus value can only be properly executed in terms of labor hours. The calculation of surplus value for each industry in terms of labor hours (s) is usually proceeded by deducting the labor hour equivalent of wages paid to productive workers of the industry (v) from the total labor hour expended by the productive workers of the industry (v+s) during any given year. To estimate the former, v, either the method of "inverse transformation", using the inverse matrix of input coefficients of input-output tables or the method of "E" ("monetary expression of labor hours") is used.[2]

However, when we estimate the national rate of surplus value, we face no serious problems if we use prices because it can be safely assumed that the inter-industrial transfers of surplus value offset each other on the level of national economy. In

2 For discussions of related issues, refer to Rieu (2006).

addition, as Shaikh and Tonak (1994) show, we can get almost identical estimates of Marxian variables regardless of whether we apply price estimates or labor hour estimates as long as we use input-output tables and reconstruct them according to Marxian categories. Using the input-output tables, rather than national accounts, is absolutely essential to get an accurate estimate of Marxian value added (v+s). As discussed below, without using input-output tables, which show intermediate inputs and demands, it would be impossible to overcome the problems of double counting or omission, which are inherent in the national accounts.

Calculation of Marxian Value Added

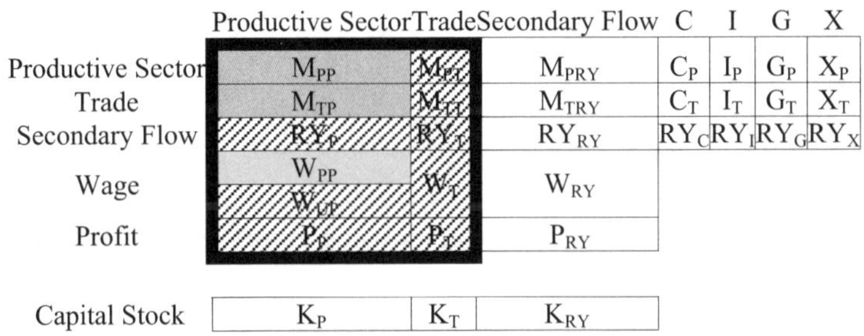

Figure 1.11 Estimation of Marxian Categories using Input-Output Tables (Shaikh and Tonak, 1994)

In addition to the estimation of variable capital (v), which has been dealt with in Section 2, estimation of the rate of surplus value also requires estimation of Marxian new value, or value added (v+s), because s/v equals ((v+s)-v)/v. This requires use of input-output tables. Figure 1.11 illustrates the reasons by mapping input-output tables with Marxian categories, following Shaikh and Tonak (1994). As shown in Figure 1.11, the bold-lined rectangle ($M_{PP}+M_{TP}+RY_P+W_{PP}+W_{UP}+P_P+M_{PT}+M_{TT}+RY_T+W_T+P_T$) corresponds to the Marxian total value (c+v+s). Note that the Marxian total value is smaller than the conventional measure of total output by the secondary flow ($M_{PRY}+M_{TRY}+RY_{RY}+W_{RY}+P_{RY}$), that is, the "product" of FIRE and public services.

The conventional measure of total output overstates the Marxian total value by double-counting the secondary flow, which has already been counted in the primary flow, that is, the product of productive sectors with the trade margin. It is also important to note that the trade margin – the "product" of the trade sector ($GO_T=M_{PT}+M_{TT}+RY_T+W_T+P_T$) – is counted as a primary rather than secondary flow, although the trade sector is unproductive of labor like the secondary flow. The simple reason is that all transactions in input-output tables are compiled in terms of "producers' price", that is, before adding the trade margin. Although this adjustment should be obvious, it was only first noticed and applied to the estimation of Marxian categories by Shaikh and Tonak (1994). Previous works on the estimation of Marxian categories using input-output tables, for example, Wolff (1987) and Jeong (1990), failed to recognize this fact. This lead them to incorrectly leave out the "product" of the trade sector (GO_T), as well as wrongly include M_{TP} (purchase of trade margin by productive sector from trade sector) in surplus value rather than constant capital, as is shown in Figure 1.12.

	Productive Sector	Trade	Secondary Flow	C	I	G	X
Productive Sector	M_{PP}	M_{PT}	M_{PRY}	C_P	I_P	G_P	X_P
Trade	M_{TP}	M_{TT}	M_{TRY}	C_T	I_T	G_T	X_T
Secondary Flow	RY_P	RY_T	RY_{RY}	RY_C	RY_I	RY_G	RY_X
Wage	W_{PP} W_{UP}	W_T	W_{RY}				
Profit	P_P	P_T	P_{RY}				

Figure 1.12 Estimation of Marxian Categories using Input-Output Tables (Wolff, 1987)

	Productive Sector	Trade	Secondary Flow	C	I	G	X
Productive Sector	M_{PP}	M_{PT}	M_{PRY}	C_P	I_P	G_P	X_P
Trade	M_{TP}	M_{TT}	M_{TRY}	C_T	I_T	G_T	X_T
Secondary Flow	RY_P	RY_T	RY_{RY}	RY_C	RY_I	RY_G	RY_X
Wage	W_{PP} W_{UP}	W_T	W_{RY}				
Profit	P_P	P_T	P_{RY}				

Figure 1.13 Estimation of Marxian Categories using Input-Output Tables (Mage, Mohun, Moseley)

The next step in the calculation of the national rate of surplus value is identifying the constant capital flow (c), and deducting it from Marxian total value (c+v+s) to get Marxian new value (v+s). As is shown in Figure 1.11, only the thick grey-colored rectangle, that is, the sum of M_{PP} (purchase of intermediate inputs by productive sector from productive sector) and M_{TP} (purchase of trade margin by productive sector from trade sector) is identified with the constant capital flow. Now, deducting the constant capital flow (c) from Marxian total value (c+v+s) makes Marxian value added (v+s), which corresponds to the bold-lined rectangle less the thick grey-colored rectangle in Figure 1.11. It is also clear from Figure 1.11 that Marxian value added is the sum of value added of the productive sector (W_{PP}+W_{UP}+P_P), the trade margin (total inputs to trade sector, or total output of trade sector (GO_T=M_{PT}+M_{TT}+RY_T+W_T+P_T)), and purchase of "secondary flow" by productive sector (RY_P).

The final step is deducting the variable capital flow (v) from Marxian value added (v+s) to arrive at surplus value (s). From the previous discussion, we know that the wages of productive (non supervisory) workers in the productive sector (W_{PP}) alone is counted as variable capital flow (v), which corresponds to the white grey-colored rectangle in Figure 1.11. It now becomes clear that surplus value corresponds to the hatched part of the bold-lined rectangle. In other words, surplus value created is distributed as profits of productive sector (P_P), wages of unproductive (supervisory) workers of productive sector (W_{UP}), purchase of "secondary flow" by productive sector (RY_P), and trade margin (GO_T).

Figure 1.11 also makes it clear that the conventional measure of value added (GDP), that is, the sum of wages (W_{pp}+W_{up}+W_T+W_{RY}) and profits (P_P+P_T+P_{RY}), overstates Marxian value added by the "value added" part of the secondary flow, that is, W_{RY}+P_{RY}, while understates it by the sum of RY_P and intermediate inputs to the trade sector (M_{PT}+M_{TT}+RY_T). Therefore, if we depend only on national accounts, which do not provide critical information about intermediate inputs, it is impossible to correctly measure Marxian value categories, c, v, and s, even if we introduce the distinction of productive and unproductive labor, as is shown in Figure 1.13. As a result, otherwise very important contributions to Marxian empirical studies, like Mage (1963), Moseley (1991) and Mohun (2004b; 2004c), are flawed. The same is true for efforts to estimate Marxian categories in terms of labor hours by applying "E", such as Gouverneur (2004), Mohun (2004c), Park (1996), and Kim (2000), because they do not use input-output tables. Indeed, the concept of "E" actually covers only the portion of value added of national accounts, for it is usually calculated by dividing GDP by total labor time expended. Therefore, recent works of Mohun (2004b; 2004c) should be regarded as a retreat from Shaikh and Tonak (1994), even though they elaborate the estimation of productive labor. In Korea, Seong (1996) offers the first rigorous application of Shaikh and Tonak (1994) to the estimation of the rate of surplus value. However, it suffers from a number of shortcomings, especially in the estimation of productive and unproductive labor, for it depends on problematic "industry by occupation" data.

Calculation of Wage Equivalent of Value Added by Petty Bourgeoisie

The last issue to be addressed is the treatment of value added by the petty bourgeoisie, including peasants and self-employed. The value added by petty bourgeoisie is counted as part of "operating surplus" of national accounts and input-output tables. However, the value added by petty bourgeoisie is actually "mixed income", reflecting both labor income accrued as a worker and property income accrued as an owner of means of production. Therefore, the former part should be separated from the "operating surplus" and added to wages if we are to correctly divide the total value added into wage ("compensation of employees" or variable capital) and profit ("operating surplus" or surplus value). I will call the portion of labor income of the value added by the petty bourgeoisie as their "wage equivalent". Without adding the "wage equivalent" of the petty bourgeoisie to the "compensation of employees" and subtracting it from "operating surplus", the former will be understated, and the latter overstated, resulting in overstated Marxian ratios like the rate of surplus value, profit/wage ratio, or the rate of profit. Moreover, without the decomposition of value added by petty bourgeoisie into labor and property incomes, the trends of these ratios will be biased downwards if the weight of value added by the petty bourgeoisie decrease over time.

The wage equivalent of value added by the petty bourgeoisie for the whole economy is calculated by the following procedure, one which is similar to that used by Shaikh and Tonak (1994): (1) calculate the average wage of employees for each industry (W_i/L_i) by dividing "Compensation of Employees"(W_i), taken from *Input-Output Tables* (or from *National Accounts*, published by the Bank of Korea, when we calculate the rate of profit by the number of employees (L_i) of the industry, reported in "Employment Tables" of *Input-Output Tables*[3]; (2) the "wage equivalent" of value added by petty bourgeoisie of each industry is estimated by applying the average wage of employees for each industry, calculated in (1), to the numbers of petty bourgeoisie (that is, the numbers of self-employed and family workers) of the industry (A_i), that is, $(W_i/L_i)*A_i$; (3) the "wage equivalent" for the whole economy is derived by summing (2), that is, $\sum(W_i/L_i)*A_i$.

Results

Figure 1.14 illustrates the results of estimation of the rate of surplus value for the Korean economy during 1980-2000 by applying the data and methods as discussed above. The rate of surplus value maintained a relatively stable level of approximately 140% in this period, except 1980, when it was 161.5%, and 1988, when it fell to 125.8%. Note that the rate of surplus value recovered soon after 1988, increasingly to 138.9% in 2000. It shows that the production of surplus value rapidly expanded during this period. These findings imply that an enormous exploitation of the working class was behind the rapid economic growth during 1980-2000.

Figure 1.15 compares the estimates of Korean rates of surplus value using different methods. It is noteworthy that the estimates of the rate of surplus value using the method of Shaikh (1994) are almost identical with those made using the method of Wolff (1987), both in level and trend during 1980-1993, even though the

---

3 For the number of workers that is needed in the estimation of wage equivalent, it is absolutely required that the data of "Employment Tables" of Input-Output Tables, not Annual Report on the Economically Active Population Survey, published by National Statistical Office, should be used. The latter is not adjusted for "full-time equivalent employees" and is inconsistent with macroeconomic value added statistics.

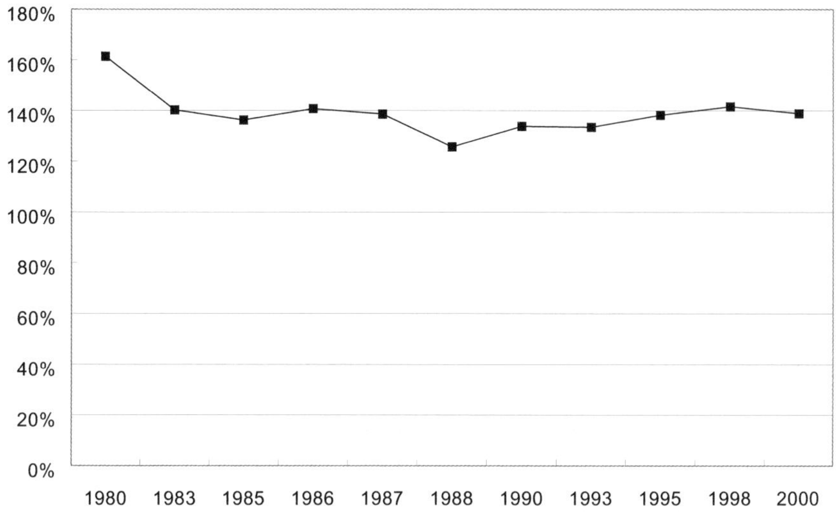

Figure 1.14 Rate of Surplus Value in Korea in all Industries in Korea, 1980-2000

latter is flawed in its treatment of the trade margin. It is also striking that the level and trend of these estimates are almost identical with the series estimated using the method of Mohun (2004), which only covers the value added part of input-output tables. However, classifying all services as unproductive labor, as was done by Jeong (1990), Park (1994) and Kim (2000), results in far higher levels of rate of surplus value, as is shown by the series of Jeong (1990). These findings suggest that how one distinguishes between productive and unproductive labor, especially concerning services, has a major impact on the results of the estimates of rate of surplus value. This is in contrast to the treatment of trade margin or the choice of data sources, that is, input-output tables or national accounts. It is also interesting that the estimates of Wolff (1987), Mohun (2004), and Jeong (1990) all rose fairly rapidly after 1995, unlike my estimates, which show only a gradual rise during the 1990s. The reason for this difference might be sought in the fact that, as is shown in Figure 1.11, my estimates do not count the secondary flow, W_{RY} and P_{RY}, which has grown rapidly during 1990s, as a part of surplus value, on the grounds that it has already been counted in the primary flow.

Figure 1.16 compares my estimates of the rate of surplus value with those of Park (1994), Seong (1996) and Kim (2000), and finds them all significantly larger. This outcome is largely explained by the fact that both Park (1994) and Kim (2000) regard all services as unproductive, while I classify a substantial part of services as productive. The reason why Seong (1996) has a larger estimate, despite using the same method of Shaikh and Tonak (1994) and *Input-Output Tables*, can be explained

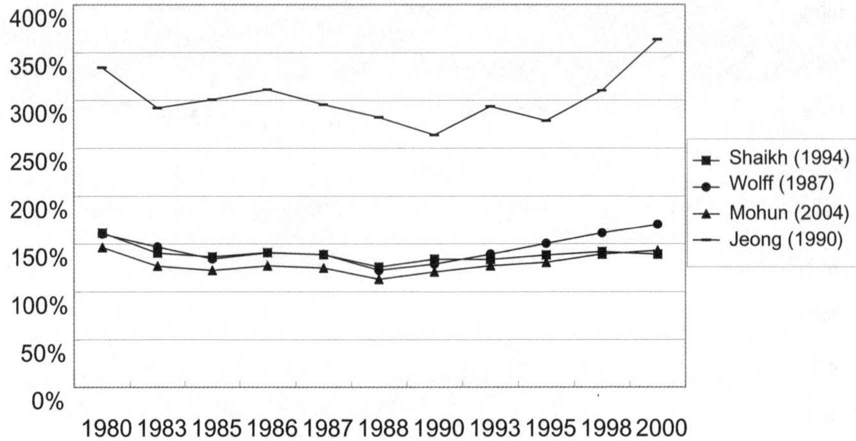

Figure 1.15 Estimates of Rate of Surplus Value in Korea Using Various Methods, 1980-2000

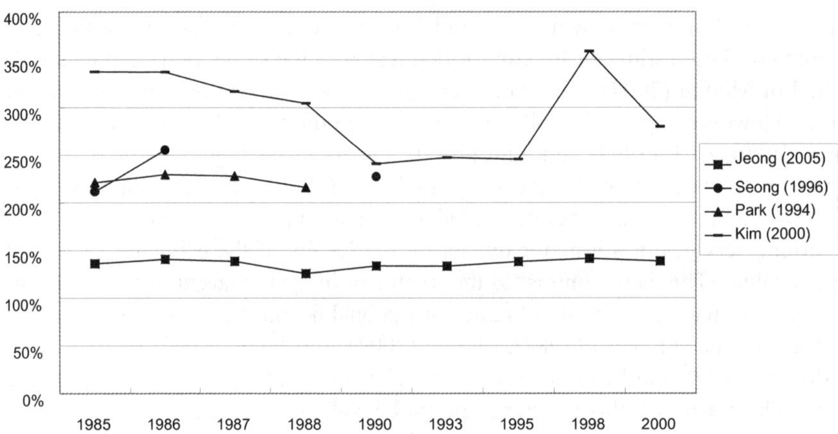

Figure 1.16 Comparison of Estimates of Rate of Surplus Value in Korea, 1985-2000

by the fact that it uses different data sources for identifying productive labor (as previously discussed.

Figure 1.17 illustrates the distribution of surplus value in Korea during 1980-2000. As shown in Figure 1.11, surplus values exploited from the working class are distributed to the following four categories: profits of productive sector (P_p),

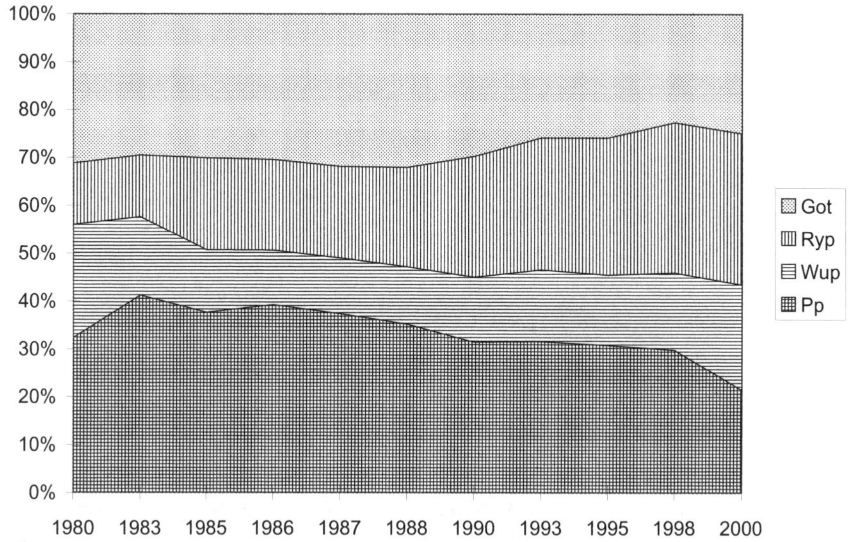

Figure 1.17 Distribution of Surplus Value in Korea, 1980-2000

wages of unproductive (supervisory) workers of productive sector (W_{UP}), purchase of "secondary flow" by productive sector (RY_P), and trade margin (GO_T). Among them, the largest category was initially P_P, which received 32.4% of the surplus value generated in 1980 and increased its share to 39.3% in 1986. However, its share began falling after 1987, becoming the smallest (!) among the four categories in 2000. After the economic crisis of 1997, P_P literally collapsed, from 29.8% in 1998 to 21.4% in 2000. Conversely, RY_P, which had received the smallest (12.8%) share in 1980, grew rapidly especially after 1990, receiving the largest share (31.6%) in 2000. W_{UP}, whose share decreased during the early 1980s, also began to gain a larger share after 1990, jumping from 16.1% in 1998 to 22% in 2000.

Figure 1.18 and Figure 1.19 show the trend and composition of total value, that is, c+v+s. As shown in Figure 1.19, the stability of the composition of total value during 1980-2000 is striking: c: v: s, which had been 59: 16: 25 in 1980, was 57: 18: 25 in 2000, respectively.

Figure 1.20 shows that the conventional measure of GDP is almost identical with Marxian value added estimated from the Input-Output Tables, as is anticipated from the findings of Figure 1.15. The ratio of GDP to Marxian value added (v+s) was close to 1 till 1995, though it slightly exceeds 1 after 1993. The reason is because the double counted and excluded parts of GDP (illustrated in Figure 1.11) almost cancel each other out, to make it approximately equal to Marxian value added.

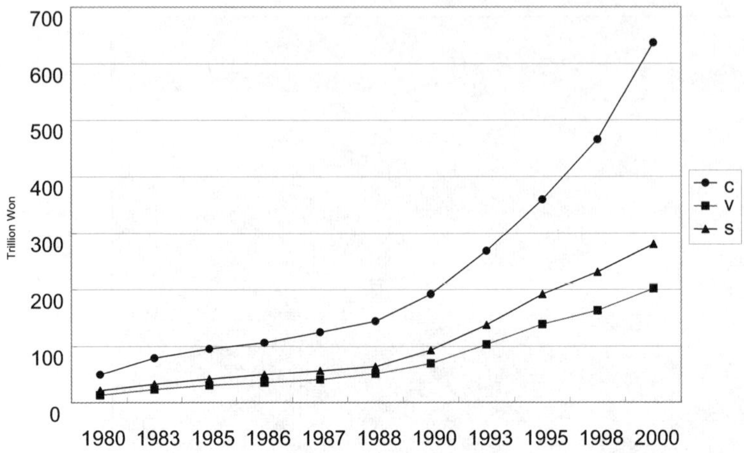

Figure 1.18 Constant Capital, Variable Capital and Surplus Value in Korea, 1980-2000

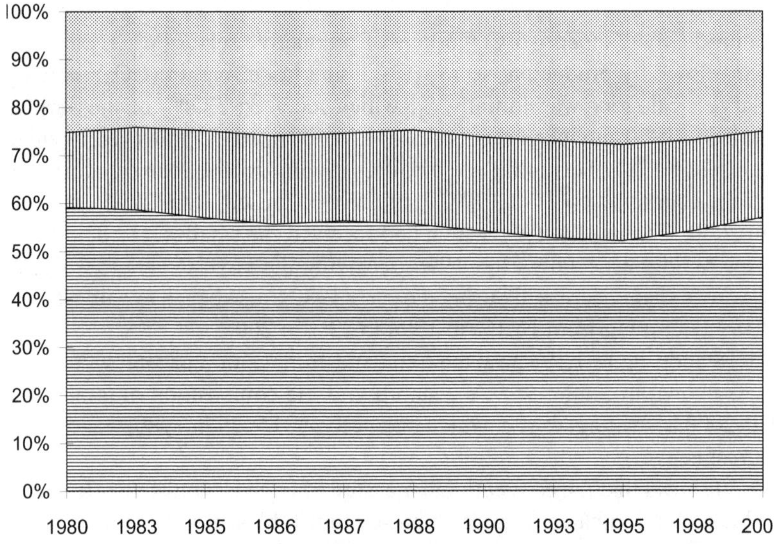

Figure 1.19 Composition of Total Value (c+v+s) in Korea: 1980-2000

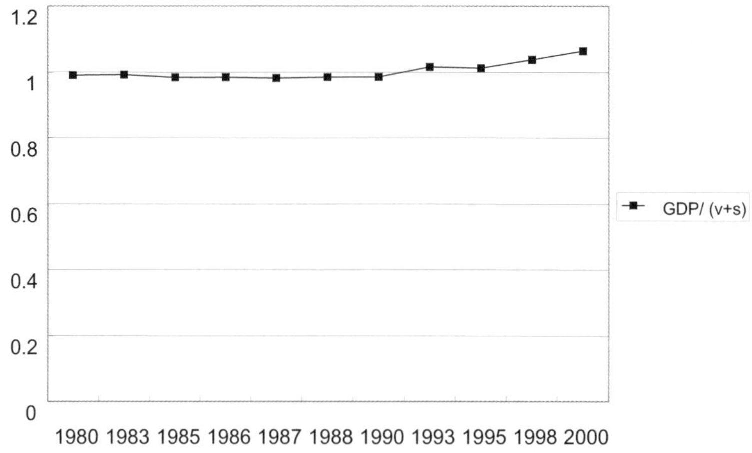

Figure 1.20 Comparison of GDP with Marxian Value Added (v+s) in Korea, 1980-2000

Rate of Profit: 1970-2002

Data and Method

This section presents estimates of the rate of profit for the non-farm business economy in Korea during 1970-2002. It is an extension and updating of Jeong (2004), which provided estimates of the rate of profit for the Korean manufacturing sector during 1970-2000. Unlike the rate of surplus value, which belongs to a high level of abstraction that reflects the deep and "hidden essence" of "capital in general", the rate of profit belongs to a lower level of abstraction that exists in the "everyday consciousness of the agents of production themselves". Therefore, the rate of profit should be defined and estimated so that it could "approach the form in which they appear on the surface of society" as closely as possible (Marx, 1981: 117). As a result, it is not necessary to introduce the distinction between productive and unproductive labor. Indeed, Shaikh (1992; 1999) and Mohun (2004a) do not distinguish productive and unproductive labor when they calculate the rate of profit, though they use a very sophisticated method to distinguish between productive and unproductive labor when estimating the rate of surplus value, as is shown in Shaikh and Tonak (1994) and Mohun (2004c). Similarly, neither Duménil and Lévy (2002; 2004) nor Brenner (1998) introduce the distinction between productive and unproductive labor in their estimation and analysis of the rate of profit. In contrast, Moseley (1991; 2004) and Seong (1996) do use this distinction in their calculations of the rate of profit.

Based on above discussion, and using the notations of Figure 1.11, I will define the rate of profit as the ratio of the total profits ($P_P + P_T + P_{RY}$) to the total capital stock (actually total net fixed capital stock, $K_P + K_T + K_{RY}$), as in equation (1-1) below, and not as the ratio of the surplus value (s) to the productive capital stock (K_p), as in Moseley (1991).

$$\frac{p}{K}=\frac{P_P+P_T+P_{RY}}{K_P+K_T+K_{RY}}=\frac{S-s_U+P_{RY}}{K_P+K_U} \tag{1-1}$$

S_U in equation (1-1) indicates the portion of surplus value distributed to the unproductive sector net of P_T (profits of trade sector). S_U amounts to the costs incurred owing to the unproductive sector (identical to the area of W_{UP}+RY_P+(GO_T-P_T) in Figure 1.11). K_U indicates the capital stock invested in the unproductive sectors, including K_T (trade sector) and K_{RY} ("secondary sector"). Equation (1-1) makes clear that, other things being equal, an increase in the unproductive sector will exert downward pressure on the rate of profit if it accompanies an increase in S_U or K_U. Although an increase in the unproductive sector could also raise the rate of profit through an increase in P_T, it is empirically found to result in furthering the falling rate of profit by Mage (1963) and Moseley (1991; 1997; 1999; 2004).

Estimating the rate of profit also requires that we deal with issues of categorization and aggregation. Limiting the focus of our investigation to the manufacturing sector has its own merit in that it enables us to get an accurate estimate of developments in the heart of the capitalist economy. However, we need to extend the scope of estimation to cover the whole national economy if we want to "approach" the Marxian concept of average rate of profit, mediated by the competition of "many capitals". This requires that we choose the most appropriate scale of aggregation. Here, I first aggregate all national industries into ten large groups that will be consistent with net fixed capital stock data, which is essential to the calculation of the rate of profit. The industries are: (1) Agriculture, (2) Mining, (3) Manufacturing, (4) Utilities, (5) Construction, (6) Transportation, (7) Services, (8) Restaurant, (9) Finance-Insurance-Real Estate, and (10) Government. By combining these industries in different ways, the following categories of estimation can be constructed:

Business Sector: (1)+(2)+(3)+(4)+(5)+(6)+(7)+(8)+(9)
Non Farm Business Sector: (2)+(3)+(4)+(5)+(6)+(7)+(8)+(9)
Productive Sector: (1)+(2)+(3)+(4)+(5)+(6)+(7)+(8)
Non Farm Productive Sector: (2)+(3)+(4)+(5)+(6)+(7)+(8)
Non Farm Material Sector: (2)+(3)+(4)+(5)+(6)

Among these categories, I believe that the Non-Farm Business Sector is the best sector to use in estimating capitalist profitability for the whole economy, because it covers all the major capitalist industries while excluding the non-capitalist sectors (Agriculture and Government). Adding Agriculture to the Non-Farm Business Sector creates the Business Sector category. However, adding Agriculture, which is largely a non-capitalist sector, will make the estimation of capitalist profitability inaccurate even if we were to correct for the "wage equivalent" of that sector. Subtracting finance-insurance-real estate from the Non-Farm Business Sector leaves the Non Farm Productive Sector.

As previously discussed, if we admit that the distinction between productive and unproductive labor is unnecessary and irrelevant for the estimation of the rate of profit, the same should hold true in terms of the distinction between productive and unproductive sectors. In this regard, Kim (2005) is inconsistent; it does not distinguish between productive and unproductive labor when estimating the rate of profit while simultaneously using that distinction to determine the sectors of the economy to include in the estimation. For similar reasons I reject using Productive, Non Farm Productive, or Non Farm Material Sector as the basis for my estimation of the rate of profit for the whole economy.

Estimating the rate of profit for the Non Farm Business Sector requires the following calculations:

1. The rate of profit of the Non-Farm Business Sector is equal to the ratio of profits (P) to the net fixed capital stock at current price (K) or P/K.
2. K is the sum of K_i of each industry, with the data drawn from Pyo (2000); $K=\sum K_i$.
3. P is the sum of P_i of each industry; $P=\sum P_i$.
4. P_i of each industry is calculated by deducting W_i (wages of each industry) from Y_i (value added of each industry); $P_i=Y_i-W_i$.
5. Y_i, is the "Domestic Factor Income" of each industry. It is equal to "Gross Output "– "Intermediate Consumption" – "Indirect Taxes" + "Subsidies" – "Consumption of Fixed Capital". The data comes from the table "Gross Domestic Product and Factor Income by Kind of Economic Activity" of the *National Accounts*.
6. W_i is the sum of "Compensation of Employees" of each industry and the "wage equivalent" of value added by self-employed and family workers of each industry. The former is taken from the same source as in (5). The latter is estimated by applying the numbers of petty bourgeoisie (self-employed and family workers) to "Compensation of Employees" per employee of each industry. The numbers of self-employed, family workers, and employees of each industry are taken from "Employment Tables" of *Input-Output Tables*.

The following calculations of working hours and various price indexes are also required to decompose the movement of the rate of profit:

1. H is the total working hours expended in the Non Farm Business Sector. It is calculated as the sum of H_i of each industry; $H=\sum H_i$.
2. H_i is calculated by applying L_i (total number of workers including petty bourgeoisie of each industry) to h_i (average working hours per employee of each industry); $H_i=L_i*h_i$. L_i is taken from "Employment Tables", and h_i is

taken from *Survey Report on Wage Structure*.

3. Py is the deflator of GDP for Non Farm Business Sector. It is calculated by dividing the GDP of the sector in current prices by the GDP of the sector in 2000 constant prices, where both series of GDP are taken from the table "Gross Domestic Product and Factor Income by Kind of Economic Activity" of *National Accounts*.
4. Pk is the deflator of K (net fixed capital stock) for Non Farm Business Sector. It is calculated by dividing K in current prices by K in 2000 constant prices, where both series are taken from Pyo (2000).

Decomposition of Rate of Profit

In order to explain the determinants of the trend of the rate of profit, it is useful to decompose the rate of profit into the product of the share of profits in total value added (P/Y) and the output-capital ratio, or "productivity" of capital (Y/K) as in equation (1-2).[4] If we assume that the share of profits (P/Y) reflects the Marxian rate of exploitation (P/W), then the output-capital ratio (Y/K) can be used as a substitute for the inverse of the Marxian value composition of capital (K/W). Equation (1-2) also can be transformed into a growth accounting equation, as in equation (1-3). These two equations help us separate the effects of distribution on the rate of profit (P/Y) from those of technological change (Y/K).

$$\frac{P}{K}=\frac{P}{Y}\cdot\frac{Y}{K} \tag{1-2}$$

$$\dot{\left(\frac{P}{K}\right)}=\dot{\left(\frac{P}{Y}\right)}+\dot{\left(\frac{Y}{K}\right)} \tag{1-3}$$

Following Mohun (2004a), the output-capital ratio (Y/K) can be decomposed as in equation (1-4). Equation (1-4) shows that this ratio is positively related to the ratio of the GDP deflator (Py) to the implicit price deflator for fixed capital stock (Pk), Py/Pk, and the real productivity of labor ((Y/Py)/H). It is negatively related to the real fixed capital stock per labor input ((K/Pk)/H), that is, "capital intensity", which is similar to the Marxian concept of organic composition of capital. Like equation (1-3), Equation (1-4) also can be transformed into a growth accounting equation, as in equation (1-5).

$$\frac{Y}{K}=\frac{Py\times\left(\frac{Y}{Py}\right)}{Pk\times\left(\frac{K}{Pk}\right)}=\left(\frac{Py}{Pk}\right)\times\left(\frac{\left(\frac{Y}{Py}\right)/H}{\left(\frac{K}{Pk}\right)/H}\right) \tag{1-4}$$

4 Equation (1-2) is a standard way Marxian empirical research decomposes the rate of profit. For example, see Shaikh (1999), Mohun (2004a), and Wolff (2003).

$$\left(\dot{\frac{Y}{K}}\right) = \left(\dot{\frac{Py}{Pk}}\right) + \left(\frac{(Y \dot{/} Py)}{H}\right) - \left(\frac{(K \dot{/} Pk)}{H}\right) \tag{1-5}$$

$$\frac{P}{Y} = \frac{Y - W}{Y} = \frac{\left(\frac{Y}{Py}\right)/H - \left(\frac{W}{Py}\right)/H}{\left(\frac{Y}{Py}\right)/H} \tag{1-6}$$

$$\left(\dot{\frac{P}{Y}}\right) = \left(1 - \dot{\frac{W}{Y}}\right) = -\frac{W}{P}\left(\dot{\frac{W}{Y}}\right) = \frac{W}{P}\left[\left(\frac{(Y \dot{/} Py)}{H}\right) - \left(\frac{(W \dot{/} Py)}{H}\right)\right] \tag{1-7}$$

Equation (1-6) makes clear that the profit share is determined by the difference between the real productivity of labor ((Y/Py)/H) and the hourly product wage ((W/Py)/H), that is, the nominal hourly wage deflated by the GDP deflator. The profit share moves positively with the real productivity of labor and negatively with the hourly product wage. Equation (1-6) also can be transformed into a growth accounting equation, as in equation (1-7)[5].

Results and Implications

Figure 1.21 shows that the rate of profit of the Non Farm Business Sector, measured by the ratio of pre-tax profits (P) to the net fixed capital stock (K), remained quite high, between 12% and 16%, from 1970-1986, with the exception of a short, though sharp fall in the early 1980s. It began a steady decline after 1987, finally hitting a low of 5.1% in 1996, and then recovering slightly. Of course, over the whole period of 1970 to 2002, the rate of profit clearly shows a falling tendency. In particular, over the period 1986-1996, the period immediately predating the 1997 crisis, the rate of profit fell dramatically from 13.3% to 5.1%. In fact, it reached its lowest level of the entire period in 1996, the year before the crisis. These facts imply that the 1997 crisis was intimately related to a broader problem of declining capitalist profitability. While the rate of profit has recovered since the crisis, its 2002 level (6.6%) still remains at only one-third the level of 1978 (16.7%). This suggests that the Korean economy remains in the middle of its long downturn.

Figure 1.22 shows that the same profit rate trend can be found whether we calculate it for Manufacturing, Non Farm Material, Non Farm Productive, Productive, or the Business Sector. More specifically, we find the profit rate falling over the entire

---

5 $$\left(\dot{\frac{P}{Y}}\right) = \left(1 - \dot{\frac{W}{Y}}\right) = \frac{1}{1-\frac{W}{Y}}\left[0 - \frac{d\left(\frac{W}{Y}\right)}{d}\right] = -\frac{W}{P}\left[\frac{1}{\left(\frac{W}{Y}\right)}\right]\left[\frac{d\left(\frac{W}{Y}\right)}{d}\right] = -\frac{W}{P}\left(\dot{\frac{W}{Y}}\right)$$

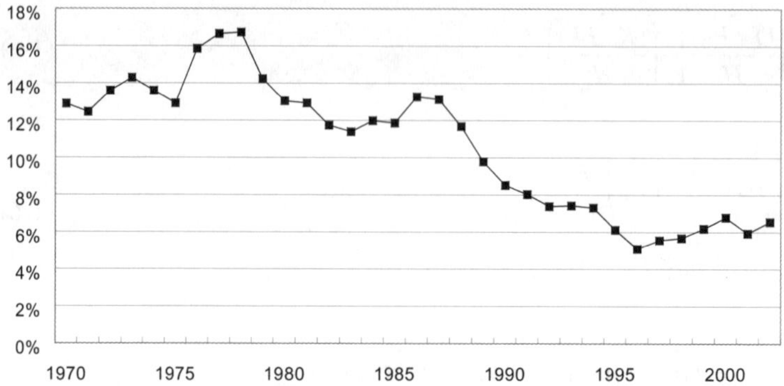

Figure 1.21 Rate of Profit in Non Farm Business Sector in Korea, 1970-2000

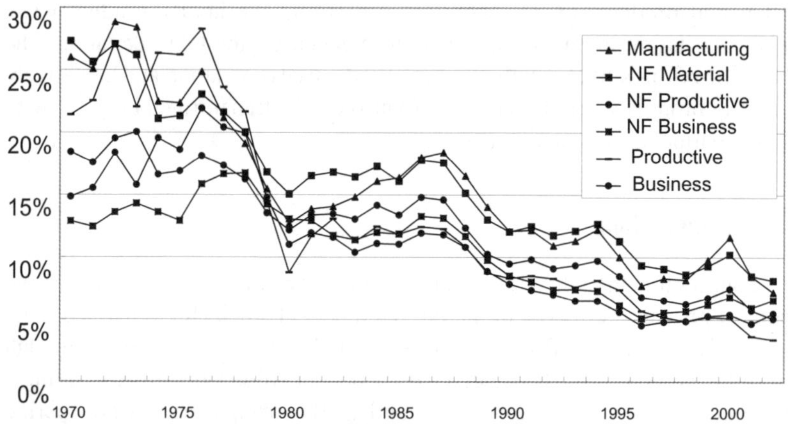

Figure 1.22 Rate of Profit in Korea, 1970-2000

period of 1970-2002. Its high point is in the 1970s, and it declines steadily from the late 1980s until the late 1990s, with a slight recovery after 1997 crisis. Figure 1.23 shows the same trend even when we calculate the rate of profit without correcting for the wage equivalent of value added by the petty bourgeoisie. As expected, without correction, the rate of profit shows a more consistent and smooth downward trend.

Figure 1.24, Figure 1.25 and Table 1.2 show the trend of the two determinants of the rate of profit (P/K)—the profit share (P/Y) and output-capital ratio (Y/K)—for the Non Farm Business Sector over the period 1970-2002. While both the profit share and output-capital ratio declined over the entire period, the movement of the output-capital ratio seems to track the rate of profit better than does the profit share. Compared to the output-capital ratio, which generally shows a long-run falling tendency like the rate of profit, the profit share first rose over the period 1970-1986,

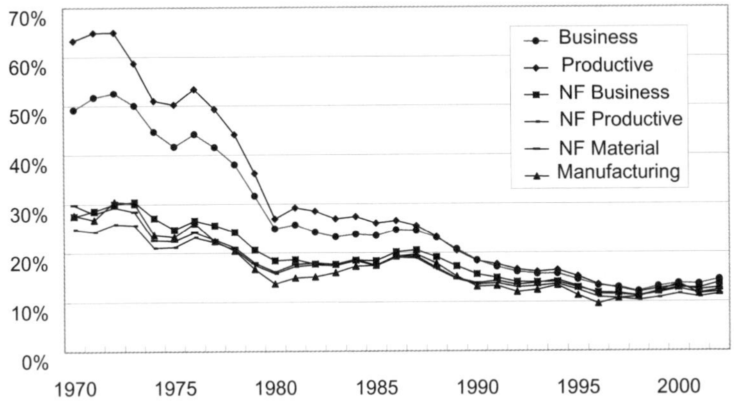

Figure 1.23 Rate of Profit in Korea, without Correcting for Wage Equivalent of Self-Employed, 1970-2002

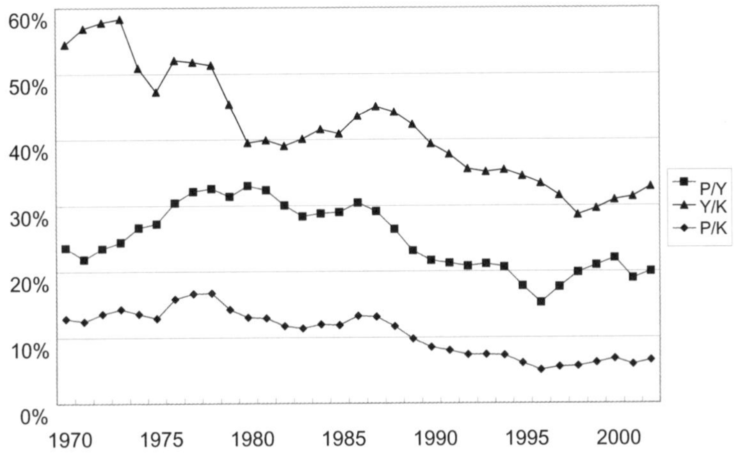

Figure 1.24 Determinants of Rate of Profit in Non Farm Business Sector, 1970-2002

before gradually falling. Table 1.2 shows that the fall in the output-capital ratio was more responsible for the falling rate of profit than was the fall of the profit share over the whole period, accounting for 58.6% of the fall in the rate of profit for 1970-2002. This outcome is consistent with the Marxian thesis of a falling rate of profit resulting from a rising organic composition of capital. At the same time, for the period 1986-1996, that is the period before the 1997 crisis, the fall in the profit share accounted for more of the fall in the rate of profit then did the fall in the output-capital ratio. Moreover, when the rate of profit began to recover after 1996, the rise in the profit share almost completely (98.5%!) explains the recovery. This implies that that the

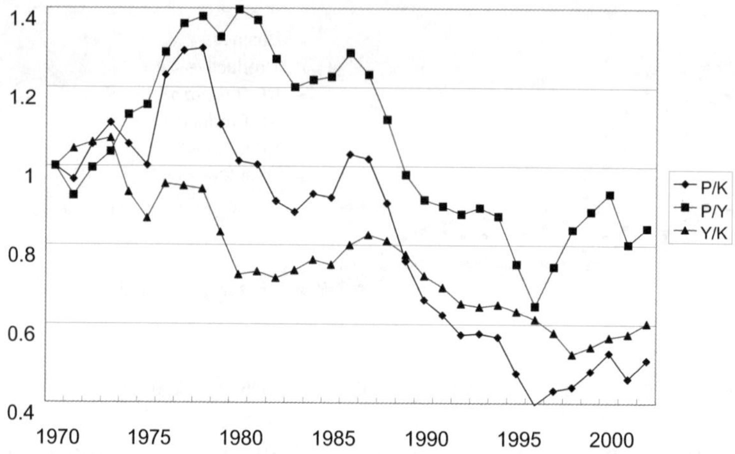

Figure 1.25 Trend of Determinants of Rate of Profit in Non Farm Business Sector, 1970-2002

Table 1.2 Decomposition of the Trend of Rate of Profit in Korea, 1970-2002

Non Farm Business Sector

	(1) P/K	(2) P/Y	(3) Y/K	P/Y	Y/K
1970-2002	-1.47%	-0.61%	-0.86%	41.33%	58.67%
1970-1986	-0.33%	0.75%	-1.09%	-226.32%	326.32%
1986-2002	-2.17%	-1.03%	-1.14%	47.54%	52.46%
1986-1996	-3.92%	-2.52%	-1.40%	64.32%	35.68%
1996-2002	1.66%	1.63%	0.02%	98.53%	1.47%

Notes: 1) The values in the columns of (1),(2),(3) are obtained by ordinary least squares regression of log x on time, measured in years of each period. The estimated value of the time coefficient is the average annual exponential rate of growth of x.
2) (1)=(2)+(3)

neoliberal restructuring after 1997 represents nothing more than the restoration of capitalist profitability through the intensified exploitation of the working class.

Another striking finding is that over the period 1970-1986, the rise in the profit share was enough to cancel out the effect of the fall in the output-capital ratio. This helped sustain a high rate of capitalist profitability during this period, as can be seen in Figure 1.24, Figure 1.25, and Table 1.2. Indeed, the profit share increased from 23.6% in 1970 to 33% in 1980, and still remained at a relatively high 30.4% in 1986. Thus, intensification of the exploitation of the South Korean working class was the foundation of the rapid economic growth under the Park Jung Hee regime.

Table 1.3 Decomposition of the Trend of Profit Share and Output-Capital Ratio, 1970-2002

Non Farm Business Sector

	(1) Y/K	(2) Py/Pk	(3) (Y/Py)/H	(4) (K/Pk)/H	(5) W/Py)/H
1970-2002	-0.86%	0.58%	1.98%	3.42%	2.17%
1970-1986	-1.09%	1.10%	1.50%	3.68%	1.22%
1986-2002	-1.14%	0.16%	2.13%	3.42%	2.44%
1986-1996	-1.40%	0.02%	2.34%	3.75%	3.08%
1996-2002	0.02%	0.40%	1.64%	2.01%	1.28%

Notes: 1) The values in the columns of (1),(2),(3),(4),(5) are obtained by ordinary least squares regression of log x on time, measured in years of each period. The estimated value of the time coefficient is the average annual exponential rate of growth of x.
2) (1)=(2)+(3)-(4)

Figure 1.26 and Table 1.3 show the trend of the determinants of the output-capital ratio of the Non Farm Business Sector. Except for the years 1996-2002, the fall in the output-capital ratio over the period 1970-2002 appears best explained by the rise in the capital intensity of production ((K/Pk)/H), which more than offset the rising real productivity of labor ((Y/Py)/H).

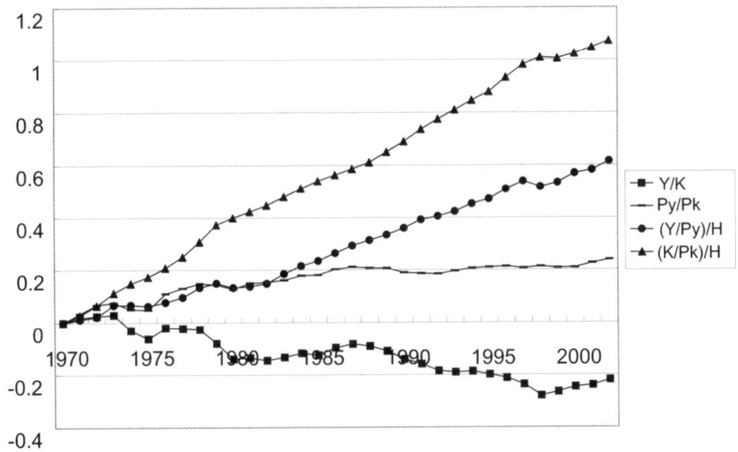

Figure 1.26 Trend of Determinants of Output-Capital Ratio in Non Farm Business Sector, 1970-2002

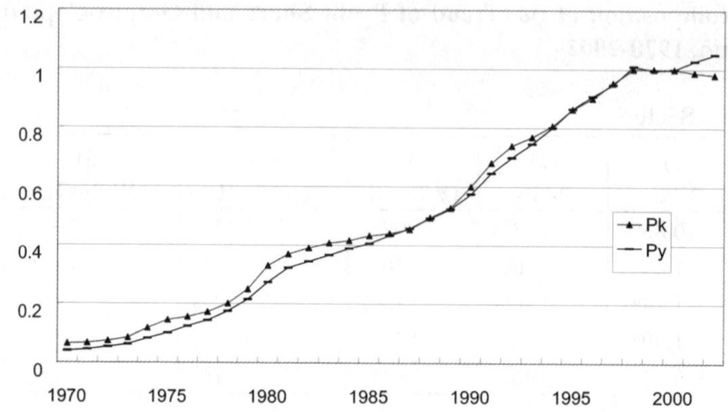

Figure 1.27 GDP Deflator (Py) and Net Capital Stock Deflator (Pk) in Non Farm Business Sector, 1970-2002

Figure 1.24, Figure 1.25, Figure 1.26, Table 1.2 and Table 1.3 also reveal that after the 1997 crisis, the recovery in capitalist profitability has been supported by both a growing output-capital ratio and a growing profit share. The higher output-capital ratio since 1997 is explained by both a rising Py/Pk and a rising real productivity of labor ((Y/Py)/H). However, as Figure 1.27 illustrates, the rise in Py/Pk (after 2000) was more the result of falling Pk than a rising Py. This falling Pk is a noteworthy development in the history of Korean capitalism, since it was the severe destruction and devaluation of capitals during the 1997 crisis and subsequent neoliberal restructuring that produced this falling Pk.

Figure 1.28 and Table 1.3 highlight the trend of the determinants of the profit share of the Non Farm Business Sector. What is striking is that during 1970-1986, the period of rising profit share, the annual growth rate of the hourly real product wage ((W/Py)H) was always lower (except in 1971 and 1979) than the annual growth rate of the real

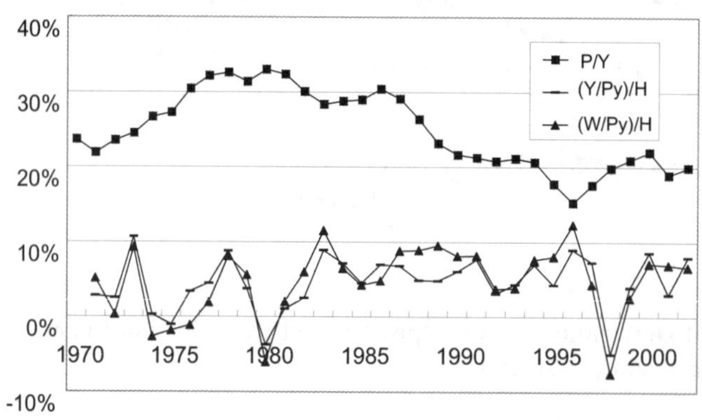

Figure 1.28 Trend of Determinants of Profit Share in Non Farm Business Sector, 1970-2002

productivity of labor ((Y/Py)/H). The thesis of "shared growth" under the Park Jung Hee regime, recently propagated by the so-called New Right, is simply groundless.

Figure 1.29 illustrates the converging trend of industrial rates of profit during 1970-2002. This outcome suggests that the Marxian tendency of equalization of rates of profit and formation of average rate of profit is becoming a reality with the development of competition and capitalism in Korea.[6]

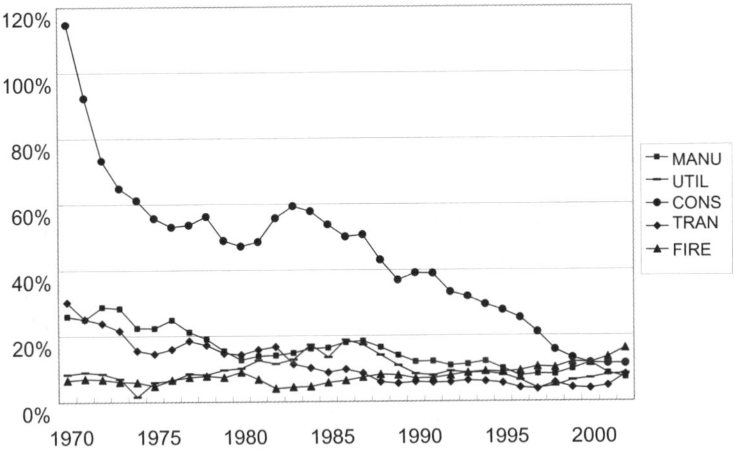

Figure 1.29 Industrial Rates of Profit in Korea, 1970-2002

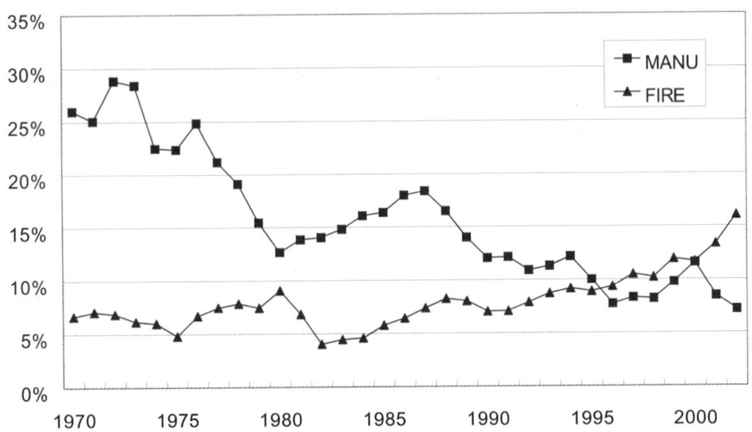

Figure 1.30 Rate of Profit in Manufacturing and Financial Sector in Korea, 1970-2002

6 For more counter-factual evidence for the so-called "strengthening monopoly" thesis, see Joo (2005).

Figure 1.30 illustrates the convergence of the rates of profit between the manufacturing sector and the finance-insurance-and real estate sector, in particular during 1970-2000. Another interesting feature is that the latter began to outstrip the former after 1996. However, these features should be interpreted as the combined results of falling manufacturing profitability and loosening "financial repression", rather than indicating a transition to the so-called "finance-led accumulation regime", as was discussed in Jeong (2004).

Conclusion

The main findings of this chapter and their implications can be summarized as follows: First, we see a downward trend in productive labor in Korea beginning in the late 1980s, from a very high level that was sustained for many years. The extraordinary high level of productive labor during the 1970s and 1980s played an important role in the country's rapid growth over this period. Second, the rate of surplus value in Korea, estimated by the rigorous application of the method of Shaikh and Tonak (1994), was maintained at a fairly stable level of 140% during 1980-2000, with a slightly increasing trend over the decade of the 1990s. Of course, the way one differentiates productive and unproductive labor, especially as it relates to services, will have a significant effect on the estimated rate of surplus value.

Third, the rate of profit for the non-farm business sector fell significantly over the period 1970-2002, from a high of 16.7 percent in 1978 to a low of 6.6% in 2002. Its decline was behind the economic crisis of 1997, as argued in Jeong (2004). The main cause of the decline in the rate of profit over this period was the fall in the output-capital ratio, thereby providing strong support for the Marxian thesis of a falling rate of profit resulting from a rising organic composition of capital. The increasing unproductiveness of the economy since the late 1980s has also exerted downward pressure on the rate of profit by redirecting the surplus value towards unproductive uses, especially in the form of payments for royalties and the wages of unproductive workers.

However, for the period 1970-1986, the so-called era of Park Jung Hee, the rate of profit was maintained at a high rate largely because of a rising profit share, which was attributable to the intensified exploitation of the working class. The recovery of the rate of profit since the 1997 crisis is also largely the result of a renewed exploitation of labor as well as devaluation of capital. These findings appear to corroborate the hypothesis of Jeong (1997) that the state capitalist social structure of accumulation that sustained high economic growth over the 1970s and most of the 1980s began to crumble beginning in 1987. The country's structural crisis continues.

Chapter 2

Uneven Development of the Rates of Surplus Value: The Case of South Korea

Dong-Min Rieu

Introduction

Attempts by Marxian economists to compute and analyze trends in Marxian ratios have generally focused on the average rate of profit (Duménil and Lévy, 1993; Moseley, 1991; Shaikh and Tonak, 1994). This is also true for those interested in trends for South Korea (Jeong, 1997). Significantly, these studies have largely ignored the issue of unequal rates of surplus value. Perhaps the main reason for this omission is that many Marxian economists view exploitation as a phenomenon that is meaningful only on a macro level. However, "Marx also remarked…that in any concrete study of wages differential rates of exploitation must be taken into account. His assumption of a single rate of exploitation was thus clearly an attempt to abstract away from a phenomenon which he did not consider to be basic to the operations of the capitalist system" (Roemer, 1978, p. 43). In addition, as discussion of the so-called "transformation problem" reveals, it is obvious that sectoral rates of surplus value are equalized only if exchange takes place in terms of values.[1] Thus, one aim of this chapter is to more fully explore the issue of the uneven development of the rate of surplus value. More specifically, with respect to the South Korean economy, this chapter will show that recent structural changes, including the economic crisis in 1997-8, have had a differential effect on sectoral rates of surplus value.

In order to establish the existence of uneven sectoral rates of surplus value in South Korea, this chapter must first overcome some theoretical shortcomings in the literature on methodological issues surrounding the estimation of Marxian ratios. Empirical research on Marxian ratios has benefited from the concept of the "monetary expression of labor time", which was developed as part of the so-called "New Interpretation" (Duménil, 1980; Foley, 1982; Lipietz, 1982). The reason is that use of this concept facilitates time-series estimation of Marxian ratios through relatively easy manipulations, as compared to the traditional approach, which employs input-output data. However, this concept has also generated several theoretical and empirical problems, in that its use has diverged rather too much from the initial perspective of the Marxian labor theory of value (Fine, Lapavitsas and Saad-Filho, 2004). To overcome these problems, this chapter will also offer a new method for measuring value productivity on a sectoral level.

---

1 The author is indebted to Lefteris Tsoulfidis for this point.

This chapter is structured as follows: Section 2 summarizes the logical structure of the "New Interpretation". After examining the applicability of the "New Interpretation" to individual sectors following the work of Gouverneur (1990), Section 3 offers an alternative method for estimating sectoral rates of surplus value. Section 4 presents some empirical results concerning the South Korean economy over the decade of the 1990s. Section 5 offers concluding remarks.

The Logical Structure of the "New Interpretation"[2]

The "New Interpretation" was presented by several scholars almost at the same time (Duménil, 1980; Foley, 1982; Lipietz, 1982). It greatly contributed to empirical research from the perspective of Marxian value theory, because its' main concept, the "monetary expression of labor time" or "value of money" (Foley, 1982), made it possible to directly connect labor value and monetary variables.

The standard postulates of the "New Interpretation" can be summarized with the help of the following two postulates:

Postulate 1. The "monetary expression of labor time" (E) is defined with regard to net product, not gross product:

$$E = \frac{py}{lx} = \frac{p_1 y_1 + \cdots + p_n y_n}{l_1 x_1 + \cdots + l_n x_n} \tag{1}$$

Here, the $1 \times n$ vectors of $p = (p_1, p_2, ..., p_n)$ and $l = (l_1, l_2, ..., l_n)$ denote prices and direct labor requirements respectively, while $x = (x_1, x_2, ..., x_n)^T$ and $y = (y_1, y_2, ..., y_n)^T$ are gross product and net product, respectively, defined as $n \times 1$ vectors. The equation relating gross product and net product is:

$$x = Ax + y \tag{2}$$

where A represents a $n \times n$ matrix of input-output coefficients.

Equation (1) implies that the "monetary expression of labor time" is equal to the ratio of total net revenue to the total amount of living labor. This postulate represents the ratio of transforming the total labor expended into the prices of the net product over the same period. As total living labor and net product are measured by hour and monetary unit, respectively, E is not a non-dimensional quantity. Its dimension is, for example, dollars per hour.

Postulate 2. The value of labor power (V_L) is defined as the ratio of the money wage (w) to the "monetary expression of labor time":

$$V_L = \frac{w}{E} \tag{3}$$

2 This section heavily draws upon Rieu (2006).

We can use these two postulates to derive the "New Interpretation". First, the profit per unit of a commodity is equal to its price minus labor and non-labor cost:

$$p - pA - wl \tag{4}$$

Since the surplus value per unit of a commodity is defined as labor expenditure minus total value of labor power (as defined in Equation (3)), it can be written as:

$$l - V_L l = (1 - \frac{w}{E})l \tag{5}$$

Of course, value and price are dimensionally different. Therefore, if we wish to discuss aggregate equalities of transformation, dimensional consistency must be obtained. The "New Interpretation" involves either multiplying value by E or dividing price by E. For example, multiplying Equation (5) by E and subtracting it from Equation (4) gives:

$$t = p - pA - wl - (E - w)l = p - pA - El \tag{6}$$

where t is the difference between profit and surplus value represented in terms of price.

Post-multiplying both sides of Equation (6) by the gross product vector x and using Postulate 1 gives:

$$tx = p(I - A)x - Elx = py - Elx = 0 \tag{7}$$

Equation (7) implies that total profit and total surplus value are equal. However, we also know, from the definition of value and net product that the following must also be true:

$$lx = \lambda(I - A)x = \lambda y \tag{8}$$

where λ is the $1 \times n$ value vector.

Therefore, Equation (7) also implies that, with regard to net product, assuming $E = 1$, the total price (py) must be equal to the total value (λy). In other words, using the two postulates modifies and directly leads to Marx's two aggregate equalities in the transformation procedure.

As recently emphasized by Fine, Lapavitsas, and Saad-Filho (2004), the "New Interpretation" can be formulated without sectoral equations. For further discussion, however, it is necessary to set the value and price equations of the "New Interpretation" as follows, where π represents the $1 \times n$ profit vector.

$$\lambda = \lambda A + l = \lambda A + wl + (1 - w)l \tag{9}$$

$$p = pA + wl + \pi \tag{10}$$

On one hand, it seems unusual to introduce the money wage rate directly into the value equation. To put it differently, w must be a scalar for dimensional consistency in Equation (9). However, as w represents hourly wage, its dimension is dollars per hour. Therefore, a parameter is needed to transform the hourly wage into a scalar with the dimension of hours per dollar. This parameter is the inverse of the "monetary expression of labor time", and it can be safely assumed to be equal to 1 for analytical convenience (Lipietz, 1985, p.40). On the other hand, Equation (10) clearly shows that the "New Interpretation" does not assume an equal rate of profit. As one of the "New Interpretation" theorists has emphasized,[3] Marxian transformation can be analyzed without assuming an equal distribution of profit across sectors.

The Estimation of the Sectoral Rates of Surplus Value

Based upon the logical structure of the "New Interpretation" as summarized in Section 2, we can derive the dynamic relationship between the value of labor power and its determinants. Equation (3), which expresses the basic relationship underlying the "New Interpretation", can be transformed as follows, where E_R denotes value-added productivity measured in real terms:

$$V_L = \frac{w}{E} = \frac{w}{pE_R} \tag{11}$$

The second equality in (11) is derived from a decomposition of E into nominal and real terms. Mohun (2004d) expressed this formula as a relationship between the change rates of two terms, as in expressed in Equation (12). Here, the notation $\dot{x}$ represents the rate of change over time of a given variable x.

$$\dot{E} = \dot{p} + \dot{E}_R \tag{12}$$

Although Foley (2005, p.40) also decomposes the monetary expression of labor time into price change and labor productivity, the derivation of a relation like that illustrated in Equation (12) does not, in fact, necessarily require the "New Interpretation". For example, Nakatani (1994) presented two measures for inflation. One was the quantity of production represented by a unit of money, which corresponds to the reciprocal of the rate of inflation. The other was the quantity of labor represented by a unit of money, which corresponds to the reciprocal of E.[4]

3 "As far as the new interpretation of the transformation problem is concerned, the required conditions are *the existence of a positive set of prices regardless of the rates of profit, guaranteeing not necessarily uniform positive wages, and a positive aggregate price of the net output*" (Italics in the original: Duménil, 1984, 348).

4 According to his empirical study, the decreasing rate of the latter turned out to be bigger than that of the former for Japanese data spanning the three benchmark years of 1975, 1980, and 1985. This suggests that $\dot{E} > \dot{p}$.

Therefore, $\dot{E}_R$ may reasonably be represented as the difference in their respective rates of change.

On the other hand, an ex-post identity exists of the following form, in which p_2 and b are, respectively, the prices of wage goods and the real wage represented as a wage basket:

$$w \equiv p_2 b \qquad \therefore \dot{w} = \dot{p}_2 + \dot{b} \tag{13}$$

From (11) and (13), it follows that

$$\dot{V}_L = \dot{w} - \dot{p} - \dot{E}_R = \dot{p}_2 + \dot{b} - \dot{p} - \dot{E}_R = (\dot{p}_2 - \dot{p}) + \dot{b} - \dot{E}_R \tag{14}$$

Therefore, the change rate of the value of labor power can be determined by three factors, namely, the structure of relative prices, the real wage basket, and the labor productivity of the economy as a whole.

Gouverneur (1990) tried to estimate Marxian ratios, including the rate of surplus value, using the method of the "New Interpretation". His approach is worth examining here, because it is closely related to the problem of applying the "New Interpretation" to individual sectors, even though he did not estimate the rates of surplus value on sectoral levels. Gouverneur (1990) transformed Equation (14) as follows, decomposing the value of labor power into the value of wage goods and the real wage:[5]

$$\dot{V}_L = (\dot{p}_2 - \dot{p} - \dot{E}_R) + \dot{b} = \dot{\lambda}_2 + \dot{b} \tag{15}$$

The change rate in the "value of wage goods" ($\dot{\lambda}_2$), however, is actually equal to the difference between the rate of increase of the relative prices of wage goods and that of aggregate labor productivity. Therefore, this expression can be taken as the change rate in the value of wage goods only with the addition of restrictions. In this regard, two points are worthy of note. First, in a steady state, where the change rates of all related variables are the same, the second equality in Equation (15) holds because, in this case, $\dot{p}_2 = \dot{p}$ and $-\dot{E}_R = \dot{\lambda}_2$. Contrary to Gouverneur's (1990, p. 8) argument, the fact that the market price and value evolve in the same direction as labor productivity increases, which is one of the typical results of the Marxian empirical literature including the work of Ochoa (1984), does not guarantee the relationship expressed in Equation (15).

Second, $\dot{V}_L < 0$ and $\dot{b} > 0$ have been included in the "stylized facts" of several studies, an inclusion that has frequently led to the inference that $\dot{\lambda}_2 < 0$. However, this interpretation should be taken with a grain of salt. Even in the case of $\dot{b} - \dot{E}_R < 0$,

5 Actually, this decomposition has been uncritically accepted by empirical studies of the South Korean economy. The initiation of this tendency may be attributed to Chung (1981), who introduced quantitative Marxian research into South Korea in the 1980s.

$\dot{V}_L$ can be positive if $\dot{p}_2$ is sufficiently larger than $\dot{p}$. This implies that, if the relative prices of wage goods increase, the value of labor power may likewise increase, even when the labor productivity of the economy as a whole increases faster than the real wage.

This situation may result either from a relatively slow increase in labor productivity in the wage goods sector, or from changes in other elements not related to changes in labor productivity. If the difference between $\dot{p}_2$ and $\dot{p}$ is not significant, then the change rate of the value of labor power is undoubtedly determined by the difference between $\dot{b}$ and $\dot{E}_R$. In particular, if we calculate $\dot{p}_2$ and $\dot{p}$ as the consumer price index and GNP (or GDP) deflator, respectively, then the difference between these indices may provide a slightly different result.

However, this discussion of the value of labor power results from the application of the concept of the "monetary expression of values"[6] to individual sectors, rather than to aggregate conditions. The following statement illustrates this point succinctly:

> It is worth noting that dividing the price of any commodity (or group of commodities) by E [monetary expression of values] gives an adequate measure of total productivity in real terms for the commodity(ies) concerned……The price/E ratios, on the other hand, express the number of hours of past and present labor necessary to produce one unit of the commodity considered: they make it possible to obtain a fairly accurate picture of the growth of total real productivity. (Gouverneur, 1990, 8)[7]

This argument, however, is misleading, in that the aggregate concept is applied to individual sectors without any mediation. It may be used to obtain approximate estimates only in special cases, so as to create a general picture of a time-series trend. In passing, it must be noted that although the "monetary expression of labor time" cannot be directly applied to an individual sector level, the value-price relation expressed in the "New Interpretation" can be specified quantitatively on a microeconomic level (Rieu, 2006).

---

6 It may be worth pointing out here that Gouverneur (1990) used the term "monetary expression of values" instead of "monetary expression of labor time". This terminology is an implicit reflection of his misleading usage of the concept discussed in the text.

7 Recently, this point of view has been revived in a more extreme form by Freeman (2004). Freeman (2004) presented an example of calculating the value magnitude of an individual (oil) sector. After calculating "the monetary expression of the living labor " by dividing total value added by the number of workers, he argues that the value of individual sector is equal to the product of the number of workers in that sector and the monetary expression of the living labor. "In my view, the simplest and most direct – but also the most rigorous – interpretation of Marx's theory of value is to say that this *is* the value of output of the oil sector" (Italics in the original; Freeman, 2004, p.59).

According to the line of reasoning elaborated by Gouverneur (1990, p. 1), the rate of surplus value in the i-th sector can be represented as follows, where l_i and w_i, respectively, denote average labor time per worker and the hourly wage:[8]

$$e_i = \frac{l_i}{w_i l_i / E} - 1 = \frac{E}{w_i} - 1 \tag{16}$$

Moreover, sectoral profit-wage ratios (σ_i 's) are given by

$$\sigma_i = \frac{E_i l_i}{w_i l_i} - 1 = \frac{E_i}{w_i} - 1 \tag{17}$$

where E_i represents the value-added productivity of the i-th sector.

From Equations (16) and (17) we can conclude that,

$$\frac{\sigma_i + 1}{e_i + 1} = \frac{E_i}{E} \tag{18}$$

where E_i is an indicator measuring the sectoral inequality in the exchange of labor quantities.[9]

For terminological simplicity, the expression $e_i + 1$ is referred to hereafter as "the rate of surplus value". From Equation (16), the change rate of the sectoral rate of surplus value may be derived as follows:

$$\dot{k}_i = \dot{E} - \dot{w}_i, \text{ where } \quad k_i = 1 + e_i \tag{19}$$

In other words, this rate of change is equal to the difference between the change rate of the hourly wage and the change rate of the "monetary expression of values". In this framework, the skill or intensity of labor is assumed to be irrelevant to value creation, or else it is assumed that complex labor has already been reduced to simple labor. Therefore, virtually all increases in the rate of surplus value result from the production of absolute surplus value in the sense that only the length of the working day matters. Although assumptions of this kind are, to a certain degree,

8 The distinction between productive and unproductive labor is not considered here, mainly for the sake of analytical convenience, as the purpose of this chapter is to present a first approximation method of calculating the sectoral rates of surplus value. Although there are still the lines of questioning the productive-unproductive labor distinction, like Laibman (1999), most Marxian economists emphasize the analytical importance of the distinction (Shaikh and Tonak, 1994; Mohun, 2003). Whether a specific sector is regarded as productive or unproductive is, however, still a moot point. With regard to the numerous trials of calculating the number of productive workers in the South Korean economy, Jeong's survey (2005) will be useful.

9 E_i was named as "rate of income" in the sense that it represents the quantity of income per unit of direct labor in the sector (Nakatani, 1994, 74).

indispensable, it is necessary and possible to measure skill-adjusted sectoral rates of surplus value using proxy variables.[10]

Denoting the degree of skill in the i-th sector as α_i,[11] and that α_i is equal to one in the sector having an average degree of skill, the adjusted rate of surplus value can be represented as follows:

$$k_i^* = \frac{\alpha_i l_i}{w_i l_i / E} = \frac{E\alpha_i}{w_i} \tag{20}$$

A comparison of Equation (20) with Equation (17) indicates that

$$\frac{\sigma_i + 1}{k_i^*} = \frac{E_i}{E\alpha_i} \tag{21}$$

This implies that the relationship between the profit-wage ratio, measured in price terms, and the rate of surplus value may be shown to depend not only upon E_i / E, but also on α_i.

In the end, the key problem is that of how to measure the magnitude of α_i at a certain point in time. If one assumes that all labor is simple in the base year, then its change rate can be computed for any other year. Therefore, the change rates of sectoral rates of surplus value are as follows:

$$\dot{k}_i^* = \dot{\alpha}_i + \dot{E} - \dot{w}_i = \dot{\alpha}_i + \dot{k}_i \tag{22}$$

That is, the change rate for a given sector is equal to $\dot{\alpha}_i$ plus the "unadjusted rate of surplus value", where the difference between the change rate of sectoral labor productivity and that of social average labor productivity constitutes a proxy for $\dot{\alpha}_i$. Here, "labor productivity" is defined as the total direct and indirect labor required for producing the commodity in question, which is essentially equal to the Marxian value, or the "vertically integrated labor coefficient", in the sense of Sraffa-Pasinetti (Pasinetti, 1973). For example, an increase in the degree of skill in the i-th sector causes a decrease in the magnitude of the value calculated using "unadjusted" labor. It can be safely assumed that the inverse of the change rate of the value magnitude calculated from input-output data is equal to the change rate of labor productivity in the sector concerned. Therefore, equation (22) may be transformed into

10 In estimating the value magnitudes for the U.S. economy using input-output data, Ochoa (1984) used sectoral wage rates as proxies for skill levels. For example, if the wage rate of the i-th sector was twice that of the j-th sector, an hour of labor in the i-th sector was assumed equal to two hours of labor in the j-th sector. This method was based upon the simplifying assumption that sectoral rates of surplus value were equalized. As the main goal of this study is to examine the uneven development of sectoral rates of surplus value, Ochoa's method cannot be adopted here.

11 For analytical convenience, labor intensity is also included in the concept of "degree of skill".

$$\dot{k}_i^* = (-\dot{\lambda}_i + \dot{\lambda}) + \dot{k}_i = (-\dot{\lambda}_i + \dot{\lambda}) + (\dot{E} - \dot{w}_i) \tag{23}$$

However, as input-output data are available only for benchmark years, the change rate cannot be estimated continuously; only the ratios for the periods between benchmark years can be estimated, for which purpose the following equations are employed,

$$\frac{k_{i,t+1}}{k_{i,t}} = \frac{E_{t+1}}{w_{i,t+1}} \div \frac{E_t}{w_{i,t}} = \frac{E_{t+1}}{E_t} \cdot \frac{w_{i,t}}{w_{i,t+1}} \tag{24}$$

$$\frac{k^*_{i,t+1}}{k^*_{i,t}} = \frac{E_{t+1}\alpha_{i,t+1}}{w_{i,t+1}} \div \frac{E_t\alpha_{i,t}}{w_{i,t}} = \frac{\alpha_{i,t+1}}{\alpha_{i,t}} \cdot \frac{E_{t+1}}{E_t} \cdot \frac{w_{i,t}}{w_{i,t+1}} \tag{25}$$

Here, the subscripts t and t+1 index discrete time.

In the same manner, the inter-temporal ratio of the degree of skill is given by

$$\frac{\alpha_{i,t+1}}{\alpha_{i,t}} = \frac{(1/\lambda_{i,t+1})}{(1/\lambda_{t+1})} \div \frac{(1/\lambda_{i,t})}{(1/\lambda_t)} = \frac{\lambda_{i,t}}{\lambda_{i,t+1}} \cdot \frac{\lambda_{t+1}}{\lambda_t} \tag{26}$$

Relation (27) obtains from the substitution of (26) into (25).

$$\frac{k^*_{i,t+1}}{k^*_{i,t}} = \frac{\lambda_{i,t}}{\lambda_{i,t+1}} \cdot \frac{\lambda_{t+1}}{\lambda_t} \cdot \frac{E_{t+1}}{E_t} \cdot \frac{w_{i,t}}{w_{i,t+1}} \tag{27}$$

In sum, we can estimate the sectoral rates of surplus value using equation (27), although this requires making the simplifying assumption that all labor is simple in the base year.

Empirical Results

Having provided a basic summary of the content of the methodology, we are now ready to estimate sectoral rates of surplus value using empirical data from South Korea in the 1990s. We begin by estimating the quantity of total direct and indirect labor required to produce commodities. The total quantity of embodied labor or the vertically integrated labor coefficient can be calculated from Equation (9):

$$\lambda = \lambda A + l = l(I - A)^{-1} \tag{9}$$

Although the dimension of λ in (9) is hour per commodity unit, the quantity of embodied labor from input-output data is measured by hour per monetary unit, say a million Won in the case of South Korea (Shaikh and Tonak, 1994, 78-88). Using input-output data from South Korea for the years 1990, 1995, and 2000, therefore, the following can be obtained. Here the asterisk implies that the corresponding quantities are measured by using monetary unit. For example, l^* is the $1 \times n$ vector of direct labor required to produce a million Won of output. Similarly, the elements of A^* matrix represent the amount of the i-th commodity used to produce a million Won's worth of output of the j-th sector. Therefore, the dimension of λ^* is hour per million Won.

$$\lambda^* = \lambda^* A^* + l^* = l^*(I - A^*)^{-1} \qquad (9)'$$

Considering the existence of fixed capital and imported inputs of production, the equation (9)' must be transformed into a more complicated one as shown in Equation (9)″:

$$\lambda^* = \lambda^*(A^{*d} + D^*) + \lambda^*_m \mu^* + l^* = \lambda^*(A^{*d} + D^*) + \lambda^* e^* \mu^* + l^*$$

$$\therefore \lambda^* = l^*(I - A^{*d} - D^* - e^* \mu^*)^{-1} \qquad (9)''$$

Here A^{*d} and D^* represent, respectively, a $n \times n$ input coefficients matrix of domestic goods and services and a $n \times n$ matrix of fixed capital depreciation. While A^{*d} can be directly obtained from input-output data, D^* must be replaced by the proxy assuming that the sectoral ratios of fixed capital formation flows are equal to those of fixed capital stocks.[12]

At the same time, it is very important to estimate the embodied labor quantity of imported goods and services, especially in the case of the South Korean economy, which heavily depends upon the imported inputs. In this chapter, using Nakatani's (1994) method, these quantities are estimated as follows:[13] e^* is a $n \times 1$ vector whose element e_i^* denotes the proportion of export of the i-th commodity to total export. Therefore, the sum of e_i^*'s is equal to 1. A scalar quantity λ_m^*, which can be obtained from premultiplying e^* by λ^*, reveals the embodied labor quantity contained in the composite good of exported commodities. Similarly, μ^* is a $1 \times n$ vector whose element μ_i^* denotes the total price of the imported inputs required to produce a certain amount of the i-th commodity.

This method rests upon the simplifying assumption that a country must export the same monetary amount of imported commodities. From this assumption, the embodied labor quantity of imported goods and services is calculated by that of the basket or composite commodity of exported goods and services. Insofar as there is

12 Although the Bank of Korea does not publish the data on capital stock matrix, more reliable estimates than this chapter can be calculated using Shin's (2005) results. It is possible, however, only for the two benchmark years 1995 and 2000.

13 In estimating the value magnitudes of the US, Japan and the South Korean economy, Nakajima and Izumi (1995) also adopted this method.

no input-output data on the whole world scale, however, this kind of assumption is indispensable.[14]

We are now able to calculate λ^*.

Table 2.1 represents the sectoral estimates of the embodied labor quantities on the level of the 28 large-sized industries in South Korea for the three benchmark years. Table 2.2 represents the sectoral rates of income, which is E_i in Equation (18). In the context of Marxian literature, it represents an index of unequal exchange across sectors.

Table 2.1 Sectoral Quantity of Embodied Labor (hour/million Won)

Code	name of sector	1990	1995	2000
1	Agriculture, forestry, and fisheries	488.3980	253.1282	187.9564
2	Mining and quarrying	117.4920	110.8462	23.7009
3	Food, beverages and tobacco	215.5154	102.1260	73.0454
4	Textile products and leather products	511.4375	173.1621	86.6273
5	Wood and paper products	206.8564	106.0510	60.9947
6	Printing, publishing and reproduction of recorded media	125.7171	81.9291	45.0588
7	Petroleum and coal products	152.7627	86.4104	71.6828
8	Chemicals and allied products	435.3710	237.0520	154.2210
9	Nonmetallic mineral products	159.6404	76.7819	38.7601
10	Primary metal products	413.1687	191.2400	109.1906
11	Fabricated metal products	165.3435	91.1885	58.3614
12	General machinery and equipment	249.4772	154.8624	99.4836
13	Electronic and other electric equipment	396.1910	259.8295	187.4797
14	Precision instruments	116.5082	62.4990	39.5153
15	Transportation equipment	255.4845	153.8424	109.8291
16	Furniture and other manufacturing products	174.8950	85.8511	44.2518
17	Electric, gas, and water services	159.9056	92.0300	44.1139
18	Construction	275.5482	124.1776	64.4030
19	Wholesale and retail trade	479.2980	263.7173	169.0138
20	Eating and drinking places, and hotels and other lodging places	589.8878	476.3975	106.1220
21	Transportation and warehousing	272.1488	159.1957	95.2309
22	Communications and broadcasting	126.4973	75.7388	40.8302
23	Finance and insurance	270.7357	179.6115	91.6329
24	Real estate and business service	403.7153	337.2703	146.3499
25	Public administration and defense	114.9531	66.3589	38.4628
26	Educational and health service	141.8511	85.2418	71.5717
27	Social and other services	418.8867	201.8606	85.8208
28	Dummy sector	203.7500	113.5272	50.7102

14 If there is an unequal exchange between countries, this method will systematically over or underestimate the value magnitude of imported goods and services. The correct estimate will be provided only by a fluke.

Table 2.2 Sectoral Rates of Income (Won/hour)

Code	name of sector	1990	1995	2000
1	Agriculture, forestry, and fisheries	3,189.78	6,150.94	8,555.24
2	Mining and quarrying	8,560.37	7,021.32	34,167.01
3	Food, beverages and tobacco	6,114.52	14,549.49	21,407.11
4	Textile products and leather products	2,159.85	5,218.54	10,622.90
5	Wood and paper products	4,722.97	12.077.43	16,157.88
6	Printing, publishing and reproduction of recorded media	4,632.13	8,255.32	10,145.70
7	Petroleum and coal products	18,013.23	116,198.67	400,302.12
8	Chemicals and allied products	6,638.68	14,406.47	25,421.75
9	Nonmetallic mineral products	5,607.28	11,531.15	19,519.39
10	Primary metal products	8,491.38	18,092.39	38,389.94
11	Fabricated metal products	3,762.50	8,938.28	12,272.07
12	General machinery and equipment	5,272.84	10,972.72	16,740.73
13	Electronic and other electric equipment	4,739.31	13,473.92	27,500.58
14	Precision instruments	3,416.97	8,333.56	11,777.32
15	Transportation equipment	7,597.60	14,381.69	21,697.16
16	Furniture and other manufacturing products	2,879.54	6,350.86	10,269.07
17	Electric, gas, and water services	24,139.33	40,657.47	75,641.41
18	Construction	6,752.66	16,753.54	14,726.13
19	Wholesale and retail trade	3,236.44	4,020.03	6,371.75
20	Eating and drinking places, and hotels and other lodging places	1,129.77	1,175.19	5,222.05
21	Transportation and warehousing	4,938.88	8,745.55	10,607.31
22	Communications and broadcasting	16,181.32	26,351.35	66,884.74
23	Finance and insurance	8,986.04	11,878.43	27,154.84
24	Real estate and business service	10,009.94	24,157.29	45,618.27
25	Public administration and defense	4,806.04	9,038.78	17,728.91
26	Educational and health service	7,347.64	16,546.09	13,776.37
27	Social and other services	1,485.06	3,087.63	6,629.04
28	Dummy sector	0.00	0.00	0.00

Finally, the corresponding sectoral rates of surplus value are estimated according to equations (24) and (27). Figure 2.1 and Table 2.3 present the results of this estimation, while Table 2.4 provides inter-temporal sectoral value ratios.

The correlation coefficients between the two rates k^* and k are 0.8022, 0.3248, and 0.6105, respectively, for the periods of 1990-1995, 1995-2000, and 1990-2000. This implies that Gouverneur-like estimates do not fully reflect the trend in the rate of surplus value, and that this is particularly true on a sectoral level. In some cases, as can be seen from Table 2.3, the direction of the change itself depends upon which indicator is chosen. In the case of transportation and warehousing (Code 21) for the years between 1990 and 2000, while the "rate of surplus value" increased by 21.1% according to a Gouverneur-like estimation, it decreased by 4.7% according

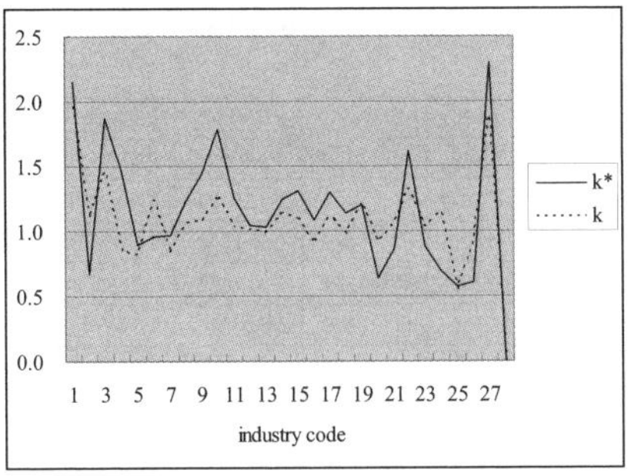

a) Year 1995/Year 1990

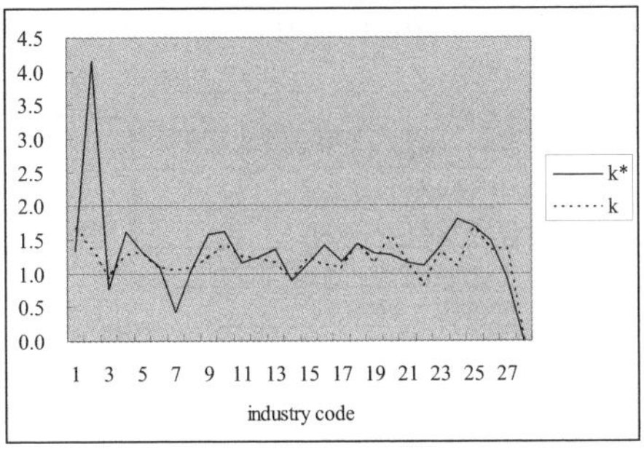

b) Year 2000/Year 1995

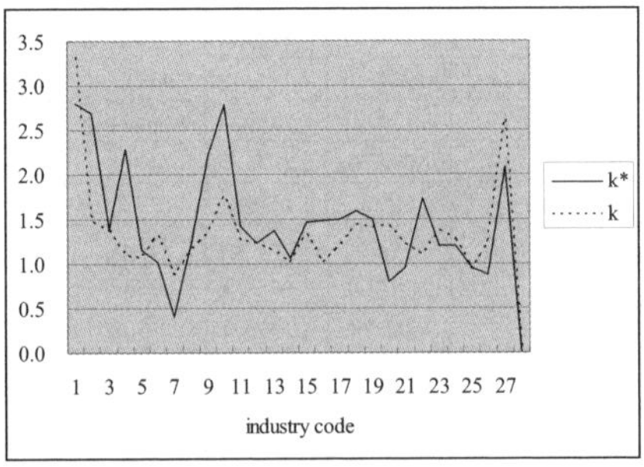

c) Year 2000/Year 1990

Figure 2.1 Inter-temporal Ratio of Sectoral Rates of Surplus Value

to the estimation approach used in this chapter. This difference results from the characteristics of α_i, for which a proxy change rate of value is used in this chapter. Therefore, differences among the sectoral change rates of value determine the direction of change.

The main shortcoming of the estimation approach used in this chapter is that it does not allow us to determine the absolute magnitudes of the sectoral rates of surplus value. However, a first approximation can be calculated under the assumption that the sectoral degrees of skill were equalized in the base year 1990. Table 2.5 and Figure 2.2 present the results for this case. In contrast to the terminology used above, the rate of surplus value in the following table is represented by e_i, rather than by k_i.[15]

15 Note that the rate of surplus value may be underestimated because the distinction between productive and unproductive labor is not considered. If we accept the Marxian conception that only productive labor can create value and surplus value, the wages paid to unproductive workers must be regarded as the deduction of surplus value produced by productive workers, not as variable capital.

Table 2.3 Inter-temporal Ratios of the Sectoral Rates of Surplus Value

Code	name of sector	k(95/90)	k(00/95)	k(00/90)	k*(95/90)	k*(00/95)	k*(00/90)
1	Agriculture, forestry, and fisheries	1.968547	1.690638	3.32810	2.147969	1.346476	2.792413
2	Mining and quarrying	1.101066	1.337811	1.47302	0.672203	4.146404	2.69107
3	Food, beverages and tobacco	1.463146	0.935287	1.36846	1.876479	0.761494	1.379632
4	Textile products and leather products	0.853943	1.279862	1.09293	1.464289	1.619052	2.288973
5	Wood and paper products	0.818052	1.288744	1.05426	0.894706	1.327553	1.146794
6	Printing, publishing and reproduction of recorded media	1.247776	1.065238	1.32918	0.959186	1.090383	1.009799
7	Petroleum and coal products	0.835079	1.050717	0.87743	0.973025	0.424313	0.398624
8	Chemicals and allied products	1.068863	1.073537	1.14746	1.223194	1.059201	1.250911
9	Nonmetallic mineral products	1.07779	1.235586	1.33170	1.441215	1.59089	2.213717
10	Primary metal products	1.260376	1.410745	1.77807	1.782622	1.615389	2.780287
11	Fabricated metal products	1.027519	1.230807	1.26468	1.259751	1.159889	1.410764
12	General machinery and equipment	1.014425	1.219005	1.23659	1.041615	1.226404	1.233371
13	Electronic and other electric equipment	0.984366	1.155235	1.13717	1.037214	1.362399	1.364351
14	Precision instruments	1.134053	0.88622	1.00502	1.242674	0.884516	1.061246
15	Transportation equipment	1.092231	1.227711	1.34094	1.313334	1.147723	1.455343
16	Furniture and other manufacturing products	0.905627	1.117662	1.01218	1.088789	1.412732	1.485103
17	Electric, gas, and water services	1.12068	1.067094	1.19587	1.300864	1.18576	1.489298
18	Construction	0.983921	1.447751	1.42447	1.139215	1.441031	1.585011
19	Wholesale and retail trade	1.226465	1.144005	1.40308	1.200778	1.290968	1.496689
20	Eating and drinking places, and hotels and other lodging places	0.919756	1.553926	1.42923	0.635805	1.280052	0.785786
21	Transportation and warehousing	1.058232	1.144667	1.21132	0.85915	1.148487	0.952683
22	Communications and broadcasting	1.333239	0.811723	1.08222	1.617768	1.105241	1.726339
23	Finance and insurance	1.034895	1.31666	1.36260	0.879812	1.403119	1.191894
24	Real estate and business service	1.145496	1.09817	1.25795	0.688296	1.813407	1.205102
25	Public administration and defense	0.553365	1.687693	0.93391	0.574075	1.711693	0.948741
26	Educational and health service	0.902467	1.341012	1.21022	0.610527	1.478577	0.871569
27	Social and other services	1.894752	1.387881	2.62969	2.30273	0.939063	2.087811
28	Dummy sector	n.a.	n.a.	n.a.	n.a.	n.a.	n.a.

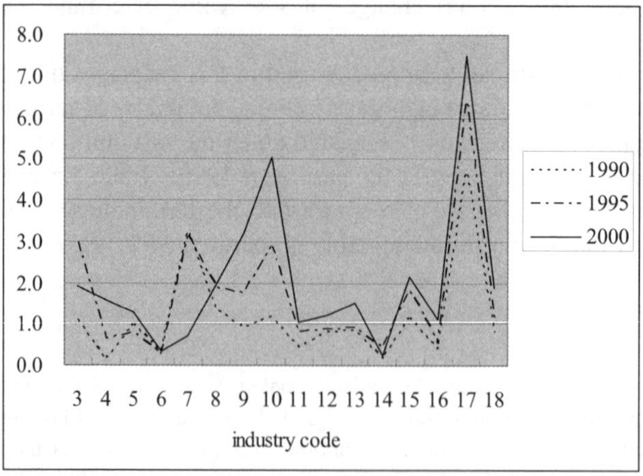

Figure 2.2 Sectoral Rates of Surplus Value

Table 2.4 Inter-temporal Value Ratios

code	name of sector	1995/1990	2000/1995	2000/1990
1	Agriculture, forestry, and fisheries	0.676167	0.938412	0.634523
2	Mining and quarrying	1.208508	0.241137	0.291416
3	Food, beverages and tobacco	0.575281	0.917951	0.52808
4	Textile products and leather products	0.430267	0.590804	0.254204
5	Wood and paper products	0.674585	0.725531	0.489433
6	Printing, publishing and reproduction of recorded media	0.959777	0.730144	0.700775
7	Petroleum and coal products	0.633198	1.850721	1.171873
8	Chemicals and allied products	0.644708	0.757495	0.488363
9	Nonmetallic mineral products	0.551749	0.580462	0.32027
10	Primary metal products	0.521647	0.652698	0.340478
11	Fabricated metal products	0.601785	0.793076	0.477261
12	General machinery and equipment	0.718537	0.742871	0.53378
13	Electronic and other electric equipment	0.700204	0.633734	0.443743
14	Precision instruments	0.673306	0.74882	0.504185
15	Transportation equipment	0.613586	0.799466	0.490541
16	Furniture and other manufacturing products	0.61368	0.591278	0.362856
17	Electric, gas, and water services	0.635603	0.672585	0.427497
18	Construction	0.637222	0.750865	0.478467
19	Wholesale and retail trade	0.753579	0.662298	0.499094
20	Eating and drinking places, and hotels and other lodging places	1.067297	0.907285	0.968343
21	Transportation and warehousing	0.908757	0.744893	0.676927
22	Communications and broadcasting	0.608034	0.548899	0.333749
23	Finance and insurance	0.867846	0.701326	0.608643
24	Real estate and business service	1.227876	0.452601	0.555738
25	Public administration and defense	0.71118	0.7369	0.524069
26	Educational and health service	1.090593	0.677844	0.739252
27	Social and other services	0.607079	1.104583	0.67057
28	Dummy sector	0.746233	0.526403	0.392819

From the above results, we are able to confirm that sectoral rates of surplus value evolved unevenly during 1990s in South Korea. In most sectors, the rate of exploitation increased, no doubt, due to the economic crisis in the late 1990s. Above all, we can confirm that it is misleading to assume away the sectoral differences in the rate of surplus value.

Concluding Remarks

Methods using input-output data have conventionally been adopted for the purpose of estimating value and surplus value in the context of the Marxian tradition. However, the conventional interpretation has reached an impasse, for example, in the form of the so-called "transformation problem", which implies that Marx's two aggregates, total value-price equality and total surplus value-profit equality do not

Table 2.5 Sectoral Rates of Surplus Value

code	name of sector	1990	1995	2000
3	Food, beverages and tobacco	1.1191537	2.97654719	1.92365189
4	Textile products and leather products	0.12773933	0.65133659	1.58136538
5	Wood and paper products	0.98593622	0.77682883	1.27745951
6	Printing, publishing and reproduction of recorded media	0.33129813	0.27696221	0.3443435
7	Petroleum and coal products	3.25096933	3.13630033	0.69453779
8	Chemicals and allied products	1.34699375	1.8708277	1.93588125
9	Nonmetallic mineral products	0.89906123	1.73695621	3.20398456
10	Primary metal products	1.17837295	2.88321649	5.05650123
11	Fabricated metal products	0.43722546	0.81054679	1.02758647
12	General machinery and equipment	0.79496779	0.86966452	1.21386146
13	Electronic and other electric equipment	0.84963128	0.91846407	1.52354622
14	Precision instruments	0.16986238	0.45375751	0.2415115
15	Transportation equipment	1.15966025	1.83635593	2.14304709
16	Furniture and other manufacturing products	0.40918552	0.53430505	1.09278568
17	Electric, gas, and water services	4.70714174	6.42421609	7.49963749
18	Construction	0.81882513	1.07203328	1.88285731

hold simultaneously. Although the "New Interpretation", once named the "New Solution" (Lipietz, 1982), develops tools for empirical analysis on a macro level, it also aims to solve the theoretical difficulties found in the conventional interpretation. Therefore, it has importance not only for the development of empirical research, but also as a means of maintaining the theoretical perspectives provided by the Marxian labor theory of value.

This chapter has attempted to combine the estimation of value magnitudes from input-output data with the insights of the "New Interpretation", to arrive at a first approximation of uneven development in the sectoral rates of surplus value. To sum up, the following points were made in this chapter. First, the relative change rate in "labor productivity" or "vertically integrated labor coefficient" was presented as a proxy for measuring the degree of skill. Although this requires a strong assumption, it can serve as a useful proxy for the relevant variables.

Second, based upon the above method, empirical estimates of sectoral rates of surplus value in the South Korean economy were provided. The results demonstrate the validity of the hypothesis that the structural changes including the economic crisis in the 1990s had a differential effect on the sectoral rates of surplus value.

Appendix: Data Sources

1. Input-Output Table: The South Korean input-output tables are based on the *1990-1995-2000 Link Input-Output Tables* published by the Bank of Korea (BOK).
2. Employed Persons by Industry: Employed persons by Industry are obtained

from Employment Matrix in the supporting tables of the Input-Output Table.

3. Sectoral Average Hours Worked per Worker and Sectoral Wage Rates: These data come from *Survey Report on Wage Structure*, Ministry of Labor. Adjustments were performed to make these data compatible with the sector classification of the Input-Output Table. Korean Standard Industrial Classification (KSIC) was changed, respectively, in the year 1984, 1991, 2000. Table A.1 summarizes this procedure.
4. Capital Consumption Data: Estimated using the information on 'fixed capital formation' found in the supporting tables of the Input-Output Table.

Table 2A.1 Classification of Industry (KSIC)

code	name of sector (input-output tables)	Primary (2000)	Primary (1991)	Secondary (1984)
1	Agriculture, forestry, and fisheries	01,02,05	01,02,05	111,112,113, 121,123,130
2	Mining and quarrying	10,11,12	10,13,14	210,230,290
3	Food, beverages and tobacco	15,16	15,16	311,312,313,314
4	Textile products and leather products	17,18,19	17,18,19	321,322,323,324
5	Wood and paper products	20,21	20,21	331,332,341
6	Printing, publishing and reproduction of recorded media	22	22	342
7	Petroleum and coal products	23	23	353,354
8	Chemicals and allied products	24,25	24,25	351,352
9	Nonmetallic mineral products	26	26	361,362,369
10	Primary metal products	27	27	371,372
11	Fabricated metal products	28	28	381
12	General machinery and equipment	29	29	382
13	Electronic and other electric equipment	30,31,32	30,31,32	383
14	Precision instruments	33	33	385
15	Transportation equipment	34,35	34,35	384
16	Furniture and other manufacturing products	36	36	390
17	Electric, gas, and water services	40,41	40,41	410,420
18	Construction	45,46	45	510,520
19	Wholesale and retail trade	50,51,52	50,51,52	610,620
20	Eating and drinking places, and hotels and other lodging places	55	55	630
21	Transportation and warehousing	60,61,62,63	60,61,62,63	711,712,713,719
22	Communications and broadcasting	64	64	720
23	Finance and insurance	65,66,67	65,66,67	810,820
24	Real estate and business service	70,71,72,73,74,75	70,71,72,73,74	830,840
25	Public administration and defense	76	75	
26	Educational and health service	80,85,86	80,85,86	920,931,932,933, 934
27	Social and other services	87,88,90,91,93	90,91,92,93	935,939,940,950
28	Dummy sector			

Chapter 3

State, Market, and Stages of Capitalism in South Korean Development

Richard Westra

Introduction

This chapter offers a Marxist approach to the post-Second World War (WW2) economic development of South Korea (hereafter, Korea) and to the debate currently playing itself out in academic development literature over the role of market and state in that process. What inspires the chapter is concern with the way debate over Korean economic development, monopolized by neoliberals and left-liberal "statists", reifies the concepts of market and state, pays no attention to the historicity of their analytical separation, and elides theoretically informed discussion of the specificity of the capitalist market and that of the specifically *capitalist* state. The intellectual currents contributing to this state of affairs are not hard to trace. In its triumphant beginning, as "modernization theory", development studies easily dispensed with problematizing capitalism arguing that liberated from the yoke of colonialism developing societies had only to imbibe socio-political patterns of developed countries and engage in free trade with them to realize similar prosperous futures. However, by the mid-1960s, as evidence mounted that little development characteristic of the dominant capitalist countries was occurring across the third world, the problematizing of capitalism began to take center stage in development debates as variations of dependency theory[1] challenged the modernization approach. Whereas modernization theory believed international relations in a post-colonial world of sovereign states had no impact on the economic futures of individual countries dependency theories argued that centuries of capitalism had shaped the world system in a fashion that promoted development at one pole and underdevelopment and poverty at another. While modernization theory viewed world economic development as a teleological process from a universal state of "backwardness" to one of capitalist modernity dependency theory maintained the apparent lack of development or apparent backwardness in much of the world was not an original condition but the outcome of capitalism orienting economies of the third world in "dependent", "extroverted" and "peripheral" ways. Finally, whereas the policy implication of modernization theory was the opening of the global economy to unmitigated free trade that of dependency theory involved some measure of "de-linking" from the world economy to build either an "introverted"

1 Dependency theory is adopted here as an umbrella term for critical theories of "underdevelopment", "imperialism", "unequal exchange" and "world system". See the expanded discussion in Brewer (1991).

capitalism under the banner of import-substitution industrialization (ISI) or, in more radical incarnations of the theory, to build a socialist economy. This then placed the spotlight upon the *state* – its' economic or class character, international orientation, and so on – as the organized force of development policy direction.

From the perspective of this chapter, despite its broad and, to be sure, ongoing critical appeal, dependency theory ran aground in two significant areas. The first area was theoretical. Marxist critics recognized a "unit of analysis" problem at the heart of the dependency approach. While Marx, it was argued, had concerned himself with the class-exploitative and asymmetric wealth distributive consequences of capitalism in every country in which capitalism spawned dependency theory shifted discussions of the logic of capitalism from "national" accumulation to international accumulation at the expense of analysis of capitalist outcomes within the context of the former. As elaborated upon elsewhere (Westra, 2004a; 2006), the purported inability of Marxist theory to advance concepts to deal with this sort of problematic led to the charge that Marxism's "meta-theoretical" pretensions compromised its whole research agenda and its ability to enhance knowledge in the development field. And, with the discrediting of Marxist theory in development studies, the problematizing of capitalism was effectively dropped from development theory. The second area in which dependency theory was challenged was over empirical evidence. Its meta-theoretical purview, it was asserted, proved incapable of grasping the fluidity of actual "situations" of development (Cardoso and Faletto, 1979). And no situation as such was accepted as more compelling than the rise in East Asia of a group of so-called newly industrializing countries (NIC's) led by the "super NIC" (Bienefeld, 1988), Korea.

What the evidence seemed to indicate was that contrary to dependency theory characterization of the world system development was possible within global capitalist relational contours. And, while dependency theory claimed only de-linking from the world economy would offer a development future for the third world, Korea's growth it was maintained stemmed from its free and open trading with the developed north. Further, whereas dependency theory had urged ISI as the path to industrialization for developing countries, Korea and other NIC's it was argued successfully adopted a strategy of export oriented industrialization (EOI). To enthusiasts, this accumulated evidence pointed to a vindication of modernization theory, now recast in terms of the role of "the market" as the world economic engine of development; a view promptly codified as the panacea for the travails of the developing world as a whole (World Bank, 1993).

Yet, with the systemic implications of dependency theory contested and its radical anti-capitalist thrust blunted one aspect of its research program survived. This being the belief that while ISI de-linking and socialism did not yield the anticipated development outcomes the development that did mark the NIC phenomenon nevertheless was hardly the result of unimpeded markets but that of the concentrated power of the state.[2] Instructive catch phrases that emerge here include the notion of the state as "developmental" (Johnson, 1996), largely orchestrating economic growth, with an "embedded autonomy" (Evans, 1995) from particularistic ruling class interests sufficient to spur these classes to dawn the mantle of national capitalist development. The state in this view "governs" the market (Wade, 1990) by selecting companies to support and fashion into world-market "winners"; a strategy that means the success of the Korean political economy is predicated not upon supposed market-rational pricing and resource allocation but "getting prices wrong" (Amsden, 1989; 1990).

To be sure, in their critique of the neoclassical economics neoliberal policy repackaged modernization theory of market efficiency and destruction of trade barriers to realize "perfect" international competition as the global development template, statists serve a valuable intellectual function. For example, statists bring history back in to the development debate through comparative examination of earlier experience with "catch-up development" where evidence is adduced to display the rationality of a follower country embarking upon state-led development (Hoogvelt, 1997, 205-7). Statists also explore questions of potential social forces making for developmental state empowerment and autonomy – political (Chibber, 1999), social class (Davis, 2004), to cite two important exemplars – in order that other countries might take these lessons and possibly duplicate the NIC experience with development. However, the statist approach also carries huge impediments to the advancement of knowledge in development studies. Firstly, the statists never question neoclassical economics as the centerpiece of economic theory of development. Put differently, what is actually meant by the term market and what peculiar ontological properties this market has which allow it to be counter-posed as a kind of "extra-human force" of development to the overtly human force of the state are left un-interrogated. In this sense the debate as a whole craftily evades questions about the capitalist specificity of this market and the specificity of the capitalist state. Compounding this, the debate circumvents the signal issue of capitalism and *its* historical development and transformation, and how the form and patterns of capitalist development impact upon the realm of possibilities for the development of any developer.

These questions, that dependency theories and early Marxist development theory groped, unsatisfactorily to be sure, towards answering, are hardly innocuous. The statist literature, as alluded to above, makes some headway in challenging the historical blindness of modernization theory and its neoliberal progeny by focusing on development sequencing. It brings to bear concepts of "early", "late" and even "late, late" development to capture instances where historical conditions warrant the state engaging in policy action to promote development as a supplement to market outcomes. The problem with this is that by accepting the fundamentally a-historical

2 For a representative cross-section on the state in the NIC phenomena, see for example, Deyo (1987); Haggard (1990); Chaudhry (1993); Woo-Cumings (1999). On South Korea specifically, see for example, Amsden (1989); Woo-Cumings (1991) and Kim (1997).

neoclassical economics as the basis of economic analysis in development theory, while historical conditions on the state side of the state/market ledger are perceived as changing, the operation of the market side is held constant. In other words implicit in the state/market debate is the view that the market, or more specifically for purposes of this chapter, the capitalism, characteristic of the economy of mid-nineteenth century Britain, early twentieth century Germany, mid-twentieth century United States (US) and late twentieth century Korea would operate in a "pure" form, as captured in economics textbooks, if unimpeded by extraneous non-market factors. Corollary to this problematic is also the lingering question of the unit of analysis. When we talk about the market, or again capitalism, within the context of discussion of development within the geo-spatial contours of a nation-state, and capitalism as an international economy with the impact of global market forces being considered in development analysis, are we talking about the same kind of market? Can our analysis then move seamlessly from discussion of the benefits of markets in national development to that of market operations globally?

Finally, there are the questions that clearly only the Marxist research agenda ever seriously posed of the fundamental disposition of capitalism and how capital is destined to shape human material existence wherever it spawns. There is also the question of the limits to capitalism: After all, capitalism is a historically constituted mode of economic life that comes into being at a particular level of development of human material wants and productive technique. And, while Marx believed it was transformable to a certain extent (something this chapter will deal with in the final section), he also understood that capitalist development necessarily would face limitations as technologies and energy sources that are not operable according to its principles of economy emerge on the horizon and as human wants spill out beyond the range of those which capitalism is able to satisfy. It is virtually impossible to imagine how issues such as these, which have the most pressing ramifications for Korea as a capitalist economy, could ever be dealt with in the context of the arid state/market debate constituting the main focus of development literature on Korea.

To remedy this intellectual state of affairs the procedure of this chapter is to first deal with the subject of the ontological uniqueness of capitalism and reveal what it is about the ontological structure of capital that constitutes the basis of the analytical separation of market and state in political economy. Here, the chapter recruits a powerful Marxist theoretical framework originating in Japan in the work of Kozo Uno (Uno, 1980). Second, the chapter expounds upon Uno's work to argue that the study of capitalist development requires a "levels of analysis" approach where the historical explanatory power of economic theory is mediated by a mid-range stage theory of capitalism. Third, the chapter explores causal matters regarding the specific operation of the capitalist market and role of the specifically capitalist state in Korean development through the lens of the theorizing of stages of capitalist development in the Uno approach. The chapter demonstrates how an adequate explanation of the NIC phenomenon in Korea is produced when the historical situation of Korean development is examined within the analytical contours of the stage specific accumulation modalities and institutional architecture of capital in the post-Second World War stage of capitalism. Fourth, the chapter seeks to make sense of the new twists and turns in the state/market debate that follow on the heels of the Asian economic crisis in the closing years of the twentieth century. The chapter will then be concluded.

The Logical Ontology of Capital and the Marxist Study of Capitalism

A Marxist approach seeking robust knowledge of Korean development must commence with inquiry into the ontological uniqueness of capitalism as a social science subject matter. More than anything, this necessitates coming to terms with capitalist *reification*. To build the argument here it is worth referring back to economic historian Karl Polanyi's highly instructive and widely cited differentiation between capitalism and pre-capitalist societies in terms of the economy in capitalism tending to become "dis-embedded" from other realms of the social – the politics, religion, ideology – with which it had been intermeshed since the dawn of human society. Less acknowledged, but even more intellectually potent, Marx also has an understanding of this peculiar attribute of the capitalist market. His conceptualizing of the "fetishism" of capital captured the tendency of capital to reify economic life. That is, for Marx, not only does the economic in capitalist society dis-embed from the social but, though capitalism is a socially and historically constituted order, the economic in capitalism comes to take on a "life of its own" and wields the social, human beings and the human life-world for its own self-aggrandizement – the augmentation of value.[3] However, it would remain the task of the Japanese political economist Kozo Uno (1980) to draw out the ultimate implications of Marx's work for social science and the analysis of capitalist development.

It is no accident that economics emerges as a field of study only in the age of capitalism: For it is precisely the reification of economic life or again, the dis-embedding of the economy from its enmeshment among other realms of the social that constitute the ontological condition of possibility for economic theory. That is, as Polanyi, Marx and Uno observe, pre-capitalist societies reproduce their economic life through interpersonal relations of co-operation, dependence, or domination and subordination. Capitalism, however, tends to dissolve all such interpersonal relations of economic existence in its organizing of human material life in impersonal, society-wide integrated systems of self-regulating markets. In this fashion, capital converts human relations of material life into what Marx refers to as "relations among things", in effect, constituting an "upside down" society in which human beings effectively abdicate their responsibility for managing their material existence to an "extra-human" force: the commodity economic logic of capital. The key social science implication for the study of capitalism flowing from this is that it is the conversion of human interpersonal relations into relations among things in the abstract operation of self-regulating markets which then "objectifies" economic

3 Postone (1996, 156) captures this aptly with the notion of capital assuming a position akin to that of the "Absolute Subject".

relations rendering them "transparent" for theory to explore.[4] A major controversy in Marxism however has been over the precise character of the theory necessary to apprehend capital's objective logic.

In his reflection upon Marx's study of capitalism in *Capital,* Uno came to understand that if the modus operandi of capitalism in history is the conversion of all use-value life, including its wellspring, human labor power, into commodities as grist for the impersonal dictates of self-regulating markets operating to augment value, then, to truly capture the objectifying logic of this process, it is incumbent upon Marxian economics to trace it out to a hypothetical conclusion in a theoretical procedure that excludes non-objective, non-economic, non-capitalist interferences. In other words, the role of economic theory is to produce a *theory of a purely capitalist society* (TPCS)[5] that demonstrates what human material life would look like if completely under the reified thrall of capital. For only in that way, in the hypothetical consummation of the objectifying logic of capital, can we genuinely know what capital *is*. The *materialist* pedigree of this theory flows not from its following all the variegated transformations and differentiations of capitalism throughout its history. Marx's *Capital* reconstructed as the TPCS is materialist because it commences with the cell-form in which capital first manifests itself in human history – the commodity as the contradiction between value and use-value – and follows the self-synthesis or material force of this contradiction to unearth the "truth" of capital in the demonstration of the immanence and objective logical interrelation of all the categories of capital. The prerequisite of the TPCS then is the historical existence of capitalism. However to fully apprehend the logical ontology of capital requires that economic theory study capital free from extra-economic extra-capitalist impurities and distortions.

But, while *Capital* recast as the TPCS captures the homogenizing logic of capital with the highest degree of scientificity possible in a social science endeavor it also leaves a gap between the study of capital's inner logic and the diverse and open ended history of capitalism. To deal with this theoretical problematic Uno argued that the study of capitalism demanded a *levels of analysis* approach where the movement in thought from the TPCS to the study of capitalism in history was mediated by a *stage theory* of capitalist development. Levels of analysis are warranted by the peculiar ontology of capital and operate in a division of labor to produce complete knowledge of capitalism (See Figure 3.1). For Uno, this was hardly an arbitrary imposition upon Marxism. *Capital* itself, he argued, manifested an implicit levels of analysis approach. *Capital* contained a theorizing of capital's inner logic, analysis of the capitalist stage of *liberalism* characteristic of mid-nineteenth century Britain,

4 As put by Albritton (1999, 35), "We can carry out this theoretical practice because we are objectified by capital but still have the potential cognitively to become knowing subjects capable of theoretically grasping what is happening to us. We can know capital as a subjectified object because we are objectified subjects".

5 The most up-to-date refinement of the TPCS is the impressive two volume work of Sekine (1997).

and a wealth of historical empirical material on the capitalism of Marx's day. Given his temporal emplacement, where it appeared capitalism was tending towards actual purity in history, and where it was assumed socialist revolution would soon suspend capital, Marx would have seen no pressing theoretical reason to elaborate upon levels of analysis. Privy to the momentous transformation of capitalism in the stage of *imperialism* however, Uno realized the indispensability of levels of analysis in Marxism.

Theory of a Purely Capitalist Society

- Abstract economic theory
- Studies inner logic of capital as *constant* of all existing capitalist societies
- Confirms possibility of *capital* viably reproducing material life of human society

Stage Theory

- "Concretization" of capital's inner logic
- Studies capital's management of core forms of *use value* production characterizing phases of capitalist development
- Theorizes the capitalist superstructure and state form supporting accumulation
- Confirms viability of stage specific structures of capital accumulation

Historical Analysis

- Empirical/historical
- Studies coming into being, transformation and passing of capitalism in history
- Confirms impact of capital in historical outcomes

Figure 3.1 Levels of Analysis in Marxian Political Economy

The cardinal problematic of development theory thus is that while the reifying logic of the capitalist market certainly exists as a *constant* of each and every capitalist society, the fact is that throughout its historical existence capitalism assumes multifarious forms, is supported historically to greater or lesser extents by non-capitalist and non-economic social practices, and is subject to resistance and challenge by human agency. Yet, rather than tasking theory with controlling the way the logic of capital is used in historical explanation as such, radical development studies have lurched from attempting to directly read capitalist history off that logic to arguing that history is too diverse and far too marked by human agency for the logic of capital to be accorded an explanatory role. Uno, however, also accepting the fact of the diversity of use value life in economic history, understood that the causal efficacy of capital's objective logic in history could be gauged if the study of capitalism in history was mediated by a stage theory of capitalist development. Stage theory as a level of analysis in Marxian political economy operates to "concretize" the logic of capital elaborated in the TPCS. That is, as in Marx's *Capital*, the TPCS views the paramount contradiction of capitalism as that between value and use value. Stage theory therefore concretizes this contradiction through its theorization of world historic stages of capitalist development as the *interplay* of capital's logic and stage specific forms of use value production.

State, Market and Stages of Capitalist Development

Put in the language of the state/market debate, capitalist development, as solely a product of the pure working of society-wide integrated systems of self-regulating markets, is something that exists only within the reified context of the TPCS. To theorize market development as such several vital theoretical assumptions are made, including holding implicit the specificity of use value, business structure and technology deployed by capital. Theory simply assumes that there exists a frictionless use value space for capital to manage for its abstract purpose of value augmentation, businesses are industrial and conduct all transactions through external market price taking, and technologies are capitalistically operable. In short, the capitalist market, as conceptualized in the TPCS reproduces human economic life on its own with no extra-market encumbrances or unmanageable *externalities*.[6] In the TPCS therefore, the state, which is an institution pre-dating capital, and hence is "alien" to capital's objective inner logic, has no place. In is precisely in this sense that the thought experiment of the TPCS, which captures the logical ontology of capital with the consummation of capital's objective tendencies, constitutes the theoretical basis of the analytical separation of market and state in the political economic study of capitalism.

As a mediating level of analysis stage theory gauges the impact of capital in history through the prism of the capitalist management of key use values

---

6 Externalities in this chapter refer to those facets of material life in capitalist society that capital is unable to manage according to its principles of self-regulating market operations as elucidated in the TPCS.

characteristic of accumulation in world historic stages of capitalist development. What stage theory makes immediately evident is that stage specific forms of use value production *refract* the logic of capital in various ways. The assumptions of docility and malleability of use value life are dropped in stage theory as managing stage specific use values shapes capital into distinct structures of accumulation. In elaborating upon these structures of accumulation stage theory is confronted by the fact that capital accumulation is beset by varying sets of externalities which demand the support of the capitalist superstructure. Thus, while the extent of superstructure support for capital differs among stages, stage theory demonstrates that capitalist development necessitates the capitalist state. It is at the level of stage theory, which analyzes structures of accumulation and accumulatory supports for capital as accumulation congeals around a particular form of use value production, that the *policy* profile of the state must be established. In fact, in the Uno approach, stages are named according to the stage specific policies supporting capital and managing capitalist externalities (See Figure 3.2).

Importantly, stage theory is also where the unit of analysis issue in the study of capitalism is addressed. The spatial dimensions of the TPCS are "global" in the sense that given the assumption of total reification where the homogenizing logic of capital has complete sway over the world there is no distinction to be made between "national" and "international" capital. In "concretizing" the logic of capital, stage theory, as has been pointed out, treats the shaping of capitalist structures of accumulation by the exigencies of stage specific forms of use value production. Stage theory also faces up to the fact of capital's need for extra-economic support for accumulation and its harnessing of the superstructural power of the state to manage or "internalize" externalities to accumulation. The refracting of capital's logic by the recalcitrance of use value further places the concern of stage theory upon the geo-spatial diversity and uneven development of capitalism. Stage theory commences its theorization of capital at the most advanced geo-spatial site of capital accumulation of a stage. Therefore each stage of capitalism theorizes a characteristic form of use value production, the dominant capitalist accumulator, the predominant form of capital of the stage and so on (See Figure 3.2). Stage theory however is neither a theory of national accumulation nor of international capital. Stage theory is a *structural* theory that builds a model of the type or predominant pattern of capital represented by a stage of capitalism, but leaves questions of the emergence and transformation of stages, as well as study of the way stage structures manifest themselves across all the various situations of capitalist development, to historical analysis as the final, most concrete and *empirical* level of analysis in Marxian political economy. Put differently, stage theory utilizes the TPCS to guide its procedure of conceptual abstraction from concrete history to produce an "abstract type"[7] of accumulation which freezes history

7 An *abstract type* is to be differentiated from an "ideal type". The latter merely systemizes empirical history. The former, on the other hand, is a category that has conceptual

Stage	Golden Age	Representative Use-value	Form of Capital	Structure of Accumulation	State Form + Management of Key Externalities
Mercantilism (British Hegemony)	1700-50	Wool	Merchant Capital	- "putting out system" - primitive accumulation - commodification of labor-power + land	- emerging legal form of *rechtsstaat* - consolidation of national market
Liberalism (British Hegemony)	1850-73	Cotton	Industrial Capital	- entrepreneurial/owner operated business - external transactions/ market price signals - internationalization of commodity circuits	- *laissez faire* "night-watchman" state domestically - colonialism + coveting of raw materials - control over colonial markets
Imperialism (Germany/USA Hegemony)	1890-1914	Steel/ Chemicals	Finance Capital	- monopoly/oligopoly - bank/industry union - joint stock company - internationalization of portfolio finance circuits	- *Sozialpolitic* welfare state - *Weltpolitik* expansionism - international competition for resources and markets - militarization + division of globe into spheres of influence
Consumerism (USA Hegemony)	1950-73	Automobile (consumer durable complex)	Corporate Capital	- oligopoly/MNC'S - economic programming/ planning transfer pricing (transaction cost issues) - "technostructure" (principal/agent issues) - global governance - fixed currencies/ capital controls - managed "free trade" - formal decolonization - internationalization of production circuits	- Keynesian developmental welfare state - projects of national development - credit, fiscal, monetary policy supporting mass consumption - class accords + social wage - vehement anti-communism

Figure 3.2 Stages of Capitalism[8]

---

validity only in the part it plays in constructing a mediating level of analysis informed by both abstract theory and history.

8 The understanding of stage thoery in this chapter develops work by Albritton (1991). While Uno had therorized three stages of capitalism – mercantilism, liberalism and imperialism – it is Albritton who is responsible for entering the stage theory of consumerism into the lexicon of the Uno approach to Marxian political theory.

if you will to sketch out the key features of capital and accumulatory supports in the stage in question. The process of abstraction centers upon a "golden age" period of several decades in which the stage specific features of capital accumulation appear in their most advanced and characteristic form. One aspect of stage theorizing thus is to theorize an international dimension of capital for a stage. The international dimension of capital constitutes an important component of development theory.[9] That is, though determining whether stage structures promote development or underdevelopment falls to historical analysis, the potential scope for development is contextualized by stage theory as stage theory offers insights into the shape and realm of possibilities of development or underdevelopment in particular geo-spatial locales of capital accumulation.

Before the chapter turns to its central focus, Korean development, it is important to crisply clarify how the three levels of analysis operate in a division of labor to produce knowledge of capitalism. First, the discrete role of *historical analysis* as a level of analysis in Marxian political economy must be understood. Historical analysis is the third, most concrete, level of theory in the Uno approach and has its own epistemological proviso. While theorizing the inner logic of capital in the TPCS is carried out by a dialectical epistemology,[10] and stage theory has a structural epistemology,[11] historical analysis is empirical. However, historical analysis is not "empiricist". To be sure, empirical observation first reveals the existence of capitalism in human history. For Marx, empirical observation also confirmed that capitalism was historically peculiar and warranted an exploration of its potential deep logical inner constituents. This was the task Marx set out for himself in *Capital* which the Uno approach recasts and completes as the TPCS. The TPCS is evidence of the reifying of human material life by capital and its wielding by capital for the abstract purpose of value augmentation. The TPCS therefore robustly demonstrates what capital is. With more precise knowledge in hand of capital and its fundamental modus operandi than was furnished by simple observation it is now possible for Marxian political economy to probe the process of capitalist development. The conceptual problematic of capturing the impact of capital's marketizing logic in history – that logic being the constant of all really existing historical capitalism – while simultaneously respecting the sheer complexity and diversity of historical situations of capitalism constitutes the ontological ground for stage theory as a mediating level of analysis. Structures of accumulation and accumulatory supports studied by stage theory provide the causal/explanatory link between the logic of capital and empirically evidentializing of historical outcomes of that logic.

9 Whether the understanding of the capitalist market deployed in the theorizing of a stage specific geo-spatial predominant capital accumulator can be applied with similar presuppositions about the viability of capitalism to the international dimension of capital will be discussed in the fourth section of this chapter.

10 On dialectics in Marxian political economy see, Albritton (1999); Kourkoulakos (2003).

11 See Albritton (1991)

The Stage Theory of Consumerism and Capitalist Development in Korea

This section of the chapter operationalizes the Unoist levels of analysis approach in the study of Korean development. Predicated upon the knowledge of capitalism provided by the TPCS we can confirm that the Korean economy of the period following the Second World War was capitalist. Precisely when Korea made the transition to capitalism and the myriad processes contributing to it would be a task for both historical analysis as well as possibly the stage theorizing of *imperialism*. Complete explanation of the rise of capitalism in Korea would benefit from historical materialist study of the pre-capitalist order and mode of production and potentially the study of Korean culture. This chapter however is interested in Korean capitalist development in the period in which the capitalist stage of *consumerism* is the most advanced world-historic form of capital. This period of capitalist development constitutes the temporal backdrop for the state/market debate; a debate it was argued in the Introduction desperately in need of a Marxist intervention. The procedure of this section will be to trace out the connections between the paradigmatic structures of capital in the capitalist stage of consumerism and those of Korean capital and to offer commentary on the interfacing of these. The structures of capital to be treated are as follows: use value; form of capital; international dimension of capital; state and superstructure; capital/labor relation.

Use Value

The TPCS which constitutes a general theory of capitalism holds use value implicit. Stage theory, as noted above, begins with theorizing the interplay of capital's abstract logic and a stage specific form of use value production confronting that logic. Consumerism, as a stage of capitalism, is characterized by the production of consumer durables with the automobile being the representative type. Automobile productions' expansive backward and forward linkages and its sheer material accouterment are unrivalled by any other capitalist production sector. As with steel in the late nineteenth century a national automobile industry is viewed as a hallmark of modern industrial development; just as the automobile is idiosyncratic of contemporary life (Law, 1991). Indeed, the automobile industry constitutes the predominant industry in global trade, and one needs to look no further than the mainstream business press to appreciate the extent to which automobile production persists as the bell-weather industry of world capitalist accumulation. As per the stage specific structure of consumerist accumulation autos rapidly emerged as the core industry of Korean capitalism. In fact, Korea "compresses" the historical process of over a century of development experienced by the developed countries from light to heavy/chemical to consumer durable industry into a few decades (Watanabe, 1992, 103-8). In the 1980s Korea's emergence as a prominent player in the world automobile industry embodies the dramatic shift that occurs in global automobile production during the last decades of the twentieth century (Bloomfield, 1991; Deyo, 1996). While the export prowess of Korea is a well-documented subject it is not generally appreciated the extent to which Korea constitutes an automobile society ranking fifth in the world in 1998 in automobiles per 1000 population (163 in that year) and evidencing an exponential increase in automobile ownership of 2228.6% between 1980 and 1998 – the largest of any country in the world during that period (Conybeare, 2003, 66). And, producing 3.7 million automobiles in 2005, Korea is today the worlds 5th largest automobile maker (Korea Development Bank, 2006).

Form of Capital

For capital to viably manage the production of a complex use value such as the automobile it is necessary that it adopt an apropos form. Corporate capital, the characteristic form of capital for the stage of consumerism differs qualitatively from both the entrepreneurial owner operated industrial capital of liberalism and finance capital's bank-dominated, bank/industry union of imperialism. Corporate capital shares the joint-stock form of finance capital but is marked by a series of novel stage specific features including: the tendency toward in-house financing, complex mixtures of vertically and horizontally integrated geographically dispersed production branches warranting the appellation multinational corporation (MNC), high degrees of management control, internalized intra-corporate transactions and transfer pricing, tripartite or corporatist labor relations, and an overall propensity toward economic planning and programming approaching the scale with which such exists in a soviet style state (Korten, 1995, 221). Before directly addressing the question of Korean capital as reflective of the above let us take a brief detour through issues raised by a literature on so-called "models" of post-war capitalism (Coates, 2000). The problematic of that literature is two-pronged: on the one hand it seeks to explore business institutional arrangements for determinants of rapid economic growth; on the other hand its aim is to identify the institutional underpinnings for the most "progressive" model of capitalism. Subsequently, its research foci are: the role of the state; corporate governance, relating to outcomes of differing configurations of corporate share ownership and corporate financing; and, the capital/labor relation. A central debate that emerges is over the extent to which a purported East Asian model differs from the US or Anglo model of capital.

In the case of corporate governance, so the argument goes, Korean *chaebol* like the Japanese *keiretsu* are marked by business networks and multi-subsidiary structures, draw increasingly upon personal relations and "trust" among grouping affiliates to share investment responsibility and risk, spawn under the auspices of a single entrepreneur/family and flourish viz. political patronage. These features, it is claimed set East Asian capital apart from the impersonal modes of corporate governance of US capital with its more arms-length supply links and reliance upon a stock market dominated by individual investors for finance. However, in following Coates (2000, 149ff.), and striving to control for factors of historical catch-up, our investigation into the existence of an East Asian model is confronted by the following: first, US corporate capital at its inception also spawns around the entrepreneur/family (Ford, Carnegie, Rockefeller, etc.) and in its heyday certainly enjoyed political patronage comparable to that of the *chaebol's* youth. Second, the evidence from Korea is that with the passing of *chaebol* founders the tendency of corporate capital is toward adopting increasingly professional management (though such often involves strata of "ivy-league" educated offspring or relations of founding families). As well, the shift of the *chaebol* toward the higher value-added production of consumer electronics and automobiles characteristic of the stage of consumerism also prompts a transformation in management style (Watanabe, 1992); transformation that is currently being reinforced by government legislation to render *chaebol* more accountable to individual shareholders (Koo, 2002).

Third, there is the complex question of ownership: On the one hand, as a noted business analyst explains (Abegglen, 1994), East Asian corporate capital is not alone in its structure of business groupings as European capital is marked by both the *keiretsu*-style bank-centered pattern and the *chaebol* form of entrepreneur/family control. Such configuring reflects the historical need of capital to tap into varying sources of investment and, in the case of Korea, the state allocation of credit to favored *chaebol* was a successful component of Korea's "late" late economic development (Cho, 1998). On the other hand, however, in terms of direct ownership, for example, by 2001, the top ten *chaebol* families owned an average of only 4.3% of shares in their group of companies (*Economist*, 2003b). Though it is also estimated that through cross-subsidiary holdings *chaebol* owning families control almost half the shares in their firms, as analysts of the US "power elite" have long contended (Domhoff, 2005), dispersed individual shareholding in the US context serves as a smokescreen for centralized control of productive wealth vis-à-vis networks of interlocking directorates and stock ownership by holding companies. And, as we are reminded, both the so-called "Nippo-Rhenish" model (that includes the *chaebol*) and Anglo-US model are simply variant responses to similar problems of managing transaction costs and that of principal and agent (Woo-Cumings, 2001; Kester, 1996); problems that I would argue are stage specific to corporate capital given its development of the joint stock form and diversified horizontally and vertically integrated organizational structure.

Finally, on the issue of supplier links, indications are, particularly in the stage specific consumer durable/auto industry, that the tight coupling of tasks which optimally requires increased horizontal integration and fostering of long term relations with suppliers acts as a powerful force for industrial convergence across models of post war capitalism (Thelen and Kume, 1999).

As Abegglen puts it (1994, 205), "this group versus individual characterization of East and West demands a good deal of qualification if it is to fit specific realities. But it does serve to identify what seems generally agreed to be a difference in fact, if in degree more than in kind". And it is precisely the question of "kind" that I argue is the crux of stage theory. Though the TPCS assumes capital is "industrial", because the actual use value complex is not specified at the level of abstract economic theory, the technology and organizational structure of industry is simply posited as operable on a capitalist basis. As the mediating level of analysis stage theory is required to theorize the form or kind of capital most representative of the stage and elaborate upon the stage specific modalities through which it is able to viably manage the characteristic use value of a stage. While the chapter will focus more pointedly upon the international structure of the *chaebol* in discussion of the international dimension of consumerist capital below it is important to emphasize here that the interweaving of vertical and horizontal integration and variations of the joint stock ownership form are called forth by capital precisely to deal with the stage specific use value – the automobile – the production of which involves more than processes of "combination" characteristic of imperialism where industry sought to control backward and forward linkages for a single product such as steel. Rather, to meet the challenge of automobile productions' diversity of inputs, economy of scale and marketing requirements corporate capital adopts an octopus-like structure of accumulation where the corporate headquarters coordinates the global activities of its varied branches as well as relations with numerous supporting industries; and does this viz. tentacles reaching through the backward and forward linkages of *each*.[12] Importantly as well, irrespective of variations in stock ownership profile (institutional vs. individual investor), this structure of accumulation is a constant for corporate capital in the way it accommodates the need of capital to increasingly internalize transactions – *get prices wrong*[13] – to manage the production of the stage specific use value. And the *chaebol* example of capital that emerges in the post war era to meet the challenges of world economic competition of the stage of consumerism clearly fits within the stage specific contours of corporate capital.

International Dimension of Capital

As touched upon above, the Uno approach addresses the unit of analysis problem at the heart of the impasse debate in terms of the *level* of analysis. That is, at the level of stage theory, capital accumulation, including the international dimension of capital is theorized as an abstract type of capital idiosyncratic of capitalist development in the stage as a whole. In this sense, though stage theory is abstracted from the representative geo-spatial site of accumulation in a stage, it is neither a theory of "national" capital or of capital as a "world system". Rather it is a theory of the stage specific modalities of accumulation in all their dimensions. In commencing analysis with the view of capitalism as a world system, dependency-type theories elide the paramount question of the extent to which capital is truly global across its history and that of the different forms international capital assumes. Yet it is precisely in reconciling the study of capital in its national and international dimensions and

12 The work of Dicken (1998, Chapter 7) on "webs of enterprise" is instructive on this question in that it demonstrates how the sort of organizational template I have suggested is characteristic of corporate capital of consumerism persists through transnational variations in modes of vertical and horizontal integration.

13 I note Wade's (1992, 294) objections to Amsden's (cited above) use of the term. The usage here is intended to convey the general tendency of corporate capital to eschew market pricing in its economic activity and to internalize economic transactions.

specifying the particular form and pattern assumed by international capital in a world historic stage of capitalism – in this case consumerism – that it is possible to grasp the stage specific world economic context of Korean capitalist development.

If there is a signal distinguishing feature of international capital in the stage of consumerism it is the internationalization of production including: foreign direct investment, international technology licensing, international subcontracting, leasing, management agreements and so on. Supporting the internationalization of production is the internationalization of finance and banking. It is the internationalization of production and spread of global commodity chains that creates a genuine international division of labor for the first time in the history of capitalism. In prior world-historic stages of accumulation international capital is characterized by the concentration of global industrial production in the hands of a limited group of core states. Both so-called "early" and "late" industrializing states within this group follow much the same development sequence exporting first light industrial commodities to foreign markets, then capital goods (Kurth, 1979), and maintain a divide viz. the world at large which is relegated to a position of raw material supplier or outlet for foreign portfolio investment. The position taken in this chapter is that the exigencies of consumerist accumulation congealing around the mass production and mass consumption of a use value complex of consumer durables (the automobile being the representative type) – whether approached in "supply side" terms of the modalities of corporate capitals' integration of diverse economic sectors and production branches or in "demand side" terms considering the requirement for capital to ensure ever-expanding effective demand – renders the geo-spatial dispersal of production a necessary condition of accumulation in the stage of consumerism from the outset.

Bracketing for the moment discussion of extra-economic forces in the consumerist international economy, Korea connects with global commodity chains on the supply side initially as assembler and producer of low cost standardized products for mass consumption. In this process Korea benefits from the emergence in the 1960's of what has been proclaimed "[o]ne of the most significant developments" of the international economy – international subcontracting (Dicken, 1998, 223). In particular, Korean development is marked by two facets of this, Original Equipment Manufacturing (OEM) and Own-design and manufacture (ODM). Through OEM Korean firms first gain valuable technical and organizational expertise under the auspices of foreign companies that market their products. With ODM Korean firms "reverse engineer" industrial processes, technology and components while producing under the design requirements of the foreign companies marketing the goods (Dasgupta, 1998, 268-72). The growth in indigenous productive capacity which the foregoing engenders can be charted empirically in the upward spike of Korea's export-import ratio in trade of industrial goods with both Japan and the world, as well as in Korea's increasing rates of domestic investment as opposed to foreign investment (Watanabe, 1992, 95-103). With respect to the demand side of global commodity chains, as suggested by Halevi and Kriesler (1998), the rise of Korea to the forefront of world market competition meets two vital challenges of the necessity of expanding effective demand in the stage of consumerism. On the one hand, it helps solve the problem of demand for Japanese industrial exports that plagued Japan in the pre-war period. On the other hand the rapid productivity growth of Korean *chaebol* in export industries; a productivity growth rate higher than even Japan, Korea's main competitor, results in a fall in prices of exports to the benefit of foreign consumers.

Of course, as has been pointed out (Abegglen, 1994), a feature distinguishing Korea from other NIC's is the weight of domestic consumption in Korean development. In this sense, the international dimension of capital of consumerism and the internationalizing of Korean corporate capital contributes to what Halevi and Kriesler (1998) dub "full range industrialization" in Korea as opposed to the extroverted economy dependency theory claimed was the fate of developing states. And, in turn, it is the full range industrialization of the Korean economy which propels Korean *chaebol* up the technological ladder as global brands and international competitors with global reach in their own right. By 1998, Korea became the 10th largest global passenger car exporter (Nam and Yang, 2003). In 2003 and 2004 Samsung Electronics leaped to global leadership with the highest market share in sales of memory chips (DRAM and flash) and flat-panel screens (*Economist*, 2005b). Korean corporate capital is also following the consumerist pattern of internationalizing its own production. From owning no foreign subsidiaries in 1991, Korean capital ranked 10th in the world in 1998 in number of international holdings, owning a total of 78 foreign subsidiaries (Kentor, 2005). Samsung, Korea's biggest *chaebol*, for example, has over the past decade invested $2.7 billion in China employing 41,000 people there in 26 factories it built (*Far Eastern Economic Review*, 2003, 26). In fact, Korea has emerged as potentially the single largest foreign investor in China making $6.25 billion in fixed investment in China in 2004 (*New York Times*, 2005).

State and Superstructure

To recapitulate, the debate over state and market in Korean political economy germinates in an intellectual milieu in which the problematizing of capitalism is accorded no explanatory role. This chapter maintains that the state/market debate itself has little explanatory purchase given its mooring in categories the historicity of which the debate never interrogates. To do so reveals how the analytical separation of state and market in the study of capitalism resides in the tendency of capital toward reifying economic life. And that the meaning of development as solely a product of the capitalist market makes sense *only* in the context of the TPCS where it is assumed by *theory* that all use value obstacles or oppositions to capital are neutralized and capital organizes a commodity economy solely according to abstract, objective market principles with the goal of augmenting value. That such a stark society never emerges in history does not invalidate the theory: for the theory only extrapolates to conclusion material tendencies of capital. Thus it is through the TPCS that we know what capital is. However, it is also on the basis of the TPCS which captures capital in its most fundamental incarnation that we are led to the inescapable conclusion that capital *never* constitutes an *historical* society solely according to is commodity economic principles. That is, whether arising from the recalcitrance of use value, class struggle, the opposition to capital of nature and so on, capitalism in history is always marked by a range of externalities that the capitalist state must necessarily internalize or manage. And it is at the level of analysis of stage theory which concretizes the study of capital as it accumulates with key types of use value production and forms of capital that specific policies supporting capitalism become the subject focus.

The stage of consumerism characterized by the automobile industry of corporate capital represents the furthest move *away* from market principles by capitalism in its history. Obvious empirical indicators of this derive from the organizational modalities and scale/scope economies of corporate capital that compel it to rely less and less on external market transactions based upon market prices thus transforming the nature of economic competition (Korten, 1995; Barnet and Cavanagh, 1994)). We can also single out the changed profile of the international economy where it is estimated that only 15% of global trade remains market based with 40% of total trade intra-firm trading of global corporations (Greider, 1997, 137-8). Further, the investment requirements of corporate capital increasingly saddle it with strategically managing the effective demand for its expensive consumer durables. Such a shift in the fundamental structure of capital expands both the range of externalities for the capitalist state to manage and the extent of extra-economic supports required by capital to successfully accumulate. To meet the policy challenges it faces the capitalist state of consumerism is equipped with an arsenal of interventions including: countercyclical demand management, investment in infrastructure, military expenditure, social welfare and insurance programs, fiscal policy, monetary policy and so forth.[14] But, while state policy to manage the externalities of the dominant form of capital is the centerpiece of analyzing the superstructure in stage theory, as Albritton (1991) argues, particularly with regards to the stage of consumerism (though to complete stage analysis generally), it is vital to assess how other social practices such as ideology, politics and law coalesce with state policy in support of capital. Of significance here are the consumerist ideologies of anti-communism and hyper-individualist mass consumption.

To be sure, the conceptualizing of a "developmental state" in the context of NIC economic growth is not groundless. But the notion that its obverse in post war

---

14 Achieving analytical clarity over the crucial stage specific interventionist role of the state in the capitalist stage of consumerism in support of capital accumulation has been thwarted in part by the historical variance in the consumerist state's application of Keynesian demand management. The US state for example has supported mass consumption less through welfare measures and more through massive doses of military spending. Japan, on the other hand, has devoted considerable largess to infrastructure and less to military and welfare spending. An instructive way of capturing the historical variance among key capital accumulators in the stage of consumerism that also holds fast to the fact that the stage specific mode of accumulation of consumerism necessitates a massive state support system for capital is to view Britain as the classic *welfare* state, the US as *military* state (though veering toward a welfare state during the Vietnam War years), and Japan as the *entrepreneurial* state (Kato, 1984).

capitalism is a sort of "night-watchman" state *is*. As Coates (2000, 223) puts it, no state can "free either itself or its class base from the generalized logics of accumulation which characterized world capitalism as a whole". And, if world capitalism in the stage of consumerism has a "logic" shaping state action, it is one that operates within the international institutional parameters of the Bretton Woods monetary system facilitating state governed projects of national development. This "economic nationalism" (Brown and Lauder, 2001, 16) in effect makes developmental policy of a sort a mainstay of state policy *per se* for consumerism. For example, the US state directs finance toward "picking winners", specifically in defense and agriculture. Also, the US state maintains a "de facto" industrial policy viz. its proclivity to bail out corporate capital when required and regulate industry with an eye to international competitive outcomes (Coates, 2000, 202-3). And despite US MNC's constituting the representative case for the internationalization of capital in consumerism, during the 1960's even the US resorted to varying forms of capital controls to support domestic interests (Simmons, 1999, 40).

Of course, it is not being argued that US policy and the targeting of industrial sectors and select businesses, allocation of credit to such, favoring of particular entrepreneurs, exerting of authoritarian control, etc. marking the Korean state are commensurate. But, again controlling for historical catch-up and the compressing of industrial epochs by Korea, we see that the development, from which the strong view of the developmental state as constitutive of capital is drawn, coincides with the growth of the *chaebol* around the steel/heavy chemical complex under the 1970's Yushin system of Park Chung Hee. In comparative perspective, it is precisely this period of the "great spurt" where West European development, for example, also experiences hypertrophied state participation in industry combined with authoritarian politics; a policy profile which then changes as these economies shift to consumer durable production (Kurth, 1979). Similarly, as chronicled (Kim, 1997; Woo-Cumings, 2001), with the receding of Korea's great spurt so state/business relations also begin to change. Examples of this ongoing process include: merging of the Economic Planning Board and Ministry of Finance as part of so-called *segyehwa* deregulation (Kang, 2000, 92-4); creation of the Financial Supervisory Commission to simultaneously manage industrial and financial sector reorganization (Woo-Cumings, 2001, 366-69); governments' transforming of regulatory institutions, creating the Korea Asset Management Corporation, for example, to deal efficiently with non-performing loan residues of the great spurt (*Economist*, 2003b). However, these and other so-called "Big Deals" initiatives (Cherry, 2005) do *not* reflect a transition to some a-historical market development but the re-channeling of state power towards managing new externalities besetting capital as it struggles to successfully accumulate around consumer durable production with all the domestic and international ramifications of this.

Within the reified context of the TPCS human subjects are simply the personification of economic categories. In this sense, while it is true that capital liberates human beings from the extra-economic compulsions they were subjected to in pre-capitalist modes of production, their individual freedom in capitalist society, to buy and sell anything including their labor power, only contributes to the collective objectification of humanity as a whole by capital which then wields human material life for the abstract purpose of value augmentation. Extra-economic practices therefore have no place in theorizing pure capitalism. At the level of analysis of stage theory, the exigencies of the capital accumulation in the capitalist management of production of stage specific use values forces theory to consider the range of extra-economic supports required by capital. In no stage of capitalism do extra-economic practices play such a prominent role in support of capital as in the capitalist stage of consumerism.

With the spread of Soviet power internationally and the growth of giant collectivities such as the welfare/warfare state domestically, the ideology of anti-communism emerges as a cornerstone of accumulation for consumerism.The impact of the ideology of anti-communism upon Korean development is immense. To maintain Korea as a bastion of anti-communism in Asia it is officially claimed that in the years 1945-65 Korea obtained $12 billion from the US equal to 100 per cent of the Korean government budget during the 1950s. However, calculating US taxpayer beneficence for the period 1945-76, one estimate has it that Korea is the recipient of $600 per capita each year for thirty years. And military aid was also considerable, amounting to $15 billion for the period 1945-76, equal to four times that directed towards Latin America during the same time period (Woo-Cumings, 1991, 44-6). What is most significant however is the global projection of anti-communism. According to Halevi (1999), as US re-armament puts a floor under its domestic economy, the Korean War contributed to the recovery of both Germany and Japan, and through the war in Vietnam, which removes the last vestiges of "old" colonialism from Asia, the world economy crystallized around three poles of capital accumulation. In the context of capital accumulation in Asia centered on Japan, capitalist development in Korea emerges as the "most significant...outside Japan because it was based on a deliberate linkage between the objective of creating a national capital in the country and the role of both Japan and the United States which accepted and sustained the above objective" (Halevi and Kriesler, 1998, 88). Besides its direct position on a Cold War fault line Korea is bound to US global anti-communism sending 300,000 troops to Vietnam, more per capita than the US itself (Woo-Cumings, 1998, 335). Korea's early export orientation noted above was thus part of US strategy seeking to reduce the dependence on aid of its anti-communist partner. By 1967, it is pointed out (Halevi and Kriesler, 1998, 86), the share of Korea's total exports by sector going to South Vietnam is: steel (94.29%); transportation equipment (51.75%); non-electrical machinery (40.77%). Finally, it is through Japan, also firmly under the US anti-communist security umbrella that, following a US brokered rapport, OEM and ODM transfer technology to Korea. And the edifice as a whole is supported by the absorptive capacity of ever-expanding domestic consumption of the US market opened to Korean exports by US anti-communist designs.

Given, the importance of mass consumption of consumer durables for capital accumulation in the stage of consumerism the spawning of an ideology of hyper-individualism and the raising of an ideology of ever-expanding mass consumption to the status of a secular religion have become its mainstay's. So-called "Asian values" of Confucian self-denial are often posited as setting Asia apart from the general dynamic of mass-consumption. Survey evidence however indicates that in the Asian region as a whole, Korea in particular is characterized by individualism, support for expanding individual rights, and the desire to achieve personal financial success (Fukuyama, 1999, 321-22). Mass consumption in Korea has been bolstered as well by a state sponsored credit boom with new personal credit cards being issued at an annual rate increase of 75% between 1999 and 2002, and in which even a Korean family pet dog is alleged to have received a credit card (*Economist*, 2003a). Mass consumption in Korea is supported further by the increasing power of advertising and the emergence of new consuming social cohorts. For example, characteristic of the practice of law in the stage of consumerism is the expansion of "rights" – gender, race, sexual orientation, and so forth – to ensure that no social group is excluded from mass consumption of consumer durables. Typical of the increasing inclusiveness of mass consumption in Korea has been its gendering in the "Missy" phenomenon where the earlier image of the demure, frugal housewife has been superseded by married women determined to remain an object of male "gaze" as their college student counterparts and encouraged to spend lavishly on themselves to that effect. Thus, today, as is pointed out, the campuses and streets of Korea are "filled with model-like women with bright red lips and high heels" (Cho, 2002, 183-86). Korea thereby has notably become an exporter of fashion and the culture of consumerism to other Asian locales such as China (*New York Times*, 2006).

Capital/labor Relation

With a use value such as the automobile, an expensive consumer durable requiring a massive capital outlay for its production and secured market for its consumption, corporate capital is pressured to arrive at a *modus vivendi* with labor making consumerism the stage of the "class accord". Antagonistic class struggle is deflected by the inclusion of labor unions in projects of economic nationalism where sanctioned worker action revolves around bargaining over wage and benefit packages and unions are effectively de-politicized as a condition of inclusion. Maintaining consensual labor relations emerges as a major externality for capital which then draws in the state as its ultimate guarantor such that the class accord becomes "tripartite" or "corporatist". The state also tops up the benefits for labor with a social wage.

In tracing out connections between the class accord of consumerism and Korean labor relations it is instructive that despite a rapid shift to an industrial society anti-capitalist struggle as occurred in Europe never foments in Korea. The source of this anomaly, according to the authoritative study of Choi (1989), is the particular phase of industrial development into which Korean workers were thrust; so-called EOI demanding homogeneity, stability and discipline in labor relations. To be sure, these conditions are met in Korea under the auspices of an authoritarian state; yet an authoritarian state that never seeks to prevent union organization among workers, rather effectively co-opting and shaping it through what Choi dubs "state corporatism". This approach proves indispensable in managing workers' collective response to stark conditions in the shift to heavy steel/chemical industrialization and then towards consumer durable production (Koo, 1993). Thus, while Korean labor is hardly quiescent, Korean workers "never questioned capitalism...with any alternative ideological apparatus" (Choi, 1989, 74). Such, it may be added, also reflects underwriting of state corporatist policy in Korea by anti-communism which, as in other consumerist states, operates to de-politicize labor as a condition of corporatist inclusion and beneficiary of increasing mass consumption. While the repression of Korean workers represented by the state corporatist model sets it apart from the paradigmatic class accord of consumerism, the divergence of Korean labor relations here owes much to the unique historical conditions of compressed economic growth. With the democratization process in Korea tripartite labor relations develop

USE VALUE COMPLEX	historical process of development compressed as Korea becomes automobile society ranking 5th in world by 1998 in automobiles per 1000 population Korean development unique among NICs in size and growth of domestic market
FORM OF CAPITAL	*chaebol* model of corporate capital assumes multi-subsidiary network structure and draws upon relations of trust among affiliates to share investment responsibility differs from corporate capital in degree of institutional vs. individual shareholding rather than in kind though controlling for factors of historical catch-up as *chaebol* move into more high value added production management style and ownership patterns approach corporate capital pattern
INTERNTIONAL DIMENSION OF CAPITAL	internationalizing of production opens door to industrialization beyond core of global accumulation on "supply side" Korea benefits from emergence in 1960s of international subcontracting arrangements of OEM and ODM + on "demand side" Korea benefits from expanding mass consumption in core *chaebol* internationalization follows MNC form of corporate capital
STATE AND SUPERSTRUCTURE	"economic nationalism" – characterizes state policy of consumerism Korean state "developmentalism" no anomaly anti-communist ideology impacts upon Korean economy directly through military demand and indirectly through US + Japanese support for Korean "full-scale industrialization"
CAPITAL/LABOUR RELATION	"class accord" of "state corporatism" through Park Chung Hee era - moving toward tripartite wage relations with shift from heavy steel production to consumer durables + following opening of democratic politics rise of "productivist welfare state"

Figure 3.3 The Stage of Consumerism and Korean Capitalism

as in other consumerist states (Koo, 2001). In fact, one of genuinely democratically elected Kim Dae Jung's first major policy initiatives was the establishment of a "tripartite commission" to consensually integrate labor into the designs of Korean corporate capital and the state (Kim, 2005). Democracy also contributes to labor's ability to exact wage increases from capital (Jeong, 1997). Finally, in line with the consumerist capital/labor relation, democratization yields an expansion of state social welfare and insurance provisioning (Tang, 2000) constituting what is dubbed a "productivist welfare state" in Korea (Holliday and Wilding, 2003).

The material of this section is summarized in Figure 3.3 above:

Neoliberalism, Globalization, and the Future of Korean Capitalism

Following the Asian economic crisis of the final decade of the twentieth century, the specific causal impetus for which I do not intend to delve into here given the ample treatment it has received elsewhere,[15] the debate over market and state has generated new sets of claims and counter claims that it is vital the chapter make some headway in sorting out. The main thrust of the debate asserts that the Asian economic crisis sounded the death knell of "Korea Inc." with its structures of "crony capitalism"[16] and suggests future Korean development demands Korea increasingly fall in line with neoliberal market reforms as represented by the US model of accumulation.[17] This strain of debate further sub-divides into argument that a) the continued policy efficacy of the Korean state belies claims of its neoliberal transformation; b) Korea is shifting to an increasingly market oriented economy as per neoliberal and modernization theory dictates, but this move is to be decried; and c) neoliberalism conceived as simply about the exorcizing of the state is misunderstood, and Korea's post-crisis neoliberal policy orientation to build new market-enhancing institutions is a positive outcome.[18] In addressing this debate, to belabor a point, corporate capital of consumerism operates at a considerable distance away from the market and, while

15 See for example Bernard (1999).

16 It can be immediately interjected here, of course, that crony capitalism is hardly a phenomena limited to Korea. Nor is it something neoliberal reforms efface: witness the Enron debacle in the US and Haliburton's contractual arrangement with the US government to "rebuild" Iraq! See, for example, Stiglitz (2001, 516) on this point.

17 To be sure, a virtual growth industry has arisen around the implications of the Asian crisis for development rivaling that writing on the Asian NIC miracle. For the knee-jerk reaction, see for example Kirk (1999). For more level-headed accounts, see for example, Lo (1999); and selections in Stiglitz and Yusuf (2001); Robison, Beeson, Jayasuriya and Kim (2000).

18 See the discussion in Pirie (2005).

		Externalities/State Policy
Key Production Activity	consumer durables (automobiles) (electronics, computers, cell phones, digital TVs, etc.) enlarged service sector with reduced purchasing power	neo-liberal deregulation/dismantling of social wage structures hollowing out of industry de-commodification of labor power + "third-worldization" of work (new slavery, putting-out, work houses, etc.) - petroleum economy/rising energy costs
Key Economic Structures	transnational corporations/banks	public subsidies/tax breaks/financial bailouts increasingly centralized economic + planning/decentralized delivery + sub-contracting increased international competition excess capacity/over-accumulation mergers and acquisitions cronyism/fraud/speculation
World Economy	increasing internationalization of production/finance predatory re-location of marketable productive capacity global shifts in poles of accumulation rise of regional blocs national economies "accumulation by dispossession" "exclusion from wage relations"	dismantling of capital controls IMF + WTO "governmentality" increasing world economic asymmetries rotating financial crises "failing of states" - rise of NNEs "nonviable" militarism and global police actions perpetual war and "terrorism"

Figure 3.4 Globalization/Neoliberalism as a Period of Transition[19]

corporate capital manifests itself in several models evincing empirical variations among them, these models of corporate capital are of a kind, differing largely in the fashion states deal with particular externalities from the burgeoning list of these that confront capital. In this sense, both the *chaebol* form of corporate capital and the more individual invested, stock market regulated model of US capitalism share a family resemblance. However, whether Korean capital shifts toward the US model or not, it remains a form of capitalism the development of which always holds only limited promise for the majority of working people. The transformation of Korean capital in wake of the Asian crisis, as touched upon in the previous section, involves a restructuring toward accumulation norms better suited to the stage of consumerism not some a-historical market capitalism. That neoliberalism recruits the concentrated power of the state is a fact but the apprehension of this as a project of creating

19 Terms used in the box "world economy" describing the disarticulated international structure of neoliberalism derive from the work of Harvey (2003); Dierckxsens (2000); De Rivero (2001).

capitalist market friendly institutional edifices is misguided. This point will be expanded upon below.

Critical approaches to the Asian crisis and its aftermath begin with the view that the crisis signals the "end" of NIC development *per se*, given how the specific constellation of politico-economic forces within which this development germinates no longer exist (Bello, 1998; Burkett and Hart-Landsberg, 1998; Cumings, 1999). In this perspective the internationalization of neoliberalism through the so-called "Washington consensus" constitutes a war of attrition aimed at remaking the world economic hierarchy. The merit of this latter view is that it breaks free of the confines of the arid state/market, neoliberal/statist monopolized development discourse and links the travails of Korean capital to wider challenges facing the global political economy. However, let us further examine this issue through the prism of the Unoist levels of analysis approach. Projects of national development entailing significant state presence which in turn find support in an international dimension of capital that maintains a balance between MNC investment prerogatives for mass production and consumption of consumer durables and national development strategies, constitute a mainstay of consumerist accumulation. This stage specific institutional architecture for accumulation is not a policy choice for capital but is necessary for the very economic viability of capitalism given the use value complex of accumulation in the stage of consumerism. However, as elaborated upon in previous work (Westra, 2003b; 2004b), the rise of neoliberalism as a global policy template reflects the contradictory desire of capital to abdicate its responsibility for managing the externalities of consumerist accumulation. This is contradictory because much of the material substructure of consumerism remains intact (See Figure 3.4). Thus, as capital seeks an alternate role for the state it is in fact undermining a fundamental condition of its existence.

From the perspective of Marxist theory and levels of analysis in political economy the fundamental question for neoliberal policy driven "globalization" is not whether the state plays some role as throughout the history of capitalism, even in the stage of liberalism, in which capitalist development asymptotically approaches its ideal image captured in the TPCS, accumulation is supported by the capitalist state. The question, rather, is whether the state is performing its historic role as a *capitalist* state. This is also the question to be posed with regards to the ongoing transformation of capitalism in Korea.

Marx referred to capitalism originating in the "interstices" of the globe. What he meant by this was that for centuries markets have existed in one form or another external to the mode of reproducing the material life of the social community. Capitalism came to form an historical society only when capital subsumed the material life of the community in systems of society-wide self-regulating markets. The subsumption of economic life by capital proceeded in tandem with the rise of the nation-state as the geo-spatial purview of the nation-state was conducive to the regularizing of economic activity required by capital to viably reproduce economic life. And the fact that though capital disavows the state in its basic principles it nevertheless co-opts the state as a "crutch" to support its historical forms of accumulation. Stage theory demonstrates that while capitalism in history closely approximates its pure market operation under the accumulatory conditions of the stage of liberalism, through the stages of imperialism and consumerism, capital accumulation moves asymptotically away from its market ideal (See Figure 3.2). Stage theory further demonstrates how the constituents of a stage – its leading use value production sector, concomitant technology bundle, geo-spatial core and institutional/policy architecture – constitute the matrix through which long term capital accumulation proceeds and provide capitalism with the modicum of coherence it requires to reproduce economic life of society viably in each stage. Judged according to this standard (See Figure 3.4), it should be evident that what is referred to as globalization does not constitute a stage of capitalism. Nor do its tendencies portend the formation of a stage. The glaring world-economic asymmetries in productivity and resource capacity mitigate the rise of anything remotely approaching neoliberal enthusiasts' image of "perfect competition". The term "global capitalism" thus cannot be used in the same sense as the term capitalism applied to accumulation viably reproducing economic life of the nation-state unit. Even if capitalism could materialize a global economy in the latter sense it would require a world capitalist state to manage its externalities. However, with its "off-ground" financialization, predatory re-location of productive capacity, so-called accumulation by dispossession, exclusion from wage relations, generating of non-viable economies and failing of states, and so forth, neoliberal impelled globalization, as I have argued (Westra, 2003b), portends the unravelling of capitalism and the transition toward an as yet undetermined social order.

It is within the forgoing context that the notion of NIC development in Korea coming to an end must be understood. Among OECD states Korea has the lowest per capita income, the longest working time for labor, increasing youth unemployment and one of the higher percentages of non-regular workers in the labor force (OECD, 2004). The Korean economy is thus caught in a twilight zone where as its political economic transformation approximated stage specific norms of capital accumulation of consumerism that did bring some benefits to working people in comparison with previous stages of capitalism the viability of consumerism itself as a stage of capitalism is in question. The neoliberal chant that there is an economic payoff to the conversion of the Korean economy to an unspecified market economy is pure ideology as this chapter makes abundantly clear. On the other hand, the world of developmental states the loss of which is bemoaned by the statists cannot be recaptured. If a future of social betterment exists for Korea as well as other states caught in the vortex of neoliberal globalization the road to it necessarily runs through a form of socialist economy.

Conclusion

This chapter introduces the Japanese Uno approach to Marxist theory to treat questions of the post-Second World War development of Korea and the neoliberal/statist debate over the role of market and state in Korea's development process. The chapter operationalizes Uno's levels of analysis approach to the political economic study of capitalism where explanation of Korean development is unfolded through the mid-range stage theory of consumerism. The stage theory of consumerism mediates the movement in thought from the logic of capital to the study of post-Second World War capitalist history in a fashion that simultaneously captures the impact of dominant structures of capital on the Korean political economy and the diversity of the Korean development situation. Further, through the prism of the levels of analysis approach to Marxism the chapter elaborates upon the historicity of the separation of economic (market) and state/superstructure in the study of capitalism and develops analysis of the capitalist state in the stage of consumerism en route to specifying the role of the state in the Korean political economy. And, the chapter demonstrates how the physiognomy of Korean capital accumulation fits neatly within the contours of the stage specific structures of capital accumulation in the stage of consumerism. If one single message is to be drawn from the chapter it is that while the view of capitalist development as a product solely of the unimpeded operation of self-regulating markets geared to augmenting value has a conceptual foundation in Marx's *Capital* recast as the TPCS what stage theory demonstrates is that following the mid-nineteenth century stage of liberalism capital accumulation moves asymptotically away from market regulation. And the neoliberal claim that today's economy of corporate behemoths, hugely expensive technological outlay's, centrally coordinated global commodity chains and so on can be operated according to pure market principles is sheer folly and masks the insidious social polarization and asymmetric concentration of wealth ensuing at the heart of the neoliberal project. The Korean economy may gain some respite by clinging to elements of the economic nationalism and developmentalism characteristic of the stage of consumerism but this effort is likely to be short-lived.

PART II
The South Korean Economy in Global Perspective

Introduction to Part II

Both neoliberals and left Keynesian/statists generally believe that all countries are capable of developing through capitalism if their respective states adopt appropriate policies. Thus the division between the two sides primarily reflects their differing understandings of what constitutes appropriate policies, with neoliberals calling for free market policies and left Keyneisan/statists calling for active state direction of economic activity. By contrast, Marxists view capitalism as an international system in which nation state policies and outcomes are shaped and limited by broader global accumulation dynamics, which are themselves shaped by the class contradictory imperatives of core capital. This section offers two chapters that seek to highlight the global dynamics that set the context for Korea's economic choices and challenges.

Most economists celebrate China as one of the most successful developers in modern times and believe that its foreign-driven, export-led growth is positively reshaping and accelerating economic activity in other countries, including in East Asia. The chapter, "China and the Dynamics of Transnational Capital Accumulation", by Martin Hart-Landsberg and Paul Burkett, rejects this "conventional wisdom". It argues that China's economic experience and the resulting restructuring of other countries' economic activity cannot be adequately understood in national or even inter-national terms. Rather, production processes in China and other countries, especially in East Asia, are being linked and collectively reshaped by broader transnational capitalist dynamics, in particular by the establishment and intensification of cross-border production networks by transnational corporations. Korea's experience is highlighted in this regard. Far from benefiting working people, these dynamics are increasing international imbalances and instabilities as well as heightening competitive pressures that work against the interests of workers in all the countries affected by them.

The next chapter, "The Changing Patterns of Accumulation and Realization in East Asia since the 1990s", by Joseph Halevi and Peter Kriesler, argues that (East) Asia has gone through two phases of capital accumulation, both largely shaped by Japanese dynamics (although in the latter under the US umbrella), and has now entered a third, this time largely shaped by Chinese dynamics. The first phase dates roughly from the late 1870s to World War 2, while the second runs from the end of the war until the East Asia currency crisis of 1997. The paper then explores the causes and consequences of this new phase through an examination of China's capital accumulation process. In particular it argues that this process, at present driven by export-oriented transnational capital, is likely to generate deindustrialization, and therefore conflict between leading transnationals and their respective states, in Europe, Japan and the United States, while intensifying China's economic dualism and technological dependency. As a result, new national, regional, and international tensions and instabilities can be expected.

Chapter 4

China and the Dynamics of Transnational Capital Accumulation

Martin Hart-Landsberg and Paul Burkett

Introduction

Most economists consider China's post-1978 economic transformation to be of historic importance. They believe that China's rapid export-led growth has made the country one of the most successful developers in modern times. They also believe that the nature, speed, and scale of China's growth is reshaping and accelerating economic activity in other countries. These claims, if true, have profound political implications. The first implies that governments pursuing economic development should adopt policies similar to China and promote greater market freedom and international integration. The second implies that unregulated capitalist dynamics continue to create new global growth centers capable of ensuring economic progress for those countries willing and able to embrace the capitalist world market. Thus, in contrast to many workers throughout the world who view China's export activity as a threat to their economic survival, most economists believe that its long run impact will be positive for all.

The data does indeed show that China has achieved unprecedented rates of growth and that its economic transformation has greatly influenced economic processes in other countries. However, we reject the mainstream understanding of the Chinese experience highlighted above and the commonly derived political conclusions. To begin with, we do not believe that China's economic experience or the resulting restructuring of other countries' economic activity can be adequately understood in national or even inter-national terms, as if China's gains afford policy makers in other countries opportunities to promote their own national restructuring in ways that benefit their respective working-class majorities. Rather, we see the transformation of production processes in China, and in the other countries whose economies are becoming linked to China, as being collectively reshaped by broader *transnational* capitalist dynamics, in particular by the establishment and intensification of cross-border production networks by transnational corporations. And, far from benefiting working people, we believe that these dynamics are increasing international imbalances and instabilities as well as heightening competitive pressures that work against the interests of workers in all the countries affected by them, including China.

In short, we believe that the conventional wisdom on China presents a flawed picture of global-capitalist dynamics and the tensions they generate, one that leaves workers with a set of political options largely limited to passive acceptance of their worsening conditions or a declaration of economic war against their counterparts in other countries, especially China. In contrast, by focusing on the nature and logic of the new transnational accumulation dynamics that are reshaping economic activity in China and other countries, it becomes easier to see the destructive nature of capitalism itself, and the need to build international solidarity and nationally complementary strategies to oppose and overcome it.

The Rise of China

Since 1978, China's GDP has grown by an average of 9.5% a year, three times the rate of the US and faster than that of any other country (*Economist*, 2004, 6). As a result, China's GDP now accounts for 13 percent of world output (based on purchasing power parity), second only to the US (*Economist*, 2004, 4). China is now the world's fourth largest industrial producer, behind only the United States (US), Japan, and Germany, and the largest producer of more than 100 kinds of manufacturing goods, including cameras, air-conditioners, televisions, washing machines, refrigerators, and toys (Lee, 2004, p.1). Even these figures understate China's importance to the world economy: in 2004, China and the US accounted for almost half of world growth (*Economist*, 2004, 3).

Table 4.1 Net Foreign Direct Investment in China, billions US$

1985	1.0
1986	1.4
1987	1.7
1988	2.3
1989	2.6
1990	3.5
1991	4.4
1992	11.0
1993	27.5
1994	33.8
1995	37.5
1996	41.7
1997	45.3
1998	45.5
1999	40.3
2000	40.8
2001	46.8
2002	52.7
2003	53.5
2004	60.6

Source: Asian Development Bank (2005).

It is also commonly agreed that China's post-1978 economic success is the result of a series of state decisions to promote the decentralization, marketization, and privatization of economic activity. Over time, and with the support of the Chinese state, this transformation has come to be largely driven and the economy shaped by the activities of export-oriented transnational corporations (Hart-Landsberg and Burkett, 2005a, Chapter 2). The important and growing role of foreign investors is highlighted in Table 4.1, which shows the rapid rise in foreign direct investment (FDI) in China, beginning in the early 1990s. In 2002, China became the largest recipient of FDI in the world. Significantly, as Table 4.2 reveals, China has been the only East Asian country to sustain its attractiveness to foreign investors.

Table 4.2 Net Foreign Direct Investment in East Asia, billions US$

	1997	1998	1999	2000	2001	2002	2003	2004
Korea	-1.6	0.7	5.1	4.3	1.1	-0.2	0.1	3.4
Singapore	1.1	4.6	8.5	1.2	-7.6	1.7	5.6	5.4
Thailand	3.3	7.4	5.7	3.4	3.5	0.8	1.5	0.7
Malaysia	5.6	2.2	2.5	1.8	0.3	1.3	1.1	2.6
Indonesia	4.7	-0.2	-1.9	-4.6	-3.0	0.1	-0.6	1.0
Philippines	-	-	1.8	1.4	1.1	1.7	0.2	.06

Source: Asian Development Bank (2005).

As a result of their ongoing investments, transnational corporations are coming to dominate the Chinese economy. For example, the share of foreign manufacturing affiliates in China's total manufacturing sales has grown from 2.3 percent in 1990 to 31.3 percent in 2000 (Hart-Landsberg and Burkett, 2005a, p. 59). Foreign firms are also coming to dominate China's export activity. The percentage of exports produced by these firms grew from 17.4 percent in 1990 to 55 percent in 2003 (Hart-Landsberg and Burkett, 2005a, p. 125; Gilboy, 2004). As a consequence of these trends, the ratio of exports to GDP has also climbed steadily, from 16 percent in 1990 to 36 percent in 2003 (Hart-Landsberg and Burkett, 2005a, p. 121; Roach, 2005). Thus, China's economic growth has become increasingly dependent on the export activity of these transnational corporations.

China and the World Economy: The Virtuous Growth Spiral

Although China's ability to attract foreign direct investment and export has the potential to make it a threatening international competitor, mainstream analysts argue that there are stronger reasons to see China as a new growth center capable of supporting a restructured international economy, with benefits for working people in all countries, rich and poor.[1] Among the most important reasons for their confidence are China's close integration with global markets and abundant supply of cheap labor. As the *Economist* explains:

> First, for such a big economy [China] is unusually open to trade and investment. This year the sum of exports and imports of goods and services is likely to reach 75 percent of China's GDP, far more than in other big countries: in America, Japan, India and Brazil the figure is 30 percent or less. At its peak Japan's trade reached only 32 percent of its GDP. Similarly the stock of total investment in China by foreign firms is equivalent to 36 percent of its GDP, compared with 2 percent in Japan.
>
> The second feature is that Chinese manufacturers have access to an almost unlimited supply of cheap labor. By some estimates, there are almost 200 million underemployed workers in rural areas that could move into industry. This surplus labor may take at least two decades to absorb, helping to hold down wages for low-skilled workers (who currently earn less than 50 cents an hour). Japan and South Korea, in contrast, absorbed their rural labor much more quickly. (*Economist*, 2004, p. 9)

In other words, China's cheap labor and massive size will enable it to keep attracting foreign investment and produce exports at low cost. But, because China's foreign production is heavily import-dependent, the resulting growth will generate a substantial demand for goods and services produced in other countries. Therefore, those governments that allow market forces to restructure their respective national economies in line with China's activities will be rewarded with new, higher value added activities and employment opportunities for their populations. This understanding of the process by which China's rise can benefit other countries explains why mainstream economists also argue for extending neoliberal policies and WTO agreements (Athukorala, 2003, 8-9). Mainstream economists generally believe that the experience of other East Asian countries provides powerful empirical support for this positive view of China's growth. They find the East Asian experience especially relevant because the countries in the region have also relied on foreign produced exports to drive their growth.

As Table 4.3 shows, China's foreign-driven growth trajectory has led the country to reorient its exports of manufactures away from East Asia (minus Japan) and toward the two most important international markets, those of the US and the European Union. And, in response, most of the other countries in the region have been forced to redirect their exports away from those markets. Fernald and Loungani (2004), for example, examined China's competitive strength in the US market by dividing the major East Asian developing countries into three groups: China (China and Hong Kong), the NIEs (South Korea, Singapore, and Taiwan), and the ASEAN-4 (Indonesia, Malaysia, Philippines, and Thailand). They found that the China group's share of the total exports of the three groups to the United States rose

1 For detailed discussion of the mainstream optimism on China, with references to the academic literature, see Burkett and Hart-Landsberg (2000, 31-36) and Hart-Landsberg and Burkett (2005a, Chapter 4). The *Economist*'s (2004) special report combines the different elements of the mainstream consensus in compact and highly readable fashion.

from approximately one-fourth in 1989 to one-half in 2002 (Fernald and Loungani, 2004, 2).

Table 4.3 Direction of Exports of Manufactures, percent of National Total

		Destination			Total Exports, billions $US
Exporting Country	Japan	USA	EU	EAS-Japan	
China					
1992	9.1	11.1	9.5	57.9	65.5
1996	17.8	20.2	14.0	34.2	123.6
2000	15.1	22.9	16.7	29.9	215.5
Malaysia					
1992	7.7	27.1	18.0	39.5	25.9
1996	11.1	23	15.1	42.7	58.7
2000	11.3	24.5	15.1	39.8	78.3
Thailand					
1992	14.0	26.4	21.3	23.7	21.5
1996	15.7	19.6	19.6	32.5	38.4
2000	13.9	22.9	17.7	32.7	50.9
Singapore					
1992	5.5	26.4	19.0	35.0	48.1
1996	7.7	21.7	14.8	45.0	103.4
2000	7.5	19.7	14.6	47.3	117.1
Indonesia					
1992	12.7	17.9	21.9	31.8	15.8
1996	15.9	18.4	19.3	30.7	25.2
2000	13.2	19.2	18.5	32.4	34.7
Philippines					
1992	13.1	65.5	4.8	12.1	5.8
1996	16.1	37.1	17.4	24.7	16.9
2000	13.7	31.1	18.3	32.7	34.8
Korea					
1992	11.7	25.9	14.3	23.9	66.3
1996	9.2	19.0	13.6	32.6	109.7
2000	9.0	23.9	15.3	31.5	148.3
Taiwan					
1992	10.5	47.1	7.3	26.5	52.9
1996	9.2	14.9	14.9	39.4	114.8
2000	10.2	26.4	18.3	37.1	159.7
Japan					
1992		29.3	20.8	31.1	312.8
1996		28.6	16.2	40.7	374.7
2000		31.2	17.1	38.2	435.1

Note: EAS-Japan includes all the countries listed above minus Japan, plus Hong Kong and Vietnam.
Source: Athukorala (2003), Table A-1, 40-41.

Table 4.4 Export Shares in US Market, in percent

	Computers, peripherals and semiconductors	Apparel and footwear	Household goods	Recreational equipment and materials	Home entertainment equipment
China and HK					
1989	7	36	24	38	19
2002	24	69	67	84	53
NIEs					
1989	72	52	66	57	64
2002	42	12	22	11	17
ASEAN-4					
1989	21	12	10	5	18
2002	34	20	11	6	30
IMPORTS from Asia, 2002	$67.8 bn	$41.1 bn	$38.8 bn	$19.4 bn	$17.1 bn

Notes: NIEs includes South Korea, Singapore, and Taiwan; ASEAN-4 includes Indonesia, Malaysia, the Philippines, and Thailand; HK is Hong Kong. This table shows the five largest industries ranked by total dollar value of US imports from these countries. The industry shares of the three groups sum to 100 for each year.
Source: Fernald and Loungani (2004, 2).

An industry level examination highlights the fact that "China has emerged as a significant exporter across virtually the entire spectrum of industries" (Fernald and Loungani, 2004, 2). This development is illustrated in Table 4.4, which shows changing export shares for the three groups in the five largest industries ranked according to the dollar value of US imports from the three groups. Thus, while China and Hong Kong accounted for only 7 percent of the total exports in computers, peripherals and semiconductors in 1989, their share rose to 24 percent by 2002, with the export share of the NIEs falling from 72 to 42 percent over the same period.

Other analysts have come to similar conclusions about China's impact on East Asian exports. For example, Holst and Weiss (2004) investigated the impact of China's export growth on the ASEAN-5 (Thailand, Indonesia, Philippines, Malaysia, and Singapore) over the period 1995-2000. They found that the ASEAN-5 suffered "substantial and widespread loss of export markets" to China in the US and Japanese markets and that "this loss tends to be greatest in the export activities in which ASEAN economies are most specialized" (1256).

In spite of these trends, mainstream economists, as noted above, do not believe that China's growing competitiveness threatens East Asian economic prospects. Rather they believe that China's very growth has encouraged and supported a successful restructuring and upgrading of regional economic activity. Lall and Albaladejo (2004) highlight this outcome by examining the changing export profiles of East Asian countries. As Table 4.5 shows, although the percentage of Chinese high-technology (HT) exports rose considerably over the period 1990 to 2000, the other East Asian countries were also able to greatly increase their own specialization in HT products, in many cases even more successfully then China. For example, Singapore raised its share of HT exports from 39.1 percent to 61.2 percent over the same period.

Table 4.5 Composition of East Asian Manufactured Exports, in percent

	RB	LT	MT	HT
China				
1990	14.3	51.9	26.9	6.9
2000	9.5	44.9	21.2	24.4
Singapore				
1990	27.8	9.6	23.4	39.1
2000	14.9	6.5	17.4	61.2
Philippines				
1990	37.6	33.7	12.9	15.8
2000	6.5	11.9	11.6	70.0
Malaysia				
1990	31.9	14.8	18.0	35.3
2000	13.1	9.6	17.8	59.4
Thailand				
1990	24.2	40.1	15.1	20.6
2000	18.4	21.5	23.8	36.3
Indonesia				
1990	54.2	32.6	11.3	1.9
2000	33.7	31.3	17.5	17.4
Korea				
1990	7.1	40.0	31.3	21.6
2000	11.7	17.1	34.0	37.1
Taiwan				
1990	6.9	41.3	26.1	25.7
2000	4.4	23.8	25.5	46.3

Note: RB refers to resource based; it includes processed foods, tobacco and wood products, refined petroleum products, dyes, leather, precious stones and organic chemicals. LT refers to low technology; it includes textiles, garments, footwear, other leather products, toys, simple metal products, simple plastics, furniture and glassware. MT refers to medium technology; it includes heavy industrial goods such as automobiles, industrial chemicals, machinery and standard electrical and electronic products. HT refers to high technology; it includes complex electrical and electronic products, aerospace, precision instruments, fine chemicals and pharmaceuticals.

Source: Lall and Albaladejo (2004, 1446).

Equally important for the mainstream argument is the fact that the new market for these NIE and ASEAN exports is increasingly East Asia itself, and especially China. Table 4.6 shows that China's trade balance with East Asia (excluding Hong Kong) went from a deficit of $4 billion to a deficit of $40 billion over the decade of the 1990s. Looking more specifically at what Lall and Albaladejo (2004) call the New Tigers (Indonesia, Malaysia, the Philippines, and Thailand), we can see that they transformed a deficit with China of $270.3 million in 1990, to a surplus in of $4.2 billion in 2000. And, this surplus was largely based on trade in HT products. In like manner, the NIEs (Korea, Taiwan, and Singapore) greatly expanded their surplus with China, from $1.4 billion to $32 billion, with the surplus based on MT and HT exports.

More recent trade developments seem to confirm this argument about China's growing ability to support regional growth. As the *Asia Times* reports, "In the past year [2003] China has taken in 40-50 percent of Asia's exports, accounting for all of Taiwan's and the Philippine's export growth last year and over 50 percent of each of Japan's, Malaysia's, South Korea's and Australia's" (Keliher, 2004).

Table 4.6 China's Net Trade with East Asia, billions US$

	1990	2000
Japan total	-2.9	-3.4
RB	0.7	1.90
LT	0.8	12.7
MT	-3.1	-11.4
HT	-1.3	-6.6
NIEs total	-1.4	-32.0
RB	0.07	-4.0
LT	-0.3	-4.6
MT	-0.9	-14.9
HT	-0.2	-8.6
Hong Kong total	10.5	32.6
RB	1.4	1.9
LT	7.4	16.5
MT	1.5	4.9
HT	0.2	9.2
New Tigers total	0.3	-4.2
RB	-.3	-2.2
LT	0.3	1.0
MT	0.1	0.07
HT	0.08	-3.1
East Asia-HK total	-4.0	-40.0
RB	0.5	-4.4
LT	0.9	9.1
MT	-3.9	-26.2
HT	-1.5	-18.3

Notes: NIEs includes South Korea, Taiwan, and Singapore; New Tigers includes Indonesia, Malaysia, Philippines, and Thailand; HK is Hong Kong. Refer to Table 5 for definitions of the four product groups.
Source: Lall and Albaladejo (2004, 1456).

The Underlying Dynamics of Regional Restructuring

This view of China, as a national success story based on its increasing export prowess, and as an anchor for regional and global growth, is seriously misleading. The reality is that China and East Asia are being jointly reshaped by a larger transnational corporate restructuring dynamic, with China serving as a processor of manufactured components imported from neighboring countries and the final production platform for the region's increasingly important extra-regional export activity. In the process, different nations' workers become pitted against each other, primarily for the benefit of transnational capital and its local subordinates in each country, thereby intensifying exploitation and worsening uneven development and overproduction problems.

Several trends help to highlight this reality. First, trade (exports plus imports) as a percentage of GNP has risen sharply from 1990 to 2003 for all East Asian countries, which means that a growing share of each nation's economic activity is being shaped by international dynamics. For example, Malaysia's trade ratio rose from 139.2 to 213.5, while Thailand's rose from 66.5 to 110.9 (Asian Development Bank, 2004, 83).

Secondly, as Table 4.7 shows, an increasing share of this trade is in parts and components rather than final products.[2] For the ASEAN-6 countries as a whole (Indonesia, Malaysia, Thailand, Singapore, Philippines, and Vietnam), the growth in parts and components exports accounted for 55 percent of the group's combined export growth over the years 1992-2000. The growth in parts and components imports accounted for 68.2 percent of their combined import growth (Athukorala, 2003, Table 4, 30-31). The experience of the NIEs was similar. China's different role as the region's main producer of final products is highlighted by the fact that parts and components accounted for only 17.9 percent of its total export growth, but 42 percent of its import growth over the same period (Athukorala, 2003, Table 4, 30-31). Thus East Asian economic activity is increasingly being narrowed to the production and trade of parts and components within a regionally structured production network.

China's emergence as the final export platform linking this network together is further highlighted by country trade patterns as shown in Table 4.8. Note that with the sole exception of Indonesia, East Asian countries have all substantially increased the share of parts and components in their exports to China. For example, the percentage of Malaysia's exports to China that are parts and components rose from 6.4 to 50.6 between 1992 and 2000. For South Korea, the corresponding percentages are 8.1 and 26.7. As Table 4.8 also shows, China is the only country, with the exception of Indonesia, that continues to sell mostly final goods to the US,

2 The trade in parts and components highlighted in this paper is measured by the amount of this trade in only two SITC categories: SITC 7 (machinery and transport) and SITC 8 (miscellaneous goods). However, these two sectors together accounted for about 70 percent of total world trade in manufactures over the period 1992-2000. And they include the goods most regularly produced through global assembly operations (Athukorala, 2003, 10).

Japan, and the EU. One consequence of China's key role in this regional production network is that it is the only East Asian country to run a deficit in its parts and components trade (Athukorala, 2003, 25). Equally revealing of the nature of the transnational accumulation process is the fact that East Asia's parts and components trade is largely concentrated in SITC 7, machinery and transport equipment, and within that sector in electronics and electrical industries (Athukorala, 2003, 14).

Table 4.7 Parts and Components, Shares of Manufactured Exports and Imports

	Total exports of manufactures US billions	% of exports parts and components	Total imports of manufactures US billions	% of imports parts and components
China				
1992	65.5	6.7	60.3	19.5
1996	123.6	9.8	102.4	21.1
2000	215.5	14.5	160.2	33.5
Malaysia				
1992	25.9	40.4	31.2	37.9
1996	58.7	42.6	61.1	47.5
2000	78.3	49.7	66.0	58.8
Thailand				
1992	21.5	21.2	27.5	26.5
1996	38.4	23.4	51.9	32.9
2000	50.9	35.9	48.3	45.3
Singapore				
1992	48.1	28.2	53.2	32.0
1996	103.4	39.7	105.9	42.8
2000	117.1	49.6	108.1	51.7
Indonesia				
1992	15.8	4.0	19.3	20.5
1996	25.2	7.4	28.3	23.8
2000	34.7	14.2	18.9	19.4
Philippines				
1992	5.8	29.3	7.2	32.6
1996	16.9	52.5	25.3	43.6
2000	34.8	64.0	24.7	55.1
Korea				
1992	66.3	17.8	48.4	26.7
1996	109.7	25.2	90.4	27.4
2000	148.3	30.6	93.1	38.9
Taiwan				
1992	52.9	20.1	37.6	29.6
1996	114.8	28.8	60.4	35.0
2000	150.7	37.8	93.6	37.3
Japan				
1992	312.8	22.9	99.2	15.4
1996	374.7	30.3	185.4	19.3
2000	435.1	30.6	209.2	24.2

Source: Athukorala (2003, Table A-1, 40-43 and Table A-2, 48-50).

Table 4.8 Parts and Components Share of Trade in Selected Markets

Share of parts and components in exports	China	ASEAN	US	Japan	EU
China					
1992		8.2	4.3	6.2	2.9
1996		17.7	7.2	11.8	6.0
2000		29.0	9.1	15.4	10.9
Malaysia					
1992	6.4	45.2	43.6	45.5	35.8
1996	16.1	57.1	40.9	35.2	44.0
2000	50.6	65.2	47.6	40.5	14.8
Thailand					
1992	6.8	57.2	17.3	25.9	11.7
1996	29.2	42.3	16.4	20.0	16.4
2000	54.0	56.9	26.3	37.6	32.2
Singapore					
1992	23.1	37.6	28.1	37.6	19.3
1996	41.9	48.3	38.5	37.9	38.8
2000	50.3	56.3	46.4	41.1	47.7
Indonesia					
1992	0.0	7.6	3.4	5.3	2.6
1996	1.1	19.5	4.3	7.2	4.0
2000	5.7	31.4	9.4	20.8	6.7
Philippines					
1992	1.8	64.4	26.0	27.0	14.8
1996	17.6	82.5	43.4	48.9	56.0
2000	81.8	87.5	52.0	52.8	66.5
Korea					
1992	8.1	38.8	20.4	18.4	13.6
1996	13.1	40.3	37.7	32.5	23.8
2000	26.7	50.0	30.5	39.7	26.2
Taiwan					
1992	18.4	26.8	18.6	19.1	21.3
1996	17.1	34.1	27.2	27.6	27.2
2000	29.8	48.9	32.8	41.6	35.0
Japan					
1992	11.7	33.4	25.7		19.3
1996	23.5	40.6	31.9		26.5
2000	32.8	46.8	27.5		27.6

Note: ASEAN includes Malaysia, Thailand, Singapore, Indonesia, Philippines, and Vietnam.
Source: Athukorala (2003), Table A-2, 48-49.

In sum, East Asian export production (itself a growing portion of total production) is increasingly narrowing to a select few operations in a select few industries in response to the changing needs of transnational corporate production networks.

One consequence is that the significant rise in the share of East Asian trade that is intra-regional does not support the mainstream claims of a growing regional independence and balance. Distinguishing between total trade and final trade (total manufacturing trade net of parts and components), we find that while the intra-regional share of total trade is going up, the intra-regional share of final trade is going down (Athukorala, 2003, Table 5, 32). The difference is most striking when looking at exports. The percentage of final exports from developing East Asia that were sold outside of the East Asian region rose from 55 percent in 1992 to over 60 percent in 2000 (Athukorala, 2003, 18).[3]

Consequences of Restructuring

We find little reason to believe that this transnational production system can support a stable and sustainable process of regional development. The most obvious problem is that East Asia's accumulation dynamic is increasingly dependent on exporting outside the region. More specifically, as more of China's economic activity, and thus the region's production, is oriented toward the US market, the region's economic health rests ever more shakily on the ability of the US to sustain ever larger trade deficits. The US runs its largest bi-lateral trade deficit with China, a deficit that has soared from $84 billion in 2000 to $162 billion in 2004. Over the same period, the overall US trade deficit grew from $375 billion to $617.7 billion; it is now approaching 6 percent of the country's GDP (US Department of Commerce, 2005). It is unlikely that the US can long finance such large and growing trade deficits. Yet, any disruption to this trade pattern would have profoundly negative consequences for the entire East Asian supply line and growth process.

However, the problems with the region's accumulation dynamics run deeper than such trade imbalances suggest. The China-based regional system of export production is also shifting economic activity away from meeting the needs of East Asian working people. And, although this system appears to promote higher value added production, the reality is that the gains tend to be limited for the various countries that compete with one another for positions in the cross-border production chains controlled by transnational corporations. An UNCTAD (2002a) study highlights several reasons for this outcome. Among the most important is that participation in these chains greatly increases third world dependence "on the decisions and performance of foreign firms and countries. This reduces policy autonomy in developing countries regarding the formulation of development strategies that emphasize national capabilities and goals" (UNCTAD, 2002a, 76). As a result, these production networks are likely to generate "less, rather than more, technology transfers. The spillovers from engaging in subcontracting or hosting affiliates of TNCs are reduced because the package of technology and skills required at any one site becomes narrower and because cross-

3 Developing East Asia includes China, Hong Kong, Indonesia, Malaysia, Philippines, Singapore, South Korea, Thailand, Taiwan, and Vietnam.

border backward and forward linkages are strengthened at the expense of domestic ones" (UNCTAD, 2002a, 76).

Many of the limitations of participation in this system are visible in China. The Chinese government has employed a variety of policies to attract export-oriented foreign investment, hoping that foreign capital would generate substantial technology transfers and industrial upgrading. However, as Edward Steinfeld (2004) describes it:

> What has moved to China en masse . . . are the manufacturing-intensive segments of particular value chains. More precisely, it is the codified, commodified, nonintegral manufacturing activities that move. . . . Chinese firms are integrating extensively with the global economy, but they remain concentrated in primarily low-end commodity manufacturing, activities for which they have few other options but to compete on the basis of intense discounting. 21% of China's $325 billion exports in 2002 may have been classified by the Chinese government as "high-tech," but even these ostensibly higher end exports were dominated by lower end parts for information technology products, or at best, mature products such as DVDs and laser printers. . . . In higher technology sectors, Chinese firms are churning out goods roughly 80% of whose value is created elsewhere. (Steinfeld, 2004, 1971-1972, 1983)

None of this has prevented the Chinese government from trying to develop national firms that can globally compete in particular activities. But it does help explain why the Chinese government's efforts to develop such "national champions" (by giving them tax, land, and credit subsidies, and assisting them in negotiations with foreign companies) have been far more successful in resource enterprises (several oil and gas companies) and heavy industries (Baosteel, for example) than in high-tech and consumer brand activities (*Economist*, 2005a, 60). A major reason for its limited success is that compared to South Korea and Japan, "the central government has allowed foreign companies into China at a much earlier stage of its development and these now control the bulk of the country's industrial exports, have increasingly strong positions in its domestic markets and retain ownership of almost all technology" (*Economist*, 2005a, 61; cf. Naughton, 1996, 21). George Gilboy (2004) highlights the strong and growing foreign dominance in China's high-tech sector as follows:

> While exports of industrial machinery grew twentyfold in real terms over the last decade (to $83 billion last year), the share of those exports produced by FFEs [foreign funded enterprises] grew from 35 percent to 79 percent. Exports of computer equipment shot from $716 million in 1993 to $41 billion in 2003, with the FFEs' share rising from 74 percent to 92 percent. Likewise, China's electronics and telecom exports have grown sevenfold since 1993 (to $89 billion last year), with the FFEs' share of those exports growing from 45 percent to 74 percent over the same period. . . . This pattern repeats itself in almost every advanced industrial sector in China. . . . FFEs increased their total share of high-tech exports from 74 percent to 85 percent between 1998 and 2002. But perhaps more significant, in the same period, they increased their share of total domestic high-tech

sales from 32 percent to 45 percent, while the share of that market held by China's most competitive industrial firms, SOEs, fell from 47 percent to 42 percent.

In sum, Chinese state policy has indeed transformed the country into a fast growing export platform, with some significant domestic production capacity. But autonomous development potential is being eroded as the state loses its planning and directing capability, and resources are taken over and restructured in and by foreign networks largely for the purpose of satisfying external market demands.

An even more damning critique of the regional restructuring process is that insofar as the region's growth is increasingly dependent on cross-cutting and competing transnational corporate production networks (whether or not directed at exporting), all of the countries of East Asia are under ever greater pressure to keep wages down and productivity up in order to sustain or improve their position within these networks. This, in turn, reinforces the bias of the system toward exports, thereby worsening export overproduction problems. And, because of its key position in transnational investment and trade networks, China has become the benchmark for competition. Therefore, workers throughout East Asia have become pitted against each other in a contest to match the level of labor exploitation achieved in China, with disastrous consequences for all. We highlight some of these negative consequences for workers in China, South Korea, and the US.

Case Study: China

Given the celebration of China's economic success one might expect to see obvious gains for Chinese workers. In fact, quite the opposite appears to be true. Despite the growth of a relatively small but numerically significant upper income group whose consumption opportunities have greatly expanded, most Chinese working people are suffering from deteriorating work and living conditions.

China's reform program, as noted above, involved a sustained effort to marketize and privatize economic activity, and to promote foreign export oriented enterprises as the leading force in the economy. The success of this effort is reflected in the fact that by 2002, foreign firms produced a greater share of industrial output then did state owned firms, 34 and 30 percent respectively (McGuckin and Spiegelman, 2004, Part I). In line with this change, the share of workers employed in state owned and operated firms fell from 81 percent to 49 percent of the urban work force over the same period (McGuckin and Spiegelman, 2004, Part II).

Unfortunately, the massive decline in state employment has not been offset by the growth in private employment. The result has been a significant increase in the urban unemployment rate. This increase does not show up in official government statistics largely because these figures exclude laid-off state workers and rural migrants now living and working in urban areas. Thus, while government statistics claim only a three percent urban unemployment rate, most independent analysts, and even the IMF, estimate the true figure to be in double digits, some as high as

23 percent (Hong Kong Confederation of Trade Unions, 2004, 19; McGuckin and Spiegelman, 2004, Part II).

Although some laid-off state workers do find new employment, few are able to improve their position. An All China Federation of Trade Unions (ACFTU) survey of re-employed state workers found that "18.6 percent were odd-job manual workers, 10 percent did various sorts of hourly work (which usually refers to activities such as picking up others' children from school); 5.2 percent had seasonal jobs; 60 percent were retailers operating stalls; and a mere 6.8 percent had obtained formal, contracted employment" (quoted in Hong Kong Confederation of Trade Unions, 2004, 12-13).

Thus, large numbers of state workers are suffering from the reform process. Many face a hopeless future, because they live in cities that are no longer central to the new foreign dominated export activity that is largely concentrated in coastal areas. As a result, they are left with few options but to demonstrate for better pensions and health care. Even those still employed must worry about competition from migrant workers and the possibility of future closures or privatization of their current enterprises if they demand too much.

While there is job growth associated with the new export oriented, foreign dominated production, most of these jobs are low paid. According to *Business Week*, a US Bureau of Labor Statistics attempt to measure average hourly compensation of Chinese factory workers "concluded [that] China has about 38 million city manufacturing workers. The 30 million on whom [the BLS consultant] found data earn an average $1.06 an hour. Another roughly 71 million suburban and rural manufacturing workers earn an average 45 cents an hour, for a blended 64 cents. In the current BLS survey, Mexico's $2.48 hourly compensation is the lowest" (Coy, 2004).

In Guangdong, where approximately one third of China's exports are produced, "base assembly-line wages . . . have been virtually frozen at about $80 per month for the past decade . . . . Factor in inflation over roughly the same period, and average pay in real terms has declined by as much as 30%" (Gough, 2005). Adding insult to injury, many of China's workers are not even being paid what they are owed. In fact, "government surveys showed that 72.5 percent of the country's nearly 100 million migrant workers were owed wages" (Lee, 2004, 2).

These problems are not likely to be corrected by government action. Rather, poor employment terms and the lack of institutional support for workers seeking to improve them flow directly from the nature of China's capitalist restoration (Hart-Landsberg and Burkett, 2005a, Chapter 3). As part of the reform process, regional and local government officials were freed from central oversight and encouraged to promote private enterprise, especially foreign enterprise, for their mutual profit. Thus, most provincial and local authorities now depend heavily for their own success on attracting and keeping profitable firms in their jurisdiction. In many cases, local government officials have actually become shareholders in these ventures. As a result, workers often find their efforts to improve conditions undermined by the very local governments that are supposed to protect them.

In response, growing numbers of rural workers are deciding to remain in the countryside. One consequence is that "factories in the Pearl River Delta region are facing a shortfall of some 2 million workers, with shortages also affecting other key manufacturing provinces, including Fujian and Zhejiang" (Holland, 2004, 42). Even more threatening to the Chinese growth strategy is the fact that workers are increasingly taking direct action in their own defense. For example, the number of mass incidents or protests is rapidly escalating. According to the Ministry of Public Security, there were 74,000 in 2004, involving more than 3.7 million people, compared with 10,000 in 1994 and 58,000 in 2003 (*Economist*, 2005b). Labor disputes, in particular, are on the rise and growing most rapidly at foreign and private enterprises, the ones that are most celebrated for driving Chinese growth (Hong Kong Confederation of Trade Unions, 2004, 29).

Perhaps most significant is the fact that workers are increasingly pressing their demands for improvement through strikes (Cody, 2004). This is a relatively new development. In the past the labor news was largely filled with stories about laid-off state workers demanding fair treatment in terms of severance payments and pension and health support. An example was the massive unrest in northeast China during the spring and early summer of 2002. The Chinese government has generally responded to such actions with policies designed to "prevent workers' protests from spreading beyond their immediate locale" (Hong Kong Confederation of Trade Unions, 2004, 7). These included the use of "media blackouts, denial of the right to demonstrate, police spies, snatch squads and 'visits' to workers' homes from various organs of the state, including the All China Federation of Trade Unions (ACFTU)" (Hong Kong Confederation of Trade Unions, 2004, 7). But this strategy is likely to lose its effectiveness as more workers initiate strike actions that directly threaten production, especially at foreign companies.

Of course, China's rapid growth has also created wealth. However, most of the domestic gains have been captured by a relatively small percentage of the population. According to the *South China Morning Post*, "The growing disparity between the mainland's urban rich and rural poor has created one of the world's most pronounced national income gaps. It is on a par with the poverty-stricken African nation of Zimbabwe . . . while some urban residents are buying luxury homes and cars, the vast majority of the 800 million peasants live on less than US$1 a day" (Cheng, 2004). And, as researchers with the Chinese Academy of Social Sciences point out, "the income disparity is evident not only between urban and rural residents, but also among urban people as well" (*People's Daily*, 2004). Although China's National Bureau of Statistics has concluded, based on survey research, that only 5 percent of the country's population can currently be considered middle class, the government confidently predicts that its economic policies will raise this to 45 percent by 2020

(*People's Daily*, 2005). However, such a prediction flies in the face of the lived experiences of the great majority of Chinese working people.[4]

Case Study: South Korea

South Korea's economy is also being rapidly restructured in line with the above described transnational accumulation dynamics, and with negative consequences for South Korean workers. This restructuring is largely a result of the post-crisis (1997-98) liberalization and deregulation of the South Korean economy (Hart-Landsberg and Burkett, 2001; Hart-Landsberg, 2004b). A major consequence is that China's growth has become the main force driving South Korea's economic activity and shaping its economic choices. In 2001, China became South Korea's number one foreign investment location; in 2004, almost half of South Korea's foreign investment went to China. In large part because of this investment, China became South Korea's number one export market in 2002, and its number one trading partner in 2003.

In the immediate post crisis period, the South Korean government relied on deficit spending to promote the country's economic recovery. But, this spending was not sustainable, both because of the rapid rise in the national debt and pressure from the IMF (*Korea Herald*, 2003b). Foreign investment also played an early role in boosting growth, providing the government with critical foreign exchange. However, much of this investment was "vulture investment" that involved takeovers of South Korean assets at fire sale prices. One consequence of this investment has been a significant denationalization of South Korean capital (Hart-Landsberg and Burkett, 2001, 414-16). Significantly, once the most attractive assets had been purchased, foreign investment rapidly and steadily declined, falling from a peak of $15.7 billion in 2000, to $6.5 billion in 2003 (Hart-Landsberg, 2004b, 93).

Desperate to reverse this decline, the South Korean government has taken steps to create a more attractive investment environment for foreign companies. It established three special free economic zones; foreign businesses that operate within them enjoy tax breaks as well as exemptions from various environmental and labor regulations. However, this policy appears unlikely to achieve its goal. One important reason is that transnational corporations are far more attracted to China, where they have access to extremely low cost labor, an extensive system of subsidies, and a lax regulatory environment. In 2004, the head of the American Chamber of Commerce in Korea made this explicit when he said, "Korea's competition is Shanghai, Hong Kong and China. Realize what your competition is, because investors can choose where to go" (Kim J-H, 2004b). He singled out the need for the South Korean government to increase "labor flexibility."

At the same time as foreign direct investment inflows have slowed, outflows of South Korean foreign direct investment have grown substantially. Over 4000 South

---

4 For a more complete discussion of the ways in which the reform process has led to deteriorating social conditions for the majority of Chinese working people, especially health care and education, see Hart-Landsberg and Burkett (2005b, 606-612).

Korean factories have moved their production out of South Korea since 1998, and the numbers have been increasing dramatically each year. According to a Korea Customs Service official, "about 70.7 percent of those production facilities have moved to China" (Kim M-H, 2003). A study by the Korea Chamber of Commerce and Industry found that "about nine out of ten companies manufacturing products in Korea have plans to invest in China in the future, as the country's low production cost and the eager-to-please regulations make the market more attractive than Korea" (Kim M-H, 2003). As a result of this trend, South Korea's net foreign direct investment actually turned negative in 2002 (see Table 4.2).

The *chaebol*, like their foreign counterparts, are also demanding that their government take more aggressive steps to weaken the country's labor movement. They have made clear that if the government does not meet their demands they will continue to move their production "across the Yellow Sea to China, where wages are lower and the demands of workers rarely result in headaches for managers" (Kirk, 2003, W1). This is no empty threat. In fact, signs of industrial hollowing are already visible. For example, South Korean firms have largely stopped buying new equipment for their domestic operations. Before the crisis, the yearly growth rate of investment in machinery in the manufacturing sector was regularly over 20 percent. It fell to 0 percent in 1999, 0.5 percent in 2000, and then -5.9 percent in 2001 and -4.9 percent in 2002. While the rate of investment turned positive in 2003 and 2004, the recovery has been quite modest, 0.6 percent and 3.2 percent respectively. To put this trend in perspective, South Korean manufacturing companies spent less on new equipment and plants in 2004 then they did in 1996 (*Korea Herald*, 2005). As a consequence, employment in manufacturing is now declining (Kim S-Y, 2005a, 1).

Beginning in 1999, in an attempt to counter these negative developments, the South Korean government started encouraging the use of credit cards to stimulate domestic private consumption by, among other things, introducing tax deductions for purchases made by credit card. The result was a major consumption boom and corresponding credit card debt explosion. The total amount of credit card spending rose from $53 billion in 1998 to $519 billion in 2002 (Lowe-Lee, 2004a, 1). Household debt rose from 87 percent of disposable income in 1999 to 131 percent in 2002 (Kim J-K, 2005).

With cash advances and credit-card loans accounting for approximately two-thirds of all consumer transactions, it was not long before many households faced unsustainable debt levels. Delinquency rates began rising sharply in 2002. Frightened by the prospect of a wave of personal bankruptcies and the danger such bankruptcies could cause the country's financial system the government finally took steps to limit credit card use in the spring of 2003. Not surprisingly, the government's success led to a sharp decline in private consumption and investment, and a recession in the first half of 2003 (Lister, 2003, 1).

As a result of these trends, South Korea is now more dependent then ever on exports to power growth. And, these exports are increasingly headed to China. Many South Korean analysts claim that the shift in export orientation from the US to China has greatly reduced the country's vulnerability to instabilities in the US market

(Lister, 2004, 1). But, as we have seen, China largely functions as a production platform for exports to the United States. In line with this orientation, most South Korean exports to China are intermediate goods used in the production of other goods. For example, studies by the Korea International Trade Association and the Korea Institute for International Economic Policy revealed that "a large portion of the final products are reshipped to third countries, with about 40 percent re-exported to the United States" (Brown, 2004, 1). Similarly, an UNCTAD examination of East Asian trade relationships concluded that South Korean exports to China now move in lockstep with Chinese exports to the US (UNCTAD, 2005, 137, 139).

In short, South Korea's economic future has become increasingly dependent on a narrowing range of exports within a framework shaped by a China-based, US-oriented system of export production. South Koreans are already paying a high price for their country's economic restructuring: poverty rates remain higher than before the crisis and inequality has hit record levels (Hart-Landsberg, 2004b, 98-99). One reason is that many corporations have taken advantage of new labor laws, which were implemented by the government to promote export competitiveness, to fire their permanent workers and then rehire them as temporary or even daily workers. As a result, the percentage of workers with irregular labor status rose from 42 before the crisis to 55 percent in 2003 (Jang, 2004, 280-81); these irregular workers receive only 53 percent of the hourly wages paid to regular workers (*Korea Herald*, 2003a). Perhaps the best summary indicator of social conditions comes from a 2004 Korea Broadcasting System survey, which found that "more than half of South Koreans feel that the current economic situation is worse than it was in late 1997 when the financial crisis shook the nation" (Kim J-K, 2004).

Case Study: United States

We have highlighted some of the ways in which East Asia's regionally structured export production network is worsening living and working conditions for East Asian workers. The primary focus of this network has been the US market, and the China-based export offensive is also generating serious problems for US workers. In the words of *Business Week*:

> "The China price." They are the three scariest words in US industry. In general, it means 30% to 50% less than what you can possibly make something for in the US In the worst cases, it means below your cost of materials. Makers of apparel, footwear, electric appliances, and plastics products, which have been shutting US factories for decades, know well the futility of trying to match the China price. (*Business Week*, 2004)

These imports and plant closures have led to a loss of manufacturing jobs in the US, more than 3 million between 1998 and 2003 (Bivens, 2004, 2; Burke, *et al.*, 2004, 4-5). And, whereas in previous years, China's exports were largely in low technology items, they are increasingly shifting to products that threaten the jobs of higher paid US workers (Burke, 2000, 6).

We have argued that the China phenomenon should be understood not in simple national or even inter-national terms but rather as a transnational capitalist process that ties together production across borders to the benefit of transnational capital and to the detriment of enterprises not connected to this process and most workers in the countries involved. Consistent with this understanding, while many US companies are being hurt by China-based production activity, other US firms are directly contributing to and profiting from that activity. Among the biggest beneficiaries are companies that use China "as a base for exporting or sourcing cheap goods, such as Wal-Mart" (McGregor, 2004). In fact, Wal-Mart alone accounts for more than 10 percent of total US imports from China (*China Economic Net*, 2004). Other US transnationals, such as General Motors, Procter & Gamble, and Motorola, are also making large profits doing business in China and with Chinese subcontractors (*Business Week*, 2004).

The role of US transnationals in advancing or deepening this China-based process to the detriment of US workers is significant and growing. According to Burke (2000, 1-2), "A 10 percent increase in the level of US direct investment in an industry in China is associated with a 7.3 percent increase in the volume of US imports from China and a 2.1 percent decline in US exports to China in that industry." Burke charts the changing orientation of US firms operating in China by comparing "exports shipped to US affiliate firms in China to imports sold to the United States from these affiliates, from 1989 to 1997" (Burke, 2000, 4). The result is that "since 1995, the value of imports from US affiliates in China has surpassed the value of US exports to these foreign affiliates. In just a few years, US multinationals operating in China have turned from net exporters to China to net exporters to the United States, a gap that will only widen with increased FDI to China, further contributing to the growing US trade deficit" (Burke, 2000, 4).

We have focused on China because of its importance for contemporary global capitalist dynamics, especially for the development of East Asian industry and the US trade deficit. However, precisely because China's new global role has largely grown out of the changing nature of transnational capitalist production imperatives, it is important to acknowledge that this transnational activity is not limited to East Asia, and that capitalist competition generates a complex array of intersecting cross-border relationships around the world. This complexity is highlighted by the results of a study done by Kate Bronfenbrenner and Stephanie Luce for the US-China Economic and Security Review Commission (Bronfenbrenner and Luce, 2004). Their main focus was on US production shifts (tied contractions and expansions of jobs) to China, as reported in English language media, during the first quarters of 2004 and 2001, respectively.[5] However, in order to situate these corporate moves in

5 Their work was not intended to be comprehensive. For example, they did not look at the coordinated expansions and contractions of production at different sites undertaken by transnational corporations (as opposed to complete closures and openings that were connected). Nor did they investigate the kind of foreign outsourcing in which US firms (whether transnational or not) shift purchases of intermediate goods from domestic to foreign

a wider geographical perspective, they also looked at "job shifts from the US to other Asian countries, Mexico, and other Latin American countries; and production shifts from Asia, Europe, and other countries into China, other Asian countries, and Latin American countries" (Bronfenbrenner and Luce, 2004, 9).

For the first quarter of 2004, they found 255 shifts announced or reported by US facilities, with 48 percent going to multiple destinations. Mexico was the location for 69, China for 58, other Asian countries for 39, India for 31, and other Latin American and Caribbean countries for 35 (Bronfenbrenner and Luce, 2004, 16). This number of production shifts out of the US represented a major leap compared to the first quarter of 2001, for which the authors found only 30 shifts to Mexico, and 25 to China (Bronfenbrenner and Luce, 2004, 17). These figures also suggest that while China is a major destination for US production, the largest number of production shifts out of the US continue to go to Mexico.

One of the most important results to emerge from this study is that production shifts, which in the past were mostly shifts that involved US based firms moving production from the US to a single foreign location, are now shifts to multiple foreign locations. But even more significant is the strategic orientation of these multiple shifts. According to the authors: "A large percentage of these shifts were simultaneous shifts to 'nearshore' countries in Latin America (primarily Mexico) and to China and other 'offshore' countries in Asia" (p. 20). In other words, for US corporations, global restructuring tended to involve both Mexico and China.

The unique role played by China in the transnational restructuring process becomes clearer thanks to Bronfenbrenner and Luce's examination of production shifts from countries other than the US. Similar to the US case, they found that a growing number of shifts from Asia and Europe also went to multiple locations, the majority of which included China. More specifically, while Asian companies tended to simultaneously shift production to China and other Asian countries, European companies tended to shift production to China and countries in Eastern Europe (Bronfenbrenner and Luce, 2004, 21).

Thus, transnational corporations from all three regions are expanding their production lines to include both near-shore and offshore operations. China is the dominant production base in East Asia, representing for many East Asian companies the best near-shore and offshore option. But for US and European companies, China is the desired offshore option, with US companies choosing Mexico and European companies choosing Eastern Europe for their respective near-shore operations. Since European and US firms have other options closer to home, their cross-border operations are not as dependent on China as are those of firms in Asia.

All of this highlights the fierce competition among transnational corporations based in the US, Europe, and Asia to expand and diversify their production networks, the effect of which is to bring different countries' workers into an overarching framework of competition both within and between different enterprises. Asian

---

suppliers. Burke, et al.(2004) show that this last form of foreign outsourcing has greatly accelerated in recent years.

capital appears to have moved fastest and furthest in this direction but US and European companies are quickly catching up. China's role is critical because while it is the dominant production base for East Asia, the region which is the most export oriented, it also plays a critical role in the transnational production networks being extended by US and European firms.

The commonality of worker experiences resulting from this dynamic is perhaps best illustrated by employment trends in both China and the US, the countries that appear to lie at opposite ends of the accumulation process. The reality is that while the US is losing manufacturing employment, so is China. As a Conference Board report notes, "While there has been much discussion about offshoring high-wage jobs from the United States to low-wage countries like China, the loss of large numbers of manufacturing jobs is actually occurring in both countries simultaneously" (McGuckin and Spiegelman, 2004, Part I). More specifically, in the 1995-2002 period, China actually lost 15 million manufacturing jobs, a 15 percent decline. Moreover, it lost jobs in "many of the same industries where the developed world has seen the greatest employment declines. For example, the United States lost 202,000 textile jobs between 1995 and 2002, a tremendous decline by any measure. But China lost many more – 1.8 million." In fact, China suffered job losses in 26 of its 38 major industries (McGuckin and Spiegelman, 2004, Part I).

Thus, growing numbers of workers in China, East Asia, and the US are increasingly captured by a common dynamic of capitalist restructuring. Wealth is being generated but working people in all the countries involved are being pitted against each other and suffering similar consequences, including unemployment and worsening living and working conditions.

Conclusion

Our analysis of China verifies the continuing dynamism of contemporary capitalism. That dynamism leads to rapid shifts in the economic fortunes of nations and the development of new production and exchange relationships within and among countries. Indeed, it is the very rapidity of change that leads many to celebrate contemporary capitalism as an engine of development. Nonetheless, we believe that a careful examination of contemporary dynamics shows that, despite its rapid growth and export success, China is not an attractive model of development from a working-class perspective. Chinese workers are facing increasingly difficult conditions even as they succeed in producing more exports. In addition, China does not anchor a development process that is beneficial for workers in other countries. Workers throughout East Asia are being knitted together in a production process that is organized to serve export markets out of the region, under the direction of transnational corporations whose interests are largely in cost reduction regardless of the social or environmental consequences. The US economy and US labor are also being restructured as part of the same process.

Our analysis also highlights the fact that this transnational capitalist restructuring, within which China plays such a critical role, is generating tensions and imbalances. For example, East Asian growth is increasingly dependent on ever-greater US trade deficits. This trend cannot continue forever. In saying this, we do not mean to predict that capitalism has reached some final crisis. Rather, our point is that these imbalances will have to be corrected, and insofar as the logic of capitalist competition goes unchallenged, governments can be expected to manage the resulting economic instabilities with policies that will only further worsen living and working conditions. Moreover, they are likely to generate explanations for the necessity of such policies that will deliberately foment racism and a destructive nationalism.

Whether workers can develop a response to this situation remains to be seen. Clearly the dynamic nature of the system tends to mask its destructive nature. So does the mainstream perspective on the Chinese experience. We need to demystify the transnational capitalist processes that are reshaping different countries' economies in order to reveal the capitalist roots of the growing social problems faced by workers around the world and the structural imbalances that threaten yet further immizeration. Finally, we need to translate this understanding into a program of action that can assist the birth of national, regional, and global movements capable of helping working people reclaim control over their lives.

Acknowledgement

This work was partly supported by a Korean Research Foundation Grant (KRF-2003-005-B00006).

Chapter 5

The Changing Patterns of Accumulation and Realization in East Asia since the 1990s

Joseph Halevi and Peter Kriesler

Introduction

In order to understand current developments in Asia, particularly the pattern of growth and accumulation, it is necessary to consider the historical development of the region. In this chapter we attempt to understand these recent developments from the stagnationist tradition in Marxist literature which is discussed in the next section. Using the stagnationist framework, three distinct phases of Asian capital are identified. The early phase was characterized by European interest in the region and with the start of Japanese industrialization, while the second phase is marked by the rise of Japan as the oligopolist power in the region. Finally, the rise of China as a significant economic force leading to structural change in the region is considered.

Historical Background

There is an important stagnationist tradition in the Marxist literature which goes back at least as far as Rosa Luxemburg. In the twentieth century it culminated in the writings of Kalecki and Baran and Sweezy. The essence of this view is that there are long run stagnationist tendencies in capitalist economies caused by the fact that the growth rate of productive capacity (ie. the rate of accumulation) is faster than the growth in the level of effective demand.

These stagnationist tendencies are reinforced with the development of the monopoly phase of capitalism. Oligopolistic corporations are associated with both a rise in the share of profits at the expense of labor's share, as well as a reduction in the drive to accumulate. As the propensity to save from profits is higher than from wages, this redistribution is associated with lower levels of effective demand, further exasperating the problem.

This is well summarized by Baran and Sweezy:

> Under monopoly capitalism....The normal condition is less than capacity production. The system simply does not generate enough 'effective demand'...to ensure full utilization of either labour or productive facilities (Baran and Sweezy, 1966, 146).

The stagnationist tradition acknowledges that these tendencies may be postponed by a Schumpeterian process of creative destruction in times of profound technological change. External markets can also act as exogenous sources of effective demand which can mitigate the stagnationist tendencies. External markets refer to demand from markets external to the sphere of production. These external markets can be either domestic or foreign. By domestic external markets, we refer, in the tradition of Baran and Sweezy, to a number of possible external sources of effective demand including advertising, finance, insurance, real estate, government expenditure and expenditure on the military[1].

Foreign external demand is the result of net exports. Countries can increase domestic demand at the expense of their trading partners, by increased exports, a point noted by both Keynes and Kalecki, who also stressed the global limitations of such policies. Keynes and Kalecki clearly understood the importance of international trade as a mechanism for exporting unemployment between nations (Keynes, 1936, ch. 16; Kalecki, 1976; Halevi, 1984). In other words, the balance of payments may become an important constraint on the growth of effective demand if countries maintain chronic deficits.

This problem was specifically addressed by the successful development of East Asia in the post-WW2 period, which relied on external markets with the newly industrializing economies (NIE's) growth strategies explicitly focused on exports.

However, even in these cases, the balance of payments may be problematic as the level of the productive stock of capital is deemed low relative to population, particularly where capital goods – including intermediate industrial products – are mostly imported. Even if a country has a large productive capacity its accumulation may be constrained by the balance of payments bottleneck which will arise when factories and services are near full capacity. If capital goods including intermediate products have to be imported, then any increase in investment will increase the size of the external deficit, which may then become an obstacle to full employment policies even if the economy is an advanced one in terms of per capita income. This is the result of fundamental problems in the international monetary system which has always placed the burden of adjustment on the deficit country, so reinforcing the stagnationist tendencies already inherent in the system (Kriesler and Halevi 1996; Halevi and Kriesler 1998).

This view should be contrasted with the dominant neoclassical view, according to which any increase in saving is a benefit to the economy rather than the burden that Marxist economics in the above traditions see it as. The reason for this is that with an underlying loanable funds vision of capital markets, the increased saving – supply of loanable funds – immediately translates into an increase in investment demand for loanable funds. It is this view, associated with the Washington Consensus, which argues that policies are needed to increase national savings as the only way of both improving growth rates and addressing current account imbalances. Similarly,

1 Kalecki also acknowledges the importance of the last two sources of expenditure.

according to this position, Japanese current account surpluses, post-1970, have led to capital outflows which, in turn, have funded investment elsewhere:

> [T]he current surplus in the Japanese balance of payments ... is a *beneficial* feature of the world economy, and ... Japanese savings, as manifested in the country's balance-of-payments surplus, can be used for Asian economic development (Healey,1991, 25 *Emphasis in original*).

Elsewhere we have discussed this position in full noting that there are serious logical and theoretical problems with these arguments (Halevi and Kriesler 1998; Kriesler and Halevi 1996) The loanable funds idea underlying it is based on the view that saving constitutes a stock of loanable funds for investment, and that savings must precede investment, so that savings causally determine investment, with the rate of interest equating the two. This idea is rejected by most heterodox economists, for reasons outlined in our earlier chapters. Rather than being of benefit to other nations, large current account surpluses are merely ways of exporting unemployment, and lead to severe contractionary pressures in the deficit countries.

Capital Accumulation in Asia: Growth to the 1990s

From the 19th century until launching in China of the Four Modernizations program in 1979, the process of capitalist accumulation in (East) Asia had gone through two phases. In 1979 it entered a crucial third phase which started to have a significant extreme impact by the end of the 1980s and gathered momentum after the Asian crisis of 1997. Thus it can be said that only around and after the 1997 financial crisis did the new regime of accumulation which was incubating in China change and sweep aside the previous one based on Japan's hegemonic role in the East Asian zone bordering China.

We can now summarize the main features of the phases of capitalist accumulation in East Asia:

Phase 1

The first phase of accumulation is characterized by both the European imperialist encroachment upon China and the industrialization of Japan strictly connected to its imperialist expansion into China, including formerly Chinese Manchuria under Tsarist Russia and into Korea. This imperialist expansion by both Europe and Japan into China and by Japan into Korea was a factor of grave retardation of the development of both countries. The logic was that of subordinating the economic structure of East Asia to capitalist accumulation in the respective metropolis. The expansion of Japan into China and Korea (1895, 1905 and 1910) was based on an alliance, both political and financial, with Britain which sustained Japan's expansion and extended large loans to Tokyo, thereby turning Japan into a major debtor.

World War 1 (WW1) solved the external debt problem of Japan, thanks to the alliance with Britain. WW1 acts as a classical external market and as an import substitution device. The search for markets restarted in earnest with the Great Depression and the related Manchuria incident in 1931. This event, which started the long war against China and, in appropriate historical terms, WW2, is the factor which propelled the heavy and chemical industry process of capital accumulation in Japan, operating therefore, in an eminently Kalecki/Rosa Luxemburg form of imperialism *cum* accumulation. At the same time however, the imperialism of Japan's capitalism had one crucial weakness regarding the structure of the balance of payments. While the Yen area was generating a surplus for Japan it was not doing so in terms of the trade with the dollar and sterling areas (Nakamura, 1983). Japan's imperialism towards China clashed more and more with the role ascribed to China by the United States (US) – defined by the open door policy elaborated in the years leading to the war against Spain in 1898 which brought the US to Asia through the conquest of the Philippines. Washington's move towards sanctions and oil embargo against Japan turned the dollar and sterling components of the balance of payments of Japan into an insurmountable obstacle out of which grew the conditions for total war. Thus Phase 1 ended in practice in 1937 when the all out war against China encroached directly on US interests in China and compelled a rather reluctant US government to set up an oil embargo against Japan which then led to Japan's decision to attack the United States.

Phase 2

What remained of Phase 1 was the structural change caused by the heavy and chemical industrialization of Japan. Kosai Yutaka has presented convincing estimates regarding the extent of the war damage (Kosai, 1986). While the damage was extremely severe in shipbuilding it turned out of to be milder in the machine producing capacity of the economy, although more serious than in the case of Germany. But Japanese capitalism lost the functional connections between markets and raw material supplies that it has been establishing through imperialism for half a century up to 1945. Thus Phase 2 can be seen as formed by three sub-periods. The first sub-period is centered on creating the conditions for an economic anchor for Japan and the second is marked by the formation of a Japanese oligopolistic zone in the East and Southeast part of Asia. The third begins in 1971 with the US abandonment of the dollar-gold convertibility. Both periods up to 1971 are characterized by US public expenditure connected – in a pure Baran-Sweezy fashion – to military expenditure and to the special institutional arrangements made by the US to have Japan quickly accepted within the General Agreement on Tariffs and Trade (GATT) in 1955. These included the signing of 13 trilateral trade treaties offering to third countries greater access to US markets provided they forwent the use of clause 35 of GATT which allowed setting up trade barriers against any country not accepting trade reciprocity (Forsberg, 2000). US policies allowed Japan to lift the balance of payments ceiling which is another way of saying that the limited availability of internationally profitable effective demand was less of a constraint on decisions concerning investment and accumulation.

Why was the United States interested in uplifting and protecting Japan even at the expense of the penetration of its own multinationals into Japan? There was indeed a grand design of reshaping world capitalism with the United States at its core flanked by two growth poles: Europe with West Germany at its center and Japan in Asia. The difference between these two poles resided in the fact that while Europe was the economic hinterland of Germany, Japan could not be ensconced in Asia because of the Chinese revolution and the national liberation movements in the region, including the VietCong led by Ho-Chi-Minh. Thus there was no natural area for Japan in the region. Japan had to be taken on board by Washington in a much more direct way than was the case with Germany, while, at the same time, the United States took upon itself the task of fighting the national liberation movements. This fact led Washington to transform the Korean War into a roll back war, and to get involved in Vietnam. Such a strategy was part and parcel of US policies to control raw materials through its own multinationals and to control world liquidity through the dollar supremacy which then was connected to a US surplus in the current account. With hindsight it seems clear that US authorities did not foresee the costs, in terms of the current account, of their own imperialism and were convinced that American technological superiority and sheer economic size would carry the day. US policies created a shelter for Japan in which the *keiretsu* could organize the much needed retooling in order to fan out into world markets without reciprocity from the Japanese side. American special procurement payments during the Korean War were the most noticeable example enabling Japan to overcome balance of payments constraints. But as shown by US historian Michael Schaller, US war expenditure in Vietnam had an equally important impact on Japan.

The second sub-phase is that of the Vietnam War which Schaller has characterized as Japan's re-entry in Asia (Schaller, 1985). Propelled by US war expenditure the area becomes structurally dependent upon Japan, first in terms of imports. The crucial pillars of the area of Japanese oligopolistic hegemony are The Republic of Korea (hereafter Korea) and Taiwan notwithstanding that, unlike later Thailand, Malaysia, and Singapore, the two countries did not develop solely and not even principally on the basis of direct multinational investment. Yet it is in relation to Korea and Taiwan during the years of the Vietnam War that the model of structurally dependent accumulation was fashioned and it has been this model, rather than the so-called "flying geese" paradigm, that continued after the end of the second sub-phase shaping capitalist power relations in East Asia (Lim, 1985; Hart-Landsberg, 1993). This factor has been recognized also by economists involved with establishment institutions and policy making bodies, but precisely for this reason they have smoothed out the implications regarding the fundamentally asymmetrical and contradictory forces at work (Hatch and Yamamura, 1996). The essence of the asymmetries lay in the role of Japan as a poor buyer but as a strong oligopolistic seller, while solutions to financial crises had to be undertaken by the US (Woo-Cumings, 1991).

In this context the third sub-phase is represented by the sharpening of US disengagement as the global coordinator of developed capitalism which began in 1971 with President Nixon's declaration of the abandonment of the Bretton Woods parity between the US dollar and gold, made Japan into the adjustment variable of US monetary and exchange rates policies. The ensuing sharp revaluation of the Yen, transformed the part of East Asia under US geopolitical and military control, into an increasingly important rear for the dominance of Japanese monopoly capital. Japan countered the devaluation of the US dollar in the 1972-79 period by further tying Asia to itself. Technology transfers to Korea for instance meant a widening trade gap in favor of Japan and an increased structural dependence of Korea. In countries – such as Thailand, Malaysia and Indonesia – structural dependence was brought about by the dominant role of the Japanese *keiretsus*.

The third sub-phase – which is specific to the American-Japanese Asia – ran for a while parallel to the beginning of the third big phase in the history of Asian capitalist development. That is, parallel to the inception and incubation of the Deng Xiaoping reforms in China. Indeed during the 1980s the events in China, while momentous in social, political and geopolitical terms, were relatively separate from the macroeconomic trends occurring in the rest of American-Japanese zone of East Asia. The impact of the Chinese situation became apparent by the end of the decade and by the time of the East Asian crisis of 1997-98 China became the real center of gravity of the Asian continent. This means that the disengagement of the US from its role as global coordinator of world capitalism must as far as the American-Japanese East Asia is concerned, be seen as part of the third and final sub-phase of Phase 2.

We have seen that the third sub-phase begins in 1971 with the ditching by the US of the dollar-gold parity and with a sharp devaluation of the US dollar against the Yen thereby pushing Japan to further extend its economic domination over non-communist East and Southeast Asia. By 1979 with the loss of Iran to the United States and the ensuing rise in oil prices US policy makers decided to fence off any threat to the dollar and enacted a high interest rates cum large military spending deficit policy. This set of policies led to a revaluation of the US currency – albeit well below the pre 1971 level – to a military led growth revival in the United States and to the opening up of an unbridgeable deficit in the current account, in which Japan and the rest of East Asia had a big share.

By 1985 the policy became unsustainable as it was generating tensions within US capitalism and also with the Europeans who, already mired in high unemployment, were witnessing a flight of capital towards the United States. On the 22nd of September of 1985 in the Plaza hotel in New York an accord was reached between the United States and the major capitalist countries on lowering US interest rates starting a steep devaluation towards the Yen which lasted till May 1995. In that monetary context, Japan's strategy towards Asia aimed at recouping – through Asia's growth and exports and Japan's own economic hegemony – the squeeze in profit margins of Japanese corporations on their exports to the US and also on the activities of transplants.

The US market has for Japan greater competition than the Asian one so that it was impossible to transfer fully the increase in the value of the Yen onto Japan's exports towards the USA. Furthermore, for the same reasons, the transplants could not pass fully the increased dollar costs of imported technologies and machinery onto their final US prices. It is in this context that East Asia, whose currencies were pegged to the US dollar, became a very important source of Japan's net balance of payments position. The Asian crisis of 1997 was a real crisis of capital accumulation determined by the dynamics of structural asymmetries and not by the factors usually mentioned in traditional studies. With the collapse of little capitalist American Japanese Asia Phase 3 of the history of Asian capitalism which had already begun in China with Deng Xiaoping reforms came to the forefront of world development.

Post Asian Crisis: Phase 3

It would be difficult to address exhaustively in this chapter the reasons why China has become the anchor of capitalist accumulation in Asia. This would require full research on why the capitalist world trusted the intentions of Deng Xiaoping's policies. Our own view is that in the case of China's entrance into the capitalist world the old Mao adage "politics in command" actually operated from the US side. Consider that when the *4 Modernizations* were launched in 1979, China and the United States were together on all the main international issues in Asia and shared opposition to the Soviet Union. They agreed in supporting the ousted Khmer Rouge in Cambodia, both vehemently opposing Vietnam's intervention there; they agreed in supporting the armed opposition to the Soviet Union in Afghanistan and they also agreed in supporting Pakistan relatively to India. Given that throughout most of the 1980s the cold war had been revived by the presidency of Ronald Reagan, the China card played a crucial role in US policy. Hence Washington was willing to grant credibility to China's capitalist reforms particularly as they were intended not just to open China to some kind of local ersatz capitalism, but especially to the multinational companies, both directly and indirectly through outsourcing.

Moving now back to economic reasoning, once this process of development of Chinese markets kick started the new industrialization, owing to the size of its internal markets, the process of structural adjustment spread throughout the economy, leading to the development of many of the stages of production involved in manufacturing. As a result of these structural changes, inter industry linkages were kept domestic, so that expansion in one sector fed through to increased demand for other developing sectors. As a result any improved export performance fed into a cumulative process spreading the benefits of industrialization through the economy, with minimal leakages abroad. (Kaldor 1989)

The first step to take for the assessment of the role that the PRC has been acquiring in influencing the tendencies in world capitalism will be to ascertain the degree of sustainability of accumulation process in China, not in relation to some normative objectives but in relation to the Marxian and Post-Keynesian notion of profitability and effective demand. This requires the analysis of dualism based on the following criteria which cannot be obtained from orthodox economics.

To what extent does China's accumulation validate or not the conditions of *comparative productivity change advantages* (Pasinetti, 1981)? These have nothing to do with the static fixed factor endowments theory of comparative advantages. Instead it is a rather Smithian dynamic principle according to which if productivity increases are not retained within the same economic system (defined in terms of its polity, currency and institutions), but are instead leaked abroad mostly through fall in export prices, the country will develop in a dualistic manner without an adequate growth of domestic demand. The adequacy of the growth of domestic demand is not measurable by aggregate GDP figures but by whether or not the growth of productivity in the leading sectors flows back in roughly equivalent increases in wages and productivity in the domestic sectors. While such a gap cannot be avoided its systemic persistence and widening will set a limit to the expansion of per capita demand of wage earners creating conditions of chronic underutilization of capacity. The *principle of comparative productivity change advantages* has a special corollary which works in reverse. We have seen that the country as a whole may find itself on an unwarranted accumulation path if the productivity of the dynamic, say exporting, sectors does not flow back as greater domestic purchasing power but is instead leaked abroad through persistently lower export prices. The corollary lies in that whenever the growth of productivity of the dynamic export oriented sectors exceeds significantly the growth of productivity of the equivalent sectors abroad, the sectors in the foreign countries cannot hold onto their own productivity growth and must shed workers as well as undertake capital flows externally. The paradox is that a less advanced industrial country has a much greater chance of developing sectors whose productivity growth is both much higher than that of the rest of the domestic economy and that of the corresponding sectors abroad.

The PRC is a unique case in the world of transfer of global capital towards an economy which in absolute terms is now bigger than France's but in relative per-capita terms is so much lower than any of the advanced OECD countries. And this situation is likely to last for quite a long period. There have been other cases of industrial development for large countries such as Brazil, Mexico and India but neither in per capita nor in absolute terms have they ever surpassed any of the big capitalist countries of Europe and of course Japan. Japan, when it began to outgrow in absolute terms the large Western European countries it did so when it reached the stage of industrial maturity with a high wage level per unit of labor. The PRC by contrast can stay for a long time on the lower end of the scale with the dynamic sectors operating according to the *principle of comparative productivity change advantages* and its reverse corollary for the industrialized world. The PRC can therefore be in absolute terms bigger than, say, Germany, while remaining in per capita terms below Turkey.

International oligopolies have here a double edged role. On one hand by investing in productive facilities they expand the array of sectors having dynamic productivity growth, but on the other hand, they tend to reinforce the dualistic features of that growth domestically and the corollary internationally. Let us make the following cases.

a) A multinational company invests in China for the local market as it is now the case for autos. In this instance the capital goods will be provided by the parent company and the domestic Chinese economy will supply the basic commodities. Profits will spring mostly from the low wage costs and from productivity gains. By contrast if after a while the foreign company starts ordering its capital goods from Chinese industries, then there is a structural flow back both in terms of productivity growth and in terms of the expansion of the array of domestic sectors. But, and this we know from advanced economic theory, even orthodox, there is no guarantee that market mechanisms will ensure such a transition. It will more likely depend on the determination of the central authorities to steer investment of multinationals into developing the capital goods sectors in China.
b) Assume a foreign multinational invests in order to export by supplying itself with capital goods ordered from the home country or from any of the high wage countries of the US/Europe/Japan "Triad". Then this means that the foreign multinational is only interested in using the lower wage costs coupled with its own price making capacity in the developed countries (markets). This case, which according to research seems to be quite significant as only 15% of the total value added of China's exports is from domestic production, just perpetuates dualism while hollowing out the corresponding sectors abroad.
c) Assume a foreign multinational subcontracts/outsources its orders in China. There may be then a greater use of domestic inputs, but the entire operation is based on the principle of maximizing the "benefits" stemming from low wages and from the price making powers of the multinational in question.

Both in the case of (b) and of (c) the expansion of per-capita income and demand in China is constrained by the strategic role played by low wages, so that demand may expand absolutely but less so in per capita terms, while at the same time hollowing out the productive basis of the advanced countries. Cases (b) and (c) are for the long term objectives of the PRC's authorities to transform China into a significant industrial and military power to be discarded. Yet they may nest into the Chinese political economy thereby creating a permanent structural fault or weakness in the way per capita income and demand progress in the country. Given the Communist Party of China's orientation to have a sort of "new economic policy" (NEP) with world capitalism, the best solution is to have multinationals which (i) invest in China for both the domestic and the export markets and (ii) produce in China the capital goods and the required technologies or at least a growing part of them. This eventuality however does not solve the question of the hollowing out of the advanced countries. At the same time however even for China reliance on foreign multinationals cannot continue for too long a period because the crucial decision making processes and crucial technological development will occur outside it. Thus only by creating its own oligopolistic multinationals will China find itself in a position of being on the path of becoming an advanced industrial and military power. But if China does not get substantial technological transfer to be incorporated into its own corporations, that is, not just for the foreign corporations operating in China, the country will not escape easily from dualism and technological dependency, while at the same time generating a hollowing out of the productive system of other economies.

Let us now consider the gravitation of foreign direct investment to China coupled with the corollary of the special principle regarding productivity change advantages. The corollary establishes the case for the hollowing out process and this leads to insurmountable problems of effective demand for the advanced countries. At this stage in what way is the link between the State and capital accumulation modified? According to the Marxian view the State defends the interests of capital in a sometimes complex process of mediation but also sometimes quite straightforwardly. Since the so called globalization cum privatization phase set in, we are in the straightforward phase and the State only mediates between the different capitalist groups. But if productive bases are hollowed out and the interests of US/Europe/Japan based multinationals and outsourcing companies resides in China, the material ground of the advanced states weakens. A contradiction develops between what is required from the State and its material capacity.

The Chinese State cannot be a substitute for the global role that the State of the advanced capitalist countries is for world capital and for the reproduction of capitalist relations: First, because it does not have the power to play that role. Secondly, and because of the first reason, the Chinese State if it really intends to stay on an advanced capital accumulation path must strengthen the material basis of its own political capacity. This will make it privilege Chinese corporations and support them in the competition on foreign markets against the very foreign companies that are investing in China. Hence lured by the Chinese State but not necessarily defended by it, the gravitation of world capitalism towards China creates a conflict between the multinationals of the Triad and their respective states in Europe, Japan and the US. In general there is no political or economic solution to this type of conflict which is already manifesting itself since the EU has defined a red danger zone encompassing the sectors which are exposed to the hollowing out process.

The US is the most vulnerable country, and this is well known. The US is counting on two factors:

1. The military one which brings about the control of crucial energy areas and prolongs the dollarization of energy products.
2. The willingness of the PRC's central bank to refinance US external deficits. Yet this second aspect contains a major inconsistency. In order to secure beyond any doubt the refinancing of its external deficits by Beijing's Central Bank US authorities must accept the institutional politicization of their external deficits. In other words the clearance of the deficit becomes a political not an economic issue. If it were left to economics the refinancing would not be guaranteed. This explains why the US monetary authorities while favoring the

opening and liberalization of the capital accounts in the balance of payments of the Asian countries under direct US influence, are quietly supportive of the Chinese position of keeping their own capital accounts closed. And recently, the previous Federal Reserve chairman, Mr. Greenspan, also came out against freeing the exchange rate of the Yuan. But this factor weakens the state capacity of the US in favor of China.

The contradictions between China and the US can be understood by referring to the different strategic view about China in the world economy held by US multinationals and the Chinese Communist Party. For the former China's position is simply that of a low cost producer, for the latter the inflow of capital and direct investment is part of a policy with world capitalism and therefore it is supposed to be just a stage in the transformation of China into a leading industrial and military power. In the long term these two views are not compatible while at the same time the actual role of China contributes both to the profits of, say, Walmart, and to the hollowing out of the US and of its State capacity.

Europe is in an intermediate position which reflects also the contradictions within Europe. The countries with heavy machinery sectors and telecommunications technologies (Germany with Austria and Switzerland, Sweden and Finland) whose trade balance in those sectors is highly positive are supportive of the Chinese pattern of growth. Financialized economies like the UK are also but for altogether different reasons. By contrast countries with still a large consumption goods sector such as Italy, Spain, Greece and France are increasingly at odds with China and they were behind the move to define a red zone of danger in terms of sectors vulnerable to being hollowed out. In this context the case of France is interesting because France is poised to sell to China its advanced weapons as well as public sector's goods such as railway technologies. Yet clearly they think that the hollowing out process is stronger than the expansion into China despite the fact that their automotive companies are heavily involved in the PRC.

At first sight East Asia and Japan are the least vulnerable because they have a substantial surplus with China. But these aspects will have to be explored in more details because reliance on exports towards China may actually create the conditions for their subsequent hollowing out. In fact a great deal of these are made by Japanese and Korean multinationals for investment purposes which will translate into a growing flow of exports from China back into Japan, Korea etc. There would be nothing wrong if the present flows of net exports were to be accompanied by significant export led growth in those countries. So that by the time exports from China become positive, those countries will have already achieved a high level of utilization of their own productive capacities. But this is not case especially for the most important of them: Japan. Furthermore exports towards China depend very much on the trade patterns between China and the US and between China and Europe. While China has changed the direct dependency of Japan and East Asia on net exports towards the U S, the process of integration is not China-centered since the effective demand loop is closed by China's net exports to the US. In this sense the PRC growth and the greater gravitation of East Asia's trade flows towards China do not change the basic picture of the US as defining the perimeter of realization.

Europe's stagnation is unlikely to be solved through the domestic boosting of effective demand. This phase is over in Europe since it is difficult in Europe to increase demand without empowering wage earners as there is much less room to channel the surplus towards sectors, such as the military industrial complex, which remain outside the range of wage earners. Hence Europe will require an increasing amount of net exports, a paradoxical situation since the greater an economic area becomes the smaller should be the importance of net external flows. But this is not the case for Europe where stagnation has acquired chronic features. Coupled with the increased importance of Chinese net exports towards the US, the problem of the refinancing of US external deficits is likely to become the catalyst of the various crisis tendencies operating in the present phase of capitalism.

In earlier work (Kriesler and Halevi 1996 and Halevi and Kriesler 1998), we considered the implications of Japanese surpluses for Asian development from the beginning of the post war period up to the beginning of the 1990s, concentrating on the role of effective demand. There we concluded that Japanese surpluses with the rest of Asia created an effective demand sink, leaking demand from that region and promoting strong stagnationist tendencies. Had the region been autarchic, the effect of this would have been to lead to low growth levels, with high levels of unemployment. The tendency was counteracted by the region's strong trade surpluses with the US, which acted as an external source of effective demand. An important additional consideration, which needs to be incorporated into this thesis, is the implications of the rise of China as a major international trading partner for effective demand in the region. As Hart-Landsberg and Burkett (Chapter 4, this volume) make clear, the emergence of China has effectively changed the structure and destination of Asian trade, but has not changed its reliance on the US as an external source of demand necessary to alleviate the region's stagnationist tendencies. In other words, the loop has changed, to incorporate China, but still ends in the US, so that there is the same problem with just one additional major link in the chain. This has been manifest by a number of important changes to trade. "China has increasingly reorientated its exports of manufacturing away from East Asia (minus Japan) and towards the two most important international markets, those of the US and the European Union" (Hart-Landsberg and Burkett, Chapter 4, this volume). As a result of the substantial increase in Chinese exports to these markets, exports from the rest of East Asia, the Association of South East Asian Nations (ASEAN), and the NIEs included, have fallen dramatically. In other words, Chinese exports to those areas have replaced those of the other Asian nations. On the other hand, East Asian exports have been reorientated towards China, so that over the 1990s, China's deficit with the area increased a thousand fold (Hart-Landsberg and Burkett, Chapter 4, this volume).

The capitalist development of China introduced new contradictions into the world system of accumulation. During the US-Japanese hegemony in the little Asia bordering China the contradictions were mainly connected to the neomercantilist orientation of Asian growth, a neomercantlism supported by the US itself over almost

40 years. The contradiction was mostly between the states involved, their national companies and the US and its multinationals. Now the contradiction is within the capitalist economies investing in China, and operates directly on the scale of the advanced capitalist world. Increased reliance on production stemming from branches operating in China undermines the connections between the State and the respective capitals in a fundamental way. How it will pan out we cannot tell as processes are always path determined. If, for example, there is a change in the willingness of America to absorb the trade surpluses of China, thus acting as an external source of effective demand then it is clear that the underlying stagnationist tendencies for the area will manifest themselves in the form of crisis lowering growth and employment throughout the region. However, it is not possible to forecast the actual outcomes, since they are dependent on economic, social and political factors which themselves will be determined by the paths of events. In particular, political attitudes in America and Europe are currently in a state of flux, and it is unclear what shape any emerging consensus, if there is one, will take. Clearly, however, it is the political consensus of these areas which will play a vital role in the economic future of Asia.

Conclusion

We can conclude by considering the significance of the emergence of China for the underlying, structural forces at work in the Asian region. As we have argued, these forces have reinforced domestic stagnationist tendencies, particularly due to the role of Japanese surpluses as a further leaking of effective demand from the other Asian economies. In the initial stages of growth and accumulation, it was the foreign external markets provided, in particular, by the US which prevented the region from collapsing due to long run problems with effective demand. The emergence of China has not essentially changed the stagnationist tendency of the Asian region. Rather it has led to changes in the structure and direction of Asian trade, but it has not changed the reliance of the region on external sources of demand (mainly the US) so as to prevent a slow down of growth and the emergence of mass unemployment. Although China has introduced new links into the chain of demand, it is not in itself an adequate source of effective demand for the region.

As a result, the underlying stagnationist tendencies of the region would lead to low growth and employment levels, except for the external sources of effective demand, dominated by America. Given the political climate in America, it is not clear whether, or for how long, it will continue serving this role, and, therefore, how long crisis in the area can be averted.

PART III
The South Korean Economy in Historical Perspective

Introduction to Part III

At the root of debates over the political economy of South Korean development and the possible crystallizing of the lessons of Korean development as a global development policy template are competing analyses of the historical experience both preceding and at the outset of South Korea's rapid industrialization. In his chapter, "Land Reform and Capitalist Development in Korea", Sang-Hwan Jang investigates the land reform experience in South Korea. Most analysts agree that land reform is essential to development and that South Korea's successful land reform played a major role in the country's rapid industrialization. However, in contrast to most scholars who claim that land reform in Korea was achieved only as a result of the Korean War, this paper argues that Korean landlords sold, at relatively low prices, a significant share of their holdings to their tenants even before the land reform legislation of 1950 was approved. Moreover, most of the remaining land transfer was achieved before the actual start of the Korean War fighting. The paper examines the social and political reasons for this unusual experience and the ways in which it laid the groundwork for South Korea's later, post-1960 rapid growth.

When the daughter of the late Park Chung Hee as leader of the conservative opposition challenged the left liberal leadership of Roh Moo-hyun the developmental record of General Park emerged as an important site of contestation in Korean politics. In their chapter contribution, "A Critical Appraisal of Economic Achievements under the Park Chung Hee Regime", Soohaeng Kim and Seung-ho Park re-appraise this record through the prism of debates on the developmental state carried on between the leading nationalist, statist, institutionalist, and left-Keynesian schools of thought on Korea. Kim and Park demonstrate how each school elides key aspects of the reality of the Park regime in their analysis and attributes these gaps to the conceptual frameworks the schools adopt. To this, Kim and Park contrast the Marxian class power perspective. They argue that only in this way can much of the mist shrouding Park's developmental pedigree be lifted. They then proceed to demonstrate how the facts of the Park regimes' developmental record fit neatly within the class power perspective they defend.

Chapter 6

Land Reform and Capitalist Development in Korea

Sang-Hwan Jang

Introduction

South Korea had accomplished rapid economic growth for over three decades, before the financial crisis in 1997-98. GDP grew by an average of 9% during the 1960s, 9.3% during the 1970s, and by nearly 10 % during the 1980s and the first half of the 1990s. At the same time, South Korea has been transformed into a highly industrialized country. The share of manufacturing in output and employment rose from only 10% in 1962 to well over 25% by the early 1990s.

What the main sources of rapid economic development and high economic growth were in Korea has long been the issue of high debate among many scholars in development economics and policy makers of developing countries around the world. The proponents of the so-called free market argued that the "magic of the market" was the most important factor for this success. Statists, who stressed the role of state for economic development (Hart-Landsberg and Burkett, 2001), argued the success accrued from effective government policies such as state-led and export-oriented industrialization policy. Amsden (1989) emphasized the importance of "industrialization through learning" initiated by the government in the case of South Korea

World Bank (1993) identified the East Asian Model as a successful mix of fundamentals and interventions. It agreed that South Korea extensively used industrial policy, but it also insisted on the importance of market-friendly policies such as ensuring low inflation and competitive exchange rates; building human capital; creating effective and secure financial systems; limiting price distortions; absorbing foreign technology. I want to stress that the state interventions of Korea were not simply responding to market failure such as economic crisis but engendering market operations themselves. When we adopt this view, the difference between the market proponents and statists would be not so decisive. Generally speaking, as Gershcenkron (1965) and many studies on economic history and economic development showed, state-led industrialization policy had been inevitable for almost all late industrialized countries, developed as well as developing countries. However, even if many developing countries introduced similar state-led industrial policies as South Korea, their performances were far different from the East Asian countries. So, we can see that state-led industrial policy is a necessary condition for rapid economic growth in Korea, but it is not a sufficient condition. Others argue that a favorable international environment for the East Asian development was the main source of South Korean success: open markets of developed countries for developing countries, massive aid endowments and public and private loans to developing countries, and so forth (Cumings, 1984). But, even though many developing countries enjoyed the same international economic environment few developed as did Korea

As for a concurrent argument over the contribution of colonial industrialization to post-liberation economic development, the fact is, Japanese colonial occupation cannot be justified. Colonial industrialization was fulfilled not by Japanese occupation but in spite of it. Japanese colonial government prohibited the Korean entrepreneurs to manage their own firms 1910-1919. After the Great Uprising of March 1, 1919 for liberation, it permitted only narrowest opportunities for them. Even though it did not exclude industrial development then that which did occur under the auspices of Japanese colonial administration was not that significant. Heo (1999) characterized economic growth under Japanese rule as "development without development". It means that development during Japanese rule never contributed to higher living standards among the Korean people. As Ho argues, it is not clear that the creation of economic infrastructure and rapid increase of agricultural and industrial production under the colonial period can be definitively linked to the post colonial economic development. So many important changes happened during the ten years after liberation: the division of the nation; United States (US) military government occupation; Korean War. These cataclysmic events made it difficult to link the legacy of the colonial period to post liberation development.

Therefore, it is incumbent upon us to investigate other factors to explain the successful growth of Korea and different performances among developing countries. It can be argued that the domestic initial conditions of each developing country at the time of industrialization were different: Class structure; natural resources endowment; accumulation of historical experiences of administrating the society, etc. It can be argued that initial conditions of South Korea were favorable for economic development: land reform in 1950 – abolishing the feudal production relationship; Korean War (1950-1953); providing the political base to repress the laboring class; the long history of Lee dynasty (1392-1910); accumulating the ability to mobilize resources; poor natural endowments and a four season climate pushing people to work hard to survive. Among them, it may be argued, land reform is possibly the most important factor.

As for the significance of land reform for economic development, the argument will benefit from a reference to the experiences of developed countries. Developed countries accomplished agrarian revolution from below as in the United Kingdom or agrarian reform from the above as in Germany. Galor et al (2003, 2005) argue that the distribution of land within and across countries affected the nature of the transition from an agrarian to an industrial economy generating diverging growth patterns across countries. They insist that some land abundant countries that were associated with the club of the rich economies in the pre-industrial revolution era and were marked by unequal distribution of land, were overtaken in the process of industrialization by land scarce countries and were dominated by other land abundant economies in which land distribution was rather equal. Theoretically, landowners have the economic incentives to resist growth enhancing educational expenditure. Their research, based on cross-state data from the High School Movement in the first half of the twentieth century in the US, uncovers empirical support for the negative effect of land inequality on public expenditure in education. In relation to this, Lee (1998) argues that, for South Korea, the expansion of education in 1945-61 contributed to high economic growth in 1960-70s. He explained that strong demand for education was motivated by the unusual homogeneity of Korean society brought out by the Liberation and the Korean War. However, Lee never considers the significance of land reform for his results.

Shin (1998) considered colonial industrialization and land reform to be the most crucial facets in the shaping of postcolonial Korean development.

> In addition to creating a more equitable social structure, Korean land reform had several significant, more direct, impacts on subsequent industrial transformation. First, it removed a centuries-old stumbling block to the rise of capitalist production relations by destroying a landlord-centered agrarian class structure. Second, by removing the once-powerful landed class, reform fostered structural conditions that enhanced the state autonomy and power crucial to subsequent industrialization. Third, it facilitated and completed the historical process of capital conversion from land to industry, started during the colonial period. Fourth, creation of a smallholder class structure produced surplus labor in rural society, which later supplied labor crucial for industrialization. Finally, land reform removed a major source of rural unrest in the first half of the 20th century and thus provided social and political stability. In short, land reform created structural conditions necessary for subsequent industrial development, including capital formation, state autonomy, a labor force, and social stability.

As Ki-Wook Shin remarked in the Session 52: Revisiting South Korea's Land Reform, at the 2001 AAS Annual Meeting, most scholars studying the economic development of Korea agree that land reform was instrumental to economic "take-off" in South Korea. It is said to remove a major obstacle to industrialization (i.e., regressive landlords), create a more equitable social structure, bring about social and political stability, enhance state autonomy, and create surplus labor, all crucial to capitalist development that took place in South Korea.

However, in spite of the significance of land reform for rapid economic development in Korea, its roots, processes, outcomes and influences have not been sufficiently examined, especially in works written in English. The purpose of this chapter then, is to investigate the historical meaning of land reform for capitalist development in Korea. Together with this, the chapter also tries to solve several issues related to the land reform itself.

Major issues related to land reform in Korea are as follows: First, what was the historical background contributing to successful land reform in Korea? Among many developing countries only few countries such as South Korea and Taiwan could fulfill land reform successfully after World War 2 (WW2). We must find out country-specific reasons for that. Second, precisely when was the land reform performed? In other words, when did the farmers actually get the distributed land? A related question is: "What is the relation between land reform and the breaking out of the Korean War"? Sakurai (1983) argued that land reform was not carried into practice until the breaking out of the War, June 25, 1950, because "Provisions for the Numbers of Family Workforce", which regulated the land size to be distributed according to the number of workforces of each farm household, was made public only June 23, two days before the Korean War. He argued that North Korea brought about the War on June 25 to carry out the land reform on its initiative before the South Korea government did it. But we must look into the total process of land reform from the promulgation of the law to the registration of the distributed land for farmers' account after all repayments – to ultimately verify his argument. Third, what were the terms and conditions of transactions for the landlords to sell their tenanted land to tenants before land reform? Many scholars insisted that landlords sold tenanted land to tenants coercively, by threatening them that land would be sold to other farmers if they would not buy the land. But we argue in this chapter that the political and social environment of those days was not favorable for the landlords. For Japanese imperialism which had supported them lost power by defeat of WW 2. Fourth, what is the historical significance of land reform for the agricultural development in Korea?

The procedure of this chapter is as follows: Section two surveys the economic and political background of land reform. Section three deals with the process of legislation and implementation of the land reform act. Section four analyzes the historical significance of land reform for agricultural and overall capitalist development in Korea.

Economic and Political Background of Land Reform

After WW2, the issue of land reform arose in most post-colonial countries. But only few countries, such as Taiwan and Korea, ultimately succeeded in accomplishing land reform. The background of the successful land reform in Korea seemed to be as follows: Feudal land ownership relations became obsolete for increasing agricultural productivity; political power of landlords who opposed the land reform became weak, on the one side; power of the bourgeois and the peasant (tenant-farmer) who demanded and carried out land reform became strong, on the other side.

The Economic Background

Firstly, there are important economic indicators to be considered in the historical background of land reform. In Korea, 77% among total population were employed in agricultural sector just after the liberation, and the rational resolution of the land problem was the most crucial problem that the new government was compelled to solve. Conflict between the various political parties and their struggle for political power rose basically from the conflict of interests surrounding the policies for the land problem.

The Land Census of 1910-23 under Japanese colonial rule basically established the landlord-tenant relationship that held at the time of liberation in 1945. Land Census included the physical measurement of arable land and the identification and registration of land ownership. The main features of it were landownership by a few big landlords, a petty tenant farming cohort, and high rate of rent payment in kind. The concentration of land ownership in the hands of landlords was accelerated during the period of severe tenancy in which a nationwide average of 50-60% of the crop to be paid in kind as rent was imposed on tenants in addition to the payment of land taxes on behalf of their landlords. As a result, the number of tenants among all farm households increased from 39% during 1913-17 to 56% in 1938. The tenanted land area also expanded from 1.6 million chungbo (one chungbo is equivalent to 0.992 hectare) in 1914 to 2.6 million chungbo (including North Korea area) in 1938.

Modern land ownership was established as the institution of Principle of "exclusive ownership for one property" in outward appearance but it was fundamentally "semi-feudal" land ownership. Most of the farmland was owned by a small number of landlords. Most farmers were tenants using traditional technology and paying rent amounting to more than 50% of gross revenue. Most tenant farmers were dominated by their landlords in terms of economic status as well as social position.

In South Korea, in the last months of 1945 just after the liberation there was a serious food shortage problem. Potential increases in food production were hindered by the tenant system. 1,450 thousand chungbo among total 2,230 thousand chungbo was tenanted land. Landlords controlled all the surplus labor of peasants under semi-feudal land ownership conditions so the development of agricultural productivity

Table 6.1 Land Area and Farm Households under Tenancy

	Land Area [a] (1000 chungbo)	Farm households [b] (1000 household)
Japanese-owned land under tenancy (A)	230 (282) [c]	554 [d]
Korean-owned land under tenancy (B)	1,220	882 [e]
Sub-total (A+B)	1,450(64.2%)	1,436(70%)
Total (South Korea)	2,230(100%)	2,041(100%)

Source: a) Bank of Korea, Annul Report of Korean Economy, 1948, pp I-29.b) Bank of Korea, Annul Report of Korean Economy, 1948, pp I-375.c) Including non-farm land, estimated as of February 1946, MOAF, 1970, p.352. d) As of February 1946, MOAF, 1970, p.340. e) Residual number. Because statistics of 1945 were not available

remained repressed. Added to this, supply shortages of fertilizer, farming machines and agricultural chemicals led to a decrease in agricultural production.

On the food demand side, so many Koreans who had left the country for foreign lands (Japan, Manchuria, etc.) in the period of Japanese rule, returned to Korea and their homes after the war. This seriously aggravated the food shortage problem. So US military government in Korea was forced to reintroduce the rice collection policy which had been highly condemned by the Korean peasants.

Hungry citizens and tenant farmers attacked the landlord class and government offices. The October Uprising of 1946, which broke out from North Gyeongsang province, spreading to other rural areas for about 2 months, was basically caused by the food shortage problem and the complaints of peasants to the suspension of land reform. Unless the government could solve this tenancy problem the problem of social unrest and food shortage was not going to be settled. Encouraging the farmers to increase the yield by distributing to them tenanted land by Land Reform was the most effective policy for that.

Political Background

Land reform can be carried out when the power of the landlord becomes weak and the power of the bourgeois and the peasant (tenant-farmer) is strong. In South Korea, the tenant farmers' struggle for land reform was strong by the accumulated historical experiences and the influence from North Korean land reform. Compared to this, the power of landlord class that had collaborated with the Japanese imperialists was rapidly weakened by the defeat of Japan in the WW2. Responding to this class conflict, the bourgeois class of US that governed Korea after liberation and new Korean government decided to implement the land reform.

Land Reform of People's Democratic Type in North Korea

The Soviet-backed North Korean authorities faced land reform at once and a central decree legalized all previous action taken spontaneously, with sweeping provisions "bestowing the right to exploit the land to those who cultivate it". On March 1946, the North Korea provisional government enacted the Land Reform Act. All Japanese and Korean collaborator-owned land, continuously tenanted land, and the land 5 chungbo above owned by the Korean landlord and religious organizations were confiscated without compensation. Confiscated area was 1,325 thousand chungbo from 422,646 household. It occupied 52% of the total arable area in North Korea and 85% of landlord owned land. These lands were distributed in their entirety to the peasants free of charge. Responding to the land reform by the government almost all landlords gave up with no resistance and fled to South Korea. So, the North Korean provisional government could fulfill the radical land reform with ease and rapidity. But the right of farmers on the distributed land was severely limited. They could only hold the "right to till" and could not sell their land. So the land reform of North Korea can be categorized as land reform of a "peoples democratic" type.

The news of Land Reform in North Korea was broadcasted by mass media and received high praise from the tenant farmers of South Korea. Junnong (National Federation of Farmers' Association), a major national farmers' organization, evaluated its concrete economic content as the fundamental method for real liberation. Democratic National United Front argued the land reform plan of North Korea was progressive, total and democratic. Establishing different systems in two areas of one country meant that severe class struggle would ensue. US military government and the new Syngman Rhee government could not but implement land reform in the face of support of farmers for North Korean land reform and possible support for the social system of North Korea should the US only back bourgeois reform in the South.

The Left and Peasant Struggle for Land Reform

After liberation, the leftist political power was very strong. According to investigations of public opinion conducted by the US military government on August 1946, among 8,453 interviewees, 70% preferred socialism and 7% preferred communism. Before US forces arrived in Korea Korean peasants tried to establish democratic government by organizing People's Committees with laboring classes on the initiatives of the left, anti-Japanese resistance. Communists and left-oriented nationalists took the leadership of the Preparatory Committee for Independence and the Korean Democratic Republic a voluntary organization for new nation building. The left and peasants had pushed anti-feudal democratic revolution of land distribution. In autumn 1945, Junnong advised tenants to pay only 30% of the crop as rent (the 3 : 7 system) until land reform.

After North Korea accomplished radical land reform on March 1946, Junnong urged that (1) "land be distributed to peasants", (2) "transfer of land ownership be prohibited", (3) "Japanese and national traitors' owned land be confiscated", and (4) "landlords' land exceeding five chungbo be confiscated, and if they want to cultivate land themselves, the same amount of land as peasants be allowed to them" (Choson Inminbo [Korea People's Daily] March 16, 1946). De facto Guerilla warfare began after the people's uprising of October 1946 was crushed. It threatened the life of the landlords and accelerated the land reform.

Land Reform Policy of Landlord Class

After the liberation from Japanese rule the political position of the landlords in Korea became weak because people blamed them for their collaboration with Japanese invaders in the colonial period. Meeting hot hostility from the tenant farmers, they could not but feel somewhat guilty for their behavior of severe exploitation under Japanese rule. Landowning class formed their own political party, the Korean

Democratic Party (KDP) in 1945 to respond to the difficult political situation after the liberation. At first, they naturally opposed the land reform and proposed the policy detail, "Restricting extreme landownership and establishing equal tilling right for the farmers".

However, in the face of the land reform of North Korea and subsequent change of the US military government policy to favor land reform in the US controlled South Korea, the KDP changed their position and ultimately accepted the reform. In September 1996, KDP announced their new land reform policy: Distributing to the farmers the farmland confiscated or purchased with suitable compensation; payment by the farmers for the distributed farmland on long period installment; enacting of the Farmland Act to prevent re-concentration of ownership. Yu Jin-O recollected that Kim Sung-Su, the top leader of KDP agreed to "the land reform with compensation and payment" when he visited Kim and told him, "The original land policy of the communist party is nationalization of the land. Their public policy of land reform without compensation and payment is cheating the farmers…[L]and reform with compensation and payment is the best way to hold the communist party in check" (Kim et al, 1989, 439). They also demanded that enough compensation be paid for the expropriation of their farmland and that the government was obliged to help them transform themselves into industrial capitalists.

Land Reform Policy of the United States Military Government

The main objective and task of United States Military Government in Korea (USMGIK) was to prevent the communist and leftist from taking power in South Korea. So it outlawed the leftist People's Republic and all its local organizations and tried to weaken the political power of the leftist camp by seeking the support of farmers. On October 5th 1945, USMGIK promulgated public Ordinance No. 9 which restricted farmland rent to one-third of total crop and required written lease agreements between landowners and tenants. Its target was to preempt the Junnong's movement which demanded that the rental rate be restricted to 30% of the crop which was to be paid in money not in kind. However, USMGIK did not have adequate administrative enforcement mechanisms thus the rent restriction ordinance was widely violated except in areas where tenants had some power and, in fact, already were paying only about one-third of their crop.

USMGIK acquired farmlands formerly owned by the Japanese through Shinhan Gongsa (New Korea Corporation), a public organization established in February 1946 to manage "enemy-owned" properties. The vested land area was 282 thousand chungbo, 13.4% of total farmland. Farmers tilling the vested land were 554 thousand, 26.8% of total farm households. USMGIK hesitated and postponed implementing land reform in contrast to the rapid land reform of North Korea. USMGIK worried about possible unrest and giving bolstering the chance of the People's Committee camp if it performed the land reform without establishing a firm administrative ability in the countryside.

However, the US had changed their position on the question of land reform in Korea to reflect a more positive line. First, it wanted to construct a barrier against communism and the leftists to secure South Korea from the political and ideological competition of the communist camp as North Korea, which successfully won support and legitimacy from accomplishing land reform peacefully. Second, it did not have the demand to import massive amount of rice from Korea as Japan, so it had no demand to protect the landlord class. Instead, it had strong motive to export its surplus agricultural product to Korea. The existence of landlord class would be unfavorable for that.

In September 1946, USMGIK announced that one of its major objectives was to implement land reform that would replace wide-spread tenancy with full ownership of the land by the individual farmer. On March 23, 1948, USMGIK Governor signed Ordinance No. 173, to prevent the rise of communist peasant movement and to get the support of the tenant farmers for the first election to be held on May 10, aimed to form new South Korea government. By this ordinance all vested land formally owned by the Japanese and transferred to USMGIK was distributed to the present tillers by the newly established National Land Administration (NLA), which had taken over the properties owned by Shinhan Gongsa. NLA began to sell the vested land to tenants in the following manner: The vested land was to be sold to its present tenants. Priority was given to those who had actually cultivated the land as tenants on NLA land as of March 1, 1948 and who wished to purchase it. Each tenant was allowed to purchase up to 2 ha of land. The payment for the land was to be equivalent to 3 times of the average annual yield of the farm, and was to be paid in 15 annual installments in kind.

Three times of the average annual yield of the farmland as the amount of payment was the market price of the farmland at that time. During Japanese occupation period, farm land price was 5-6 times of annual yield. But it dropped to 3 times of annual yield after liberation in 1945. Landlords did not want any more to buy the farmland but only wanted to sell out the land, and the farmers did not have enough money to buy the farmland. The landlords and the peasants anticipated the official distribution of farmland in the near future. This increasing supply and contracting demand of farm land pushed the market price of it down to 3 times annual yield. Interestingly, the situation of class struggle had changed the transaction price of the tenanted land. In this respect, it could be argued that USMGIK implemented "market-based" land reform, "confiscation with full compensation, distribution with payment". But later, by the Agricultural Land Reform Amendment Act of 1950, the payment amount for vested land was to be based on the same criteria as the repayment amount for the land owned by Korean landlords, 1.5 times annual yield to be paid in 5 annual installments in kind.

NLA was to continue to extend production credit and family emergency credit at low interest rates to the tiller-purchasers and also to continue assisting them with the improvement of farmland. The Vested Land Management Special Account was opened as a separate book-keeping system designed to properly manage the collection of repayments from new land owners and to control land development expenditures. This Account was incorporated into the Land Reform Special Account in 1952.

The USMGIK's redistribution of the vested land influenced the tone of every political party's land reform policy and promoted landowner's selling out lands. It provided the new government with an effective model for the land reform of Korean-owned land.

Land Reform Policy of New Korea Government

President Syngman Rhee of new government established in August 1948 basically followed the land reform policy of USMG. He was compelled to secure loyalty from the people to respond to the influences from North Korea. At the same time, he wanted to reduce the political power of his rival, landowning class. And he wanted to get the support of the farmers who occupied the majority of the population at that time to preserve long lasting political power. President Rhee appointed Cho Bongam, a former communist, progressive politician, as the first Minister of Agriculture and Forestry to secure thorough land reform.

Cho represented the land reform proposal of the moderate. In 1946, Collaboration between the Left and the Right made 7 principles of land reform: confiscation with compensation, purchase on gradual decrease, and distribution without payment etc. It was the symbol of the compromise between the Left and the Right. But land reform bill of expropriation of landowner with compensation and distribution to tenants with repayment was raised to the Interim Legislative Assembly on February 1947. As Pang (2001) argued, "progressive nationalists" advocated state intervention in the economy and cooperation among opposing classes. Such views of progressive nationalists influenced land reform in South Korea after 1945. Some of them worked as the reform-minded bureaucrats in the Ministry of Agriculture and Forestry of the Rhee government who were instrumental to enacting and executing land reform.

Legislation of Land Reform Act and its Implementation

Legislation and Revision of Land Reform Act

In December 1946, the USMGIK formed Korea Interim Legislative Assembly (not truly elected, but mostly appointed by the USMGIK) and tried to deal with land reform problem. In December 1947, the Land Reform Bill was raised to the Interim Legislative Assembly. But the Interim Assembly composed of the vested interests, refused to enact it on the excuse that the new Korea government must perform land reform. So USMG decided to implement land reform for the vested land alone in March 1948, as noted above.

In May 1948, the new National Assembly of the Republic of Korea (ROK) was formed by the general election and the Assembly promulgated the ROK Constitution in July 1948. Article 86 for agricultural land reform was listed in the Constitution as following: "Farmland shall be distributed to self-tilling farmers. The method of distribution, the extent of possession and the nature of restrictions of farmland shall be determined by law." Thus, the land-to-tillers principle was incorporated into the Constitution and the old exploitative form of tenancy became unconstitutional. The Ministry of Agriculture and Forestry submitted the Land Reform Bill on November 1948. There were hot debates among the congressmen and the government, about the ceiling of land ownership, amount of compensation for the landlords and repayment by the farmers, the numbers of years for compensation and repayment. There were various proposals for the Land Reform Bill. Among them, the bill of Ministry of Agriculture and Forestry made public by Cho Bong-Am was most favorable to the tenant farmers and the bill of National Assembly (Industry Committee mostly composed of the landowners) and its Amendment Act was most favorable to the landowners (Table 6.2). Finally, Agricultural Land Reform Act was enacted by the Assembly in June 1949. Agricultural Land Reform Amendment Act (ALRAA) was enacted on March 10, 1950.

Table 6.2 Proposals of Various Land Reform Bill

(% of Annual Yield)

	Vested Land (USMG)	MAF Bill	Office of Planning Bill (government)	National assembly Bill	First Act (1949.6.21)	Amendment Bill (Industry Committee)	Amendment Act (1950.3.10)
Ceiling of ownership	2 chungbo	2 chungbo	3 chungbo	3 chungbo	3 chungbo	3 chungbo	3 chungbo
Years of compensation	15 years	10 years [1]	10 years	10 years	5 years	6 years	5 years
Amount of compensation	300	150	200	300	150	240	150
Amount of annual compensation	20	15	20	30	30	30	30
Years of repayment	15 years	6 years	10 years	10 years	5 years	8 years	5 years
Amount of repayment	300	120	200	300	125	240	150
Amount of annual repayment	20	20	20	30	25	30	30
Government subsidy	-	30	-	-	25	-	-

Note: 1) after 3 years of deferment
Source: Kim et al., 1989, A Study on the History of Farmland Reform, Korea Rural Economic Institute (KREI).

Based on the Constitution, the Agricultural Land Reform Amendment Act was drafted and actually became effective on March 10, 1950. The important measures of the ALRAA were as follows: The government bought farmland owned by non-farmers, according to the principle of land-to-the-tiller. Maximum farm size was set at 3 ha, and any farmland in excess of this limit had to be sold to the government.

Farmland sold to the government was distributed to small farmers and former tenants who wished to continue farming. Farmers who received land from the government were to repay the price of the land to the government within five years. The government was to compensate landlords for their farmland. The major points of the new system were the maximum limit in the size of land holdings, and the institutionalization of the land-to-the-tiller principle.

Why was the compensation and repayment decided at 1.5 times of annual yield? Market price of paddy land was 6 times annual yield in around 1940, that of dry land was 5.5 times annual yield. But it dropped to 3 times annual yield after liberation, and the private transaction price between the landlords and her tenants was 1-2 times annual yield. It was about 30% lower than the general market price, considering the right of cultivation for the tenant farmers

Why was the ceiling of land ownership decided at 3 chungbo per farm household? The Land Reform Act prescribes the land of under 3 chungbo of self-cultivating or self-managing farm household should not be appropriated. Several young progressive congressmen proposed a revised bill which state that a ceiling which is not to be appropriated must be dropped to 2 chungbo. The grounds of their argument was that, on the condition that average area cultivated by farmer is around 1 chungbo, if the ceiling was decided at 3 chungbo, the equality of land ownership could not be secured and that area could not be cultivated with the help of farmhand. But the conservative congressmen supported the 3 chungbo bill and thus the 2 chungbo bill was not passed in the Assembly. The maximum farm size of 3 chungbo has been questioned by many policy makers and farmers' organizations, and it has been abolished in 1993.

Implementation of Land Reform

Farm Household Survey

Just after the enactment of the Land Reform Act on June 21 1949, the government conducted a survey on the situation of land ownership to identify the specific land to be distributed. Only 601,049 chungbo were identified as the tenanted land to be distributed to the tenant farmers (Table 6.3). It was far less than 1,220 thousand chungbo, the Korean-owned land under tenancy just after the liberation. During the period of 1945-1950, much of the tenanted land had been sold out by the landlords.

The Date of Implementation of Land Reform

As noted in the introduction, some argued that the Rhee Government did not begin implementation of land reform until one week before the Korean War broke out on June 25, 1950 (Sakurai, 1983; Putzel, 1992, 81). The process of land reform proceeded as follows: identification of the land to be purchased and distributed, purchase, distribution, dispute resolution, repayment by the farmers, compensation to the landlords, registering the land to each farmer's account. It can be argued that the

Table 6.3 Object Area of Distribution: Korean-owned Land (June 21, 1949)

	Paddy Land	Dry Land	Total	Number of Farm Household
A. Area of Farmland	1,236,559	834,018	2,070,577	2,473,833
B. Object of Distribution	363,132	237,917	601,049	-
Tenanted Land	361,918	235,511	597,429	526,195
Above 3 chungbo	1,323	2,406	3,619	-
B/A (%)	29.4	28.5	29.0	21.3

Source: Ministry of Agriculture and Forestry, Statistical Manual for Land Reform (1951, 42-43).

date of implementation of land reform must be the date when the government gave notice to the farmers about the distributed land and issued them written certificate of it. Jeong (2003) argued that the date of enforcement of land reform must be the date when government issued the repayment certificate to the tenants and land bonds to the landlords. However, it took some time to resolve the dispute between the landlord and tenant. And repayment by the farmers and compensation to landlords took a long time.

When we apply this definition to the time of implementation of land reform, it must be April 1950, before the Korean War. Provincial government office issued and released the certificate that informed each tenant of the specific land the government distributed to him, on the condition that the dispute about the decision would be resolved in due course. There were very few farmers whose distributed land would be settled according to "Provisions for the Numbers of Family Workforce" made public on June 23, two days before the break of the Korean War. For the upper ceiling of farmland ownership of 3 chungbo was somewhat large scale at that time. So issuing the certificate of distribution nearly meant the actual implementation of land reform. On May 27, 1950, Ministry of Agriculture and Forestry ordered provincial government to issue the bill for repayment to the farmers on June 9. Thus, some provincial government issued the bill for the repayment for the distributed land around mid June before the Korean War.

Land Reform by North Korean Government during the Korean War

North Korea government claimed that, by the end of August 1950, land reform was complete in the provinces of Gyeonggi, North and South Chungchong, North Cholla, and in most of South Cholla. And it is estimated that, by the time the North Korean Army withdrew to the North, 573,000 chungbo, or 95% of planned total had been redistributed according to the government land bill. According to Kim (2005), they organized 18,000 rural committee (more than 140 thousand members joined it) which made "basic investigation document for each farm household" and decided the land to be distributed. The principle was as follows: The land which the peasant bought from the Syngman Rhee puppet government or from the landlords must not be confiscated. But if nothing was paid for that land, it should not be recognized as being bought.

So it seems that they redistributed the land which South Korea government noted the tenant the land to be distributed to him before the War. But it did not have great meaning for the average farmers, because land reform by South Korea government was accomplished already. And the farmers can not exercise their full ownership for the distributed land. They had only the right to cultivate and did not have the right to sell it. It only added some few things, redistributing some land to farmhands, etc.

Distributed Area by Land Reform

Distributed area of Korean-owned farmland was 342,345 chungbo, farm households who received distributed land were 1,016,238 housholds. Distributed area of vested land from the Japanese was 262,502 chungbo, farm households who received vested land were 655,032 households. Total Distributed area was 604,876 chungbo, farm households who received any distributed land were 1,671,270 households (Table 6.4).

Table 6.4 Total Area of Distributed Land

(household, chungbo)

	Farm households	Number of plot			Distributed area		
		Paddy land	Dry land	Total	Paddy land	Dry land	Total
Purchased land	1,016,238	1,270,792	856,986	2,127,778	233,089	109,276	342,365
Vested land	655,032	883,043	459,000	1,342,043	188,746	73,756	262,502
Total	1,671,270	2,153,835	1,315,986	3,469,821	421,835	183,032	604,867

Source: Ministry of Agriculture and Forestry, "Table of Payment Amount for the Distributed Land", 1970.

Together with this, many tenant farmers were transformed to land-owned farmers by the land reform. Full land-owned farmers increased from 285 thousand (14.2%) in 1945 to 925 thousand (37.4%) in 1949, to 1763 thousand (80.7%) in 1951, and full tenant farmers decreased from 1,010 thousand (50.2%) in 1945 to 85 thousand (3.9%, estimated) in 1951(Kim et al., 1989: 1034).

Excluded and Pre-sold Area by Landlord

Korean landlords were not cut from one cloth but consisted of diverse groups from pure landlords, half-landlords/half-capitalists to agricultural capitalists. Their responses to agrarian reform during and after colonial rule were not monolithic but diverse and complex.

Landlords tried to escape the shock of land reform by selling out their tenanted land. It is estimated that they sold 713,000 chungbo, 49.2% of total tenanted area, 60.7% among the Korean-owned tenanted land, from 1945 to 1950 land reform (Kim et al., 1989, 1029). 63.8% were sold out from January 1948 to July 1949, after it became obvious that land reform to be executed in the near future (Table 6.5). But some large landlords, who had the experiences of managing non-farm enterprises during the Japanese rule, responded more sensitively to the change of the political situation for the land reform. For example, the family of Oh Gun-Ki in Chonnam province sold out 51.5% of their tenanted land from January to May in 1946 directly before and after the land reform in North Korea, March 1946. And among them they sold out 33.0% from November 1947 to March 1948, just after the sub-committee of Legislative Assembly proposed Land Reform Bill (Hong, 2001). The sale price of the tenanted land by the landlords was not favorable to them. It was about 100-200% of annual yield, cut 30% from the market price.

Table 6.5 Change of Tenanted Area before and after Land Reform

(1,000 chungbo, %)

Year	Total Farmland	Tiller-owned	Tenanted Area			Ratio of Tenanted area	Ratio of full tenants
			Korean-owned	Japanese-owned	subtotal		
Before Land Reform							
1945.12	2,226	779	1,174	273	1,447	65.0	48.9
1947.12	2,193	868	1,052	273	1,325	60.4	42.1
1949.6	2,071	1,400	597	74	671	32.6	21.0
After Land Reform							
1951.12	1,958	1,800	159(74)		159	8.1	-
1957	2,015	1,924	91		91	4.5	-
1960	2,041	1,798	243		243	11.9	6.7

Note: 74,000 chongbos in the ( ) among the tenanted area in 1951 is legally excluded area on the Land Reform Act.

Source: For 1945: The Korea Development Bank, Ten Years History of the Korea Development Bank (1955). For 1947: Ministry of Agriculture and Forestry, "Reference Materials for Land Reform" (1949). For 1949: Ministry of Agriculture and Forestry, "A Summary Sheet of Farm Household Survey" (1951). For 1951: Korea Rural Economic Institute (1989). A Study on the History of Farmland Reform in Korea. For 1957: Ban Sung-Hwan, "Empirical Study on the Transfer of Land after Land Reform," Studies on Agricultural Economics, Korea Agricultural Economics Association (1958). For 1960: Ministry of Agriculture and Forestry, Agricultural Census (1960; 1964).

Repayment for the Distributed Land

Repayment by the tenant farmers for the distributed land began from summer and autumn harvest of 1950, and ended in 1970. The quantity paid within the scheduled period (1950-54) was 792,609 M/T (unpolished rice base), only 59% of planned total. At the end of 1956, it rose to 81.2 % of the target amount. The reason for the delay were bad harvest, high burden of provisional land tax (15-28% of total harvest, 10-23% in case of distributed land) during the war, etc. Unpaid quantity to the year 1958 was decided to be paid in cash or the land bonds, much favorable conditions for the farmers, compared to paying in kind.

The amount of total repayment as 1.5 times of average annual yield was greatly advantageous for the beneficiaries, the tenant farmers. In the past, they had to pay one half of total yield each year without any prospect of getting the property right for the land. But now, they could get property right for distributed land by paying only 30% of annual yield for five years.

Compensation for the Purchased Land

Compensation was paid not in kind but in cash calculated by the regulated legal crop price. Government issued land bonds to the landowners for compensation for the purchased land. It ruled that government should pay 30% of average yield in cash evaluated at the annual legal government purchase price for five years. It was done following the rule of diminishing compensation. Diminished quantity was 113,165 M/T, about 10% of total compensation amount, 1,163,308 M/T.

Compensation had been suspended long. Compensated quantity within the scheduled period (1951-55) was only 49.8% of planned total. It rose to 85.1% in 1960. Total compensated quantity was 1,216,000M/T. It was 2,072,392,000 won in amount. Landowners suffered dual loss. One was from the difference between the legal price and market price, and the other was from the inflation by the suspension of the compensation induced by the suspension of repayment by the farmers. In 5 years, originally scheduled, only 49.8% were compensated, the remaining 50.2% was compensated not at current market price but at fixed rate of average legal price (142.5 won per one 'seok'[1] of unpolished rice) during 1950-54. As a result of this arrangement, it could be estimated that landowners had been compensated only about 10-25% of their rightful amount.

Aiming to weaken the landlords' opposition of the land reform, the government promised to protect the landowners who might be sacrificed by land reform and to help them to be transformed to industrial capitalists. Article 10 of Agricultural Land Reform Act regulated "the government can provide the landowners, who are appropriated their land by this Act, with the prior opportunities to participate in the business helpful to the economic development, according to their hope, ability, etc."

1 'Seok' is the traditional standard of weighing rice in Korea. One 'seok' is approximately 180 liters.

And article 31 of Enforcement Ordinance of the Act noted that "the landowner can apply to buy or participate in the enterprises such as government held manufacturing factories, mines, breweries, printing offices, polishing factories, orchards, nursery gardens, reclaimed lands etc., according to his hope and ability".

But in reality, almost all landowners could not be transformed into industrial capitalists except for a few large landowners. This is primarily because the scale of many landowners' property was small and they lacked ability to manage modern enterprises. As well, there were not enough manufacturing facilities for them to buy nor effective demand to promote economic development. According to Lee (1998), among 418 large landlords appropriated more than 20 chungbo, about 30% were estimated to be transformed to the industrial capitalists.

Land Reform and Capitalist Development in Korea

Abolishment of Semi-feudal Landownership

In the post colonial period, the type of land reform can be categorized into two types: "people's democratic land reform" and "bourgeois land reform". The change of land tenure without abolishing (semi-) feudal land ownership cannot be included in the category of land reform. Decrees and the policy of promoting self-owned farmers under Japanese occupation are basically not land reform either. Land reform in Korea was "bourgeois reform from the above". Its historical significance resided in, at first, abolishing semi-feudal landlords' ownership and establishing farmer's ownership. The specific historical character of it was anti-feudal, bourgeois democratic reform.

Land reform of 1950 was different from the Land Census Project (1910-18) under Japanese occupation. The Land Census Project included physical measurement of arable land and the identification and registration of land ownership. By the Land Census Project, the Japanese colonial government provided the ownership to the landlord class who had gathered the rent, but it deprived the tenants of the right of cultivation.

The bourgeois character of Land reform in Korea is obvious, considering that it chose the policy of confiscation with compensation and distribution with repayment, excluding the farmhands from the subjects to be distributed land. "Land to the Tillers" principle and the land-owning farming system had been established as a fundamental ideal of the farmland system since the Land Reform in 1950.

In comparing the composition of farm households by size of farmland under cultivation before and after the land reform, it is revealed that the percentage of households farming less than one chungbo increased from 75% in 1947 to 79% in 1953. Thus, it can be argued that the land reform contributed to the fragmentation of farm size in Korea (Table 6.6). But land reform must be distinguished from agrarian reform, targeted at the overall development of agricultural productivity and agricultural production structure.

Table 6.6 Farm Households by Farm Size under Cultivation (%)

Category of Farm	1945	1947	1951	1953	1960	1970	1973
Under 0.5 chungbo (A)		42.2	42.7	44.9	42.9	31.6	32.4
0.5-1.0 chungbo (B)	72.1	33.3	35.8	34.2	30.1	31.7	31.5
1.0-2.0 chungbo (C)		18.8	17.1	16.5	20.7	25.8	26.3
2.0-3.0 chungbo (D)	23.8	5.3	4.2	4.3	6.0	5.0	4.8
3.0 chungbo & over (E)	4.1	1.4	0.1	0.1	0.3	1.5	1.5
Non-crop farms	-	-	-	-	-	4.4	3.5
Total Farm Household	100.0	100.0	100.0	100.0	100.0	100.0	100.0
(A+B)	72.1	75.7	78.5	79.1	73.0	63.3	63.9

Source: Pak, (1956, 82) and Ministry of Agriculture and Forestry (1974, 28-29)

Increase of Food Supply though the Growth of Agricultural Productivity

Foreign aid much contributed to the farmland development project focused to irrigation facilities in 1950s, at same time two measures were arranged. One was the establishment of the Special Accounts for Land Reform Project, and the other was long-term borrowing by issuing Industry and Reconstruction Bond by the government.

Some part of fiscal revenue procured by the land reform was invested and contributed to improving the infrastructure of agricultural production. According to Special Accounts for Land Reform Project Act (April 2 1952), payments by the farm household for the distributed vested land, administration cost excluded, were directly invested into the land development project. By revising the Special Accounts for Land Reform Project Act (January 2 1958), payments by the farm household for the distributed Korean-owned land, after deducting the compensations for the landlords, were also invested to the construction of irrigation system. This was possible because the government received repayment in kind, but the compensation to the landlords was accomplished in cash calculated by the legal rice price. In other words, it was the government purchasing price instead of current market price.

Land Reform opened the possibility of agricultural productivity increase. But too much import (aid) of surplus agricultural produce from Unites States, expropriation by the provisional land tax, exploitation by usury capital, etc., hindered the realization of that possibility. But the confluence of all these factors came to a head in the 1960s. Let us compare the agricultural production performances in 1930-34 under Japanese colonial rule and those in 1960-64 after Land Reform. By expanding irrigation system, the ratio of rain-dependent paddy land decreased to 19.4% from

Table 6.7 Settlement of Special Accounts for Land Reform Project

(1000 won)

	Vested Land	Korean-owned Land	Total
Total revenue (a)	1,934,449	3,904,795	5,839,244
Repayment by farmers	1,696,537	3,618,683	5,313,220
Other revenue	237,912	286,112	524,024
Total expenditure	1,934,449	3,904,795	5,839,244
Compensation (b)	-	2,072,392	2,072,392
Administration cost	641,911	896,283	1,538,194
Agricultural Investment	975,930	724,990	1,700,920
Government revenue	316,608	211,130	527,738
Project Surplus (a-b)	1,934,449	1,832,403	3,766,582

Source: Kim et. al., (1989, 1054).

34.3%. Rice yield per 10a increased to 1.54 seok. Land utilization rate rose from 140.7% to 150.8%. The ratio of double-cropping use of paddy land rose from 21.7% to 46.6%. The area of cultivating vegetable and fruit expanded sharply. All of them can be evaluated as the development of a small commodity economy established by the Land Reform.

As for the effect of land reform on the improvement of agricultural productivity, Woo (2001) argued as follows: "It will be shown that Land Reform largely failed to raise agricultural productivity. This was primarily because the government failed to replace the role that landlords played in agriculture (providing crop information, credit, new technology etc.). Although land reform increased incentives for peasants and brought about rural stability, the government did not go far enough to establish proper institutions to take the leadership that many landlords took before reform. Thus the Rhee government largely failed to transfer potential benefits of the Land Reform into economic development in the 1950s". But it seemed this argument did not consider the fact that tenanted land under the Japanese rule was comparatively fertile land, so the extent of agricultural production increase on it could be smaller than farmer-owned land. Rice production increased from 2 million ton to 3.5 million ton in that period. And Land Reform provided the basis for the success of policies of food production increase in 1960s and 1970s. Particularly, when the government promoted the introduction of high yield rice species, the farmers responded sensitively to that and there were no adverse side effects such as increasing landless laborers.

Promotion of the Capitalist Industrialization

Abolishment of Feudal Status System

Land Reform decisively contributed to capitalist development in Korea. First, Land Reform secured the condition for the free movement of labor by destroying the feudal standing system that had existed previously. So-called "free labor" should be supplied for capitalist development through a dual process. Wage workers sprang out from the workforce freed from the fetters of standing system and at the same time from the concentrated ownership of property. The feudal status system was formally abolished by the Gabo Reform in 1894, but it actually persisted in the form of the resident servant or man-servant subordinated to the family of landlord class. Farmhands employed by large-scale or middle farmers were also in somewhat of a subordinated position. Tenants, who were legally free but economically not independent, were personally subordinated to landlord class in some aspects.

The personal relationships of domination and subordination were abolished by the Land Reform and the Korean War. When landlords were deprived of their land, they lost the power of domination over the rural workforce. Korean War accentuated the destruction of feudal standing system, but it might not easily have been destroyed without the economic revolution of land reform. As the result, the pre-modern class-consciousness almost completely disappeared in Korea in a fashion comparable to the developed countries. This social environment provided every individual with a high opportunity to give full play to their abilities and it also contributed to accelerating social mobility. This condition cannot is not something found readily in other developing countries (Jeong, 1995)

Supply of Well-educated Workers

Second, a well-educated workforce, such a crucial source of economic development, was engendered as an effect of land reform. Absent the burden of paying rent to a fundamentally extravagant and parasitic landlord class the farmers had the wherewithal to provide for educational expenses for their children. Many commentators allege that the driving force of Korea's high growth resides in its abundant cheap workforce of good quality. The composition of this workforce is primarily the children of farm households. In 1950-1960, they called the university "tower of cattle bones". It refers to the fact that many farmers suffered much, including selling their cattle to pay the tuition for their children's higher education. But, this fact can also be interpreted in terms of the farmer's actual financial ability to provide the high tuition.

The number of universities and colleges increased from 19 in 1945 to 63 in 1960 and their student enrollments increased from 7,819 to 97,819 in the same period (Table 6.8). The main background of this increase was the rise of the income level of the farmers who were transformed into land-owners by the land reform process.

Table 6.8 Increase of Students in High School and Above (1945-1960)

	1945	1952	1955	1960
Academic High School	50,343 (100)	59,421 (118)	141,701 (358)	164,492 (327)
Vocational High School	33,171 (100)	74,463 (224)	118,911 (358)	99,071 (299)
University and College	7,819 (100)	34,089 (436)	80,391(1,028)	101,045(1,292)

Source: Economic Planning Board, Population Survey 1960, Vol.1, (1963, 395).

At the same time, by the help of government education expenditure investment, the student population of elementary school and middle high school also increased sharply. As a result, among the countries of GNP per capita of approximately $90, the school attendance rate of 5-14 aged students in Korea was 59%, much higher than the average 22% in 1950s. During 1960-65, the school attendance rate of 15-19 aged middle school students in Korea was higher than the average, and the school attendance rate of higher education student in Korea is nearly the same level compared to countries, whose GNP per capita was 3-4 times higher than Korea.

Table 6.9 Increase of Students in Elementary and Middle School

(1000 person)

	Total Population	Elementary School Student		Middle School Student		Total	
		Number (B)	B/A (%)	Number (C)	C/A (%)	Number (B+C)	(B+C)/A (%)
1953	21,546	2,247	10.4	339	1.6	2,586	12.0
1954	21,913	2,664	12.2	420	1.9	3,084	14.1
1955	21,502	2,877	13.4	475	2.2	3,352	15.6
1956	21,350	2,921	13.7	359	2.1	3,380	15.8
1957	21,948	3,188	14.5	444	2.0	3,632	16.5
1958	22,524	3,262	14.5	398	1.8	3,660	16.2
1959	23,513	3,550	15.1	472	2.0	4,022	17.1

Source: Mason et al. (1980). Ministry of Education, Education Yearbook, various years.

This educated workforce contributed to the economic growth of the 1960-80s. During the period of rapid industrialization, many rural people moved to urban areas dramatically accelerating urbanization. The ratio of urban population among total rose from 18.4% in 1950 to 41.2% in 1970 and to 74.4% in 1990 (Table 6.10). The rural-to-urban migrants during 1960-75 were around 6,860,000 in total, 450,000 annually (Table 6.11). Among them well-educated young generations occupied the majority.

Table 6.10 Ratio of Urban Population and the Non-farm Employed (1950-1990, %)

	1950	1960	1966	1970	1975	1980	1985	1990
Urban population / total	18.4	28.0	33.6	41.2	50.9	57.3	65.4	74.4
Urban economically active population / total	-	24.6	32.7	37.8	42.6	52.5	63.3	-
Urban employed / total	-	21.9	29.7	36.9	40.6	50.6	62.5	-
Non-farm employed / total	20.6	34.3	42.8	49.2	51.0	62.2	72.2	81.7

Sources: Economic Planning Board, Population and Housing Census Report, various years.
National Statistical Office, Statistical Yearbook, various years
National Statistical Office, Second Special Survey of Employment Structure (1987).

Among the migrants to the city, the 5-34 aged occupied 60-80%. Particularly among the unaccompanied the ratio of the 15-24 aged was above 60-70%. The education level of the migrants to the city was higher than the average rural residents. The case study for 1966-70 showed that, as for the level of education of the migrants to the city, those whose education was the middle school and above was 45%, higher than 17.8% of the resident in country side. Because the Korean War established the strong political hegemony of capitalist class against the labor class, workers could not have basic rights of independent organization, collective bargaining and collective action until the great democratization uprisings in 1987. Domestic and foreign capitalists could employ a well-educated and obedient workforce during the period of high economic growth. It was much more favorable condition than existed in other developing countries.

Facilitating the Formation of Capitalist Class

After the liberation, USMGIK and the government of Korea privatized the vested properties confiscated from the Japanese and placed these at the disposal of a new capitalist class. Wealthy people, merchants and ex-landlords could buy these properties at favorable rates by paying land bonds. Among total land bonds issued to landlords, more than 50% were used for this purpose. In order to meet the difficult situation of a drastic drop in the value of their rent in money terms by high inflation many landlords sold their land bonds at the market price, far lower than its face value.

Favorable privatization of vested properties, together with foreign aid and preferential financing, as the main background for the early formation of *chaebols* (big family-controlled conglomerates) in the 1950s (Gong, 1993). *Chaebols* would

Table 6.11 Rural-to-urban Migrants (1965-1990)

(1,000 person, %)

	1965-70			1970-75			1975-80			1980-85			1985-90		
	M	Fm	Total	M	Fm	Total	M	Fm	Total	M	Fm	Total	M	Fm	Total
Rural-to-urban	896	940	1,827	806	949	1,754	1190	1334	2,524	1,125	1,300	2,424	1,128	1,201	2,329
Seoul	384	429	813	238	359	647	352	423	775	327	396	723	266	293	551
(ratio)	43.3	45.7	44.5	35.7	37.8	36.9	29.6	31.7	30.7	29.1	30.5	29.8	23.6	24.4	23.7
Capital Region	439	490	929	370	463	833	502	595	1097	498	594	1092	500	537	1037
(ratio)	49.5	52.1	50.8	45.9	48.8	47.5	42.2	44.6	43.5	44.3	45.7	45.0	44.3	44.7	44.5
Urban-to-rural	199	188	387	264	294	558	324	358	681	430	459	889	364	379	743
Net Rural-to-urban Migrant	688	752	1,440	541	655	1,196	866	977	1,843	694	841	1,535	764	908	1,586

Note: based on the place of residence 5 years ago.
Source: Economic Planning Board, Population and Housing Census Report (Section of the movement of population), various years, National Statistical Office, Population and Housing Census Report (Section of the movement of population), various years

Table 6.12 Education Level of Rural-to-urban Migrants (1965-90, %)

	1965-70			1970-75			1975-80			1980-85			1985-90		
	male	female	total	male	female	total	male	female	total	male	female	total	male	female	total
Illiteracy	4.8	13.4	9.5	4.0	10.2	7.7	3.1	8.6	6.2	2.3	7.7	5.4	1.7	7.3	4.7
Elementary	36.9	56.9	47.9	33.1	48.9	42.4	23.0	33.5	29.1	12.1	17.7	15.3	8.2	13.0	10.8
Middle school	27.3	20.6	23.6	30.1	28.3	29.1	31.2	35.9	33.9	25.4	32.4	29.4	15.3	18.5	17.0
High school	23.0	8.0	14.7	24.9	11.4	16.9	34.2	20.2	26.2	47.3	38.6	42.3	53.3	52.6	52.9
University	8.1	1.1	4.2	7.8	1.2	3.9	8.5	1.8	4.7	12.9	3.5	7.6	16.7	5.7	14.6

Source: Mason et al., 1980; Ministry of Education, Yearbook of Education, various years

play the role of the main capitalist actors in the period of high economic growth supported by the government.

As Hong (2001) argued, landlords' position in response to agrarian issues including Land Reform was far more complex and sophisticated. This is largely because Korean landlords were not cut from one cloth but consisted of diverse groups from pure landlords to half-landlords/half-capitalists to agricultural capitalists. Accordingly, their response to agrarian reform during and after colonial rule, was hardly monolithic, but diverse and complex. Almost all landlords simply lost out with the Land Reform but some landlords who were engaged in non-agricultural activities during the colonial period were able to transform themselves into industrial capitalists.

Conclusion

The Korean economy accomplished impressive economic growth for several decades since 1960. Some argue that this economic growth followed from strengthening free market mechanisms while others emphasize the role of the state and state-led industrialization policy. My argument is that the successful land reform was the most important foundation for yielding the favorable initial conditions contributing to rapid economic development of South Korea.

Among the various conditions of the successful land reform in South Korea the radical land reform of what I have dubbed the people's democratic model, of March 1946 in North Korea, was crucial. After liberation the landlord class could notregain sufficient political power to oppose the land reform because of their collaboration with Japanese imperialism. The USMGIK hesitated and postponed land reform in the early period for its hegemony was weak and the power of the leftist and peasant movement was very strong at the provincial level. But, after the land reform in North Korea, USMGIK changed its policy line to favor land reform. On March 1948 it distributed vested land from the Japanese to the tillers and this policy basically decided the procedure of land reform of Korean-owned land in the hands of the Syngman Rhee government of 1950. The main purpose of the land reform was to prevent people's democratic type land reform and subsequent social revolution by providing an alternative path of bourgeois type land reform.

The process of land reform in Korea in 1945-1960 abolished the feudal tenant system totally. It established a farming system based on independent land owners. Overall, it had the nature of anti-feudal, bourgeois democratic reform. The contributions of land reform to rapid economic development were as follows:

First, land reform brought about the increase of agricultural productivity by drawing in agricultural investment from the government and by offering important incentives to the farmers. As a result, the agricultural sector was able to supply food necessary to meet the increasing demand from the rampant industrialization and urbanization of the 1960s and 1970s.

Second, land reform contributed to the bringing up of well-educated workers by enabling the farmers to provide their children with the necessary education to be an efficient labor force. This, well-educated, efficient and, of course, obedient workforce, provided the most favorable conditions for the industrial capitalists.

Third, land reform promoted the formation of a new capitalist class. The wealthy persons purchased the vested property from the government with land securities which they in turn bought at heavily discounted cheap prices from the landlords.

Chapter 7

A Critical Reappraisal of the Park Chung Hee System

Soohaeng Kim and Seung-Ho Park

Introduction

South Korean (hereafter Korean) society experienced a combination of high economic growth and terrible political dictatorship during the period of Presidents' Park Chung Hee (May 1961 – October 1979) and Chun Doo Hwan (August 1980 – October 1987). The peculiar socio-economic system that emerged during the period is designated by us as the Park Chung Hee system or the Park system. The Park system was instated in the aftermath of the coup led by General Park Chung Hee on the 16th of May in 1961 and came to an end in October of 1987 due to the successful civil-society democratic movements and massive workers' struggles against capitalists.

A reappraisal of the Park system as Korea's version of the so-called Asian development model[1] became an important topic of academic interest when the Korean economy spiraled into crisis at the end of 1997. The two major competing views on the general causes of the crisis were each based on their own particular interpretations of the Park system. One view maintained that the moral hazard and the crony capitalism formed under the Park system was the key cause of the crisis. On the other hand, the opposing view argued that dismantling of the peculiarities of the Park system (e.g. the wide-spread state interventions) due to national and international efforts at liberalization of the financial and currency markets brought about the crisis.[2] Currently, discussions on the Park system have re-emerged as an important topic of Korean national debate, partly because the late Park's daughter has become the leader of the opposition party, the Grand National Party (GNP), and partly because economic growth has faltered.

In this chapter, we first introduce and criticize the three main perspectives on interpreting the Park Chung Hee system. They are *autonomous national economy perspective*, *developmental state perspective* and *developmental dictatorship*

1 The Asian development model contains the following three interrelated features. Firstly, the industrial sector finances its investments mainly through bank loans rather than issuing bonds and stocks. Secondly, the government intervenes in the selection of strategic industrial sectors and provides "policy loans" to the targeted sectors. Thirdly, as a consequence, close ties of coordination and cooperation exist between government, banks and firms. The government, of course, occupies the most powerful position.

2 See Kim and Cho (1999).

perspective. In laying out part of the argument in advance, it is our position here that since those perspectives do not connect the high economic growth under the Park system with the anti-communist defense of the world capitalist system under United States (US) auspices they remain oblivious to the crucial fact of the absolute necessity of the basic political and economic structures of the Park system to ensure rapid "capitalist" development within the context of the North-South Korean confrontation and the world-wide *cold war*. Furthermore, since those perspectives do not pay much attention to the widening and deepening class struggles between capital and labor accompanying the rapid capitalist development they do not understand that the terrible political dictatorship was an inevitable component of that development. Due to these faults, they attribute the causes of the high rates of growth in the post-war Korean economy to superior state interventions in the economy (state economic policies and policy enforcements) and the administrative prowess of Park Chung Hee himself. These theories go as far as to actually proclaim that the high growth might have been achieved without the political dictatorship.

The second task this chapter seeks to accomplish is to offer an analysis of the historic formation, development, and collapse of the Park system by taking explicit account of Korean capitalist development as it unfolded within the context of the world-wide cold war and domestic class struggles. In what this chapter refers to as the *class relations perspective* we intend to place the inevitable combination of rapid economic development and terrible political dictatorship within a proper theoretical context.

Autonomous National Economy Perspective (ANEP)

The ANEP has been engaged in criticizing the Park Chung Hee government's economic policies since the 1960s. According to the ANEP: a) the foreign capital dependent export-oriented economic development by the Park government would intensify the external dependency of the Korean economy and destroy the internal nexus of its division of labor, leading to an "abnormal" and "crippled" economic structure; b) it would lead to recurring foreign debt crisis; c) foreign capital dependency would in turn foster excessive exploitation of workers and peasants in order to improve international competitiveness for exports; d) it would strengthen the comprador dictatorial regime in order to suppress the revolts by workers and peasants; e) eventually, introduction of foreign capital and external dependency would crush the Korean economy due to the outflow of Korea's "economic surplus" in the forms of repayments of principals and interests on the foreign debts.

The supporters of ANEP claim that "it has been trying to overcome the realities of Korean capitalism which has been pursuing merely quantitative economic growth on the basis of dependent economic structure. It has been criticizing the Park government's policies from the aspect of establishing real autonomous national economy and protecting the interests of the masses" (Shin, 2000, 316). In this regard it is evident that the ANEP drew inspiration from third world revolutions of the

1950s and 60s in which states sought to "de-link" from the world economy as per the policy implications of neo-Marxist dependence theory.

During 1960s and 1970s there emerged a sort of social consensus in Korea that the paramount national task was the establishment of an autonomous national economy that would guarantee the alleviation of poverty. However, on the policies of how to achieve it, there arose an opposition between the military government and the economic bureaucrats on the one hand and the progressive intellectuals and student activists on the other hand. The former espoused the view that introduction of foreign capital and promotion of exports were inevitable in the case of Korea where capital equipment and natural resource endowments were lacking. Progressive intellectuals and student activists, on the other hand, claimed that these developmental policies would deepen external dependency and the comprador nature of the government. The ANEP was popular among anti-government students and intellectuals because of the strengthening dictatorship and the wretched conditions of the working poor.

However, the ANEP did not clarify precisely what in fact was entailed in the notion of a "real autonomous national economy" or how such an economy would be established. To be sure, its supporters always maintained in confidence that this concept in fact depicted a national self-sufficient economy liberated from US imperialism and based on the Korea reunification. They claimed, though, that as discussions on the US imperialism and Korean reunification were a criminal offense against the National Security Act at that time, and the first exponent of the ANEP, Hyun-Chae Park, took part in the Korean War as a communist partisan, the ANEP necessarily had to leave the concept vague. An intensive study on Hyun-Chae Park's ideas reveal the following: Hyun-Chae Park's study paradigm on the autonomous national economy was to clarify the relationships between class contradictions under capitalism, national liberation under the divided Korean peninsula, and political democracy as a precondition for solving the class contradiction and the national division (Rieu 2002). In any case, as the ANEP had asserted that in the absence of the rise of an autonomous national economy in Korea the economy would break down, when this failed to occur and high growth continued through the late 1960s it gradually lost popularity

But, how did the ANEP at least attempt to explain the achievement of the "merely quantitative" high economic growth under the Park system? According to the ANEP, the US political and military interests under the cold war between capitalist and communist blocs pushed the Park government to achieve the highest possible rates of economic growth in order to win the developmental race with North Korea. And, it was within the context of US coercion of Korea to dispatch military forces to Vietnam in 1965, and to normalize diplomatic relations with Japan in 1965, that the Korean government was able to inject significant amounts of foreign capital into the Korean economy; a fact which contributed to the one-sidedly quantitative and dependent economic growth.[3] In essence, the US imperial interests in the world-

3 The total foreign debts increased rapidly from 83 million US dollars at the end of 1961, to 3,590 million dollars at the end of 1972, 20,290 million dollars at the end of 1979 and

wide cold war contributed to the solid establishment of the Korean anti-communistic dictatorship, and the Korean military dictatorship eager to obtain a modicum of legitimacy from the Korean people and to win an economic race between South and North Korea pursued the foreign capital dependent export-led growth (Shin, 2000, 349-350).

Even the ANEP's emphasis on the "dependent and abnormal nature" of Korean capitalism faced several criticisms. First, the ANEP perspective entails the following conceptual constituents: a) neo-colonial domination by the US one-sidedly expropriates Korean capital, b) due to the outflow of its economic surplus Korean capitalism will stagnate or fall into a perpetual crisis, and c) the higher degree of exploitation and repression of the masses is a direct result of imperialist domination and expropriation. Several young Marxists like Woo-Jin Yang and Jang-Pyo Hong criticized the ANEP position in the following fashion: a) the bourgeois structure of domination and exploitation has been formed by Korean capital itself, albeit dependent on foreign capital; b) Korean capital has been intensifying its exploitation over workers, which has led to workers' revolts and also to government's interventions in the labor unrest; and c) Korean capital has been expanding its ability to accumulate in spite of the outflow of its economic surplus (Yang and Hong, 1991).

Secondly, in paying excessive attention to the "abnormal" characteristics of Korean capitalism (for example, investment that did not facilitate development of backward and forward industrial linkages in the Korean economy, and agriculture which was sacrificed through government enforced low price policy for agricultural products as well as its opening of the domestic market to US surplus-agricultural products such as wheat, cotton and sugar), the ANEP program for change ended up focusing so narrowly upon questions of self-sufficiency and self-contained development through mutual stimulus between the producer goods department and consumer goods department that it occluded the problem of class antagonism arising in the conditions of rapid capitalist development. Concern with the above would then have led ANEP to accept that a more socially beneficial program of change required formulation of a "new" non-capitalist economic system rather than the vague "autonomous national economy".

Thirdly, though the ANEP accepted that anti-communism demanded by US imperialism necessitated political dictatorship and high economic growth, it failed to adequately theorize the connective logics of this economic growth and political dictatorship or grasp the historical specificity of the phenomenon. This lacuna in ANEP analysis may be traced to its blindness toward the potential and actual class struggles arising from the sort of rapid capitalist development occurring in Korea and also, because ANEP never appreciated that the contents of the US military and political subjugation involved the plantation and extension of specifically capitalist social relations of production. In other words, if we lose sight of the essential feature of the Park system under which the nexus of US imperialism and anti-communism had intended to speed up economic growth by means of strengthening capitalism;

to 46,760 million dollars at the end of 1985 (Economic Planning Board, 1986).

something which necessarily involved exacerbating the capital-labor antagonism, we will never understand the strong struggles of workers and democratic citizens against the Park Chung Hee government and the factors of its final demise.

Developmental State Perspective (DSP)

DSP emphasizes the states' effective interventions in its explanation of the success of so-called "catch-up" industrialization in East Asia (Johnson, 1982, 1987; Wade, 1990; Amsden, 1990; Evans, 1995).

According to DSP, the Park government was able to achieve high economic growth because the Korean state under Park's control remained autonomous or independent from internal and external interest groups such that it could formulate and execute fair economic policies adequate to the requirements of Korean economic development. DSP enumerates these successful economic policies, including: nationalization of commercial banks; government directed credit allocation policy; repressive labor policy; state support of a combination of import-substitution and export-orientation (Jang, 1999); formation of domestic industrial linkages and meeting of economy of scale requirements by strengthening the *chaebol*; allocation of government support predicated upon a firm's competitive performance (Lee, 1999); coordination of competitive private investment plans; and, industrial restructuring through "protective" trade policy (Chang, 2002). Although DSP attributes these policies to the absolute or relative autonomy of the Park government DSP does not deal with the difficult concept of the relative autonomy of the state theoretically.[4] Therefore, DSP may be criticized as a theoretical example of "state fetishism".

It can certainly be accepted that in May 1961 when the Park's military coup occurred the size and power of the industrial working class was small, and peasants, ordinary citizens, intellectuals, students, as well as businessmen, were rendered obedient in the face of the threat of military violence. However, the so-called autonomy of the Park government was limited in several aspects: It was severely limited vis-à-vis the US government due to the following: Based upon the military confrontation between South and North Korea in the world-wide cold war the US government obtained the legal right to control both Korean and American military forces by the one-sided Mutual Defense Treaty between it and Korea. US military and economic aid was the main pillar of the Park government budget and introduction of foreign capital and foreign markets for Korean exports relied critically on the favor of the US government (Sohn 1991, 187-190)

The much vaunted autonomy of the Park government from the big capital was also severely limited. Since the petty-bourgeois ideology of Park was never concerned with mobilizing the popular power of the masses it had to curry favor with the big capital of the *chaebol*. Lacking in business know-how the Park government had to allocate capital for the strategic industries to the *chaebol* under conditions

4 Refer to Part one of Sohn (1991) for a theoretical explanation of 'relative autonomy of the state'.

where those receiving the government largesse were also called upon to assist in its disbursing of funds. According to the Fair Trade Commission (2001), the Park government had promulgated the Fair Trade Law from the mid-1960s in order to lessen the abuses of monopoly and oligopoly by the *chaebol*, but failed due to the protests of the nascent corporate behemoths. The Law was finally enacted in a muted form in 1980.

In addition to our critique of the DSP claim of the autonomy of the Park government from capital it must also be understood that the arguments over the efficiency and cleanliness of the Park government are not sustainable. Rather, our view is that the Park regime was corrupt and wasteful.[5] As President Park personally wielded ultimate power on every aspect of Korean society, and the machinery of coercion of the Park state tried to detect all dissident activity in society, the rampant irregularities and corruption could not easily be revealed and corrected. Numerous demonstrations by students, intellectuals, religious persons, workers and the poor occurred against the Park political dictatorship, Korea-Japan diplomatic normalization, and the harsh living standards of the Park era. Large scale military forces were occasionally stationed on university campuses. Combat police forces routinely had to use tear gas in dispersing student demonstrations and the government fabricated many espionage cases at critical moments in order to weaken demonstrations,[6] as well as to put pressure on the courts to impose severer sentences and penalties on the convicted. During Park's reign of eighteen years martial laws were declared successively in May 1961,December 1962, October 1963, June 1964, August 1965 and October 1971 (garrison decree in Seoul), December 1971 (national emergency), October 1972, 1974-79 (emergency acts), and October 1979 when he was killed by the KCIA director, Kim Jae-Kyu.

An Institutionalist Revision of the Developmental State Perspective: Developmental Dictatorship Perspective (DDP)

According to the DDP, a mode of national industrialization under the aegis of the state, dubbed "developmentalism", is a historical necessity for every country en route to entering the club of modern industrial societies. In this analysis, the DDP draws upon

5 Consider the wealth of the former KCIA director, Kim Hyung-Wook, who exiled to the USA in 1973 and criticized Park Jung Hee but disappeared in Paris in 1979 probably by a KCIA plot.

6 The National Intelligence Service, the renamed KCIA, has formed a truth-searching civilian committee on the past big suspicious national security cases under the Roh Moo-Hyun government. The committee revealed in December 2005 the truth of the People's Revolutionary Party Case (in 1964), the National Union of Democratic Youth and Students Case (in 1974) and the Reconstruction Case of the People's Revolutionary Party (in 1974), and in January 2006 the truth of the East Berlin Espionage Case (in 1967). All the cases were KCIA's fabrications and exaggerations for intimidating the protesters against the Park's dictatorship.

the DSP in maintaining the need for so-called developmentalism at an early stage of economic development. But the DDP criticizes the DSP in the following ways (Lee, 2003, 27-31): Firstly, it is pointed out that because the DSP focused narrowly on the society-state dichotomy in which society is viewed as riven by competing private interests, and only the state represents the public interests, it does not see the dangers of political reaction by the developmental state. Secondly, as the DSP stresses only the differences between capitalism and socialism, it does not pursue comparative studies of different capitalist countries and fails in recognizing national diversities of institutional forms. Thirdly, as the DSP focuses on state guidance of the market and state/market symbiosis, the DDP argues it does not apprehend the potential for conflict between the state and capital. Fourthly, according to the DDP, the DSP lacks appreciation of the international circumstances which permitted the successful economic growth of developmentalist Korea. For instance, the DSP does not grasp the organic connection between political-military elements (the cold war context) and economic elements marking the Park Chung Hee system.

The DDP then proceeds to define the Park government's developmental dictatorship as a mode of developmentalism specific to Korea, the characteristics of which are: "i) developmental bloc between military-political powers and socio-economically dominant powers, limiting political freedom and excluding masses' participation; ii) the state's nationalistic integration and mobilization of the people by putting its legitimacy on economic results rather than on procedural democracy; iii) system for economic development aiming at the autonomy of national economy by means of effective guidance of the market by the state, growth-oriented cooperation among the state-market-institutions, and selective external open doors"(Lee, 2003, 25).

The DDP, in other words, does not grasp the inevitability of political dictatorship in the drive to high economic growth. "In order to achieve the highest goal of social development, i.e. industrialization, in a small backward country with scarce natural resources but with abundant quality labor forces, a certain authoritarian regulation might be needed in integrating the will of people, mobilizing and distributing resources, and guaranteeing profit opportunities to capitalists" (Lee, 2003, 51). In fact, the DDP abandons any attempt to theorize the combination of development and dictatorship in the Park system, and just develops an analogy of their relationship to "light" and "shadow" aspects of development. The shadow aspect, or dictatorship of the Park system, then is then relegated to a position of lower causal efficacy.

The DDP in fact identifies the primary element for the Park system's economic success in the specific forms of "autonomous" institutions (e.g. industrial policies, connections between the state-market-institutions, selective external liberalizations),[7] and pinpoints its secondary element in the *chaebol* system and workers' voluntary devotion. Workers, trusting government's promise of "growth first and distribution later" and consenting to its "growth first" projects, sacrificed themselves to the

7 The DDP is very much technologically and economically determinist in its heavy dependence upon these so-called relatively autonomous institutions.

rapid industrialization voluntarily so the story goes (Lee, 2003, 50-51). Of course, it might seem obvious that the notion of workers' voluntary devotion or sacrifice to rapid industrialization through accepting lower wages and longer working hours is a nonsensical idea but the Reappraisal of Korean History Project by the Institute for Society and Culture, Seonggonghoe University, has tried to develop this idea.[8] The DDP raises the question of why the political repression existing in most third world countries with the exception of Korea has failed to promote industrialization, and answers it in the following way: As dictatorship is not compatible with demands for democracy, it must accommodate or distort implicitly or explicitly the common will of the people (the masses' demands) in order to obtain the minimum political supports. The Park government tried to achieve the task by separating forcefully the political and economic problems. The slogan of "growth first, distribution later" is a quite appropriate tactic for this. As this political promise should be based on the guarantee of distribution of wealth some day it is necessary to maintain political control of the fruits of economic growth. In the end, the guarantee of later distribution is a method for intensifying political dictatorship and government interventions. Hence, the common will of the people for industrialization was deliberately taken advantage of by the Park government (Kim ed., 2001, 133-134).

The DDP's idea of workers' voluntary sacrifice seems to be based on Gramsci's concept of hegemony by consent *or* coercion. However, as evidenced by the New Village Movement of rural areas and factories, the consent by peasants to participate in building roads without payment and the consent by workers to give up holidays without compensation were not voluntary but coerced by state or the factory managers. The slogans such as "Let's modernize our fatherland!" and "Let's have better life!" were not the common will or collective will of the people (or a social consensus) but the Park's governing ideology. In fact, the Park government's ruthless dictatorship and insane anti-communism deterred people from participating voluntarily in any social movement (Hong, 2003).

It seems that the DDP tries to gloss over the viciousness of the Park dictatorship by attributing the agonies and sacrifices of people under the Park system to people's voluntary consent and devotion. However the DDP view can not explain the wide-spread struggles against the Park government and capitalists and the eventual collapse of the Park system in October 1987. Clearly the DDP view is a great distortion of history.[9]

8 It has produced three books on Korean model for capitalist development formed in the Park era: Kim ed. (2001), Yoo ed. (2003), and Yoo ed. (2006).

9 You may note here how this sets the stage for the DDP to advocate a form of "bourgeois nationalism" as a new vision for the future Korea.

An Alternative Appraisal of the Park Chung Hee System: The Class Relations Perspective (CRP)

The above perspectives – ANEP, DSP and DDP – regard the Park system as a specific historical mode of "industrial" development. But it is very important to recognize that the Park system was in fact, more precisely, a historical form of *capitalist* development. This is because capitalist development relies not only on improvements of productive forces as the one-sided views of ANEP, DSP and DDP on industrial development understand, but also on the establishment and expansion of antagonistic social relations of production, i.e. capital-labor class relations. As Marx puts it:

> In the colonies, property in money, means of subsistence, machines and other means of production does not as yet stamp a man as a capitalist if the essential complement to these things is missing: the wage-labourer, the other man, who is compelled to sell himself of his own free will ... Capital is not a thing, but a social relation between persons which is mediated through things ... Capital is a social relation of production. It is a historical relation of production (Marx, 1976, 932 and note).

Therefore, it is one-sided and wrong for the ANEP to emphasize the autonomous national economy without paying attention to the accompanying class relations, and for the DSP to glorify state intervention in improving productive forces; and further, for the DDP to single out the role of institutions in the rapid economic development. Only under well established capitalist social class relations of production and capital's domination over labor do productive forces develop rapidly by means of greater exploitation of labor leading to increased accumulation of capital. This point is extremely important in avoiding technological and economic determinism. As Marx says:

> At a certain stage of development, the material productive forces of society come into conflict with the existing relations of production or–this merely expresses the same thing in legal terms–with property relations within the framework of which they have operated hitherto. From forms of development of the productive forces these relations turn into their fetters. Then begins an era of social revolution. The changes in the economic foundation lead sooner or later to the transformation of the immense superstructure (Marx, 1987, 263).

Technology, economic institutions, and national self-sufficiency policies under capitalism can influence productive forces only through capital-labor class relation (relations of production) or class struggle. Furthermore, neo-colonial interventions by imperial states influence class relations and class struggle, thus leading to stagnation or development of productive forces in the third world (Park, 2004). The intervention by the US in Korea must be viewed in this light. In the same way as productive forces and relations of production complement and contradict each in a unified mode of production, economy and politics complement and contradict each other in a unified social formation. Therefore, following Marx's dictums we propose that economic development and political dictatorship under the Park system were internally connected, and the class struggles at the levels of economy and politics transformed the combination of development and dictatorship finally leading to the demise of the combination itself for a higher combination of development and democracy.

To accurately reappraise the Park system we first have to study the historical formation of class relations favorable to rapid accumulation of capital under the Park system. Capital-dominant class relations were formed through the Right-Left confrontation just after the surrender of Japanese colonial power, the agricultural reforms, and the Korean War. Secondly, we have to examine the active roles played by the US government and the North-South division of Korea in shaping capital-labor relations as well as strategies for economic development. The US government has been the most important "internal" factor in shaping class relations, because it ruled South Korea militarily for three years (1945-48); it has stationed a sizeable military force in South Korea; it forced South Korea to dispatch soldiers to Vietnam and to normalize diplomatic relations with Japan in 1965; it supplied a huge amount of military and economic aid; it has granted large scale foreign loans to Korea and opened the gigantic US market for Korean exports. In the similar way North Korean activities toward South Korea have given very good excuses to the Park government to take political and military actions which have severely influenced class relations. Thirdly, we argue that the Park system's developmental dictatorship involved historically concrete forms of class struggle such that it necessarily had to collapse amidst the explosive unfolding of these class struggles in 1987. Fourthly, we will show that recent discourses on revival of the dead Park system reflect efforts for the dominant classes to form a grand coalition against the masses by means of invoking bourgeois nationalism in the face of cutthroat competition under conditions of current globalization.

Historical Precondition for the Park System: The Establishment of Capital-dominant Class Relations

The class struggle just after the Liberation (August 1945), farmland reform and the Korean War (1950-53) dramatically changed class relations in South Korea. The Korean War with farmland reform had dissolved the feudalistic estates system by getting rid of the landlord class and played the role of bourgeois revolution normally required in transition from feudalism to capitalism (Jeong, 2000).[10] In particular, the Korean War annihilated left-wing political and academic elements on the one hand, and established anti-communism as a formidable ideological barrier to the

10 Of course, in agriculture small-scale peasants became dominant. Since they produced mainly staple food (rice) whose price was controlled by the government and they had to buy capitalistically produced manufactured goods in the market, they were absorbed into capitalist relations of production. According to the progress in industrialization, the large-scale surplus laborers in the countryside supplied low wage, long working hour, industrial labor-power.

mass movements on the other hand. Thus, capital-dominant class relations had been firmly formed just after the end of the Korean War.[11]

From the Liberation in 1945 to the end of the Korean War, the US and North Korea were dynamic elements involved directly or indirectly in the class struggle in South Korea. The farmland reform enforced by the US. Occupation Forces and the Syngman Rhee government was a result of South Korean people's revolutionary struggle which had been stimulated by thorough land reform in North Korea. And the advanced Labor Relations Act promulgated in 1953 was not a simple transplantation of an American law but was compelled by North Korean Law and workers' struggle (Kim, 2003). However, as the North-South Korean division became the frontline of the world-wide cold war confrontation and the capital-dominant class relation was consolidated in South Korea, the necessity of the advanced Labor Relations Act disappeared completely. The pro-government Korean Federation of Labor Unions controlled workers and repressed their movements during the 1950s (Kim, 1999).

The labor movement was partially reactivated by the April students' revolution in 1960,[12] and the South-North reunification movement was begun again by students and progressive intellectuals. But the two movements were crushed by the May military coup in 1961 led by Park Chung Hee.

An Inevitable Combination of Development and Dictatorship

The emergence of the combination of development and dictatorship was partly due to the US government policy of making Korean development a show-case for capitalist development in rivalry with the socialist camp, and partly due to the military Park government's anxiety over obtaining a modicum of legitimacy from the Korean people and US policy-makers by means of rapid economic growth.

The US government changed priorities in its foreign policy from military to economic in 1957 when rivalry between the two camps in the cold war era accelerated and as the rapid industrialization of the Soviet Union, China and North Korea stimulated many third world countries to adopt their style of "socialist" development. The US government began to urge the Syngman Rhee government to formulate a long-term economic development plan in order to deter communist revolution and to achieve economic stability in South Korea. The Chang Myon

---

11 This class configuration is quite different from that prevalent among Latin American and South Asian countries where the landlord class remains dominant. It is one of the reasons why these countries could not achieve rapid capitalist development and why they could form state corporatism between indigenous capitalists and industrial workers against landlord class.

12 According to Government statistics, the actual number of labor unions increased by 203 to a total of 914 in 1960. And the number of actual union memberships increased by 40 thousand to 321 thousand. Labor disputes also increased from 95 cases in 1959 to 227 cases in 1960. In particular, the teachers began to organize labor unions which had been forbidden by Education Public Servants Act and Private Schools Act (Kim, 1999).

government, following the April students' revolution in 1960, formulated a 5-year economic development plan, which was later modified by the Park government (Lee, 1999). The US government's pressure on the Korean government in economic matters was intensified by the successful Cuban revolution in 1959 which inspired wide-spread class struggles in Latin America and increasingly directed US economic aid there. The US government began to think about transferring part of its burden of Korean aid to the Japanese government and urged the Park government to normalize its relations with Japan (Lee, 1999). The Park government finally normalized Korea-Japan relations in 1966 and Japanese public and private capital rushed into Korea.

In short, the direct confrontation with North Korea made it indispensable to maintain and expand stable capitalist class relations in South Korea, which in turn required long-term capitalist economic growth. Thus, the successive 5-year economic development plans in the1960s may be regarded as a kind of "class struggle from above" in which neo-colonial powers like the US and Japan became involved directly in engendering capitalist class relations and capital accumulation in South Korea.

In addition, Park's coup forces, which had toppled the democratically elected Chang Myon government after the students' revolution, had to achieve rapid economic growth in order to bolster its weak legitimacy both internally and externally. President Kennedy's *ex-post* approval of Park's coup was based on the recognition that Park's military government could successfully implement economic development plans (Lee, 1999).

The success in recording high economic growth depended much more heavily on the introduction of foreign capital, which was made easier by the Korea-Japan diplomatic normalization and the dispatch of Korean soldiers to Vietnam, than on the policy change from import-substitution to export-orientation.[13] But without capital-dominant class relations the inward foreign capital could not have created high economic growth. Due to the dangerous South-North confrontation and the political and social instability (continuous students' demonstrations), foreign capitalists did not want to build their factories in South Korea and the Park government introduced foreign capital mainly through borrowing foreign money-capital whose repayments were in fact guaranteed by the dominant power of the US in South Korea. Even at the end of 1980 the amount of foreign direct investment was only 1.1 billion US dollars while the total foreign debts reached 27.2 billion dollars (Economic Planning Board, 1986: 22, 28). The much lower scale of foreign direct investment was a blessing in the sense that the Park government could invest the foreign money-capital in its designated priority industries.

Just after the coup, the Park government declared anti-communism as its national policy number one, arresting 930 suspected communists (mainly anti-government protesters) and crushing workers' struggles for the right-to-live and the students' North-South reunification movement. The labor policy of the Park system in 1960s

13 The policy change was necessary as the US reduced its military and economic aids and replaced the aid by public and private loans.

was more repressive than in 1950s (Kim, 1999). The Park government succeeded in reestablishing the capital-dominant class relation.

The formation of *chaebols* was an inevitable byproduct of rapid capitalist development which was regarded as a means of class struggle from above. The Rhee government assisted in forming *chaebols* by selling enemy (Japanese) properties cheaply to the formative companies after Japanese surrender in 1945, and by allocating disproportionate amounts of American aid materials and aid dollars to them. The Park government entrusted the main priority investment sectors to them and provided *chaebols* with government guarantees for their foreign capital borrowing. As well, *chaebol* were given low interest loans and favorable tax treatment as inducements to export to global markets. The intimate relationship between government and banks and *chaebols* was thus formed. The *chaebol* system developed through the 1950s and 60s, and was solidly established by the early 1980s after incorporating heavy-chemical industries in 1970s (Kim, 2003). Export-led industrialization required crucial economy of scale considerations in raising international competitiveness and the Park government nurtured the *chaebols* as large-scale monopoly capital.

When we analyze the historical development of the Park system from the aspect of capitalist class relation, we can grasp the internal connection among imperialism, political dictatorship (politics) and development (economy). Maintenance and expansion of capitalist class relations in Korea under the world-wide cold war and the South-North Korean confrontation required rapid capitalist development. And the US and Japanese governments assisted the Park government in attracting foreign money-capital while the Park government firmly reestablished capital-dominant class relations through its terrible political dictatorship; this enabling capitalists to exploit direct producers (peasants and workers) ruthlessly, permitting big capitals to expropriate small-and-medium capitals, and entrusting all available internal and external resources to big capital – the *chaebols* – for investing in growth and export industries. In this way the high economic growth associated with the so-called Korean "miracle" was achieved.

Dynamics of Class Struggle and Vicissitudes of Developmental Dictatorship

The Park system succeeded in achieving high economic growth with export-oriented industrialization in the field of light industries such as textiles, wigs and plywood in the1960s. Workers suffered from low level of wages and long hours of working under dirty and cramped conditions. These cruel situations agitated the workers' struggle. In particular, Chun Tae-il's self-immolation by fire on the 13th of November 1970, at the Seoul Peace Market, in protest against excessive exploitation of textile female workers, played the role of initial trigger for labor and student movements (Cho, 2003). Subsequent large-scale demonstrations against exploitation and dictatorship by workers, students, intellectuals and religious persons began to have some impact on the capital-dominant class relations. But the Park government counteracted this "class struggle from below" by the more repressive and reactionary Yushin system in 1972 in which Park enacted legislation permitting him to keep presidency as long as he liked and enabling him to control the Parliament by appointing a third of total members by himself. Of course, the incursion of 31 North Korean guerrillas into Seoul on January 21, 1968 and the change in US policy on North Eastern Asia following the Nixon Doctrine in February 1970[14] also contributed to the strengthening of the Park dictatorship (Lee, 2003).

The working conditions which characterized the Park system in 1960s and 1970s were: the lowest level of wages, the longest working day, and the highest number of industrial accidents in the world. These severe conditions could be imposed upon workers partly due to the existence of a large-scale surplus population in rural areas, and partly due to the petty-bourgeois passiveness of the workers' consciousness engendered under conditions of the anti-communistic political dictatorship. Moreover, as no public social safety net existed, people had to rely on their family members. Frequently, some members of a family had to give up all possibilities of gaining an education to earn a livelihood for their family. In 1960s, the booming textile industry required many young female workers who sacrificed themselves for their families (Park, 1999).

From the end of 1960s, workers had begun to engage in scattered but spontaneous struggles for the right-to-live. Chun Tae-il's suicide by fire in 1970 stimulated protests by workers, the city poor,[15] small peddlers, illegal settlers on the hills and the unemployed. It conveyed the urgency of labor problems to students, intellectuals and religious persons and urged them to participate in democratic labor union movements in 1970s. In particular, the female workers employed in the worst working conditions of such exporting industries as the textile industry led independent democratic labor union movements (Chun, 2004). In spite of the rapid increase in exports and the rapid expansion of exporting companies, the wage-level comparison between industries for domestic demand and for exports was 100 : 65.1 in 1974 which changed to 100 : 63.9 in 1977 and 100 : 69.7 in 1979 (Lee, 2004, 344). Such ratios demonstrate that the excessive exploitation was centered on female workers in exporting light industries.

The Yushin system proclaimed in October 1972 was the worst form of developmental dictatorship as it ensured the conditions for rapid capitalist development in the face of the increasing democratization and labor movements. The Yushin system denied workers' right to combine.[16] This denial in the field of the economy was completely consonant with the denial of people's right to choose the President and Members of Parliament in the field of politics. Thus, struggles

14 Nixon implied that the US government would strongly support the friendly governments irrespective of whether they were democratic or repressive.

15 More than 30,000 city poor whom the Park government had removed from illegal settlements in Seoul to the hill sides of Kwangjoo, Gyeonggi-do organized a violent riot on August 3, 1971 to demand their livelihoods.

16 It was a retreat even from US Occupation Forces' labor act prohibiting workers' combination just after the Liberation in August 1945 (Kim, 2003). However, this ban remained intact until the end of the Chun Doo-Hwan developmental dictatorship in 1987.

for democracy and for the right-to-live went together. And religious circles such as the City Industrial Mission, the Catholic Labor Youth Movement and the Christian Academy mediated the two struggles (Lee, 2004).

Political and economic class struggles against the Yushin system exploded again at the time of the Korean economic crisis which was triggered by the world oil crisis following the Iranian revolution in 1979.[17] In August 1979, 170 female workers of the YH Trading Co. went on a sit-down strike at the head office of the opposition New Democratic Party in protest against the pull-out of their foreigner-invested company. When the police tried to break up the strike, one female worker plunged to death from the fourth floor of a building. The opposition party blamed the police and the government for the incident but the Court under the government pressure suspended the leader of the opposition party (Kim Young Sam) from performing his duties, which in turn led to resignation of all the congressmen of the opposition parties. In October 1979 large-scale street demonstrations by students and citizens broke out in Pusan and Masan, and due to an internal discord about how to deal with these demonstrations, Park Chung Hee was shot to death by his KCIA boss on October 26, 1979.

The Yushin system ended as a result of the typical dynamics of class struggle. However, the class struggle from above by the dominant classes in confrontation with the explosive struggle for the right-to-live by workers, and the struggle for full-scale democracy by students and intellectuals, took the form of another military coup led by Chun Doo Hwan and assisted by US military forces. The old developmental dictatorship by the Park government could be handed off only to a more repressive Chun government, which had to crush the Kwangjoo (Chullanam-do) uprising by killing many people in May 1980. Nevertheless, struggles for democracy and for the right-to-live had continued and reached a climax in 1987, when the Park Jung Hee system was completely destroyed. The civilian democratic revolution in June 1987 forced the Chun government to accept direct election of the President, and the massive workers' struggle in the autumn 1987 led to the founding of enormous numbers of labor unions and obtained big concessions from capital and government.

Though we had a transitional period during 1988-93 under President Roh Tae Woo, the following Presidents, Kim Young Sam (1993-98), Kim Dae Jung (1998-2003) and Roh Moo-Hyun (2003-08) have been protecting the democracy.

Recent Talks on Revival of the Park Chung Hee System

Recently, the dead Park Chung Hee system has been revived as an important topic of political and economic discussion. In 2002, the late Park's daughter, Park Keun-Hae, became leader of the opposition Grand National Party. Right-wing politicians and scholars have so successfully manipulated the images of the late Park by positively evaluating the economic results of the Park system that the opposition party swept

---

17 The Park government took advantage of large-scale oil dollar recycling during the first world oil crisis in 1973 and used the money for construction of heavy-chemical industries.

the conservative areas like Gyeongsangbuk-do and Gyeongsangnam-do in the 2005 general election.

Furthermore, as the incumbent Roh Moo-Hyun government has admitted the inevitability of accelerating neo-liberal globalization and of anti-labor legislation (for flexibility of labor market) in order to spur recovery of the Korean economy from the stagnation and disturbances of the IMF restructurings after the 1997 Korean crisis,[18] Roh's government has been cultivating a historic compromise between the past industrializing forces (mainly Park admirers) and the present democratizing forces to form a grand coalition of dominant classes against workers and the masses. In the past the evaluation of the Park system was put forward rather passively by supporters of the early industrializing conservative forces simply for the recognition of their role in Korean miracle. But now, even the democratizing, progressive forces are trying to hold a hegemonic position in the grand coalition of dominant classes by revaluating the positive role of the Park system in Korean miracle.

In these situations, it was as the DDP advocated: that a kind of bourgeois nationalism would serve as the new vision for the future Korea (Lee, 2003). The DDP had attributed economic achievements of the Park system to state-capital cooperation and workers' devotion to the state nationalistic mobilization and distribution. Now the DDP urges a state-capital-labor coalition to unite against the unlimited international competition in order to make Korean capitals (*chaebols*) rule the world. This all seems to be the perfect right-wing propaganda effort though the DDP praises this view as neither extreme right nor extreme left. The DDP emphasizes a social consensus among the state and capital and labor. However, it underestimates the burdens on the shoulders of workers and the masses imposed by this coalition.

Polarization between the rich and the poor, capitalists and workers, big capitals and small capitals, regular workers and irregular workers, cities and countries, city dwellers and peasants has been exacerbated recently due to the present government neoliberal policies. Korean society is full of discontents and rivalries and struggles. The struggle to transform the present class relation is urgently needed. The class struggle being waged now will decide the future course of Korean economy and politics.

18 Kim and Cho (1999) analyze the root causes of the Korean crisis and suggest an alternative economic reform.

PART IV
The South Korean Economy into the Future

Introduction to Part IV

What lies ahead for Korea and its people? Neoliberals and left-Keynesian/statists generally offer differing assessments about future growth prospects for the Korean economy based largely on their different assessment of the policies future Korean governments are likely to implement. As such both groups tend to think in terms of national interest and the technical challenges surrounding policy formulation within the existing structures of capitalism. The importance of class and political struggle for evaluating, envisioning, and shaping outcomes (including non-capitalist ones) is downplayed if not actually dismissed as irrelevant. By contrast, for Marxists capitalism itself is a class contradictory system whose very nature threatens working class interests, requiring an ever-widening process of class-based struggle to achieve its transformation. This section offers two chapters that seek to highlight the class structured processes that currently threaten the living and working conditions of growing numbers of Koreans as well as the importance of, and challenges to, building resistance to them.

In the first chapter, "The South Korean Economy: Problems and Prospects", Martin Hart-Landsberg argues that the Korean economy is undergoing an economic restructuring based on neoliberal, free-market principles. Mainstream economists claim that this process was a necessary and successful response to Korea's devastating 1997-1998 crisis. This article challenges this claim. It critically exams the economic and social consequences of Korea's current neoliberal restructuring; highlights the ways international capitalist dynamics and US policy initially promoted and then undermined Korea's growth; describes the role played by US and International Monetary Fund policymakers in shaping Korea's post-crisis restructuring; and considers the challenges facing Korean workers in their struggle to advance a new economic strategy.

The next chapter, "When Capital Becomes Society: The Re-composition of Capitalist Work and New Labor Activism in Korea", by Dae-oup Chang, examines the re-composition of capitalist work in Korea. Based on Marx's understanding of capital as a form of social relations of extraction of abstract labor, Chang shows the continual reorganization of capitalist labor in Korea by tracing the interactions between the movement of capital and the movement of labor. Focusing on the recent movement of capital that precipitated the massive irregularization of capitalist work since the 1997 crisis, Chang shows how capital has increasingly imposed its logic of reproduction on the individual and thereby society. Among other things, this development represents capital's attempt to utilize new methods to overcome the constant pressures generated by the recent accumulation crisis. However, rather than viewing this development as a one-way process whereby labor is recomposed by the movement of capital, Chang also illustrates the ways in which labor moves beyond the social arrangement of exploitation to recreate itself through the newly emerging labor activism of irregular workers that is growing outside of the structure of established labor unions in Korea.

Chapter 8

The South Korean Economy: Problems and Prospects

Martin Hart-Landsberg

Introduction

The South Korean economy continues to undergo an economic restructuring based on neoliberal, free-market principles. Mainstream analysts both inside and outside of South Korea (hereafter Korea) have viewed this restructuring as a necessary response to the country's devastating 1997-98 crisis that, according to the conventional wisdom, was caused by a legacy of state-generated "cronyism" and resulting economic inefficiencies. Ordinary South Koreans are said to support the restructuring and to be enjoying the benefits of the transformation so far completed.

Unfortunately this understanding of the crisis and, by extension, the benefits of neoliberalism is seriously flawed. While it is true that "crony capitalism" played an important role in the crisis, other domestic factors such as shifting state-*chaebol* relations of power and exploding class struggle were more important. The mainstream focus on Korean dynamics also masks other, possibly greater causes of the crisis, namely US government actions and international capitalist instabilities. In particular, US policy was instrumental in both enabling South Korea's past growth and causing its recent crisis. US policy also played a critical though often overlooked role in shaping Korea's post-crisis policy response. Tragically, this neoliberal restructuring is significantly worsening living and working conditions for growing numbers of Koreans and undermining the long-term stability and development prospects of the Korean economy.

To this point, worker opposition to the restructuring process remains largely focused on resisting state policies designed to promote labor flexibility, privatization, deregulation, and foreign ownership. So far, this defensive position has produced few and limited victories. In large part this is because many Koreans believe that their country's economic history of rapid growth and industrialization demonstrates that international capitalism provides a supportive environment for national development. In line with this understanding, current economic problems are generally blamed on misguided state efforts to override market forces and direct economic activity. Thus, many Koreans support policies designed to make domestic economic activity even more responsive to international market forces. As a result, working class resistance appears to many Koreans as contrary to the national interest, slowing down if not actually complicating the needed economic restructuring.

If Koreans are to escape this political dead end, activists must encourage a more critical understanding of international capitalist dynamics and the relationship between those dynamics and the fortunes of the Korean economy. In this article I show the ways in which international capitalist dynamics shaped and then undermined past Korean growth processes and continue to distort and limit current Korean economic options. Hopefully, if Koreans better understand how the tensions and contradictions generated by the dynamics of international capital accumulation have contributed to Korea's current economic problems, they will see why neoliberal policies, which increase dependence on those dynamics, need to be resisted. And, as a result, they will be encouraged to work collectively to advance new visions of economic organization underpinned by greater regional and international working class solidarity.

South Korea's Economic Situation

South Korea's post-crisis economic restructuring has, by design, produced an economy that is more deregulated and liberalized than in the past. According to those who applaud this outcome, it ensures that Korean economic dynamics will be more in tune with global market forces and thus better able to generate and sustain high rates of growth. They point to the rapid recovery in Gross Domestic Product (GDP) in the years immediately following the country's 1997-98 economic crisis to demonstrate the correctness of their position (see Table 8.1).[1] However, underlying dynamics point to a far more negative assessment of South Korea's economic policies and their potential to serve majority interests.

Table 8.1 South Korean Growth, in percent

Year	GDP growth
1998	-6.7
1999	10.9
2000	9.3
2001	3.1
2002	6.3
2003	3.1
2004	4.6
2005	3.8

Source: Korea Insight, Korea Economic Institute.

Korea's economic recovery has rested on four pillars: government deficit spending, foreign direct investment, consumer spending, and exports. Large and growing government deficits were the first factor helping to promote economic

1 See, for example, Gruenwald (2003).

recovery. Central government spending as a percentage of GDP rose sharply from a surplus of 0.1 percent in 1996 to deficits of 1.3 percent in 1997, 3.8 percent in 1998, and 4.6 percent in 1999. While an appropriate response to economic crisis, deficit spending is not a long-term solution to economic problems.[2] While deficit spending could again be used to prop up the economy in an emergency, public debts have now grown quite large. For example, the ratio of government debt to GDP rose from 16.2 percent in 1997 to 39.6 percent in 2002 (Korea Herald, 2003b). Additional government obligations weigh heavily on government finances, including a massive shortfall in public pension reserves and debt obligations incurred to support foreign exchange stabilization and financial sector restructuring. Therefore, it is unlikely that the government will find it easy to repeat the massive deficit spending of the recent past.

Table 8.2 Foreign Direct Investment into South Korea, billions US$

Year	Foreign Direct Investment Inflows
1996	3.2
1997	7.0
1998	8.9
1999	15.5
2000	15.7
2001	11.8
2002	9.1
2003	6.5
2004	12.8
2005	11.6

Source: Korea Insight, Korea Economic Institute.

In the years immediately following the crisis, foreign investment also played an important role in boosting growth by providing the government with critical foreign exchange. However, much of this investment was "vulture investment" that involved takeovers of Korean assets at fire sale prices (Hart-Landsberg and Burkett, 2001, 414-16). Once the most attractive assets were purchased, foreign investment began to rapidly decline (see Table 8.2). One outcome of this investment has been a significant denationalization of Korean capital. As of 2004, "foreign controlled banks accounted for 21.7 percent of the domestic banking sector in terms of total assets," up from 10.2 percent in 2000 (Lowe-Lee, 2005, 2). That same year, "foreigners accounted for nearly 42 percent of the nation's total market capitalization," with overseas investors holding majority shares in most large publicly trade firms, including Samsung Electronics and Hyundai Motor

2 In fact, the South Korean government was pressured by the IMF to return to a surplus position beginning in 2000.

Company (Kim So-young, 2005b). The Korean economy is, as a result, now more closely integrated into transnational production networks and, thus, international market dynamics.

The Korean government has embarked on a major campaign to reverse the decline in foreign investment.[3] In August 2003, it established three free economic zones in Inchon, Pusan, and Kwangyan in an effort to make Korea the "business hub of East Asia." Foreign businesses that operate within these zones will enjoy tax breaks as well as exemptions from various environmental and labor regulations. Foreign enterprises will also have the sole authority to build and operate educational and health institutions. In addition, the government is prepared to offer foreign high-tech investors a cash grant equal to 20 percent of the value of their total investment.

This policy appears unlikely to achieve its goal; as of mid-2005, the government has succeeded in attracting only one foreign investor to the Inchon zone. A major reason is that other countries, especially China, are offering even more attractive investment packages. In fact, the Korean government now finds itself on a slippery slope. Foreign companies, seeking guarantees that the benefits offered to them will be permanent, are asking that the investment-friendly regulations be extended to the entire country and include all firms, domestic as well as foreign (Lowe-Lee, 2004b; Alvis, 2005). The president of the European Union Chamber of Commerce in Korea made clear what was at stake: "The EUCCK thinks the peace meal opening of several localized free economic zones within Korea is far from sufficient to make foreign direct investment here an alternative option to foreign direct investment in China" (Yoo Soh-jung, 2005).

Meanwhile, as foreign direct investment inflows have slowed, outflows of South Korean foreign direct investment have grown. Over 4000 factories have moved their production out of Korea since 1998, and the numbers have been growing dramatically each year. According to a Korea Customs Service official, "about 70.7 percent of those production facilities have moved to China" (Kim Mi-hui, 2003). A study by the Korea Chamber of Commerce and Industry found that "about nine out of ten companies manufacturing products in Korea have plans to invest in China in the future, as the country's low production cost and the eager-to-please regulations make the market more attractive than Korea" (Kim Mi-hui, 2003). As a result of this trend, Korea's net foreign direct investment actually turned negative in 2002, and was close to zero in 2003 and 2005 (Asian Development Bank, 2006).

As government deficits and foreign investment declined and as significant sectors of Korean industry set up shop in China and elsewhere, Korea's economic growth

3 Foreign investment did rebound in 2004 and remain substantial in 2005, although at levels significantly below those in 1999 and 2000. The 2004 gain was largely attributable to one significant acquisition, Citigroup's purchase of KorAm Bank, South Korea's seventh largest lender. The 2005 total was also influenced by one major acquisition, Standard Chartered's purchase of Korea First Bank. This focus on finance is underscored by the fact that 2005 FDI in manufacturing fell by more than 50 percent from the previous year. See Stangarone (2006, 1).

became increasingly dependent on domestic consumption. Strong private domestic consumption often reflects sound economic fundamentals. However, this was not the case for Korea. Korean private consumption spending, with the encouragement of the government, was largely based on debt, especially credit card debt. The government began pushing credit card use in 1999 by, among other things, raising the limits on cash advances and introducing tax deductions for purchases made by credit card. The result was a major consumption boom and corresponding credit card debt explosion. The total amount of credit card spending rose from $53 billion in 1998 to $519 billion in 2002 (Lowe-Lee, 2004a, 1).

This credit card spending enabled Korea to limit the negative consequences of the US economic downturn in 2001 and avoid its own recession, but at great cost. The country had the world's fast growing household debt, which soared from 18 percent of GDP in 1999 to 62 percent in 2001, "a rise which even in the profligate US took a decade" (*Economic Intelligence Unit*, 2002). With cash advances and credit card loans accounting for approximately two-thirds of all consumer transactions, it was not long before many households faced unsustainable debt levels. Delinquency rates began rising sharply in 2002. According to the US-based Korea Economic Institute, "The credit card excesses . . . created spiraling social problems. Local newspapers and TV report continuously on increasing number of suicides, violent crime, kidnappings, and prostitution, all due to over-borrowing on credit cards" (Lowe-Lee, 2004a, 1).

Frightened by the prospect of a wave of personal bankruptcies and the danger such bankruptcies could cause the country's financial system, the government belatedly took steps to limit credit card use in the spring of 2003. While it appears the government has succeeded in avoiding a major banking crisis, it will be a long time before a new wave of consumption will drive the economy forward. Household debt has reached 70 percent of GDP. Approximately 40 percent of all households carry debts that outweigh their assets and many face risk of default (Choi, 2003). In fact, the government's success at limiting credit card use led to a sharp decline in private consumption, which in turn had a negative effect on business investment. The top five *chaebol* slashed their investment spending by 30.5 percent in 2003; the top 18 reduced their investment by an even greater 33.5 percent (Kim Ji-ho, 2004b). Not surprisingly, South Korea suffered a recession in the first half of 2003 (Lister, 2003, 1).

As a result of the above trends, Korea is now more dependent then ever on exports to power growth. Korea's post-crisis restructuring had already increased the export orientation of the economy. The export share of the manufacturing sector rose from 35.9 percent in 1997 to 45.9 percent in 2001 (*Business Korea*, 2002, 13). In 2003, with domestic consumption and investment down, exports accounted for 98.2 percent of the country's growth (Kim Ji-ho, 2004a). The situation did not change in 2004 as exports continued to carry the economy, consumer spending declined for much of the year, and investment stagnated.

This greater external orientation represents more than just a deepening of pre-crisis trends, however. As a result of changes in the international economy, Korea's export (and investment) orientation has shifted from the United States to China. In 2001, China became South Korea's number one investment location. In 2002, China became South Korea's number one export market. In 2003, China became South Korea's number one trading partner. In short, China has now become the anchor for Korea's economic future (see Table 8.3).

Table 8.3 South Korea's Trade Orientation, in percent

Year	Share of exports to China	Share of exports to China and Hong Kong	Share of exports to the United States
1992	3.5	11.2	23.6
1993	6.3	14.1	22.1
1994	6.6	14.8	21.4
1995	7.3	15.9	19.3
1996	8.8	17.4	16.7
1997	10.0	18.6	15.9
1998	9.0	16.0	17.2
1999	9.5	15.8	20.5
2000	10.7	16.9	21.8
2001	12.1	18.4	20.8
2002	14.6	20.9	20.2
2003	18.1	25.7	17.7
2004	19.6	26.7	16.9
2005	21.8	27.3	14.5

Source: Korea Trade Statistics, Korea International Trade Association

As a result of this new orientation, many Korean analysts claim that the Korean economy has greatly reduced its vulnerability to instabilities in the US market and threats of trade sanctions from the United States (Lister, 2004, 1). This is wishful thinking because China now largely functions as a major production platform for multinational corporations that export to the United States (Hart-Landsberg and Burkett, 2005, Chapter 4). Most exports from South Korea to China are intermediate goods used in the production of other goods. Studies by the Korea International Trade Association and the Korea Institute for International Economic Policy have shown that "a large portion of the final products are reshipped to third countries, with about 40 percent re-exported to the United States" (Brown, 2004, 1).

More problematic perhaps, South Korea's new China orientation is likely to promote a narrowing and premature hollowing out of the country's industrial base. South Korea is currently running a trade surplus with China. However, China is quickly becoming a major competitor to Korean exports in other markets. According to the Korea Economic Institute, "Within the next decade, Chinese firms are expected to out-compete Korean producers of low-end electronics equipment at home and abroad. Institutes and business organizations already report drops in domestic sales of Korean home appliance products" (Cooper, 2003, 54). Studies by private and state research institutes in Korea raise the same warning, concluding that "China's export competitiveness was in some cases greater than that of Korea in sectors such as machinery, electronics/home appliances, textiles, and some information products" (Cooper, 2002, 1).

Moreover, this competition is not limited to low-end manufacturing, as developments in the Chinese auto industry make clear. In 1997, when South Korea was the fourth largest automobile-producing nation, China was not in the top ten. Now, China has passed Korea to become the fourth largest producer, out-producing South Korea every year since 2002. According to an official of the Korea Automobile Manufacturers Association, "China has been accelerating its auto output because major global carmakers have been scrambling to produce vehicles in that country to tap the world's fastest-growing auto market" (Kim Hyun-chul, 2004). Even more threatening to Korean economic interests, given that cars account for nearly 30 percent of Korea's exports, is the fact that foreign producers are now beginning to use China as a production base for their own automobile exports (Bradsher, 2005).

In sum, Korea's economic future has become increasingly dependent on a narrowing range of exports within a framework shaped by a foreign-dominated, China-based, US-centered system of export production. This development greatly increases the country's vulnerability to another major crisis. For example, the Chinese economy has its own instabilities that threaten its continued high-speed growth. Problems in China, whether economic or political, will have serious consequences for the Korean economy (Hart-Landsberg and Burkett, Chapters 3 and 4; Kim Ji-ho, 2004a).

In addition, both South Korean and Chinese prospects for export growth continue to depend on the stability and import capacity of the United States. The post- 2001 economic recovery in the United States has been weak. The United States has been running bigger and bigger trade deficits: $261 billion in 1999, $363 billion in 2001, $618 billion in 2004, and $726 billion in 2005. These deficits are not sustainable. The US dollar is now falling and interest rates are beginning to rise, which will likely have a negative effect on US growth and imports. It is unlikely that the Korean economy will be able to escape the negative consequences.

South Korea's Social Conditions

Sadly, most Koreans are already paying a high price for their country's neoliberal restructuring. According to a study by the Korea Development Institute, the country's middle class is shrinking: 70.2 percent of all households were classified as middle income in 1994, 68.5 percent in 1997, and only 65.3 percent in 2000 (Sim, 2003, 10). Even though the country's poverty rate has fallen from its 1999 high, it remains considerably higher than before the crisis (Soh, 2003). Inequality actually continues to grow. For example, Korea's Gini coefficient rose from 0.283 in 1997, to 0.316 in 1998, 0.341 in 2003, and 0.344 in 2004 (Lowe-Lee, 2006, 2). The other major measure of inequality, the ratio of top-to-bottom income quintiles, shows a similar trend. In the first quarter of 2005, "the ratio of the top group's [monthly] income to that of the bottom group widened to 5.87, the highest figure since 1982 when this ratio began to be compiled" (Editorial, 2005a, 6).

One reason for these trends is that Korea's post-crisis growth has not produced any significant improvement in labor market conditions. Before the crisis, approximately 58 percent of Korean workers had permanent labor status, which meant that they had employment contracts lasting for at least one year. Following the crisis, many corporations took advantage of new labor laws to fire their permanent workers and rehire them as temporary or even daily workers—part of the "flexibilization" of the workforce. The percentage of permanent workers fell to approximately 48 percent in 1999 and has generally remained at that level. Contingent or non-permanent workers are paid, on average, only 52.9 percent of the wages paid to permanent workers (Crotty and Lee, 2001; Korea Herald, 2003a). Not surprisingly, then, disposable income in Korea currently accounts for only 65.4 percent of GDP, compared with 82.2 percent in the United States and 82.5 percent in Japan (Kim Jung-min, 2005, 1).

A 2004 Korea Broadcasting System survey on the economic state of the nation provides perhaps the clearest evidence of the failure of neoliberalism to satisfy majority needs. As reported by the *Korea Times*, the survey found that:

> More than half of South Koreans feel that the current economic situation is worse than it was in late 1997 when the financial crisis shook the nation. . . . In particular, 52.6 percent of the respondents said that their current living standards are worse than six years ago, while only 9.9 percent felt their living conditions would improve. The survey also showed that polarization between rich and poor has been accelerating, with more people in low-income brackets believing the living conditions have deteriorated. (Kim Jae-kyoung, 2004)

Workers, not surprisingly, are fighting to defend their working and living conditions. According to the *Korea Herald*, the year 2003 "is likely to be remembered as a time marred by the worst labor discontent since 1990, with labor disputes occurring almost every day" (Kim Sung-mi, 2003). As of November 2003, "labor conflicts involved a record number of 131,563 workers, up 43.8 percent from 91,630 a year earlier" (Kim Sung-mi, 2003). The Korean government claims that in 2003 labor unrest at the six largest manufacturers cut overall output $19.2 billion and exports by $1.5 billion (Kim Ji-hyun, 2004a). Worker demonstrations and strikes continued throughout 2004 and 2005, in protest against deteriorating working conditions and government initiatives designed to encourage greater labor "flexibility" and limit unionization, especially among public sector, irregular, and migrant workers.

President Roh Moo-hyun, although thought to be "pro-labor," appears to be continuing the hard-line anti-worker policies of previous administrations. A case in point: 190 workers were arrested for their labor activism during his first eight months in office (Kim Sung-mi, 2003). Even more harmful, his administration has allowed the large *chaebol* to use civil rather than labor laws to crush labor resistance. This has enabled companies to put union funds and worker salaries under temporary attachment while they wait for final court rulings about the legality of labor actions. Many families of labor activists have been forced into bankruptcy leading, in a number of cases, to worker suicides (Jang, 2004).

As Korea's economic reliance on foreign direct investment and exports has grown, the government apparently believes that it has little choice but to view labor solely as a cost of production that must be reduced or more effectively exploited. Thus, even if the government succeeds in attracting new foreign investment and boosting exports, the likely outcome will be only immiserizing growth, not a reversal of current negative social trends.

The Dynamics of Growth

How did Korea get into this situation? This is not a simple question to answer. After all, South Korea enjoyed one of the fastest growing economies in the world until its 1997-98 economic crisis. As one indicator of its economic success, South Korea became a member of the Organization of Economic Cooperation and Development (OECD) in 1996.

Mainstream economists are generally content to answer this question by blaming "crony capitalism" for leading the country into crisis. While the crisis is indeed central to understanding the contemporary Korean situation, this explanation of its cause is seriously flawed. The focus on cozy and corrupt relations between state and business leaders draws attention away from other more critical domestic developments such as shifting state-capitalist relations of power and intensified class struggle. And it totally ignores the unstable nature of international capitalist dynamics and the dominance of US power, factors which were at least as, if not more important than, the above mentioned national ones in triggering the crisis and shaping the later restructuring process.

Although supporters of neoliberal policies initially denied it, state policy was far more important than market forces in helping Korea achieve an annual average increase in real GDP of 9 percent during the 1960s, 9.3 percent during the 1970s, and nearly 10 percent during the 1980s and first half of the 1990s (Hart-Landsberg, 1993, Part I). Control over the country's financial system was perhaps the single most important factor enabling the state to successfully direct the economy. Government planners were able to use their power over both the allocation and cost of capital to promote exports as the priority activity for all firms.

At the same time, the government regularly targeted new areas for development by encouraging the establishment of domestic firms, protecting them with both trade restrictions and limits on foreign direct investment and then, when judged capable, requiring them to export as well as meet domestic needs. The government was also not hesitant about undertaking key investment activities itself through public enterprises, as in the case of petroleum, chemicals, and iron and steel. However, for political reasons, the government eventually decided to allow a small group of *chaebol* to dominate production of the new industries. By 1988, the combined revenues of the top four *chaebol* equaled approximately 47 percent of Korea's total GNP (Hart-Landsberg, 1993, 38).

Although Korea was widely celebrated as an economic model, working people paid a high price for their country's economic growth. Military dictatorship kept workers disorganized and on the defensive for most of the 1960s and 1970s through control of the only legal labor federation, a maze of ever more restrictive labor laws, and increasingly violent interventions into labor disputes by the Korean Central Intelligence Agency and special labor police. Government efforts to contain growing labor militancy in the 1980s and 1990s included frequent mass arrests and several major military assaults against workers.

Generally overlooked in most discussions of the Korean experience was the dependency of Korea's rapid economic growth and industrial transformation on favorable international conditions, most importantly substantial support from the United States as well as Japan. Korea's initial economic strategy called for building a "self-reliant economy" through import substitution. Given the country's low level of development, this strategy was expected to produce a large trade deficit requiring significant foreign exchange support. The US, unwilling to finance this strategy, used its influence to press the Korean government to adopt instead an export-oriented growth strategy. The Japanese government, fearful that a self-reliant Korea might become a fierce competitor, also supported this change in strategy.

Korea's mid-1960s shift to an export-led growth strategy did not solve the country's balance of payments problems. However, its willingness to comply with US and Japanese demands did ensure ample financial assistance, thereby enabling the government to sustain the country's rapid industrial development. For example, as part of their 1965 normalization treaty, Japan gave Korea $200 million in public loans, $300 million in grants, and at least $300 million in commercial credits. Hundreds of millions of dollars of additional loans and grants followed over the rest of the decade (Hart-Landsberg, 1993, 145).

The US government provided even greater financial assistance, in large measure in exchange for Korea's participation in the US-led war against Vietnam. The US paid secret dollar bonuses to Korean soldiers, which generated $185 million in remittances over the period 1965-73. The Korean government and business community earned almost $1 billion dollars more, over the same period, for military and civilian activities in Vietnam and increased exports to Vietnam. The country earned an additional $1.1 billion from US military activities in Korea itself, including local spending, provision of goods, and construction. During the key transition years of 1966 to 1969, approximately 30 percent of Korea's foreign exchange earnings came from Vietnam-related activities (Hart-Landsberg, 1993, 147-8).

In the early 1980s, after Korea suffered a major economic collapse and was in political chaos, the US and Japanese governments again offered critical financial assistance. Two weeks after the Kwangju Uprising had been brutally crushed, the US Export-Import Bank finalized terms to extend more than $600 million in import credits to the new military dictatorship headed by Chun Doo Hwan. The heads of Chase Manhattan Bank and First National Bank also traveled to South Korea to pledge their financial support. Not long after, the Japanese government extended a massive $4 billion loan under exceptionally generous terms (Hart-Landsberg, 1993, 148, 223).

US and Japanese support for Korea was not limited to financial assistance. Japanese corporations provided critical technology and components to the large *chaebol*, enabling them to rapidly upgrade production and boost exports. For example, during the 1980s, Korean firms depended on Japanese corporations for between 40-60 percent of their machines, 60 percent of their parts, and 50 percent of their licensed technology. The level of dependence was far greater for those firms producing critical higher value-added exports, like cars, ships, and electronics (Bello and Rosenfeld, 1990, 114). The additional US economic contribution included a willingness to provide open markets for South Korean exports. Thus, in 1986, Korea's first ever trade surplus of $4.2 billion was made possible because of the country's bilateral surplus of $7.3 billion with the US.

However, the international conditions that encouraged US and Japanese support for Korean growth were not sustainable. More specifically, capitalist dynamics eventually generated instabilities and tensions that reached a boiling point in the mid-1980s. US and Japanese government and corporate responses to these instabilities and tensions led to the creation of a new international environment hostile to Korea's growth strategy, thereby helping to set the stage for the country's 1997-98 economic crisis.

The Dynamics of Crisis

The post-World War 2 (WW2) political successes of the US government in shaping an international capitalist world system favorable to American economic interests set in motion dynamics that eventually threatened those same interests. For example, as a result of the successful rebuilding of Japan and Europe, US corporations began facing growing competition within their home market. The US trade balance finally slipped into deficit in 1971, and with the US government continuing its war efforts in Vietnam, the sustained outflow of dollars finally led to the collapse of the dollar standard in 1973 and a rapid decline in the value of the dollar in 1977-78. Beginning in the 1980s, the US government started to take aggressive actions, especially against Japan, to stop the deterioration in the US trade balance and the hollowing out of the US manufacturing sector. In September 1985, it pressured the Japanese government into supporting a rise in the yen relative to the dollar as part of the Plaza Accord. The yen appreciated by almost 50 percent over the period 1985-88, creating serious economic problems for Japanese corporations.

The severity of US economic problems led the US government to object to Korea's export drive as well. In 1983, it began pressing Korea to drop its tariffs, end its quantitative restrictions on imports, liberalize its service sector, and improve its protection of intellectual property rights. That same year it initiated anti-dumping suits against Korean color TV exports and forced Korea to agree to so-called voluntary restrictions on its steel exports. By the middle of the decade it was forcefully demanding that the Korean government open the country's beef, rice, and cigarette markets to US goods. In 1988, with Korea's bilateral trade surplus growing rapidly, the US government demanded that Korea revalue its currency. That same year the US Congress passed the Omnibus Trade and Competitiveness Act, which required the US trade representative to take action against countries deemed to be "unfair traders". In 1989, the US trade representative threatened Korea with trade penalties if it continued to use special taxes and tariffs to block imports of US goods and placed the country on the special trade watch list each of the next three years.

Fearful of angering the US government and losing access to the American market, the Korean government began opening its markets. It also allowed the won to rise by 16 percent relative to the dollar in 1988 and by another 3 percent over the first half of 1989. The Japanese, upset at losing US market share to Korea in the years following the Plaza Accord, also took action to blunt Korea's economic challenge. For example, in 1990, the Japanese government banned the export of 200 advanced technologies to Korea until 1995 (Bello, 1992, p. 88). These developments proved disastrous for the Korean economy. Export growth fell from 36.2 percent in 1987 to 28.4 percent in 1988, 5.7 percent in 1989, and 3 percent in 1990. Corporate profits also fell. In 1988, VCRs surpassed color TVs to become Korea's leading electronics export. Yet, Korean producers lost money on every single VCR sold that year in the US (Hart-Landsberg, 1993, 161). Overall manufacturing profit rates fell each year from 1989-1992 (Brenner, 2002, 162).

As noted above, Korea's economic problems were not solely caused by changes in the external economic environment. Internal contradictions were also at work. Korean export growth had benefited greatly from a highly exploitative labor regime. Over time, however, industrialization created large working class-dominated cities and massive industrial enterprises that eventually encouraged labor solidarity and an explosion of labor organizing. Massive strike waves swept the country in 1987 and 1988, resulting in significant wage increases in most manufacturing industries.

The higher labor costs no doubt contributed to the economic difficulties of Korean manufacturers, especially exporters. At the same time, it was the changing international conditions that made this development so threatening. Given that the Korean state could not force a change in US or Japanese policies, it had little choice but to concentrate its economic recovery efforts on actions designed to reverse the labor movement's victories.

These international and national developments also contributed to a weakening of Korea's system of state planning. As the state found it increasingly difficult to protect the domestic market from imports and ensure the competitiveness of Korean exports, the *chaebol* became increasingly unwilling to accept continued state direction and control over their activities. Because the county's growth dynamic had concentrated production and wealth in their hands, the *chaebol* had grown powerful enough to resist state mandates that threatened their profitability. They therefore demanded and won, over the first half of the 1990s, new borrowing and investment freedoms. One of the most important was the freedom to borrow internationally without government approval. Another was the freedom to invest abroad. From 1968 to 1980, cumulative Korean foreign direct investment totaled less than $250 million. In 1990 alone it was $1 billion. It rose to $3 billion in 1993. Between 1993 and 1996, it grew at an annual rate of 53 percent. In 1996, reported overseas direct investment totaled $6.22 billion (Burkett and Hart-Landsberg, 2000, 158).

The government did not make these changes in economic policy, along with others that allowed greater foreign investment in Korean stock and bond markets, solely in response to domestic pressures. US demands also played a critical role. A case in point: the US threatened to block Korea's entrance into the OECD unless it opened its financial markets for the benefit of US banks and brokerages (Kristof, 1999).

There was one final international development that may have been the most serious in terms of undermining Korean growth. In response to US pressure for a higher yen, Japanese corporations, with the encouragement of the Japanese government, initiated a massive process of foreign direct investment designed to regionalize their production. Southeast Asia was one of the key locations for this investment. This investment transformed Malaysia and Thailand into significant exporters of relatively advanced manufactured goods and thus competitors of Korea (Hart-Landsberg and Burkett, 1998). By the late 1980s, Malaysia's exports of electronics were replacing those from South Korea in the Japanese market (Burkett and Hart-Landsberg, 2000, 159).

Driven by competitive pressures, Japanese and other foreign investors were on the move again in the early 1990s, this time to China. And, as it did with many Southeast Asian nations, this investment helped to transform China into an increasingly successful exporter of manufactures. The share of foreign-produced exports in China's total exports rose from 17 percent in 1991 to 41 percent in 1996, leading to a rapid growth in China's exports of electronics and electrical goods (Tham, 2001, 3). Thanks to its integration in international production networks, low wages, and a 1994 currency devaluation, China quickly captured market share in both the US and Japan at the expense of Thailand and Malaysia as well as South Korea (Grilli, 2002, 184, 186).

Eventually, contradictions generated by this continuing expansion of regional export centers became unmanageable. Too many countries were producing the same goods for sale in the same markets. The resulting regional overproduction led to a decline in unit export prices and then to a sharp fall in export earnings (Grilli, 2002, 182). For example, the unit export prices of Korea's heavy and chemical products, which were the country's main exports, fell by more than 46.3 percent over the years 1996-98. As a result, South Korea's export growth rate fell from 30.2 percent in 1995 to 3.8 percent in 1996 (Grilli, 2002, 182).

Korea began running ever-larger current account deficits and accumulating greater foreign debt. The current account deficit rose from $4.5 billion in 1992 to $8.9 billion in 1995, and to a record $23.7 billion in 1996. *Chaebol* profits were also forced downward: the forty-nine largest business groups recorded total profits of just $32 million on combined sales of $274 billion in 1996, for a rate of profit of 0.1 percent (Moon, 1997, 57). The *chaebol* sustained their operations only by going deeper into debt. And, thanks to the liberalization of foreign borrowing, an increasing percentage of funds came from foreign lenders. By 1997, Korea's foreign debt totaled over $160 billion dollars, with approximately $70 billion due for repayment in less than a year.

Relatively powerless to reverse these trends, the Korean state again focused its efforts on labor. It blamed the country's increasingly well organized labor movement for the growing economic problems and attempted to crush it with new, more restrictive labor laws passed in a secret December 1996 National Assembly meeting. This attempt was met with a massive general strike, which only further reduced the country's export earnings. A number of major Korean firms were forced to declare bankruptcy in the first half of 1997. These bankruptcies, in turn, threatened to destabilize the country's banking system.

As massive capital outflows triggered crises in Thailand, Malaysia, Indonesia, and to a lesser extent the Philippines, caused in large part by investor fears of growing balance-of-payments problems, foreign investors also found reason to worry about the stability of Korea. Many therefore sold their stocks and bonds, cut back their investment, and refused to rollover existing loans. With insufficient reserves, the Korean government was forced to respond to this flight of capital by raising interest rates and cutting spending. However, its efforts to halt the run on the won failed; by mid-November 1997 the currency was rapidly losing value, and the economy headed into crisis.[4]

The Dynamics of Restructuring

The severity of Korea's crisis and the nature and extent of the restructuring that followed were also critically influenced by the changed international environment. For example, South Korea's foreign minister traveled to Japan on an emergency mission to arrange an official loan and the rollover of Japanese commercial bank loans. The foreign minister refused to help (Blustein, 2001, 128). The US government

4 Two World Bank economists summed up the severity of the crisis as follows: "As a result of this crisis, Korea experienced the harshest economic recession of its entire post-war history. Industrial production dropped by 12 per cent between August 1997 and August 1998, while business investment decreased by 28.3 per cent in the third quarter of 1998 when compared to the same period of the previous year. Corporate bankruptcies reached an unrecorded high of 3,197 firms during December of 1997 [compared with a monthly average of 965 during 1996]. Layoffs were extensive, leading to 7.4 percent unemployment in August 1998." See Ferri and Kang (1999, 198-199).

was no more helpful. In fact, the US government sought to take advantage of the crisis to pursue its own restructuring agenda (Crotty and Lee, 2004, 8-10, 31-32).

In response to a Korean request for assistance, the IMF sent Hubert Neiss to Seoul in late November 1997. However, as business journalist Paul Blustein relates, "It soon became apparent that the deal Neiss was negotiating would fail to satisfy one interested party – the US Treasury. As one IMF economist recalled, 'Treasury thought Neiss was giving the shop away'" (Blustein, 2001, 141). Therefore, the United States sent Treasury Undersecretary David Lipton to Seoul to monitor the negotiations. Lipton became a constant, although indirect, participant in the negotiations, and he successfully stalled a final agreement, with the result that the crisis deepened. An agreement only became possible when it included conditions that the US government wanted. After the IMF agreement was finally signed in early December, a Treasury official boasted to reporters in Washington D.C. that the agreement "will bring about substantial changes in the Korean financial sector, which in turn have the potential to open up the Korean economy and move it toward one that is much more dependent on the operation of market forces" (Blustein, 2001, 149).

Responding to IMF/US pressure, the Korean government agreed to further open the country's money, stock, and bond markets to foreign investors and new sectors to foreign direct investment. It also agreed to foreign buyouts of strategic firms (even if hostile), the deregulation of the foreign exchange market, the removal of tariff and non-tariff barriers on imports, a massive privatization program, and significant changes in the country's labor laws giving firms greater freedom to fire workers and employ temporary workers in their place (Crotty and Lee, 2001). In essence, the government agreed to abandon the strategies and tools that had previously defined its once-celebrated state-directed growth strategy.

The Korean government implemented this full reform package in large part because its already weak negotiating position was made weaker still by the terms of the initial IMF agreement and US policy. As some analysts pointed out at the time, initial IMF demands for higher interest rates and cuts in government spending, far beyond what the Korean government had proposed, sharply raised business costs and slashed domestic demand. As a result, many healthy firms were pushed into bankruptcy, thereby worsening the crisis.[5]

At the same time, the IMF agreement failed to reassure foreign investors that South Korea would have sufficient foreign exchange to meet its international obligations. In part this was because the US government was reluctant to support it with promised funds (Blustein, 2001, pp. 178-182). Thus, the Korean currency continued to fall throughout December, further intensifying the crisis. As Korea approached financial collapse, a new agreement was finally reached in late December. The IMF agreed to speed up its contribution, the US government agreed to provide additional financial

5 For example, the IMF forced the South Korean government to raise interest rates from 13 percent in early December 1997 to 34 percent one month later. See Crotty and Lee (2004, p. 4; 2001, 6-7).

support, and major commercial banks agreed to rollover or extend existing inter-bank loans. This new agreement was reached, however, only after the South Korean government accepted an "IMF-Plus" plan that committed it to an accelerated and deeper reform program than the one agreed to in early December (Blustein, 2001, 199). While external pressures largely drove the reform process, the support of powerful national interests also pushed the government to accept IMF/US dictates. The large *chaebol* were eager to gain their freedom from state directives and restrictive labor laws. Some of the mandated structural changes, especially those dealing with labor, were just what they wanted.

What Lies Ahead?

The US government appears generally content with Korea's more free-market orientation. As the US Congressional Research Service explains, "The intensity of the disputes [between the two countries] has diminished considerably since the late 1980s and early 1990s, in part because South Korea has enacted a set of sweeping market-oriented reforms as a quid pro quo for receiving a $58 billion package from the International Monetary Fund following the near collapse of the Korean economy in 1997" (Manyin, 2004, 2).

Even so, the US continues to pressure the Korean state into new market openings and a further retreat from industrial policy. A case in point: the Korean government wants to establish mobile communications as a strategic growth industry for the country. To encourage rapid investment, it announced its intention to establish mandatory technological standards for wireless telecommunications services. However, US technology firms do not support the chosen standards and fear that this will shut them out of the Korean market. The US trade representative responded by declaring Korea a "key country of concern," raising the specter of possible trade sanctions. As a result, the Korean government appears to have abandoned its plans for standardization (Manyin, 2004, 10-11).

US multinational corporations and many Korean *chaebol* also appear supportive of Korea's neoliberal restructuring, largely because it has opened up new private profit-making opportunities for them. At the same time, they also continue to press for even more deregulation, liberalization, and privatization, which the government cannot easily resist. Korea is now trapped in a self-reinforcing downward spiral. The post-crisis neoliberal restructuring has increased the economy's dependence on foreign investment and exports. Thus, foreign firms and *chaebol* exporters are in an excellent position to demand further concessions that, if granted, will only reinforce this same dependency.

Business analysts continue to claim that neoliberal reforms will improve the performance of the Korean economy and the well-being of its citizens. But, as highlighted above, neither has proven true. Changed international capitalist dynamics undermined Korea's past growth strategy and continue to limit the country's economic options. Neoliberal policies, which only increase Korea's dependence on these dynamics, can hardly be expected to help promote a broad-based national development agenda. This conclusion is strengthened by the nature of current US and Korean business demands. In 2004, the head of the American Chamber of Commerce in Korea explicitly laid out expectations for the South Korean government: "Korea's competition is Shanghai, Hong Kong and China. Realize what your competition is, because investors can choose where to go" (Kim Ji-hyun, 2004b).

The *chaebol* share this perspective. Above all, they, like their US counterparts, seek more "flexible" labor conditions, which ultimately means government initiatives designed to weaken the labor movement. They have made clear that if the government does not meet their demands they will continue to move their production "across the Yellow Sea to China, where wages are lower and the demands of workers rarely result in headaches for managers" (Kirk, 2003, W1). This is no empty threat. As reported by the *Korea Herald*,

> Korean industries are moving overseas faster than firms in other advanced economies, and the so-called industrial "hollowing out" will likely become a serious problem by 2007, Korea's leading business organization argued . . . Industrial migration, which in the past took place mostly in light industries such as shoe-making and apparel industries, is rapidly spreading to other sectors, including the electronics, telecommunications, metal and machinery industries, it noted. (Kim Hyun-chul, 2003)

In fact, signs of industrial hollowing-out are already visible. For example, Korean firms have largely stopped buying new equipment for their domestic operations. Before the crisis, the yearly growth rate of investment in machinery in the manufacturing sector was regularly over 20 percent. It fell to 0 percent in 1999, 0.5 percent in 2000, and then -5.9 percent in 2001 and -4.9 percent in 2002. While the rate of investment turned positive in 2003 and 2004, the recovery has been quite modest, 0.6 percent and 3.2 percent respectively. To put this trend in perspective, South Korean manufacturing companies spent a total of 74.4 trillion won in new equipment and plants in 2004, 4.3 percent less than the 77.7 trillion won spent in 1996 (Editorial, 2005b). As a consequence, employment in manufacturing is now declining (Kim So-young, 2005a, 1).

The administration of President Roh Moo-hyun has been doing all it can to satisfy business demands. In addition to the creation of special economic zones, it has also been pursuing bilateral investment agreements and free trade agreements with many countries, including Japan and the US. It has been one of the strongest advocates for a maximum WTO agenda, which includes full implementation of the Singapore issues. It remains committed to a program of privatization. And, it continues, despite its initial promise to remain neutral in labor disputes, to break strikes through compulsory arbitration, police interventions, and the encouragement of corporate use of civil suits. Such policies are unlikely to improve either the stability of the Korean economy or living and working conditions for most Koreans. Rather they can be expected to reinforce existing trends that promote inequality, poverty, and national industrial disarticulation.

Korea's economic fortunes are now ever more tightly tied to the dynamics of international capitalism. As a result, Korea's current growth strategy has placed workers on a treadmill, requiring them to accept worsening living and working conditions in a self-defeating attempt to attract higher levels of foreign investment and boost exports. To this point, working class activism appears focused on building militant trade unions and defending labor rights broadly defined. While these are important goals, workers will likely find their efforts frustrated and marginalized as long as overall government policy remains within the limits set by contemporary capitalist dynamics. Unless these dynamics are themselves rejected by large numbers of people, even liberal governments that identify with worker demands will end up taking the path of least resistance, which means bowing to capitalist imperatives and opposing these demands.

Thus, resistance to government policies must be tied to efforts to build new working class-based social movements capable of articulating and advancing new economic visions. This is no simple task.[6] It is also not one faced by Korean workers alone. Unfortunately, despite the fact that capitalist globalization has proven destructive of development possibilities throughout the world, and growing numbers of people are demonstrating in opposition to neoliberal policies, no movements have yet been able to successfully place alternative social visions on their respective national political agendas and win large scale support for them. As a result, Korean activists continue to find themselves forced to break new ground under difficult conditions, with few national experiences to inspire or inform their efforts.

That said, the arguments advanced in this paper do provide insights into the kind of organizing that must inform movement building efforts. Most importantly, they make clear that opposition to government policies must be built in ways that promote popular understanding of the fact that contemporary capitalist dynamics structurally undermine development possibilities in Korea (as well as in other countries). This will encourage South Koreans to see worker resistance as a step towards, rather than an obstacle to, the needed transformation of the country's political economy.

Finally, given the nature of contemporary capitalist dynamics, organizing efforts must also encourage awareness that new social visions and the institutional structures necessary to realize them are most likely to emerge out of a process of social change that strengthens regional working class solidarity and, on that basis, encourages new forms of regional planning and regulation over economic activity. In sum, without recognizing and confronting the shifting and contradictory nature of international capitalism, Korea will likely be dragged further down a path that leads away from the future desired by most Koreans.

6 For a discussion of some of the challenges facing the Korean Confederation of Trade Unions and the Democratic Labor Party see Hart-Landsberg (2005).

Chapter 9

When Capital Becomes Society: The Re-composition of Capitalist Work and New Labor Activism in Korea

Dae-oup Chang

Introduction

This article aims to examine the re-composition of capitalist work in South Korea (hereafter Korea). Based on Marx's understanding of capital as a form of social relations of the extraction of abstract labor, this article will show the continual reorganization of capitalist labor in Korea by tracing the interaction between the movement of capital and labor. Particular focus will be on the recent movement of capital that precipitated the massive irregularization of capitalist work. This article shows how labor has been subsumed to the logic of the reproduction of the social conditions of capital accumulation after the Asian economic crisis. However, it does not examine this process as a one-way process of labor being recomposed by the movement of capital. Rather, I illustrate this process by closely looking at the way in which labor moves beyond the social arrangement of exploitation by founding itself on the newly emerging labor activism in Korea.

The Movement of Capital

Capital as a Social Relation

Capital is in a constant movement. Capital moves by taking different forms. It changes itself into labor force (variable capital), it can take form of constant capital (means of production), and also can even become invisible through the various forms of imaginary money transactions between buyers and sellers. It moves beyond national border, buys out new companies, restructures production organization, replaces human labor with machinery and so on. Why does capital move then? Capital is, at first glance, a certain amount of money. However, we are not calling just any money capital. To be capital, money should be set in motion, either in the production process (productive capital) or in the speculative market (money capital), so that capital can valorize. In short, capital is money in motion that bears more money at the end of the valorization process (M-C-M'). The fact that capital is money-in-motion does not mean that money moves around as if it were a living thing. It is important that we understand capital not as a 'thing'. Capital is not just certain amount of money set in motion. Capital is capital only in relation to capitalist labor. "Capital, without labor, ceases to exist" (Holloway, 1996, 140). Without being a particular social relation, capital is just some amount of money, which cannot valorize, therefore cannot be counted as capital. In this regards, capital is a form of social relation between owners of money and owners of labor power, through which a particular form of social labor is organized and mobilized toward production of surplus value (Marx, 1990).

Capital as a form of social relation is in fact a developed form taken by the very basic social relations between commodity owners (in this case, money owner and labor- commodity owner) – therefore, value relations. Marx in *Capital* starts founding his explanation of capitalist social relation by exploring "value". Through his early critique of private property, Marx shows us that the social categories, such as exchange value and private property, are not naturally given but determined as a result of specific interconnections between people. The absence of an understanding of the value-form as the specific way in which individual labors, as well as individuals themselves, are connected with one another specifically was, for Marx, the origin of the misunderstanding of the whole capitalist society.

> ...Adam Smith and Ricardo, treat the form of value as something external to the nature of the commodity itself. The explanation for this is not simply that their attention is entirely absorbed by the analysis of the magnitude of value. It lies deeper. The value-form of the product of labour is the most abstract, but also the most universal form of the bourgeois mode of production; by that fact it stamps the bourgeois mode of production as a particular kind of social production of a historical and transitory character. If then we make the mistake of treating it as the external natural form of social production, we necessarily overlook the specificity of the value-form, and consequently of the commodity-form together with its further developments, the money-form, the capital form, etc (Marx, 1976, 174).

For Marx, value is the mode of existence of labor, the human activity in capitalist social relations. Marx defines labor in general as "a condition of human existence which is independent of all society" (Marx, 1976, 133). However, "what matters here is only the specific manner in which the social character of labour is established" (Marx, 1971, 32). To understand "value", we must look at the commodity, the container of value. Commodity has a dual nature: it has usefulness as product of useful labor, while it also has socially recognized "value" as product of abstract labor (Marx, 1976). While the characteristics of human labor as concrete labor is subordinated to labor as abstract labor, the characteristics of the commodity as use-value is also subordinated to the characteristic of the commodity as value. Concrete forms of labor "can no longer be distinguished, but are all together reduced to the same kind of labour, human labour in abstract" in the form of value (Marx, 1976, 128). It is the nature of the commodity being a product of (homogeneous and commensurable) abstract labor that defines a useful thing, a product of human laboring practices, as a commodity that can be exchanged, sold and bought in the market. The laboring activity of woman and man is socially recognized only insofar as it is producing or it helps to produce "value" and, to do so, they are laboring within a particular form of social relation (Negri, 1994, 9; Cleaver, 2002, 138-42). Therefore, in a more fundamental sense, "capitalist" labor is value-producing labor, before surplus value producing labor (Clarke, 1991a). Social relation of abstract labor is the social relation that value represents. Value is to be understood as a basic form of capitalist social relation between commodity owners, through which a particular form of social labor is organized and mobilized toward production of value that is "socially" recognized (Marx, 1976).[1] And the development of the value-form marks the development of capitalist social relations distinguished from other social systems.[2] The most developed value-form can be found in money. All commodities express their value in the same body of a commodity and then express their value "in a unified manner" (Marx, 1978, 146). As money universally represents socially recognizable value, i.e. abstract labor, money becomes a dominant form of social relations. In developed capitalist production process, money is set in motion, buying materials, labor forces and so on. "Value" takes the form of relation between commodity of labor power and money owner. Capital as money set-in-motion means also capital is value-in-motion (Neary, 2002) and capital contains all this social relations behind it. The fact that capital is a form of social relation, more specifically social relations in a tension based on the domination of abstract labor over living labor, (or money-in-motion or more fundamentally value-in-motion) gives us the starting point of understanding the reason why capital is in continual movement.[3]

---

1 This social relation, as Marx explains in his exposition of the value-form, appears to be the relation between commodities containing value, the nature of which is abstract labor by producers. Having said that it is abstract labor, it means that it is not important who does that particular laboring activity. Although value is on the basis of the relation between commodity producers and owners, these relations between people are replaced by relations between things, commodities. Once money functions fully and starts mediating exchange, this fetishism gets worse, removing all the traces of the relations between human beings behind the relations between things. This is commodity and money fetishism. Capitalist social relations appear in the form of relations between things. Worse still, this social relation between things becomes the only reality that every one faces everyday. All the business, state policies and social ideas are built up on the basis of this false-but-real sociality (Rubin, 1990, 6).

2 This understanding of value, not as a quantitative amount but as *a social relation* appeared in all his major critical works. It appears most apparently in *the Economic and Philosophical Manuscripts of 1844* and *The Comments on James Mill*. It was developed through all his major works on the critique of political economy such as *Poverty of Philosophy*, *Wage Labour and Capital* and *A Contribution to the Critique of Political Economy,* and it was finally completed in *Capital.*

3 This reading of Marx suggests that Marx's theory of value did not aim at completing that of Ricardo and classical political economy, which "has indeed analyzed value and its magnitude, however, incompletely, and has uncovered the content concealed within these forms", by explaining the way in which a certain amount of individual labor is transformed into price in money (Marx, 1976, 173-4; see also Elson, 1979, 123). Rather, for Marx, the question of value-form is about "why this content has assumed that particular form, that is to say, why labour is expressed in value, and why the measurement of labour by its duration is expressed in the magnitude of the value of the product" (Marx, *Capital* Vol. 1, 1976, 174).

Capital under Constant Pressure to Move

It is nothing unusual that individual capitals, companies, suffer from the problems of overproduction and growing competitive pressure in the market. In fact, this competitive pressure is based on the basic reproductive mechanism of capital: domination of abstract labor over living labor. In capitalist production, the production of social needs (living labor) is subordinated to the need for capital to make profit (abstract labor): the subordination of production of useful things to production of commodities. No social needs without the perspective of producing profit attracts investment whereas profit making perspectives attract too many businesses. Therefore, it is the destiny of capital to survive competition. Only those individual enterprises that are able to utilize more effective methods to keep the price competitive without degrading product quality can win and take the superior position in the competition. Although only a few firms could reach the superior position, and enjoy the competitive edge, it is the *perspective* and desire to reach the highest possible place that drives all enterprises to try more. This vicious cycle between more competition and overproduction is not strange to capitalist development but a basic rule of capitalism. However, this does not mean that this development can go on without consequence. While many new firms get into a new round of competition, many collapse and disappear. Furthermore, the continual investment in the means of production, in the attempts to dominate market, would result in the *over-accumulation of capital* at the industry, national and international level. If it happens on a large scale, the general profit rate starts going down. If the markets are not expanding fast enough to consume the products or if domination over the existing markets is not secured, accumulated productive forces cannot avoid becoming idle. In the face of constant pressure, individual capitals have to move. They continuously restructure their company to maximize efficiency and minimize operating cost. They are vigorously looking for new markets either by going beyond the region and national borders or inventing new social needs.

The basic reproductive mechanism of capital not only causes pressure from over-accumulation, but also produces pressure from workers who, as living labor, sell their abstract labor and whose lives cannot be sustained without being abstract labor (labor commodity). In capitalist ideal, the exchange relation between workers and capitalists appears to be an equivalent and free contract relation between capital and commodity labor as two different sources of revenue or two different individuals who own the functionally differentiated sources of revenue, namely commodity labor power and money-commodity. In reality, the exchange relations are rather reproduced by the attempt of capital to repeatedly present the ideal theory as if it were the given reality. In this framework, there is no need for collective intervention from unions or protection from the state since they undermine the free contract between free labor and capital. However, it does not take much time in the production process for workers to realize that the "labourer is no longer free, for the reproduction of capital depends on the capitalist controlling the process of production and compelling the labourer to work beyond the necessary labour time" (Clarke, 1991b, 191). Under the production of surplus-value as "the absolute law of this mode of production", the reality is that the exchange relations between workers and capitalists can be made only to the extent that labor-power "preserves and maintains the means of production as capital, reproduces its own value as capital, and provides a source of additional capital in the shape of unpaid labour" (Marx, 1976, 769). The ideal of free contract relations now appears in the form of the "rule of the capitalist over the workers", the "rule of things over man, of dead labour over the living, of the product over the producer" (Marx, 1976, 991). The contradiction of capitalist labor eventually precipitates spontaneous and, if more developed, organized forms of struggle of the workers. Workers' struggles impose pressure not only on the direct labor cost of individual capital, but also what we call the "social cost of exploitation" (Holloway, 1996).[4]

In the face of these constant pressures individual capitals are moving into many directions for survival and expansion. One of the common ways of surviving in competition is squeezing the workers by lengthening the working day or intensifying labor (*absolute surplus value exploitation*). However, there is certain limit in doing so because there is absolute limit to force the workers to work beyond human capacity and, if it goes too far, workers would not let it happen. Therefore, while trying to squeeze workers from time to time, individual capitals continually compete with each other to introduce effective means of production on the basis of *new technology*. However, specific development of technology for the labor process and development of the technical division of labor are not naturally given by technological innovation or great invention itself. Rather, the specific social forms that technological development continually takes are shaped by the development of production relations and the organization of production (Marglin, 1983). The specific form of the development of capitalist technical division of labor and the development of technology is derived primarily by the attempt of the capitalist class to enhance the conditions of surplus value production through innovating her/his control over the work process and individual workers. Introduction of mechanization and technology, new division of labor, and introduction of the factory system, "taylorism" and "fordism" are amongst those attempts to sustain accumulation in the face of the intrinsic pressures. If individual capitals are striving to enhance its control over labor and productivity of labor, there are two benefits. First, individual capital, which does it well, is able to reduce the production cost, so that it earns extra money. Furthermore, as a result of the competition for better labor productivity, general improvement in labor productivity in the industries that produce goods for workers' living will reduce their living cost, therefore release collective capital from the pressure of increasing real wages. If workers need less money to survive,

4 Social cost of exploitation includes not only direct labor cost, but also indirect cost that capital has to pay, either in terms of paying money or spending time (which is again money for capital) to reproduce its social domination over living labor. This includes health care, child care, income tax, cooperate tax, severance payment and donation to the political party that secure the interest of certain sectors of capitalist, and so on.

capital can take more. This is *relative surplus value production*, a way capital moves out of the pressures. In utilizing all these methods, capital is moving into another space, time and aspects of our social life. It turns all the things around our life into commodities and the whole society into a commodity producing and consuming sphere, getting all of society "permeated through and through with the regime of the factory" (Negri, 1994, 10). Movement of capital is not just movement of some amount of money from here to there, but more importantly *movement of social relation*, i.e. the expansion, re-composition and restructuring of social relation. In what follows, we will be looking at the traces of the movement of capital in Korea.

What Happened to Korea? The Constant Movement of Capital

The Early Settlement of Capitalist Social Relations in Korea

The initial formation of capitalist social relations in Korea had three main historical moments: Japanese colonization and liberation, the subsequent US control over Korea, and the Korean War. Japanese colonization initiated capitalist development in Korea by depriving the means of production and subsistence from farmers, turning traditional land-ownership into capitalist private property rights and commodifying the products of labor as well as labor power. The colonial capitalist development also had specific features. The integration of the mass of the population into capitalist relations was limited as the majority of the population made their living from within tenant-landlord relations and paid their rent to the landlords primarily with grains. Industrial workers were mobilized and allocated by the colonial state. The Japanese colonial period also resulted in the immature development of Korean capital, since the vast majority of capital invested in Korea was by and for Japanese capital. The sudden end of the colonial capitalist development caused a deep crisis of the further development of capitalist social relations in the aftermath of the liberation. Most of all, it was the emerging workers' and peasants' movement that challenged the capitalist and landlord classes. It was the provisional government of the US military that played the most significant role in stabilizing the crisis through 1) establishing the Korean state 2) redistributing state-vested property to Korean capitalists and 3) demolishing the labor and peasant movements. Further development of capital relations was conditioned by the devastating Korean War. During and in the aftermath of the war, the social power of the landlord class also massively declined due to the land reform in the South. By contrast, the state apparatus survived the war against the "communist threat to freedom" and achieved a significantly increased organizational power as well as legitimacy.

During the post-war period, capital accumulation in Korea relied on the development of domestic firms that had access to raw materials and financial resources supplied by the US aid and domination over the non-competitive domestic markets. In order to secure the exclusive allocation of raw materials and loans, it was necessary for individual capitals to hold a direct alliance with the state in controlling aid and raw materials. Indeed, the state kept playing a significant role in further capitalist development by suppressing the collective power of the working class, therefore guaranteeing unilateral labor relation at the work places. This marked the beginning of the politicized capital relations. It was the Park Chung Hee government which accomplished the particular configuration of capitalist social relations by suppressing the collective power of the working class and exercising its leadership against individual capitals.[5]

Under Park's regime, Korean economic development was momentous, relying on the maximized leadership of the state against individual capitals and suppressive control over collective labor as well as the unlimited supply of labor from the a surplus population. Particular elements of the capitalist development began to develop from the 60s in Korea namely the big *chaebols* and the state's leadership in economic development. During this period, capitalist industrialization deepened with industrial workers doubled in number while extreme exploitation by intensifying labor and

5 According to developmental state theories, the basis of the so-called autonomous developmental state was laid by this transition in the early 60s. However, the transition, beginning with the emergence of Park's military government, was not the development of an autonomous state. Rather it was marked by the highly politicized formation and reproduction of capital relations, in which the state exercised its force to secure maximized exploitation of the working class by capital. The understanding of the Korean state as a developmental state autonomous from capital in the statist argument is a mere mystification. This mystification is based on a particular methodology deriving the nature of the state as an a-historical institution from the relations between the state as an institution and capital as a group of capitalists. In this understanding, capital is understood not as a social relation but as a collective of individuals. If understanding capital as a social relation, the state-capital relation is to be understood as relations between the state and the totality of social relations, i.e. between the state and the reproduction of capital-labour relations. Marxist-structuralist state theory, which the developmental state theory criticizes for its economic determinism, also fails to understand the state-capital relation as relation between the differentiated but complementary forms of the manifestation of the totality of social relations, by concentrating the concept of the relative autonomy of the state as a set of institutions against individual capitals. The state, as a form of social relations through which unequal class relations are inverted into equal relations between individuals, helps the reproduction through capital-from in which unequal relations are inverted into equal relations between different sources of revenue. However, it is distinguished from the reproduction through capital-form, in that it turns the social relations into civil relations between politically equal relations of individuals without regard to the source of revenue individuals own. The state, which identifies itself completely with capital, can only be temporary and needs to rely on extraordinarily predatory methods, since it undermines the basic reproductive process on the basis of commodity fetishism. The mythical developmental autonomy in Korea and other Asian countries draws from the fact that the state could control not only the workers but also a group of individual capitals and therefore the state appeared to be autonomous from class characteristics of social relations. If capital is understood as a social relation and the state-capital relation as relations between the state and totality of social relations, the very concept of developmental autonomy cannot be established.

extending working day was sustained under the auspice of the authoritarian state. The state exercised its power to the extent that it gradually provoked politicized class struggle: the democratic labor movement and the democratization movement from the end of the 1960s. After the assassination of President Park, emerging class struggle could no longer be controlled by the state. The aspirations of the working class appeared in massive re-unionization in a few months. Although the crisis was stabilized by another military coup, the subsequent development of class struggle shows that the early settlement of capital relations was getting into a deep crisis.

Capital and Labor Moves Beyond

From the-mid 1980s, the state could not control the re-emerging class struggle as effectively as Park's regime did in the 1960s and 1970s. Meanwhile, as individual capitals, which succeeded in large-scale accumulation through heavy industrialization in the 1970s, were now able to find external funds without the mediation of the state, the state's grip on financial flows, and therefore control over individual capitals, began to weaken. This means that capital started moving beyond the early settlement of capital relations while labor was being organized into a collective social force. During the period between 1987 and 1997, the deconstruction of the early settlement of capital relations accelerated. It was marked by the increasing movement of capital in and out of Korea and the movement of labor challenging both the unilateral labor relations at the workplace, and the state's suppressive labor policies.

After the three-years boom between 1986 and 1988, the limit of capital accumulation on the basis of absolute surplus value exploitation and state control over collective labor became apparent. Capital began to suffer from both growing cost of exploitation and difficulty in exporting products into the increasingly competitive global market. Facing this difficulty, capital moved forward through the liberalization of financial flows for credit expansion, which would revitalize capital accumulation by enabling individual capitals to introduce new means of production and new products. It was at this time that the dependence of capital investment on foreign loans, which grew from $31.7 billion in 1990 to $104.7 billion in 1996 with a high dependence on short-term loans, reached a critical point. On the other hand, the relocation of productive facilities to other countries was accelerated with enormous FDI outflow that steeply increased from $598 million in 1989 to $4,449 million in 1997 (UNCTAD, 2002b). This liberalization led to the end of capital allocation by the state, which had been a primary element of the early settlement of capital relations in Korea. Meanwhile, the state attempted to control labor by tightening its authoritarian control over trade unions and, most of all, institutionalizing flexible measures that individual capitals introduced in order to effectively control individual workers. However, rather than bringing a fresh basis of capital accumulation, these measures caused instability of the financial basis of the *chaebols* due to growing dependency on short-term credit and more militant resistance of the working class, which appeared in the first ever nation-wide general strike in 1997. Finally, the fall of the early configuration of capital relations and the contested transformation of capital relations, amalgamated with the growing tendency to over-accumulation in the global markets, expressed themselves in the form of a general crisis of the reproduction of capital relations. Capital accumulation, which had been sustained by massive credit expansion but not accompanied by successful renewal of the social conditions of capital accumulation at last revealed its limit in the form of massive bankruptcies of individual capitals. The crisis was a dramatic expression of the failure of capital in revitalizing the social conditions of accumulation and overcoming the intrinsic contradiction of capitalist social relations i.e. the subordination of living labor to abstract labor. It was not until the restructuring period in the aftermath of the general crisis that a new social basis of further capital accumulation took a shape. The new condition of capital accumulation was based on the freer movement of capital, which went beyond the barrier of state regulation as well as organized labor.

Capital Moves and Labor Recaptured: Irregularization of Labor after the Economic Crisis

Capital Moves toward Irregular Labor

The economic crisis revealed that the way in which capital moved during the last 10 years was not successful enough to overcome (in fact suppress the emergence of) the intrinsic contradiction of capitalist social relations. The response of the Korean state to the unfolding of the crisis, with a strong commitment to the IMF's stabilization and structural adjustment policies, was focusing on removing all the barriers of capital movement in pursuit of better profitability from one to another production process, product, industrial sector, and country. Stabilization policies kicked the debt-ridden individual capitals out of the markets. On the other hand, they forced individual capitals to withdraw from planned investment, cut wages, downsize production and utilize mass lay-offs in attempts to stay away in the unfolding of the crisis. All these created about 2 million job loss within two years after the crisis. Indeed, the formal form of capitalist work, protected by regulations and the trade unions, was seen as an obvious barrier to the attempt of capital to move internally as well as externally. The deregulation of labor, which mostly appeared in the form of irregularization, became therefore an essential historical condition of further expansion of capital.

Focus on irregular capitalist work is a recent phenomenon. On the one hand, it is the increasing number of the non-traditional employment in developed countries that cause the "informalization" or "irregularization" debate. On the other, the growth of the so-called informal "sector" or "economy" in developing countries provokes discussions about non-traditional capitalist work. The former discussion tends to deal with labor in the informal sector as a temporary phenomena resulting from underdevelopment. Meanwhile, the latter tends to consider irregular work in the framework of "industrial relations" and identifies capitalist work with regular work, ultimatizing regular work. Therefore, both have limit in understanding the relation between the increasing movement of capital as a global phenomenon and the irregularization of labor.[6]

Perhaps, to understand the relation, it would be useful to begin with the historical formation of "regular capitalist work". At the beginning of capitalist development, capitalist work existed in various forms, which we now might call "informal or irregular", such as seasonal manufacturing or agricultural jobs, work at family-run business, and so on. For most of the population, making a living was reliant pre-dominantly on self-subsistence and only partially on commodity producing labor. It was not until the emergence of large-scale manufacturing and the labor movement that the concept of "standard" form of capitalist work emerged. Most of the elements of the formal form of capitalist work, such as "regular hours and pay, the provision of designed workplace, with pensions and sick pay arrangements and often the opportunity to join trade union" (Bradley at al., 2000, 52), came into being since then. Formal employment then became a dominant form of capitalist work at least in developed countries. Furthermore, all the terminology of industrial relations, such as collective bargaining, collective agreement, workers council, and tripartite committee, were developed on the basis of the particular historical arrangement of capitalist work.

Even then, for capital, regular, protected capitalist work is not at all the healthy form of *capitalist* work since, in capitalist ideal, the exchange relation between workers and capitalists appears to be a free contract relation. Intervention in the exchange relations should be exceptional because it denies the ideal of capitalism. Therefore, although "formal employment" has become the definition of capitalist work, the standard form of capitalist work is confined within a few developed countries and certain industrial sectors and various forms of irregular employment survived. Irregular form of "employment" here refers to the wide range of people whose working relation is based on direct and indirect "wage relations". This irregular "employment" however does not cover the "un-waged" form of capitalist work, such as many forms of self-employment.[7] Normally, self-employed are related to employers or corporation service users not through wage relations but through commercial relations even if they are working for the corporations. Although their relations with employers are vague and untraceable and sometimes practically *do not exist*, they are still doing capitalist work because their work functions to reproduce capital (by reproducing labor power of others, contributing to realizing produced

6 As far as we take irregular labour as a "temporary" or something "atypical" against capitalist work, the response of the labor movement against irregularisation will have a clear limit. It is important to understand that the industrial relation of regular labour is a historical product. It is also important not to confine capitalist labour relation within a clear form of wage relations. Capitalist labor relation is basically value relation. A more flexible theorisation and discussion of the future strategy of the movement of labour are possible by understanding value relations as labor relations. In this article, we deal with both regular and irregular work as a historical form taken by the movement of labor and capital.

7 Indeed, a large part of self-employment tends to develop as capital tries to avoid legal responsibility in employing formal workers.

value, etc). It is also obvious that the reproduction of their labor is subjected not to the concrete achievement of their work but to the "amount" of money s/he earns. In many cases, they do not have any means of production and employee. Furthermore, many of them are getting in and out of employment relations and stay unemployed in between. Many self-employed are as vulnerable as informal employees in that they cannot enjoy social protection such as social insurance, not to mention union protection.

The irregularization of capitalist work at global level involves two main aspects. For the workers in developed countries, it mostly, but not exclusively, means a process of the dissolution of formal employment. Increasing number of workers previously in standard form of employment become disposable workforces. In addition, many functions and services previously handled by corporations have been transferred to the self-employed – however, without completely losing corporate control over the work. It affects not only workers who have previously enjoyed the privilege of job protection, but also new comers as new jobs are predominantly irregular. In this way, the size of the population under formal capitalist employment, i.e. the so-called 'traditional' working class, is decreasing therefore undermining the basis of traditional trade union movement.[8] Lack of protection for irregular jobs ultimately means that *labor forces are individualized in relation to capital*. Employment relations become literally individual relations between individual capitalist and workers. In developing countries, irregular work is due to the non-availability of formal capitalist work for the population who are newly integrated into the increasingly dominant capitalist social relations. Irregularization in this sense is a particular process in which the population working previously in non-or-partial capitalist labor relations is integrated into commodity production relations and the market. In this case, irregularization is also a particular form in which capitalist work becomes truly global. In sum, the portion of irregular work against capitalist work is increasing globally. This means that capital must be united only with a particular sort of capitalist labor treated as a truly mere factor of production. In this way, capitalist labor, which was formally contained within the factory or industrial area in developed countries, is internalized in individual workers without regard to employment relations and working places and spreads into all over the society, becoming truly social and global.

Irregularization of Capitalist Work in Korea after the Asian Crisis

The reconstruction of capital relations began with the Kim Dae Jung government's attempts to reform of the so-called rigid labor market. The crisis offered the surviving individual capitals a great opportunity to introduce the "flexible" labor. This includes irregular employment contract, more competition-based personnel management and

8 This is the reason why many sociologists are prematurely talking about "the end of work" and saying "farewell" to the working class. However, the size of the population actually involved in "capitalist work" is not decreasing but increasing. This is the case if we consider tens of millions of Chinese workers not involved in waged work.

pay systems, the full utilization of which had been blocked by the unions' domination over the workplaces since the upsurge of the militant labor movement in the late 1980s. In the meantime, the state also institutionalized the market-based employment relations. Since then, the so-called numerical employment adjustment became a routine practice, rather than an emergency measure, so as to control unemployment as a whole within a certain degree. Facing this reformulation of workplace labor relations, the unions appeared to be impotent. The utilization of mass lay-off as a management tool as well as the operation of work agencies was legalized through tripartite social contract between employers, workers and the government, including the militant KCTU. In turn, the government recognized the teachers' union, removed the ban on unions' political activity and allowed the unionization of public servants under the condition of not exercising their right to take collective actions (KCTU, 1997, 180). After this controversial agreement, individual unions, such as Hyundai Motors Union, had difficult time to struggle against mass lay-off. Strike against lay-off has been illegalized, as the structural adjustment measures, according to the government, could not be subjected to collective action. Workers in non-organized companies were suffering even more. For example, LG electronics laid-off more than 30% of its workforce while Samsung reduced 10,000 work forces between 1996 and 1999, without facing a single protest.

The number of workers under the irregular employment has been growing throughout the 1990s in Korea. However, it was from the beginning of the serious recession in 1996 that irregularization began to accelerate. Temporary and daily contracted workers, the number of which accounted for about 41percent of total employment at the beginning of 1996, outnumbered that of standard-regular workers, accounting for 52 percent of total wage-workers in 2001.[9] Although the figure has slightly decreased due to the economic recovery in 2002, these forms of employment still accounted for about 49 percent of total employment in 2003. According to Kim's analysis that looks into various indirect and abnormal forms of employment, such as dispatched workers, disguised freelancers, on-call workers, home-based work, whose legal employment relation is uncertain and therefore can be hardly protected by law, a total of 772 million workers were estimated to do informal work in 2003 (Kim, Y. S., 2004). This accounts for 55.4 percent of total employment in Korea. Regardless of the nature of relations with employers, most of the irregular workers appear to have temporary contract (about 97.9 percent of total informal workers).

Although the service sector shows a high density of irregular employment (retail 71.8 percent, hotel and catering 94 percent, domestic work 100 percent), massive increase in irregular employment came mostly from the sectors where traditionally regular workers were dominant. In these sectors, there has been a widespread employment strategy that 1) dismisses the full-time permanent workers, 2) changes the posts into irregular ones without changing job specification, 3) and fills up the

9 The regular or standard employment means, in Korean labour survey, employee that works more than one year and receives regular wage including basic pay, bonus and over time payment. Therefore, the statistics reflects only short-term informal workers.

vacancies either by re-employing the sacked workers or by employing new graduates.[10] In the banking and financial sector, about 15 percent of the total workforce was made up of those re-employed (KILSP ed., 2000, 118). New jobs in this sector have been predominantly irregular. 4,640 out of 6,612 new employments in 1998 were informal and 4,671 out of 5,501 in 1999 (Kwon, 2001, 91). As a result, in 2003, the banking and financial sector employed 310,000 irregular workers that accounted for 44.6 percent of total employees. In the public sector, about two thirds of the laid-off full-time permanent job holders have been re-employed as irregular workers, including part-timers, temporarily contracted, dispatched and sub-contracted workers, which increased 46.1 percent during the four years after the crisis (KFTPSU, 2002, 9). In 2003, about 20 percent of the total employment in the public sector was estimated as irregular, comprising 234,000 workers (*Labor News*, 23rd February 2004).

In the manufacturing sector, dispatched and in-house-subcontract workers whose employment contracts are mostly temporary, are the major forms of irregular employment. This expansion can be attributed to the legalization of temporary-work agencies in 1998. In theory, these forms of employment are supposed to be under strict regulation and allowed only for 26 particular forms of skilled-labor. However, dispatched labor is utilized in almost every industrial sector without regard to the nature of work because the Ministry of Labor does not monitor illegal dispatching. Worse still, in cases that labor dispatching is found illegal, the "law for protection of dispatched workers" cannot protect workers. Firms increasingly utilize those indirect forms of employment by affiliating small subcontract firms and work agencies, the survival of which is entirely subjected to yearly or monthly contracts with the mother companies. In many cases, large-scale enterprises establish sub-contract firms and work agencies by themselves (Ahn et al. 2001, 182-6). By making the employment relations more indirect and untraceable, the management can escape from their legal obligation as direct employers and therefore can adjust the number of work forces easily. Also, by putting together irregular and regular workers on the same production line, management can precipitate more competition between them and thereby tame the organized regular workers. "Out-sourcing" methods also contribute to the changing employment structure. As many processes of the production of components for assembling manufacturers, particularly the car-making companies such as Hyundai, Kia and Daewoo, have been given to small and medium sized external subcontractors which rely heavily on cheap daily and temporary workers,[11] the proportion of permanent jobs in the mother companies are likely to decrease (KILSP ed., 2000, 121-2). Likewise, the establishment of quasi-independent subsidiaries within a firm contributes to changing large numbers of

---

10 During a one-year period from June 1998, 80 % of those who could escape from unemployment had been re-employed as temporary and daily workers (Lee and Hwang, 2000, 289).

11 The wages of workers employed in external sub-contract firms producing parts for major car-making companies are merely 60% of those of workers in the major companies (KLISP ed., 2000, 125).

workers employed in the mother company into in-house-subcontract workers whose contract is no longer guaranteed for renewal (KLISP ed, 2000, 118-26).

On top of this, non-employed (or disguised as non-employed) capitalist work also increases. This can be found in the number of self-employed that increased from 4,105,000 in 1996 to 4,413,000 in 2003. This means 7.5 percent growth during the period, in comparison to a mere 3.5 percent increase between 1989 and 1996. Except a very few high-income freelancers, such as consultant or translators, most of the workers are involved in very small size businesses. In many cases, the self-employed do have certain employment relations. It is called "special employment" (Teuksugoyong), which refers primarily to service workers who are legally not workers but self-employed, in spite of their employment relations with certain companies. These forms of employment have been regarded largely as non-workers since the firms introduced freelance-like employment contracts in the early 1990s, to bypass the labor standard law. The private tutoring industry, which employs more than 100,000 teachers tutoring more than 6 million students by visiting their homes, is the biggest in this sector. Also, caddies in golf resorts, ready mixed concrete and other construction-related lorry drivers, and delivery service providers are not legally recognized as workers but self-employed although their commercial relations to the consumers in fact subject them to managerial authority in terms of pay, workload, hours and code of conduct.

Another group of irregular workers, often completely neglected, is migrant workers, whose employment contract is apparently and irreversibly temporary. Started with importing workers from foreign subsidiaries of Korean companies, Korea has about 400,000 migrant workers from 95 different countries (Jeong, 2004, 107). Those migrant workers are not allowed to change their workplaces, cannot stay more than three years in Korea and are often paid well lower than the legal minimum wage. As soon as they move to another workplace in search for better wage and humane treatment, they become illegal workers. Reflecting the inhumane condition, there were about 140,000 non-registered migrant workers in 2004. As disposable workforces that have no rights to protect themselves, migrant workers have to tolerate the situation that finds them being actually placed at the bottom of the downward spiral of irregular workers. If adding them to the number of irregular workers, the proportion of irregular workers in the total workers can be much higher.

Despite it all, Labor Moves: The Possibility of a New Labor Activism

Capital becomes Society

The conditions of irregular workers show exactly the reason why capital moves toward irregular work. They are excluded from union or legal protection. As a result, wage gap between regular and irregular employees is widening. The average wage of irregular workers was a mere 51 percent of that of the formal workers in 2003, in comparison to 53.7 percent in 2000. Only about 11 percent of irregular employees received overtime payment. These workers were excluded also from social insurance schemes. More than 70 percent of irregular employees were not covered by national pension scheme, health and employment insurance. Worse still, workers in irregular forms of employment worked longer than formal workers, averaging 44.1 hours per week in 2003, in comparison to 41.8 hours of formal workers (Kim, Y. S. 2004). Due to the temporary and mobile nature of these forms of employment, the union density of irregular workers was merely 2.4 percent, in comparison to 22.7 percent of formal workers in 2003 (Kim, Y. S. 2004, 31-2). Consequently, capital can save the social cost of exploitation enormously.

Worse still, through facilitating irregular work, capital successfully puts workers in competition to each other. One of the challenges to organizing irregular workers is the attitude of regular workers toward irregular workers' unionization. Irregular workers have to establish their own unions, often without support from the existing formal workers' unions, as formal workers see irregular workers as a threat to their jobs. Those conflicting relations between regular and irregular workers appeared clearly in the case of the Korea Telecom contracted workers' strike. The formal workers' union not only refused to accept contracted workers but also practically attempted to disturb the establishment of an independent irregular workers' union. In the case of Korea Career subcontract workers' strike in 2001, the KCTU affiliated regular workers' union co-operated with the employer in breaking the in-house-subcontract workers' union.[12] Irregular workers' attempt to organize union without support from existing formal unions often developed into a long-term struggle for union recognition. Indeed, it makes organizing extremely difficult as irregular workers earn their living on a daily and monthly basis. The Korea Telecom Contracted Workers Union, after 290 days of strike action with more than 1,300 contracted workers, ended up with a bitter failure: dismissal of all the involved workers.

The irregularization of capitalist work and the growing antagonism between regular and irregular workers are results of the continuing attempts of capital to renew the social condition of accumulation. It was achieved through the dramatic economic crisis. Irregularization undermined the labor movement, which has been based on enterprise unionism and solidarity between enterprise unions, by imposing divisions within and outside firms. With increasing irregularization, working for same company no longer means belonging to same company. This dilutes the strong belongingness among the workers, which has been the basis of militant enterprise unionism. Competition for secure jobs and increasing time to search for jobs broke down not only the basis of the student movement but also workers communities as every worker is competing over the question "who is going to be laid-off and how

12 According to Korean Labor Law, as far as the existing formal union's articles allow informal workers to join the union, informal workers could not establish their own union since the plural unionism is illegal at the enterprise level. In Korea Telecom, the formal workers did not allow the informal workers to be members of the formal workers' union.

not" (Chang 2002)? This shows that the logic of capital is incarnated in individual workers laboring for capital in and outside of factory, permeating into once solidarity-seeking relations between workers. After the ten years of transition, capital became society while society continuously defines itself according to the logic of profit making. Irregular work requires a worker to be always stand-by capitalist labor for abstraction. This "always availability" for abstraction makes other non-abstract forms of labor less feasible. The result is that workers are exploiting themselves, without even being forced directly by capital. When capital moves, it involves changes in social relations. It puts people into a new set of social relation, turns employees into unemployed, partners of the unemployed into employees, farmers into factory workers, housewives into women workers, schoolgirls into migrant workers, and a community into a ruin. As capital moves, labor is recaptured in new forms.

However, this does not mean the new social arrangement as a result of the movement of capital can resolve the intrinsic contradiction of capitalist social relations. Indeed the re-composition of social relations is not a one-way process. Rather, capital is destined to be "engaging in a continuous struggle to maintain the social conditions deemed necessary for profitability" (Cowie, 1999, 2). Capital movement also creates new forms of labor activism as Neary pointed out:

> …as project of capitalist development deepens in response to the critical antagonism which it generates, and those critical antagonism broaden out of the factory to the level of society, the form of labor is also recomposed in ways which challenge the critical responses that were appropriate to its previous manifestation. Labor moves not simply by making strategic alliances with other disparate groups; but rather, the production of labor as a critical antagonism within capitalist social relations generates appropriate forms of critical resistance in and against not only the obvious instrument of capital, but also its own, i.e. labor's institutional forms (Neary, 2002, 169).

It is in this sense that the consequence of the contemporary transition of capital relations in Korea still remains to be seen. The restructuring of capital relations is unlikely to guarantee a smooth further reproduction of capital relations in Korea. There is an initial form of labor activism challenging the society as capital, through which the unresolved contradiction of the newly created basis of capital accumulation reveals itself.

Irregular Workers Organizing

The new labor activism challenging the new configuration of capital relations develops in various forms. There is growing recognition about the importance of solidarity building with irregular worker from within the traditional labor movement. There are a number of cases in which irregular workers were successfully organized in cooperation with regular workers' unions, particularly in small and medium sized firms. Firstly, there are cases in which the existing formal workers' unions aggressively integrated irregular workers into unions, in an attempt to prepare effective struggles against the flexible measures of employment adjustment. Successful unionization in this form took place in service, (Lotte Hotel, AC Nielson Korea), garment (E-Land) and metal industry (INI Steel) (Kim, H. J. 2002). There are also cases in which regular workers' unions actually nurtured an independent irregular workers' union. In both cases, the formal workers' unions made a great effort to organize irregular workers and persuade their own members to recognize the irregular workers' union and union membership. The Sinho Paper Manufacturing Union is a good example of an elaborated preparation of a formal workers' union in supporting irregular workers' unionization. During more than two years of preparation, the union organized 'a special committee for organization of irregular workers' and offered various educational training programs for union activists among irregular workers (Kim, H. J. 2002, 53-7). On the other hand, E-Land Union's case shows that the segregation between irregular and regular workers could be overcome by developing solidarity through a coordinated strike (Hong, 2002).

There are also struggles through which traditional non-workers became recognized as workers, therefore widening the basis of organizing labor. A good example can be found in the struggle of "disguised freelancers". Private teachers in Jeneung Education, the biggest private tutoring firm, established the Jeneung Education Teachers' Labor Union (JETLU) in 1999 after a month-long strike against the government and the employer who did not recognize the teachers as workers therefore refused to recognize the union. Furthermore, the JELTU achieved a collective agreement with the employer in 2000. This was an important step because it shows that many self-employed are actually eligible for collective action and bargaining, and other union rights in so far as their work is tied to a certain relation of control. Many other, "self-employed", are also organizing trade unions in spite of an on-going dispute about their legal status as "workers". Most of their unions are still outlawed but affiliated with the KCTU.

As capital expands into society without regard to direct employment relations, organizing at the society level has been an important method to empower workers. These "social organizing" initiatives are developing in the form of ultra-firm level organization. There are 8 general unions (Ilbannojo). Another form of ultra-firm level unionization is an occupational union in industries exclusively employing irregular workers, such as daily-construction workers. The Seoul Daily Construction Workers' Union, established in 1988, is an early example. This form of unionization is gaining increasing significance since it is in these petty-scale enterprises that most irregular workers are concentrated. Now, 5 regional-based general unions exist, including Gyungi Province Trade Union, Seoul General Trade Union, Masan-Changwon General Union, Chung-Nam General Trade Union and Pusan General Trade Union. They offer umbrella union membership, legal consultancy and support to informal workers without regard to the type of occupations (Park, 2002, 86-99). These initiatives are effective in organizing individual workers whose workplace is too small to organize an enterprise union and exercise collective actions against the employers. The alternative way is to set up branches of the general union in small sized firms. There are also general unions, such as Seoul Women's Trade Union, Korean Women's Trade Union and Seoul-Gyungi Equal Trade Unions, which aim to organize particularly women workers who account for more than 70 percent of irregular workers. They support individual women workers to struggle against sexual discrimination and the deterioration of working conditions by offering union education, conducting collective bargaining and providing legal advice. A recent case of this form of organizing is the migrant workers union. Migrant workers in Korea set up the "Struggle Network for Migrant Workers' Labor Rights and Freedom of Migration and Working" in 2000. This developed into "Equality Trade Union – Migrants" Branch in 2001. After organizing 300 days of sitting protest publicizing labor rights abuses against migrant workers in Korea, they were finally able to launch an independent union in April 2005. For these social organizing initiatives, bargaining is also becoming more and more "social", not confined within direct employment relations, but reaching to users and public, including local governments and public institutions.

Organizing informal workers has also been supported by voluntary organizations that exist outside trade union. In the case of migrant workers, small migrant workers supporting organizations and its coalition (Joint Committee for Migrant Workers in Korea) have played an important role. Also, there are organizations supporting irregular workers' movement. A coalition of these organizations is now developing into a nation-wide movement by organizing a nation-wide alliance namely the "National Alliance for Removing Insecure Labor". While the existing confederations are increasingly alerted to overcome the formal-male-worker-centered unionism, the irregular workers' movement, in spite of its short history, is already beginning to go beyond firm and occupational boundaries and build itself on the basis of solidarity among different forms of capitalist work.

Conclusion: Labor moves Beyond

Capital is a form of social relations through which labor is organized into a particular social form: abstract labor. The domination of abstract labor over living labor is the basis of capitalism but at the same time the origin of its instability. Facing constant pressure from its own mode of existence, capital has to move to survive and reproduce itself. The movement of capital is the movement of social relations. Indeed, it is the social relations that define labor as capitalist labor. This means the movement of capital involves the movement of labor. This article explored the recent transition of capitalist work by looking at the way in which capital moves in response to the emerging pressures on accumulation as a manifestation of the intrinsic contradiction of capitalist labor. The social relations of exploitation of abstract labor have undergone transformation during and after the Asian economic crisis and capital increasingly permeates into society by imposing its logic of reproduction on individual workers and thereby society. The current irregularization reflects the attempts of capital to utilize new methods to overcome the constant pressure of the crisis of accumulation by maximizing the internal and external mobility. These methods presuppose that there should be no barrier against the movement of capital. Targeted as a main barrier, formal capitalist work, protected by legal regulation and trade union, has been under attack. However, as far as capital relies on the extraction of abstract labor for its accumulation, this renewed domination of capital over society does not necessarily mean a completion of the domination. The newly emerging labor activism shows that labor also moves beyond the social conditions of accumulation imposed by the movement of capital, even before they are consolidated, by questioning the existing institutional forms of the movement of labor.

Appendix

Major Political and Economic Events in Korea, 1945-2006

1945. 8.15.	Emancipation from Japanese colonial rule
1948. 4. 3.	People's uprising in Cheju against the general election restricted to South Korea; approximately 50,000 killed
1948. 8.15.	Inauguration of Republic of Korea, Syngman Rhee elected as the first President
1948. 9. 9.	Inauguration of Democratic People's Republic of Korea, Kim Il Sung elected as the first President
1950. 3.25.	Land reform decree abolishing the semi-feudal tenant system
1950. 6.25.	Start of the "Korean War"
1952. 5.24.	Agreement on Economic Coordination Between ROK and USA ("Meyer Agreement"); Combined Economic Board established to enhance US control over Korean economic policy
1953. 7.27.	Armistice Agreement ending the Korean War fighting
1953.10. 1.	Mutual Defense Treaty Between ROK and USA
1960. 4.19.	April Revolution against the Rhee government's election rigging and corruption
1960. 8.23.	Chang Myon elected as Prime Minister and head of the 2nd Republic
1961. 5.16.	Military coup d'état led by general Park Chung Hee overthrows the Chang government
1961. 7.22.	Inauguration of the Economic Planning Board
1962. 1. 5.	Inauguration of First Five-Year Plan for Economic Development
1963.10.15.	Park Chung Hee elected as the President of 3rd Republic
1965. 1.26.	Dispatch of ROK army to fight in the Vietnam War
1965. 6.22.	Normalization Treaty with Japan signed
1967	Second Five-Year Plan for Economic Development
1969.10.23.	Inauguration of Export Free Zones
1970.11.13.	A textile worker, Jeon Tae-Il, burnt himself to death in protest against lack of enforcement of labor laws

1971.12.27.	"Special Law for State Security" to repress opposition movements
1972. 7. 4.	July 4th Joint Communiqué by North and South Korean Governments for Peace and Reunification
1972. 8. 3.	Private loan payments frozen by government decree
1972.10.17.	Inauguration of "Yushin System"
1973. 1.12.	Government initiation of heavy and chemical industrialization
1975. 5.14.	Government emergency decree # 9 to eliminate opposition movements
1977	Fourth Five-Year Plan for Economic Development, exports reach $10 billion
1978	Publication of "The Theory of National Economy" by Hyun-Chai Park, one of Korea's earliest and most celebrated radical economists
1979.10.16.	People's uprising against "Yushin System" in Pusan and Masan
1979.10.26.	Assassination of Park Chung Hee by Jae-Kyu Kim, Director of Korean Central Intelligence Agency
1979.12.12.	Military coup d'état led by general Chun Doo Hwan
1980. 5.18.	Peoples' uprising in Kwangju against Chun Doo Hwan's military coup d'état; brutally crushed, approximately 5,000 people killed.
1980.10.7.	Government ordered adjustment to reduce excessive and duplicated investments in heavy and chemical industries
1987. 6.10.	People's uprising for the amendment of the constitution for the direct election of the President
1987.7-9.	Workers' struggle for the recognition of democratic unions and higher wages
1987.10.	Inauguration of the Korean Social and Economic Association, an association of heterodox economists
1988. 2.	Inauguration of Roh Tae Woo's pseudo-civil government
1988. 9.17.	Seoul Olympics
1989.10. 4.	Introduction of public concept of landownership
1991. 9.17.	North and South Korea simultaneously join the UN
1992. 8.24.	Normalization Treaty with the People's Republic of China
1993. 2.25.	Inauguration of Kim Young Sam's "Civilian" government
1993. 8.12.	Introduction of "Real Name System" for financial transactions
1994. 2.24.	Deregulation of foreign exchange controls (first-stage)
1994. 7. 8.	Death of Kim Il Sung, succeeded by his son, Kim Jong Il
1994.11.17.	Government declaration of the age of globalization ("SeGyeHwa")

1995.11.11.	Inauguration of Korean Confederation of Trade Unions (KCTU)
1996.11.26.	Membership in the OECD
1996.12.26.	General strike led by the KCTU against government attempts to amend the labor law to make layoffs easier
1997. 1.23.	Bankruptcy of Hanbo Steel, 14th largest chaebol
1997. 7.15.	Government organized financial bail-out of KIA Group, 8th largest chaebol; eventually sold to Hyundai Motor Company,
1997.12.	Foreign currency crisis and IMF intervention, followed by severe financial and economic crisis
1998. 2.25.	Inauguration of Kim Dae Jung's "People's" government
1998. 5.25.	Abolition of limits on foreign equity investment
1998. 7. 3.	Privatization of public companies
1998.12. 7.	Neoliberal restructuring of chaebol system
1999. 5.	Abolition of limits on the use of credit card cash advances to boost domestic consumption, resulting in an explosion of household debt and credit delinquencies
2000. 1.30.	Inauguration of Democratic Labor Party
2000. 6.15.	June 15th Joint Communiqué by North and South Korean Governments for Peace and Reunification
2001. 1.	Injection of public funds to restructure the financial sector
2002. 6.13.	Two Korean middle-school girls, Hyosoon and Miseon, killed by the U.S. Army in Korea, igniting anti-American sentiments and "candle demonstrations"
2003. 2.25.	Inauguration of Roh Moo-hyun's "Participatory" government
2003. 5.23.	Inauguration of Marx Communale, an association of socialist scholars and activists
2003.10.29.	Increase on land tax to halt speculation on real estate
2004. 1.16.	The 1st 5-Year Plan for Balanced National Development
2004. 2.13.	Dispatch of Korean troops to Iraq
2004. 2.16.	Korea-Chile Free Trade Agreement
2004. 3.12.	Roh Moo-hyun impeached by National Congress
2004. 4.15.	Democratic Labor Party won 10 seats in the National Assembly
2006. 1. 1.	Roh Mu-hyun declared "social polarization" the main issue of national concern
2006. 1. 3.	U.S and Korean governments begin Free Trade Agreement negotiations
2006. 5.31.	Crushing defeat of Roh's (Uri) party in local elections

Source: Compiled from various sources by Seongjin Jeong

References

Works in English

Abegglen, J. (1994), *Sea Change: Pacific Asia as the New World Industrial Center*, (New York: The Free Press).

Aglietta, M. (1979), *A Theory of Capitalist Regulation*, (London: New Left Books).

Albritton, R. (1991), *A Japanese Approach to Stages of Capitalist Development*, (Basingstoke: Macmillan).

Albritton, R. (1999), *Dialectics and Deconstruction in Political Economy*, (Basingstoke: Macmillan).

Albritton, R. and Simoulidis, J. (eds.) (2003), *New Dialectics and Political Economy*, (Basingstoke: Palgrave).

Albritton, R., Bell. J., Bell, S. and Westra, R. (eds.) (2004), *New Socialisms: Futures Beyond Globalization*, Innis Centenary Series: Governance and Change in the Global Era, (London: Routledge).

Albritton, R., Itoh, M., Westra, R. and Zuege, A. (eds.) (2001), *Phases of Capitalist Development: Booms, Crises and Globalizations*, (Basingstoke: Palgrave).

Alvis, J. (2005). "Korea as A Business Hub in Northeast Asia", *Korea Insight* 7: 6.

Amsden, A. (1989), *Asia's Next Giant: South Korea and Late Industrialization*, (New York: Oxford University Press).

Amsden, A. (1990), "Third World Industrialization: 'Global Fordism' or a New Model?", *New Left Review* 182.

Amsden, A. (1994), "Why Isn't the Whole World Experimenting With the East Asian Model to Develop?: Review of World Bank's East Asian Miracle Report", *World Development* 22: 4.

Anelauskas, V. (1999), *Discovering American as It Is,* (Atlanta: Clarity Press).

Aoki, M, Murdock, K. and Okuno-Fujiwara, M. (1998), "Beyond *The East Asian Miracle*: Introducing the Market-Enhancing View", in Aoki et al. (eds.).

Aoki, M, Kim, H-K and Okuno-Fujiwara, M. (eds.) (1998), *The Role of Government in East Asian Economic Development*, (Oxford: Clarendon).

Arrighi, G. (1994), *The Long Twentieth Century*, (London: Verso).

Asian Development Bank. (2004), *Key Indicators 2004*, May, www.adb.org/statistics.

Asian Development Bank. (2005), *Asia Regional Information Center Indicators*. http://aric.adb.org/.

Asian Development Bank. (2006), *Asia Regional Information Center Indicators*, http://aric.adb.org/.

Athukorala, P. (2003), "Product Fragmentation and Trade Patterns in East Asia", *Working Paper* 2003/21, Division of Economics, Research School of Pacific and

Asian Studies, Australian National University, October.

Ayers, R. and Clarke, D. (1998), "Capitalism, Industrialization and Development in Latin America: The Dependency Paradigm Revisited", *Capital and Class* 64.

Balassa, B. and Williamson, J. (1987), *Adjusting to Success: Balance of Payments Policy in the East Asian NICS*, (Washington D.C.: Institute for International Economics).

Ban, S. (1979), "Agricultural Growth in Korea, 1918-1971", in Hayami et al., (eds.).

Baran, P. and Sweezy, P. (1966), *Monopoly Capital*, (New York: Monthly Review Press).

Barnet, R. and Cavanagh, J. (1994), *Global Dreams*, (New York: Simon & Schuster).

Bello, W. (1992), *People and Power in the Pacific*, (London: Pluto Press).

Bello, W. (1998), "East Asia: On the Eve of the Great Transformation?", *Review of International Political Economy* 5: 3.

Bello, W. and Rosenfeld, S. (1990), *Dragons in Distress: Asia's Miracle Economies in Crisis*, (San Francisco, CA: Institute for Food and Development Policy).

Bellofiore, R. (ed.) (1998), *Marxian Economics: A Reappraisal*, Vol.2, (New York: St.Martin's Press).

Bellofiore, R. (ed.) (1999), *Global Money, Capital Restructuring and the Changing Patterns of Labour*, (Cheltenham: Edward Elgar).

Berger, S. and Dore, R. (eds.) (1996), *National Diversity and Global Capitalism*, (Ithaca: Cornell University Press).

Bernard, M. (1999), "East Asia's Tumbling Dominoes: Financial Crises and the Myth of the Regional Model", in Panitch and Leys (eds.).

Bienefeld, M. (1988), "The Significance of the Newly Industrializing Countries for the Development Debate", *Studies in Political Economy* 25.

Bivens, J. (2004), "Shifting Blame for Manufacturing Job Loss", *Briefing Paper* 149, Economic Policy Institute, April, http://www.epinet.org/briefingpapers/149/bp149.pdf.

Blaug, M. (2003), "The Formalist Revolution of the 1950s", *Journal of the History of Economic Thought* 25: 2.

Bloch, H. (ed.) (2003), *Growth and Development in the Global Economy*, (Cheltenham: Edward Elgar).

Bloomfield, G. (1991), "The World Automotive Industry in Transition", in Law (ed.).

Blustein, P. (2001), *The Chastening: Inside the Crisis that Rocked the Global Financial System and Humbled the IMF*, (New York: Public Affairs).

Bonefeld, W. and Holloway, J. (eds.) (1996), *Global Capital, National State and the Politics of Money*, (Basingstoke: Macmillan).

Bradley, H., Erickson, M., Stephenson, C., Williams, S. (2000), *Myths at Work*, (London: Polity).

Bradsher, K. (2005), "Next Wave from China: Exporting Cars to the West," *New York Times*, 25 June, on line.

Brenner, R. (1998), "Uneven Development and the Long Downturn: The Advanced Capitalist Economies from Boom to Stagnation, 1950-1998", *New Left Review* 229.

Brenner. R. (2002), *The Boom and the Bubble, The U.S. in the World Economy*, (London: Verso).

Brenner, R. (2004), "New Boom or New Bubble", *New Left Review* 25.

Brewer, A. (1991), *Marxist Theories of Imperialism: A Critical Survey*, (London: Routledge).

Bronfenbrenner, K. and Luce, S. (2004), "The Changing Nature of Corporate Global Restructuring: The Impact of Production Shifts on Jobs in the U.S., China, and Around the Globe", Submitted to the U.S.-China Economic and Security Review Commission, 14 October, http://www.uscc.gov/researchpapers/2004/cornell_u_mass_report.pdf.

Brown, C. (2004), "Trade Sector Leads Korea's Economic Growth in First Half of 2004", *Korea Insight* 6: 8.

Brown, P. and Lauder, H. (2001), *Capitalism and Social Progress: The Future of Society in the Global Economy*, (Basingstoke: Palgrave).

Burke, J. (2000), "U.S. Investment in China Worsens Trade Deficit", *Briefing Paper* 90, Economic Policy Institute, May, http://www.epinet.org/briefingpapers/FDI/FDI_BP.pdf.

Burke, J.Epstein, G and Choi, M. (2004), "Rising Foreign Outsourcing and Employment Losses in U.S. Manufacturing, 1987-2002", *PERI Working Paper Series* 89, Political Economy Research Institute, University of Massachusetts at Amherst, October.

Burkett, P. (1999), *Marx and Nature*, (New York: St. Martin's Press).

Burkett, P. and Hart-Landsberg, M. (1998), "East Asia and the Crisis of Development Theory", *Journal of Contemporary Asia* 28: 4.

Burkett, P. and Hart-Landsberg, M. (2000), *Development, Crisis, and Class Struggle: Learning from Japan and East Asia*, (New York: St. Martin's Press).

Burkett, P. and Hart-Landsberg, M. (2003), "A Critique of 'Catch-Up' Theories of Development", *Journal of Contemporary Asia* 33: 2.

Business Korea. (2002), "Falling Exchange Rate and Profitability", July.

Business Week. (2004), "Special Report, The China Price", 6 December, on line.

Camdessus, M. (1997), "The Asian Crisis and the International Response", Speech delivered at the Institute of Advanced Business Studies (IESE), University of Navarra Barcelona, Spain, 28 November.

Cardoso, F. and Faletto, E. (1979), *Dependency and Development in Latin America*, (Berkeley: University of California Press).

Cathie, J. (1997/1998), "Financial Contagion in East Asia and the Origins of the Economic and Financial Crisis in Korea", *Asia Pacific Business Review* 4: 2/3.

Chang, D. (2002), "The Korean Labour Relations in Transition: Authoritarian Flexibility?", *Labour, Capital and Society* 35: 1.

Chang, H. and Yoo, C. (2002), "The Triumph of Rentiers? The 1997 Korean Crisis in a Historical Perspective", in Eatwell and Taylor (eds.).

Chaudhry, K. (1993), "The Myths of the Market and the Common History of Late Developers", *Politics & Society* 21: 2.

Cheng, A. (2004), "Rich-Poor Gap Among the Worst, Study Finds", *South China Morning Post*, 26 February, on line.

Cherry, J. (2005), "'Big Deal' or Big Disappointment? The Continuing Evolution of the South Korean Developmental State", *The Pacific Review* 18: 3.

Chibber, V. (1999), "Building a Developmental State: The Korean Case Reconsidered", *Politics & Society* 27: 3.

China Economic Net. (2004), "Implications of Wal-Mart's Procurement in China", 26 November, on line.

Cho, B. (2004), "The Nature of Financial Capital, the Financial System, and the Finance-led Accumulation Regime", Conference Paper, New Political Economy Group, 29-30 July.

Cho, H. (2002), "Living with Conflicting Subjectivities: Mother, Motherly Wife, and Sexy Woman in the Transition from Colonial-Modern to Postmodern Korea", in Kendal (ed.).

Cho, J. (1964), "Post-1945 Land Reforms and their Consequences in South Korea", Ph.D. Dissertation, Indiana University.

Cho, L., Kim, Y. and Shin, I. (eds.) (2002), *Restructuring the Korean Financial Market in a Global Economy*, (Seoul: Korea Development Institute).

Cho, Y. (1998), "Government Intervention, Rent Distribution, and Economic Development in Korea", in Aoki et al. (eds.).

Choi, G. (2003), "What Lies Ahead for the Korean Economy?", *Korea Herald*, 27 January, on line.

Choi, J. (1989), *Labor and the Authoritarian State*, (Seoul: Korea University Press).

Chung, J. (1981), "La Théorie de La Baisse Tendencielle du Taux de Profit", (Louvain-la-Neuve: Institute des Sciences Economique, UCL).

Clarke, S. (1990), "The Marxist Theory of Overaccumulation and Crisis", *Science and Society* 54: 4.

Clarke, S. (1991a), *Marx, Marginalism and Modern Sociology: From Adam Smith to Max Weber*, (London: Macmillan).

Clarke, S. (1991b), "State, Class Struggle, and the Reproduction of Capital", in Clarke (ed.).

Clarke, S. (ed.) (1991), *The State Debate*, (Basingstoke: Macmillan).

Cleaver, H. (2002), "Work is Still Central Issue!", in Dinerstein and Neary (eds.).

Coates, D. (2000), *Models of Capitalism: Growth and Stagnation in the Modern Era*, (Cambridge: Polity Press).

Cody, E. (2004), "Workers in China Shed Passivity, Spate of Walkouts Shakes Factories", *Washington Post*, 27 November, on line.

Conybeare, J. (2003), *Merging Traffic: The Consolidation of the International Auto Industry*, (Lanham: Rowman & Littlefield).

Cooper, C. (2002), "Does China Pose an Economic Threat to Korea?", *Korea Insight* 4: 1.

Cooper, C. (2003), "Trade Winds Blow From West to East", in Korea Economic Institute (ed.).

Cowie, J. (1999), *Capital Moves: RCA's Seventy-Year Quest for Cheap Labour*, (NewYork: The New Press).

Coy, P. (2004), "Just How Cheap Is Chinese Labor?", *Business Week*, 3 December, on line.

Crotty, J. (2002), The Effects of Increased Product Market Competition and Changes in Financial Markets on the Performance of Nonfinancial Corporations in the Neoliberal Era", *PERI Working Paper Series* 44.

Crotty, J. and Lee, K. (2001), "Economic Performance in Post-Crisis Korea: A Critical Perspective on Neoliberal Restructuring", *PERI Working Paper Series* 23, http://www.umass.edu/peri/pdfs/WP23.pdf.

Crotty, J. and Lee, K. (2002), "A Political-Economic Analysis of the Failure of Neoliberal Restructuring in Post-Crisis Korea", *Cambridge Journal of Economics* 26.

Crotty, J. and Lee, K. (2004), "Was the IMF's Imposition of Economic Regime Change in Korea Justified? A Critique of the IMF's Economic and Political Role Before and After the Crisis", *PERI Working Paper Series* 77.

Crotty, J. and Lee, K. (2005), "The Effects of Neoliberal 'Reforms' on the Post-Crisis Korean Economy", *PERI Working Paper Series* 111.

Cumings, B. (1981), *The Origins of the Korean War, Liberation and the Emergence of Separate Regimes*, Vol. 1, (Princeton: Princeton University Press).

Cumings, B. (1984), "The Origins of the Development of the Northeast Asian Political Economy: Industrial Sectors, Product Cycles, and Political Consequences", *International Organization* 38: 1.

Cumings, B. (1999), "The Asian Crisis, Democracy, and the End of 'Late' Development", in Pempel (ed.).

Dasgupta, B. (1998), *Structural Adjustment, Global Trade and the New Political Economy of Development*, (London: Zed Books).

Davis, D. (2004), *Discipline and Development: Middle Classes and Prosperity in East Asia and Latin America*, (Cambridge: Cambridge University Press).

Davis, M. (2004), "Planet of Slums", *New Left Review* 26.

de Brunhoff, S. (2003), "Financial and Industrial Capital: A New Class Coalition", in Saad-Filho (ed.).

De Rivero, O. (2001), *The Myth of Development: Non-viable Economies of the 21st Century*, (London: Zed Books).

Deininger, K. (2003), *Land Policies for Growth and Poverty Reduction*, (Washington D.C.: The World Bank and Oxford University Press).

Deyo, F. (1987), *The Political Economy of the New Asian Industrialism*, (Ithaca: Cornell University Press).

Deyo, F. (1996), "Introduction: Social Reconstructions of the World Automobile Industry", in Deyo (ed.).

Deyo, F. (ed.) (1996), *Social Reconstructions of the World Automobile Industry*, (London: Macmillan).

Daimond, L. and Shin, D. (eds.) (1999), *Institutional Reform and Democratic Consolidation in Korea*, (Stanford, CA: Hoover Institution Press).

Dicken, P. (1998), *Global Shift: Transforming the World Economy*, (London: The Guilford Press).

Dierckxsens, W. (2000), *The Limits to Capitalism: An Approach to Globalization without Neoliberalism*, (London: Zed Books).

Dinerstein, A. and Neary, M. (eds.) (2002) *The Labour Debate: An Investigation into the Theory and Reality of Capitalist Work*, (Aldershot: Ashgate).

Dirlik, A. (1997), *The Postcolonial Aura: Third World Criticism in the Age of Global Capitalism*, (Boulder, CO: Westview Press).

Domhoff, G. (2005), *Who Rules America? Power, Politics, and Social Change*, (New York: McGraw-Hill).

Duménil, G. (1980), *De la Valeur aux Prix de Production*, (Paris: Economica).

Duménil, G. (1984), "The So-Called 'Transformation Problem' Revisited: A Brief Comment", *Journal of Economic Theory* 33.

Duménil, G. and Lévy, D. (1993), *The Economics of the Profit Rate*, (Aldershot: Edward Elgar).

Duménil, G. and Lévy, D. (2002), "The Profit Rate: Where and How Much Did It Fall? Did It Recover? USA 1948-2000", *Review of Radical Political Economics* 34: 4.

Duménil, G. and Lévy, D. (2004), "The Real and Financial Components of Profitability (United States, 1952-2000)", *Review of Radical Political Economics* 36: 1.

Durand, C. (1990), "The Exhaustion of Developmental Socialism: Lessons from China", *Monthly Review* 42: 7.

Eatwell, J. and Taylor, L. (eds.) (2002), *International Capital Markets*, (Oxford: Oxford University Press).

Economic Intelligence Unit. (2002), "Drastic plastic? The Credit Card Boom", 3 June, on line.

Economist. (2003a), "A Survey of Asian Finance", 8 February.

Economist. (2003b), "A Survey of South Korea", 19 April.

Economist. (2004), "The Dragon and the Eagle", 2 October.

Economist. (2005a), "The Struggle of Champions", 6 January.

Economist. (2005b), "Special Report: Samsung Electronics", 15 January.

Economist. (2005c), "Rebuilding Failed States: From Chaos to Order", 5 March.

Economist. (2005d), "The Cauldron Boils", 29 September, on line.

Editorial. (2005a), "Sluggish Income Growth", *Korea Herald*, 21 May.

Editorial. (2005b), "Economy at the Crossroads", *Korea Herald*, 2 June, on line.

Elson, D. (1979), "The Value Theory of Labour", in Elson (ed.).

Elson, D. (ed.) (1979), *Value: The Representation of Labour in Capitalism*, (London: CSE Books).

Escobar, A. (1995), *Encountering Development: The Making and Unmaking of the Third World*, (Princeton, NJ: Princeton University Press).

Evans, P. (1995), *Embedded Autonomy: States and Industrial Transformation*,

(Princeton: Princeton University Press).

Far Eastern Economic Review. (2003), "China Breaks with its Wartime Past", 7 August.

Fernald, J. and Loungani, P. (2004), "Comrades or Competitors? On Trade Relationships Between China and Emerging Asia", *Chicago Fed Letter* 20.

Ferri, G. and Kang. T. (1999), "The Credit Channel at Work: Lessons from the Financial Crisis in Korea", *Economic Notes* 28: 2.

Fine, B., Lapavitsas, C. and Saad-Filho, A. (2004), "Transforming the Transformation Problem: Why the 'New Interpretation' Is a Wrong Turning", *Review of Radical Political Economics* 36: 1.

Foley, D. (1982), "The Value of Money, the Value of Labor Power, and the Marxian Transformation Problem", *Review of Radical Political Economics* 14: 2.

Foley, D. (2005), "Marx's Theory of Money in Historical Perspective", in Moseley (ed.).

Forsberg, A. (2000), *America and the Japanese Miracle: The Cold War Context of Japan's Postwar Economic Revival, 1950-1960*, (Chapel Hill, NC: University of North Carolina Press).

Freeman, A. (2004), "The Case for Simplicity: a Paradigm for the Political Economy of the 21st Century", in Freeman et al. (eds.).

Freeman, A., Kliman, A. and Wells, J. (eds.), (2004), *The New Value Controversy and the Foundations of Economics*, (Cheltenham: Edward Elgar).

Fukuyama, F. (1999), "Asian Values, Korean Values, and Democratic Consolidation", in Daimond and Shin (eds.).

Galor, O., Moav, O. and Vollrath, D. (2003), "Land Inequality and the Origin of Divergence and Overtaking in the Growth Process: Theory and Evidence", *Working Paper*, Hebrew University, Dept. of Economics.

Galor, O., Moav, O. Vollrath, D. (2005), "Land Inequality and the Emergence of Human Capital Promoting Institutions", *Economics Working Papers* 2005-03, Brown University.

Gerschenkron, A. (1962), *Economic Backwardness in Historical Perspective*, (Cambridge: Belknap Press).

Giddens, A. and Held, D. (eds.) (1983), *Classes, Power and Conflict*, (Basingstoke: Macmillan).

Gilboy, G. (2004), "The Myth Behind China's Miracle", *Foreign Affairs*, July-August, on line.

Gough, N. (2005), "Trouble on the Line", *Time Asia*, 31 January, on line.

Gouverneur, J. (1990), "Productive Labor, Price/Value Ratio and Rate of Surplus Value: Theoretical Viewpoints and Empirical Evidence", *Cambridge Journal of Economics* 14: 1.

Gouverneur, J. (2004), *Understanding the Economy*, on line.

Greider, W. (1997), *One World Ready or Not: The Manic Logic of Global Capitalism*, (New York: Touchstone).

Griffin, K. and Gurley, J. (1985), "Radical Analyses of Imperialism, The Third World, and the Transition to Socialism: A Survey Article", *Journal of Economic*

Literature 23.

Griffin, K. and Khan, A. (2000), "Poverty and the Distribution of Land", *Working Paper*, 00-09, Department of Economics, University of California, Riverside.

Grilli, E. (2002), "The Asian Crisis: Trade Causes and Consequences," *The World Economy* 25: 2.

Gruenwald, P. (2003), "Korea and the IMF", in Korea Economic Institute (ed.).

Haggard, S. (1990), *Pathways from the Periphery*, (Ithaca: Cambridge University Press).

Halevi, J. (1984), "Structure Economique et Demande Effective", *Economie Appliquee*, 37: 1.

Halevi, J. (1999), "The Accumulation Process in Japan and East Asia as Compared with the Role of Germany in European Post-war Growth", in Bellofiore (ed.).

Halevi, J. and Fontaine, J. (eds.) (1998), *Restoring Demand in the World Economy: Trade, Finance and Technology*, (Aldershot: Edward Elgar).

Halevi, J. and Kriesler, P. (1998), "History, Politics, and Effective Demand in Asia", in Halevi and Fontaine (eds.).

Hardt, M. and Negri, A. (2000), *Empire*, (Cambridge: Harvard University Press).

Hardt, M. and Negri, A. (2004), *Multitude*, (New York: Penguin).

Hart-Landsberg, M. (1993), *The Rush To Development: Economic Change and Political Struggle in South Korea*, (New York: Monthly Review Press).

Hart-Landsberg, M. (2004a), "International Conditions and South Korean Capital Accumulation, 1987-2003", Conference Paper, Institute for Social Sciences of Gyeongsang National University, 22 May.

Hart-Landsberg, M. (2004b), "The South Korean Economy and U.S. Policy", *Asian Perspective* 28: 4.

Hart-Landsberg, M. (2005), "South Korea: The State of Political Struggle", Monthly Review Webzine, 15 September, http://mrzine.monthlyreview.org/hartlandsberg150905.html.

Hart-Landsberg, M. and Burkett, P. (1998), "Contradictions of Capitalist Industrialization in East Asia: A Critique of 'Flying Geese' Theories of Development", *Economic Geography* 74: 2.

Hart-Landsberg, M and Burkett, P. (2001), "Economic Crisis and Restructuring in South Korea: Beyond the Free Market-Statist Debate", *Critical Asian Studies* 33: 3.

Hart-Landsberg, M. and Burkett, P. (2005a), *China and Socialism: Market Reforms and Class Struggle*, (New York: Monthly Review Press).

Hart-Landsberg, M. and Burkett, P. (2005b), "China and Socialism: Engaging the Issues", *Critical Asian Studies* 37: 4.

Harvey, D. (2003), *The New Imperialism*, (Oxford: Oxford University Press).

Harvey, D. (2006), *Spaces of Global Capitalism: A Theory of Uneven Geographical Development*, (London: Verso).

Hatch, W. and Yamamura, K. (1996), *Asia in Japan's Embrace: Building A Regional Production Alliance*, (Cambridge: Cambridge University Press).

Hayami, Y., Ruttan, V. and Southworth, H. (eds.) (1979), *Agricultural Growth in*

Japan, Taiwan, Korea, and Philippines, (Honolulu: The University Press of Hawaii).

Healey, D. (1991), *Japanese Capital Exports and Asian Economic Development*, (Paris: OECD).

Holland, T. (2004), "Labor Pains", *Far Eastern Economic Review* 23, September.

Holliday, I. and Wilding, P. (2003), *Welfare Capitalism in East Asia: Social Policy in the Tiger Economies*, (Basingstoke: Palgrave).

Holloway, J. (1996), "The Abyss Open: The Rise and Fall of Keynesianism", in Bonefeld and Holloway (eds.).

Holst, D. and Weiss, J. (2004), "ASEAN and China: Export Rivals or Partners in Regional Growth?", *World Economy* 27: 8.

Hong Kong Confederation of Trade Unions. (2004), *Chinese Labor and the WTO*, http://www.ihlo.org/.

Hong, Y. (2002), "Unity Between Formal and Informal Workers at E-Land, Korea", *Asian Labour Update*, http://www.amrc.org.hk/alu/Alu40/014004.htm, Hong Kong: Asia Monitor Resource Centre.

Hoogvelt, A. (1997), *Globalization and the Postcolonial World: The New Political Economy of Development*, (Baltimore, MD: The Johns Hopkins University Press).

International Monetary Fund. (1997), "Aim of Korea Program is to Stanch Immediate Crisis, Permit Return to Stability and Growth", *IMF Survey* 26: 3, 15 December.

Jang, S. (2004), Continuing Suicide Among Laborers in Korea", *Labor History* 45: 3.

Jeon, Y. and Kim, Y. (2000), "Land Reform, Income Redistribution, and Agricultural Production in Korea", *Economic Development and Cultural Change* 48: 2.

Jeong, S. (1997), "The Social Structure of Accumulation in South Korea: Upgrading or Crumbling?", *Review of Radical Political Economics* 29: 4.

Jeong, S. (2004), "Trend of Capital Accumulation in Korea after the 1997 Crisis: A Marxian Analysis", Paper presented for *The 4th International Marx Congress*, Paris, 1 October.

Jeong, S. (2005), "Trend of Marxian Ratios in Korea: 1970-2003", Conference Paper, Institute for Social Sciences, Gyeongsang National University, 20 May.

Jeong, S. and Shin, J. (1999), "Debates on the Economic Crisis within the Korean Left", *Rethinking Marxism* 11: 2.

Johnson, C. (1982), *MITI and the Japanese Miracle: the Growth of Industrial Policy, 1925-1975*, (Stanford, CA: Stanford University Press).

Johnson, C. (1987), "Political Institutions and Economic Performance: The Government-Business Relationship in Japan, South Korea and Taiwan", in Deyo (ed.).

Johnson, C. (1996), *Japan: Who Governs? The Rise of the Developmental State*, (New York: W. W. Norton).

Kaldor, N, (1989), *Further Essays on Economic Theory and Policy*, (New York: Holmes & Meier).

Kalecki, M. (1943), "Political Aspects of Full Employment", in Kalecki (1990).

Kalecki, M. (1944), "Three Ways to Full Employment", in Kalecki (1990).

Kalecki, M. (1945), "Full Employment by Stimulating Private Investment?", in Kalecki (1990).

Kalecki, M. (1976), *Essays in Developing Economies*, (Hassocks: Harvester Press).

Kalecki, M. (1990), *Collected Works of Michal Kalecki. Volume 1. Capitalism: Business Cycles and Full Employment*, edited by J. Osiatynski and translated by C. Kisiel, (Oxford: Oxford University Press).

Kang, C. (2000), "Segyehwa Reform of the South Korean Developmental State", in Kim (ed.).

Kato, T. (1984), "A Preliminary Note on the State in Contemporary Japan", *Hitotsubashi Journal of Social Studies* 16: 1.

Keliher, M. (2004), "Replacing U.S. in Asian Export Market", *Asia Times*, 11 February, on line.

Kendal, L. (ed.) (2002), *Under Construction: The Gendering of Modernity, Class, and Consumption in the Republic of Korea*, (Honolulu: University of Hawaii Press).

Kentor, J. (2005), "The Growth of Transnational Corporate Networks: 1962-1998", *Journal of World-Systems Research* 11: 2.

Kester, C. (1996), "American and Japanese Corporate Governance: Convergence to Best Practice", in Berger and Dore (eds.).

Keynes, J. (1936), *The General Theory of Employment, Interest and Money: The Collected Writings of John Maynard Keynes: Volume VII*, (London: The Macmillan Press, 1973).

Kiely, R. (1995), *Sociology and Development: The Impasse and Beyond*, (London: UCL Press).

Kim, E.-M. (1997), *Big Business Strong State: Collusion and Conflict in South Korean Development, 1960-1990*, (Albany: State University of New York Press).

Kim, H. (2003), "*Chaebol* Lobby Warns of Exodus", *Korea Herald*, 27 June, on line.

Kim, H. (2004), "China Outstrips Korean Car Production", *Korea Herald*, 2 February, on line.

Kim, Ji-ho. (2004a), "Morgan Stanley Warns of Economic Slowdown in China", *Korea Herald*, 24 March, on line.

Kim, Ji-ho. (2004b), "*Chaebol* Investment Falls 33.5%", *Korea Herald*, 12 July, on line.

Kim, Ji-hyun. (2004a), "Labor Unrest Slashes Output, Exports", *Korea Herald*, 17 February, on line.

Kim, Ji-hyun. (2004b), "Flexibility in Labor Top Priority", *Korea Herald*, 22 May, on line.

Kim, J.-K. (2004), "Hardship More Serious than 6 Years Ago", *Korea Times*, 26 May, on line.

Kim, J.-K. (2005), "South Korea's Consumption Growth Lowest in OECD", *Korea Times*, 3 January, on line.

Kim, Jung-min. (2005), "Economy Expanded Slowest in Two Years during First

Quarter", *Korea Herald*, 21 May.

Kim, Mi-hui. (2003), "Factories Relocating Abroad to Cut Costs", *Korea Herald*, 25 October, on line.

Kim, S. (ed.) (2000), *Korea's Globalization*, Cambridge, (Cambridge: Cambridge University Press).

Kim, S.-H. and Cho, B. (1999), "The South Korean Economic Crisis: Contrasting Interpretations and an Alternative For Economic Reform", *Studies in Political Economy* 60.

Kim So-young. (2005a), "Manufacturing, Construction, Retail Sectors Lost Jobs", *Korea Herald*, 19 May.

Kim So-young. (2005b), "Foreign Investors Increase Stakes to Gain More Input", *Korea Herald*, 20 June, on line.

Kim Sung-mi. (2003), "Labor Conflict May Hit 13-Year Peak", *Korea Herald*, 13 November, on line.

Kim, Y. (2005), "*DJnomics* and the Transformation of the Developmental State", *Journal of Contemporary Asia* 35: 4.

Kirk, D. (1999), *Korean Crisis: Unraveling of the Miracle in the IMF Era*, (Basingstoke: Palgrave).

Kirk, D. (2003), "Contract at Hyundai Raises Sights of Korean Workers", *New York Times*, 19 August.

Kitschelt, H., Lange, P., Marks, G. and Stephens, J. (eds.) (1999), *Continuity and Change in Contemporary Capitalism*, (Cambridge: Cambridge University Press).

Kleinknecht, A., Mandel, E. and Wallerstein, I. (eds.) (1992), *New Findings in Long-Wave Research*, (New York: St.Martin's Press).

Koo, H. (1993), "The State, *Minjung*, and the Working Class in South Korea", in Koo (ed.).

Koo, H. (2001), *Korean Workers: The Culture and Politics of Class Formation*, (Ithaca: Cambridge University Press).

Koo, H. (ed.) (1993), *State and Society in Contemporary Korea*, (Ithaca: Cornell University Press).

Koo, B. (2002), "Corporate Restructuring and Financial Reform in Korea", in Cho et al. (eds.).

Korea Development Bank. (2006), http://www.kdb.co.kr/, 16 February.

Korea Economic Institute. (ed.) (2003), *Korea's Economy 2003*, (Washington, D.C.: Korea Economic Institute).

Korea Herald. (2003a), "Labor Group Seeks Equality for All Workers", 16 January, on line.

Korea Herald. (2003b), "Korea's State Debt Tripled Over 5 Years", 8 September, on line.

Korea Herald. (2005), "Economy at the Crossroads", 2 June, on line.

Korea Insight, Korea Economic Institute, http://www.keia.org/2-1-insight.html.

Korean Confederation of Trade Unions (KCTU). (1997), *The KCTU Proposal for an Agreement to Overcome the Economic Crisis*, http://www.kctu.org/arguments/

sp004.htm.

Korten, D. (1995), *When Corporations Rule the World*, (West Hartford, Connecticut: Kumarian Press).

Kosai, Y. (1986), *The Era of High-Speed Growth: Notes on the Postwar Japanese Economy*, translated by J. Kaminski, (Tokyo: University of Tokyo Press).

Kourkoulakos, S. (2003), "The Specificity of Dialectical Reason", in Albritton and Simoulidis (eds.).

Kriesler, P. and Nevile, J. (2003), "Macroeconomic Constraints with Globalization", in Bloch (ed.).

Kriesler, P. and Halevi, J. (1996), "Asia, Japan and the Internationalization of Effective Demand", *Economies et Societes, Monnaie et Production*, Series M.P 10.

Kristof, N. and Sanger, D. (1999), "How U.S. Wooed Asia to Let Cash Flow In", *The New York Times*, 16 February, on line.

Kurth, J. (1979), "The Political Consequences of the Product Cycle: Industrial History and Political Outcomes", *International Organization* 33: 1.

Kusnets, P. (1982), "The Dramatic Reversal of 1979/1980: Contemporary Economic Development in Korea", *Journal of Northeast Asian Studies* 1: 3.

Labour News. (2004), 23 February.

Laibman, D. (1999), "Productive and Unproductive Labor: A Comment", *Review of Radical Political Economics* 31: 2.

Lall, S. and Albaladejo, M. (2004), "China's Competitive Performance: A Threat to East Asian Manufactured Exports?", *World Development* 32: 9.

Law, C. (1991), "Motor Vehicle Manufacturing: the Representative Industry", in Law (ed.).

Law, C. ed. (1991), *Restructuring the Global Automobile Industry*, (London: Routledge).

Lee, C.-H., Lee, K. and Lee, K.-K. (2002). "Chaebols, Financial Liberalization and Economic Crisis: Transformation of Quasi-Internal Organization in Korea", *Asian Economic Journal* 16: 1.

Lee, C.-K. (2004), "'Made in China': Labor as a Political Force?", Presentation at the 2004 Mansfield Conference, The University of Montana, Missoula, 18-20 April, http://www.umt.edu/mansfield/Ching%20Kwan%20Lee%20paper.pdf.

Lee, J.-W. (1998), "Economic Growth and Human Development in the Republic of Korea, 1945-1992", *Occasional Paper*, 24, United Nations Development Program.

Lenin, V. (1916), "Notebook on Imperialism", *Collected Works*, Vol.39, (Moscow: Progress Publisher).

Lim, H. (1985), *Dependent Development in Korea 1963-1979*, (Seoul: Seoul National University Press).

Linder, S. (1986), *The Pacific Century: Economic and Political Consequences of Asian-Pacific Dynamism*, (Stanford, CA: Stanford University Press).

Lipietz, A. (1982), "The So-Called Transformation Problem Revisited", *Journal of Economic Theory* 26: 1.

Lipietz, A. (1985), *The Enchanted World: Inflation, Credit and the Global Crises*, (London: Verso).

Lipietz, A. (1987), *Mirages and Miracles*, (London: Verso).

Lister, J. (2003), "Korea's Economy in Recession: Is it Technical?", *Korea Insight* 5: 9.

Lister, J. (2004), "Outlook for Korea's Economy", *Korea Insight* 6: 1.

Lo, D. (1999), "The East Asian Phenomenon: The Consensus, the Dissent, and the Significance of the Present Crisis", *Capital and Class* 67.

Lowe-Lee, F. (2004a), "A New Financial Crisis: Credit Card Excesses", *Korea Insight* 6: 2.

Lowe-Lee, F. (2004b), "Economic Trends: Foreigners Weary About Free Economic Zones", *Korea Insight* 6: 6.

Lowe-Lee, F. (2005), "Economic Trends: Growing Presence of Foreign Capital Worries Domestic Financial Institutions", *Korea Insight* 7: 4.

Lowe-Lee, F. (2006), "Economic Update: Income Gap Widens", *Korea Insight* 8: 3.

Mage, S. (1963), "The Law of the Falling Tendency of the Rate of Profit", Ph.D. Dissertation, Columbia University.

Manyin, M. (2004), "South Korea-U.S. Economic Relations: Cooperation, Friction, and Future Prospects", *CRS Report for Congress*, updated 1 July, Library of Congress, Washington D.C.

Marglin, S. (1983), "What Do the Bosses Do? The Origins and Functions of Hierarchy in Capitalist Production", in Giddens and Held (eds.).

Martin, J. and Torres, R. (2001), "Korean Labor Market and Social Safety-net Reforms: Challenges and Policy Requirements", Paper presented at the Forum on Labor Market Reforms in Korea, Korea Labor Institute, Seoul, February.

Marx, K. (1971), *A Contribution to the Critique of Political Economy,* (London: Lawrence and Wishart).

Marx, K. (1976), *Capital*, Vol.1, (New York: Penguin).

Marx, K. (1978), "The Value-Form", *Capital and Class* 4.

Marx, K. (1981), *Capital*, Vol.3, (New York: Penguin).

Marx, Karl. (1987), "Zur Kritik der Politischen Oekonomie", *Karl Marx-Frederick Engels, Collected Works,* Volume 29, (New York: International Publishers).

Mason, S. and Council on East Asian Studies (1980), *The Economic and Social Modernization of the Republic of Korea*, (Cambridge: Harvard University Press).

McGregor, R. (2004), "Competition in China Keeps Foreign Profits Low", *Financial Times*, 5 December, on line.

McGuckin, R. and Spiegelman, M. (2004), "China's Experience with Productivity and Jobs: Benefits and Costs of Change", Parts I, II, III, IV, *Research Report* R-1352-04-RR, The Conference Board, June, http://www.conference-board.org/publications/reports.cfm.

Mitchell, C. (1949), "Land Management and Tenancy Reform in Korea under the U.S. Army Occupation", Ph.D. Dissertation, Harvard University.

Mitchell, C. (1952), "Land Reform in Asia: a Case Prepared for the NPA Agriculture Committee on National Policy", National Planning Association.

Mohun, S. (1998), "Unproductive Labor and the Rate of Profit in Australia 1966/67-1991/92", in Bellofiore (ed.).

Mohun, S. (2002), "Productive and Unproductive Labor: A Reply to Houston and Laibman", *Review of Radical Political Economics* 34: 2.

Mohun, S. (2003), "Does All Labour Create Value?", in Saad-Filho (ed.).

Mohun, S. (2004a), "The Australian Rate of Profit 1965-2001", *Journal of Australian Political Economy* 52.

Mohun, S. (2004b), "On Measuring the Wealth of Nations: the U.S. Economy, 1964-2001", Mimeo.

Mohun, S. (2004c), "Distributive Shares in the U.S. Economy, 1964-2001", Mimeo.

Mohun, S. (2004d), "Theory and Measurement: How Do Recent Developments in Value Theory Help?", Paper presented for *The 4th International Marx Congress*, Paris, 1 October.

Moon, I. (1997), "Seoul is Still Teetering on the Edge", *Business Week*, 29 December.

Moseley, F. (1991), *The Falling Rate of Profit in the Postwar United States Economy*, (New York: St.Martin's Press).

Moseley, F. (1997), "The Rate of Profit and the Future of Capitalism", *Review of Radical Political Economics* 29: 4.

Moseley, F. (1999), "The Decline of the Rate of Profit in the Post-war United States Economy: Due to Increased Competition or Increased Unproductive Labour", *Historical Materialism* 4.

Moseley, F. (2004), "Marxian Crisis Theory and the Postwar U.S. Economy", Conference Paper, Institute for Social Sciences, Gyeongsang National University, 22 May.

Moseley, F. (ed.) (2005), *Marx's Theory of Money*, (New York: Palgrave Macmillan).

Nakajima, A. and Izumi, H. (1995), "Economic Development and Unequal Exchange among Nations: Analysis of the USA, Japan and South Korea", *Review of Radical Political Economics* 27: 3.

Nakamura, T. (1983), *Economic Growth in Prewar Japan*, translated by R. Feldman, (New Haven: Yale University Press).

Nam, S. and Yang, J. (2003), "Potential Impact of Changes in Consumer Preferences on Trade in the Korean and World Motor Vehicle Industry", Korea Institute for International Economic Policy, Working Paper, 03-08.

Naughton, B. (1996), "China's Emergence and Prospects as a Trading Nation", *Brookings Papers on Economic Activity* 2.

Navarro, V. (1992), "Has Socialism Failed? An Analysis of Health Indicators under Socialism", *International Journal of Health Services* 22: 4.

Neary, M. (2002), "Labour Moves: A Critique of the Concept of Social Movement Unionism", in Dinerstein and Neary (eds.).

Negri, A. (1994), *Labor of Dionysus*, (Minneapolis: University of Minnesota Press).

New York Times. (2005), "South Korea Becoming a Big Asian Investor", 20 October.

New York Times. (2006), "China's Youth Look to Seoul for Inspiration", 2 January.

Ochoa, E. (1984), "Labor-Values and Prices of Production: an Interindustry Study of the U.S. Economy, 1947-1972", Ph.D. Dissertation, New School for Social Research.

OECD. (2004), *OECD Economic Surveys: Korea*, (Paris: OECD).

Olsen, G. (1974), *U. S. Foreign Policy and the Third World Peasant: Land Reform in Asia and Latin America*, (Westport: Praeger Publishers).

Overbeek, H. (2000), "Transnational Historical Materialism: Theories of Transnational Class Formation and World Order", in Palan (ed.).

Pak, K. (1956), "Economic Analysis of Land Reform in the Republic of Korea, 1954-55", Ph.D. Dissertation, University of Illinois.

Palan, R. (ed.) (2000), *Global Political Economy: Contemporary Theories*, (London: Routledge).

Panitch, L. and Leys, C. (eds.) (1999), *Global Capitalism versus Democracy: Socialist Register*, (London: Merlin Press).

Park, S. (1995), "Land Reform in Korea: A Reappraisal of Previous Research and A Proposal for A New Research Strategy," *Humane Studies*, Humane Studies Institute of Yeungnam University.

Pasinetti, L. (1973), "The Notion of Vertical Integration in Economic Analysis", *Metroeconomica* 25.

Pasinetti, L. (1981), *Structural Change and Economic Growth: A Theoretical Essay on the Dynamics of the Wealth of Nations*, (Cambridge: Cambridge University Press).

Pempel, T. (ed.) (1999), *The Politics of the Asian Economic Crisis*, (Ithaca: Cornell University Press).

People's Daily. (2004), "Income Gaps Have to be Closed", 25 February, on line.

People's Daily. (2005), "China's Middle Class Defined by Income", 20 January, on line.

Pirie, I. (2005), "The New Korean State", *New Political Economy* 10: 1.

Postone, M. (1996), *Time, Labor and Social Domination*, (Cambridge: Cambridge University Press).

Prosterman, R. and Hanstad, T. (2000), "Land Reform: A revised Agenda for the 21st Century", *RDI report on Foreign Aid and Development* 108, Rural Development Institute.

Putzel, J. (1992), *A Captive Land: The politics of Agrarian Reform in the Philippines*, (New York: Monthly Review Press).

Randal, V. and Theobald, R. (1998), *Political Change and Underdevelopment*, (Durham: Duke University Press).

Rieu, D. (2005), "Estimating the Sectoral Rates of Surplus Value: Methodological Issues", in this volume.

Rieu, D. (2006), "A Reexamination of the Quantitative Issues in the 'New Interpretation'", *Review of Radical Political Economics* 38: 2.

Roach, S. (2005), "What if China's Slows?", *Global Economic Forum*, Morgan Stanley, 23 May, on line.

Robison, R., Beeson, M., Jayasuriya, K. and Kim, H-R. (eds.) (2000), *Politics and Markets in the Wake of the Asian Crisis*, (London: Routledge).

Roemer, J. (1978), "Differentially Exploited Labor: A Marxian Theory of Discrimination", *Review of Radical Political Economics* 10: 2.

Rubin, I. (1990), *Essays on Marx's Theory of Value*, (New York: Black Rose Books).

Saad-Filho, A. ed. (2003), *Anti-Capitalism: A Marxist Introduction*, (London: Pluto Press).

Sachs, J. (1997), "IMF is a Power unto Itself", *Financial Times,* 11 December.

Sakurai, H. (1983), "Why Did the Korean War 'Break Out' on June 25, 1950? A Summary of a New Hypothesis", Mimeo.

Savran, S. and Tonak, E. (1999), "Productive and Unproductive Labour: An Attempt at Clarification and Classification", *Capital and Class* 68.

Schaller, M. (1985), *The American Occupation of Japan: The Origins of the Cold War in Asia*, (New York: Oxford University Press).

Sekine, T. (1997), *An Outline of the Dialectic of Capital*, 2 Vols., (London: Macmillan Press).

Shaikh, A. (1992), "The Falling Rate of Profit as the Cause of Long Waves: Theory and Empirical Evidence", in Kleinknecht et al. (eds.).

Shaikh, A. (1999), "Explaining the Global Economic Crisis", *Historical Materialism* 5.

Shaikh, A. and Tonak, E. (1994), *Measuring the Wealth of Nations*, (Cambridge: Cambridge University Press).

Shin C.-S. (2005), "Capital Stock Matrix for the Korean Economy: 1995-2000", *Seoul Journal of Economics* 18: 1.

Shin, G. (1998), "Agrarian Conflict and the Origins of Korean Capitalism", *American Journal of Sociology* 103.

Shin, J. and Chang, H. (2005), "Economic Reform after the Financial Crisis: a Critical Assessment of Institutional Transition and Transition Costs in South Korea", *Review of International Political Economy* 12: 3.

Sim, S. (2003), "Income Gap Widened Sharply", *Korea Herald*, 17 February.

Simmons, B. (1999), "The Internationalization of Capital", in Kitschelt et al. (eds.).

Smith, M. (1991), "Respecifying Marx's Value Categories: A Theoretical and Empirical Reconsideration of the 'Law of the Falling Rate of Profit'", *Studies in Political Economy* 35.

Smith, M. and Taylor, K. (1996), "Profitability Crisis and the Erosion of Popular Prosperity: The Canadian Economy, 1947-1991", *Studies in Political Economy* 49.

Soh, J. (2003), "Gap Between Rich, Poor in Urban Areas Widens", *Korea Times*, 7 January, on line.

Song, B. (1990), *The Rise of the Korean Economy*, (New York: Oxford University Press).

Stangarone, T. (2006), "Investment Down, but More Free Trade in Korea's Future", *Korea Insight* 8: 2.

Steinfeld, E. (2004), "China's Shallow Integration: Networked Production and the New Challenges for Late Industrialization", *World Development* 32: 11.

Stiglitz, J. (2001), "From Miracle to Crisis to Recovery: Lessons from Four Decades of the East Asian Experience", in Stiglitz. and Yusuf (eds.).

Stiglitz, J. and Yusuf, S. (eds.) (2001), *Rethinking the East Asian Miracle*, (Oxford: Oxford University Press).

Sylos-Labini, P. (1969), *Oligopoly and Technical Progress*, translated from the Italian by E. Henderson, (Cambridge: Harvard University Press).

Tang, K. (2000), *Social Welfare Development in East Asia*, (Basingstoke: Palgrave).

Tham, S. (2001), "Can Malaysian Manufacturing Compete with China in the WTO?", *Asia-Pacific Development Journal* 8: 2.

Thelen, K. and Kume, I. (1999), "The Effects of Globalization on Labor Revisited: Lessons from Germany and Japan", *Politics and Society* 27: 4.

U.S. Department of Commerce. (2005), "U.S. Aggregate Foreign Trade Data", http://www.ita.doc.gov/td/industry/otea/usfth/tabcon.html.

UNCTAD. (2002a), *Trade and Development Report 2002*, (New York: United Nations).

UNCTAD. (2002b), *World Investment Report 2002: Transnational Corporations and Export Competitiveness*, (New York: United Nations).

UNCTAD. (2005), *Trade and Development Report 2005*, (New York: United Nations).

Uno, K. (1980), *Principles of Political Economy: Theory of a Purely Capitalist Society*, (Brighton: The Harvester Press Ltd).

Wade, R. (1990), *Governing the Market: Economic Theory and the Role of Government in East Asian Industrialism*, (Princeton: Princeton University Press).

Wade, R. (1992), "East Asia's Economic Success: Conflicting Perspectives, Partial Insights, Shaky Evidence", *World Politics* 44.

Wade, R. and Veneroso, F. (1998), "The Asian Crisis: the High Debt Model vs. the Wall Street-Treasury-IMF Complex", *New Left Review* 228.

Warren, B. (1980), *Imperialism, Pioneer of Capitalism*, (London: NLB).

Watanabe, T. (1992), *Asia: Its Growth and Agony*, (Hawaii: University of Hawaii Press).

Westra, R. (1996), "Periodizing Capitalism and the Political Economy of Post-War Japan", *Journal of Contemporary Asia* 26: 4.

Westra, R. (2001), "Phases of Capitalism and Post-Capitalist Social Change", in Albritton et al. (eds.).

Westra, R. (2002), "Marxian Economic Theory and an Ontology of Socialism: A Japanese Intervention", *Capital and Class* 78.

Westra, R. (2003a), "Social Theory, Economic Crisis, and the Japanese Political Economy: a Review Article", *Review of International Political Economy* 10: 2.
Westra, R. (2003b), "Globalization: The Retreat of Capital to the 'Interstices' of the World?", in Westra and Zuege (eds.).
Westra, R. (2004a), "The 'Impasse' Debate and Socialist Development", in Albritton et al. (eds.).
Westra, R. (2004b), "Globalization and the Pathway to Socio-Material Betterment", *Review of Radical Political Economics* 36: 3.
Westra, R. (2006), "The Capitalist Stage of Consumerism and South Korean Development", *Journal of Contemporary Asia* 36: 1.
Westra, R and Zuege, A. (eds.) (2003), *Value and the World Economy Today: Production, Finance, and Globalization*, (Basingstoke: Palgrave).
Whang, I, (1982), "Administration of Land Reform in Korea", *Working Paper* 8301, Korea Development Institute.
Wolff, E. (1987), *Growth, Accumulation, and Unproductive Activity*, (Cambridge: Cambridge University Press).
Wolff, E. (2003), "What's Behind the Rise in Profitability in the US in the 1980s and 1990s", *Cambridge Journal of Economics* 27: 4.
Woo-Cumings, M. (1991), *Race to the Swift: State and Finance in Korean Industrialization*, (New York: Columbia University Press).
Woo-Cumings, M. (1998), "The Political Economy of Growth in East Asia: A Perspective on the State, Market, and Ideology", in Aoki et al. (eds.).
Woo-Cumings, M. (2001), "Miracle as Prologue: The State and the Reform of the Corporate Sector in Korea", in Stiglitz and Yusuf (eds.).
Woo-Cumings, M. (ed.) (1999), *The Developmental State*, (Ithaca: Cambridge University Press).
World Bank. (1993), *The East Asian Miracle: Economic Growth and Public Policy*, (Oxford: Oxford University Press).
World Watch Institute. (2004), *State of the World*, (New York: Norton).
Yoo, S. (2005), "EUCCK Gets Frank to Lure Foreign Investment", *Korea Herald*, 7 April, on line.

Works in Korean

Academy of Korean Studies (ed.) (1999a), *Korean Industrialization and Economic Structure in 1960s*, (Seoul: Baeksanseodang).
Academy of Korean Studies (ed.) (1999b), *Political and Social Changes in 1960s*, (Seoul: Baeksanseodang).
Ahn, B. (1989), "Korean Economy as a Medium Developed Capitalism", *Movement for Thoughts and Literature* 2.
Ahn, J.-Y., Cho J.-M. and Nam, J.-R. (2001), *The Reality of Irregular Work and Policy Imperatives,* (Seoul: KLI).
Ban, S. (1958), "Empirical Study on the Transfer of Land after Land Reform",

Studies on Agricultural Economics, Korea Agricultural Economics Association.
Bang, K. (2001), "Ideological Roots of South Korean Land Reform", in Hong (ed.).
Bank of Korea. *Input-Output Tables*. www.bok.or.kr.
Bank of Korea. *National Accounts*. www.bok.or.kr.
Chang, H. (2002), "Reconsideration of East Asian Industrial policy", in Lee and Chun (eds.).
Chang, H. and Jung, S. (2005), *Solving the Entangled Korean Economy*, (Seoul: Bookie).
Cho, Y. (2003), *A Single Spark: The Biography of Chun Tae-il*, (Seoul: Korea Democracy Foundation).
Chon, S. (2001), "Economic Policy and Land Distribution under U.S. Military Occupation", in Hong (ed.).
Chun, B. (2002), "The Flexibilisation of Labour Market after Economic Crisis", *Monthly Labour Trends* 4.
Chun, S. (2004), *Not-Ended Song by Helpers*, (Seoul: Hangyeore Newspaper Ltd).
Economic Planning Board. (1986), *White Paper on Foreign Debts*, (Seoul: EPB).
Fair Trade Commission. (2001), *The 20-years History of Fair Trade Commission*, (Seoul: FTC).
Gong, J. (1993), *A Study on the Capitalist Class in the 1950s*, (Seoul: Baeksanseodang).
Heo, S. (1999), "Critique on the Theory of Development and Expropriation", *Critical Review of History*, Autumn.
Hong, S. (2001), "Land Reform and the Transformation of Korean Landlords", in Hong (ed.).
Hong, S. (ed.) (2001), *Studies on Korea Land Reform*, (Seoul: Yonsei University Press).
Hong, Y. (2003), "Park Jung Hee in the Era of Democracy", in Lee (ed.).
ISS of GSNU. (ed.) (2000), *Korean War and Korean Capitalism*, (Seoul: Hanul).
Jang, H. (1999), "Formation of Korean Development Strategies and Industrial Policies in 1960s", in Academy of Korean Studies (ed. 1999a).
Jang, S. (1984), "An Empirical Study on the process of Land Reform (1)", *Studies on Economic History* 8.
Jang, S. (1985), "An Empirical Study on the process of Land Reform (2)", *Studies on Economic History* 9.
Jang, S. (2000), "Land Reform and capitalist development in Korea – focused on the case of Gyeongnam Province", *Studies on Development Economics* 6: 1.
Jeong G. (2004), "The Present Situation and Movement of Migrant Workers in Korea", in Korean House for International Solidarity (ed.).
Jeong, B. (2003). "Reappraisal of Korea Land Reform – Date of its Completion, Driving Force and Character", *Critical Review of History*, Winter.
Jeong, J. (1995), "Dissolution of Pre-modern Residual of Social Status System after Liberation", *Journal of Institute for Social Science* 13: 1, Gyeongsang National University.

Jeong, J. (2000), "Korean War and Dissolution of Pre-modern Class Relations", in ISS of GSNU (ed.).

Jeong, S. (1990), "Analysis of Marxian Ratios in the Korean Economy," Ph.D. Dissertation, Seoul National University.

Joo, M. (2005), "Competition and Monopoly in Korean Capitalism: 1987-2002", *Review of Social and Economic Studies* 25.

Jun, G. (1996), "A Reappraisal of Korea's Land Reform Using Henry George's Paradigm", in Oh (ed.).

Kang, M. (ed.) (2000), *History of Korean Capitalism*, (Seoul: History Critique).

KCTU. (1997), *Year Book of 1997*, (Seoul: KCTU).

KCTU. (ed.) (2002), *A Collection of the Analyses of Cases of the Struggle of Irregular Workers*, (Seoul: KCTU).

Kim, H. (2002), "An Analysis of Cases of Enterprise-Level Unionisation", in KCTU (ed.).

Kim, H.-K. (1988), *Monopoly Capital and Wage Labor in Korea*, (Seoul: Kachi).

Kim, J. (2000), "A Study on the Structural Changes in the Production and Distribution of Value in the Korean Economy", Ph.D. Dissertation, Hanyang University.

Kim, J. (ed.) (2001), *Formation and Dissolution of the Korean Capitalist Development Model*, (Seoul: Nanumuijip).

Kim, K. (2003), *Was Chaebol Reform Finished*, (Seoul: Hanul).

Kim, S., Chun, K., Jang, S. and Park, S. (1989), *A Study on the History of Farmland Reform*, (Seoul: KREI).

Kim, S.-K. (2005), "Marxian Theory and the Trend of Capital Accumulation in Korea", Conference Paper, Korean Social and Economic Association.

Kim, S.-S. (1999), "Labour Policy and Capital-Labour Relations of 1960s in Korea", in Academy of Korean Studies (ed. 1999a).

Kim, S.-S. (2003), "Labour Policy and Capital-Labour Relations during the Park Jung Hee Era", in Lee (ed.).

Kim, T. (2005). "Land Reform by North Korean Government on the Occupied Territory in South Korea during Korean War," *Critical Review of History*, Spring.

Kim, Y. (2004), "The Size and Condition of Irregular Workers", *Labour Society Bulletin* 82.

Kim, Y. (2005), "The Extent and Realities of Irregular Workforce in 2005", *Labour Society Bulletin* 105.

Korea International Trade Association, *Korea Trade Statistics*, http://global.kita.net/.

Korean Federation of Transportation, Public and Social Service Union (KFTPSU). (2002), *A Report on Irregular Workers in KFTPSU Affiliated Firms*, (Seoul: KFTPSU).

Korean House for International Solidarity (ed.) (2004), *Report of Workshop for the Human Right of Workers in Korean Corporations Abroad and Meeting with Returned Migrant Workers*, (Seoul: KHIS).

Korean Institute for Labor Studies & Policy (KILSP) ed. (2000), *Structural Adjustment and Counter-Strategy to Workplace Control*, (Seoul: Nodongjeonseon).

Kwon, H. (2001), "An Evaluation of the Employment Policy of the Kim Dae-jung Government", in Kwon et al. (eds.).

Kwon, H. et al. (eds.) (2001), *An Evaluation of Labour Policy of the Kim Dae-jung Government*, (Seoul: FKTU).

Lee, B.-C. (1999), "Park Jung Hee Regime and Formation of Developmental State Model: Policy Change in the Mid-1960s", *Studies in Economic Development* 5: 2.

Lee, B.-C. (2003), "Political Economy of Developmental Dictatorship and Korean Experiences", in Lee (ed.).

Lee, B.-C. (ed.) (2003), *Developmental Dictatorship and the Park Jung Hee Era*, (Seoul: Changbee).

Lee, B.-H. and Hwang, D. (2000), "The Change in the Labour Market Structure after the Economic Crisis", in Yoon and Yoo (eds.).

Lee, I. and Chun, B. (eds.) (2002), *East Asia in the Openness: Industry and Policy*, (Seoul: Hanul).

Lee, J. (1994), "Postwar Land Reform and Capital Conversion Problem of the Landlord Class", Master's thesis, Yonsei University.

Lee, J. (2003), "Formation of Yushin System and North-South Korean Division", in Lee (ed.).

Lee, Wan-Beom. (1999), "Formulation of the First 5-Years Economic Development Plan and U.S. Role in It", in Academy of Korean Studies (ed. 1999a).

Lee, Won-Bo. (2004), *History of Korean Labour Movement 5: Labour Movement in Economic Development Period 1961-1987*, (Seoul: Jisikmadang).

Ministry of Agriculture and Forestry. (1949), *Reference Materials for Land Reform*, (Seoul: MAF).

Ministry of Agriculture and Forestry. (1951), *Summary of Farm Household Survey*, (Seoul: MAF).

Ministry of Agriculture and Forestry. (1964), *Agricultural Census: 1960*, (Seoul: MAF).

Ministry of Agriculture and Forestry. (1974), *History of Land Reform*, (Seoul: MAF).

Ministry of Labor, *The Survey Report on Wage Structure*, various years, (with Raw Data).

National Statistical Office, *Annual Report on the Economically Active Population Survey*, various years. www.nso.go.kr.

National Statistical Office, *The Report on Mining and Manufacturing Survey*, various years, (Seoul: NSO).

Oh, D. (ed.) (1996), *Patterns of Industrialization (2)*, (Seoul: Seoul National University Press).

Pang, K. (2001), "Ideological Roots of the South Korean Land Reform", in Hong (ed.).

Park, H. (1994), "A Study on the Movement of the Rate of Profit and Economic Growth in the Korean Economy", Ph.D. Dissertation, Chonnam National

University.
Park, H. (1978), *Theory of National Economy*, (Seoul: Hangilsa).
Park, J. (1999), "Social Environment and Social Welfare Policy in 1960s", in Academy of Korean Studies (ed. 1999b).
Park, S. (2004), *A Critical Reformulation of Left Theories of Modern Capitalism*, (Seoul: Hanul).
Park, Y. (2002), "An Analysis of Cases of Ultra-Firm Level Unionisation", in KCTU (ed.).
Pyo, H. (2003), "Estimates of Capital Stocks by Industries and Types of Assets in Korea (1953-2000)", *Journal of Korean Economics Analysis* 9: 1 (with unpublished update data).
Rieu, D. (2002), "A Study on the Formation Process of the National Economy Discourse", *Economy and Society* 56.
Seong, N. (1996), "A Study on Effects of the State Finance on the Economic Growth and Redistribution", Ph.D. Dissertation, Korea University.
Shin, G. (2001), "Social Origins of Land Reform in South Korea", in Hong (ed.).
Shin, Y. (2000), "A Critical Review of Economic Growth under the Park Regime", in Kang (ed.).
Sohn, H. (1991), *New Conception on Korean Politics*, (Seoul: Pulbit).
Woo, D. (2001), "Economic Consequences of Land Reform", in Hong (ed.).
Yang, W. and Hong, J. (1991), *Analysis of Korean Capitalism*, (Seoul: Ilbit).
Yoo, C. (2003), "Political and Institutional Conditions for Financial Repression", in Lee (ed.).
Yoo, C. (ed.) (2003), *History and Crisis of the Korean Model for Capitalist Development*, (Seoul: Hamkeiknunchaek).
Yoo, C. (ed.) (2006), *Searching for a Korean Economic Model of Innovation and Integration*, (Seoul: Hamkeiknunchaek).
Yoon, J. and Yoo, C. (eds.) (2000), *Political Economy of Structural Adjustment*, (Seoul: Pulbit).

Works in Japanese

Fine, B. (2003), "Beyond the Developmental State: Towards a Political Economy of Development", in Hirakawa et al. (eds.).
Hirakawa, H., Noguchi, M. and Sano, M. (eds.) (2003), *Beyond Market-Driven Development: A New Stream of Political Economy of Development*, (Tokyo: Nihon Hyoron Sha).
Nakatani, T. (1994), *The Economics of Value, Price and Profit*, (Tokyo: Keiso Sobo).

Index